SECURITY, ECONOMICS, AND MORALITY IN AMERICAN FOREIGN POLICY

Contemporary Issues in Historical Context

William H. Meyer

University of Delaware

Upper Saddle River, New Jersey 07458

Library of Congress Cataloging-in-Publication Data

Meyer, William H.
  Security, economics, and morality in American foreign policy: contemporary
issues/William H. Meyer.
    p. cm.
  Includes bibliographical references (p.) and index.
  ISBN 0-13-086390-4
  1. United States—Foreign relations—1945–1989.   2. United States—Foreign
relations—1989   3. United States—Foreign economic relations.   4. National
security—United States. I. Title.
  E840.M49 2004
  327.73—dc21

                                                        2003046754

Editorial Director: Charlyce Jones-Owen
Editorial Assistant: Maureen Diana
Marketing Manager: Heather Shelstad
Executive Managing Editor: Ann Marie
  McCarthy
Full Service Liaison: Fran Russello
Permissions Supervisor: Kathleen
  Karcher
Manufacturing Buyer: Sherry Lewis
Cover Design: Joseph Sengotta

Cover Photo: Chad Baker/
  Photodisc/Getty Images, Inc.
**Composition/Full-Service Project
  Management:** Lithokraft/Marty
  Sopher
Mgr. Prod/Formatting & Art: Guy
  Ruggiero
Printer/Binder: R. R. Donnelley and
  Sons Company
Cover Printer: Phoenix Color Corp.

Credits and acknowledgments borrowed from other sources and reproduced,
with permission, in this textbook appear on page 321.

Pearson Education LTD., London
Pearson Education Singapore, Pte. Ltd
Pearson Education, Canada, Ltd
Pearson Education–Japan
Pearson Education Australia PTY,
  Limited

Pearson Education North Asia Ltd
Pearson Educación de Mexico,
  S.A. de C.V.
Pearson Education Malaysia, Pte. Ltd
Pearson Education, Upper Saddle
  River, New Jersey

10   9   8   7   6   5   4   3   2   1

ISBN: 0-13-086390-4

CONTENTS

8 DEBT CRISES, THE ASIAN MELTDOWN, AND U.S. POLICY TOWARD THE IMF AND WORLD BANK   194

by Daniel M. Green

ACKNOWLEDGMENTS

Chapter 10 originally appeared in *Human Rights and International Political Economy in Third World Nations* (Praeger, 1998); that book is an imprint of Greenwood Publishing Group, Inc., Westport, Conn.
Research for chapter 3 was funded in part by a grant from the U.S. Department of State's Fulbright Scholars Program.

DEDICATION

This textbook is dedicated to the best professors that I ever knew: the late Jim Murray, who taught me foreign policy; the late Vernon Van Dyke, who taught me human rights; and John Nelson, who taught me to be a scholar.

William H. Meyer
Newark, Delaware

LIST OF ABBREVIATIONS

ABM	antiballistic missile
AD	assured destruction
ADA	Atomic Development Authority (Baruch Plan)
AFP	Alliance for Progress
AID	Agency for International Development
ANC	African National Congress
APEC	Asia-Pacific Economic Cooperation
ARVN	Army of the Republic of Vietnam (South Vietnamese army)
BPA	Basic Political Agreement
BUR	bottom-up-review
BWC	Biological Weapons Convention
BWIs	Bretton Woods Institutions
CAAA	Comprehensive Anti-Apartheid Act
CBNs	chemical, biological, and nuclear weapons
CE	constructive engagement
CENTCOM	U.S. Central Command
CENTO	Central Treaty Organization (Baghdad Pact)
CFCs	chlorofluorocarbons
CNN	Cable News Network
CO2	carbon dioxide
CSCE	Conference on Security and Cooperation in Europe
CTB	Comprehensive Test Ban Treaty
CWC	Chemical Weapons Convention
DSB	Dispute Settlement Board
DSM	Dispute Settlement Mechanism
ESAF	Enhanced Structural Adjustment Facility
EPA	Environmental Protection Agency
EU	European Union
FEP	foreign economic policy
FSRs	former Soviet republics
FTAA	Free Trade Area of the Americas
G-7	Group of Seven (Canada, France, Germany, Japan, Italy, UK, USA)
GATS	General Agreement on Trade in Services
GATT	General Agreements on Tariffs and Trade
GCC	Gulf Cooperation Council

GDP	gross domestic product
GSP	Generalized System of Preferences
HIPCs	highly indebted poor countries
HROs	humanitarian relief organizations
IAEA	International Atomic Energy Agency
IBHR	international bill of human rights
IBRD	International Bank for Reconstruction and Development (World Bank)
ICBM	intercontinental ballistic missile (land-based)
IFIs	international financial institutions
ILO	International Labor Organization
ILSA	Iran-Libya Sanctions Act
IMF	International Monetary Fund
INF	intermediate-range nuclear forces
IPA	International Police Academy
ITO	International Trade Organization (Havana Charter)
JNA	National Army of Jugoslavia (Yugoslavia)
KLA	Kosovo Liberation Army
LDCs	less-developed countries
LRB	long-range bomber
MAD	mutual assured destruction
MFN	most favored nation
M.I.P.S.	"maintenance of international peace and security" (UN Charter)
MIRV	multiple independently targetable reentry vehicle (multiple warheads)
MNCs	multinational corporations
MTNs	multilateral trade negotiations
NAFTA	North American Free Trade Agreement
NATO	North Atlantic Treaty Organization
NEP	New Economic Policy
NGO	nongovernmental organization
NICs	newly industrialized countries
NIEO	New International Economic Order
NIIO	New International Information Order
NMD	national missile defense
NPT	Nonproliferation Treaty
NSA	National Security Act
NSC	National Security Council
NSC-68	National Security Council Memorandum #68
NTBs	nontariff barriers
NTR	normal trade relations
NUTS	nuclear utilization theories
NWO	new world order

OAS	Organization of American States
OPC	Operation Provide Comfort
OPCW	Organization for the Prohibition of Chemical Weapons
OPEC	Organization of Petroleum Exporting Countries
OPR	Operation Provide Relief
OPS	Office of Public Safety
OSCE	Organization for Security and Cooperation in Europe
OSH	Operation Support Hope
PDD 25	Presidential Decision Directive #25
PLO	Palestinian Liberation Organization
PRC	People's Republic of China
PTB	Partial Test Ban Treaty
RDF	Rapid Deployment Force
ROK	Republic of Korea (South Korea)
RPF	Rwandan Patriotic Front (Tutsi army)
RSA	Republic of South Africa
RTAA	Reciprocal Trade Agreements Act
SAF	Structural Adjustment Facility
SALs	structural adjustment loans
SALT	Strategic Arms Limitation Treaty
SDC	Sustainable Development Commission
SDI	Strategic Defense Initiative
SDRs	special drawing rights
SEA	Single European Act
SLBM	submarine-launched ballistic missile
START	Strategic Arms Reduction Treaty
TRIMs	trade-related investment measures
TRIPs	trade-related intellectual properties
UDHR	Universal Declaration of Human Rights
UK	United Kingdom (Great Britain)
UN	United Nations
UNAMIR	UN Assistance Mission in Rwanda
UNCED	UN Conference on Environment and Development
UNDPO	UN Department of Peacekeeping Operations
UNEP	UN Environmental Program
UNESCO	UN Educational, Scientific and Cultural Organization
UNISOM II	UN Operation in Somalia
UNITAF	United Task Force
UNPROFOR	UN Protection Force (Bosnia)
USSR	Union of Socialist Soviet Republics (Soviet Union)
USTR	United States Trade Representative
Y2K	year 2000
W-P	Weinberger-Powell Doctrine
WTO	World Trade Organization

PREFACE

Every destination is determined, at least in part,
by the road that lies behind us,
the road already traveled.

"You know where it ends, yo, it usually depends on where you start."[1]

Global political trends and American foreign policy are changing in more ways, and changing more quickly, than at any other time in history. Because the world is changing so rapidly, we are in greater need of understanding the recent past. What is the status of U.S. foreign policy at the outset of the new millennium? What are the important trends and likely future prospects for American policy? To answer these questions, we must begin by looking at our past. To know where we are headed, we must first know where we have been. Where we end up usually depends on where we started. Every destination is determined in part by the path already traveled. Knowing the history of certain Cold War events is indispensable for understanding foreign policies of the present and the future. The overall goal of this book is to provide the historical background necessary for students to understand contemporary and future American foreign policies.

This book employs a historical approach for understanding U.S. foreign policy in three areas: security policy, economic policy, and ethical dimensions of foreign policy. For each of these three areas there is a separate subsection in the text. Each subsection begins with a history of American foreign policy in that area. Each section then proceeds to separate chapters on the most important and most salient areas of contemporary foreign policy. This book was produced by a joint effort involving seven people in the Department of Political Science and International Relations at the University of Delaware. Roughly half of the text was contributed by the book's principal author and editor, William Meyer. Six chapters come from the works of other current or former members of the department.

Part I begins with a two-chapter history of defense policies since World War II, including the Cold War conflicts in Korea and Vietnam. Looking at the Korean War of the 1950s helps us to understand important contemporary U.S. policies, such as current troop deployments in South Korea and American fears of a possible missile attack from North Korea in the twenty-first century. Similarly, a look back at the Vietnam War informs a proper understanding of contemporary U.S. intervention doctrines, such as the Weinberger-Powell Doctrine. Chapter 3 then moves to a history of nuclear defense policies and arms control. Chapter 3 also considers the topic of strategic defense. Reviewing the evolution of two theories of nuclear deterrence (e.g., MAD vs. NUTS) helps one understand why the United States is now engaged in a long process of reducing nuclear arsenals and why America is wrestling with a debate over national missile defense. Chapters 4 and 5 look in more detail at U.S foreign policy in the Middle East and at post–Cold War humanitarian intervention.

The Middle East warrants inclusion as the only region in this text with a separate chapter, due to America's geopolitical interests. Everyone understands the importance of oil to U.S. national interests. The Middle East deserves close attention due to the Gulf War of 1990–91 (in addition to the aftermath of that war) and due to the ongoing U.S. war against terrorism. Chapter 4 was written by Bahram Rajaee, the University of Delaware's resident expert on American foreign policy toward the Middle East.[2] Chapter 5 on humanitarian intervention is by Robert DiPrizio, now teaching at the U.S. Air Force's Air Command and Staff College. DiPrizio previously did research on post–Cold War intervention tactics at the University of Delaware.[3]

Part I concludes with a chapter by Mark J. Miller on American foreign policy in regard to terrorism. The importance of this topic is familiar to all Americans since the tragic events of September 11, 2001, a date that no American will forget. The events of that day have had a profound impact on U.S. foreign policy as well. Immediately after September 11, a common claim in the media and by political pundits was that "everything has changed." This is true in one crucial sense. After 9/11, Americans lost their sense of the invulnerability of American soil. Despite the nuclear balance of terror during the Cold War, few Americans ever felt threatened by direct foreign attack while inside the fifty states. That certainly has changed. But in so many other respects, the assertion that everything changed after 9/11 was an exaggerated (though understandable) claim. As Mark Miller points out in chapter 6, even current U.S. foreign policy for fighting terrorism has its roots in decisions (and mistakes) made during the Cold War.

The events of September 11, 2001, also revealed the interrelated nature of the three previously mentioned areas of foreign policy: security policy, economic policy, and the ethical dimensions of foreign policy. Security policy was shaken to its foundations by these attacks on the American homeland. Symbols of America's economic power, the World Trade Center towers, were the principal targets of the terrorists' attacks. The moral legitimacy of America's methods for conducting its war against terrorism was a subject of debate immediately after 9/11, especially in regard to the treatment of Al-Qaida and Taliban prisoners held at the Guantanamo Bay military base. Human rights groups such as Amnesty International and Human Rights Watch leveled accusations that some of these prisoners had been tortured.[4] In that respect, 9/11 reinforced the consensus among the authors of this text that defense policies, economic policies, and ethical policies are inextricably intertwined; hence the logic of this book's format.

Part II of this text begins with a history of America's foreign economic policies, broken down into the areas of trade policy and monetary policy. Follow-up chapters in part II by Daniel Green and Candace Archer go into more detail on contemporary policies toward the IMF and the WTO. Green has been researching U.S. policy toward international financial institutions for many years.[5] Archer has specialized in research on economic regimes, including the GATT/WTO trade regime.[6]

Part III addresses a mixed bag of topics that are often overlooked in textbooks on American foreign policy: human rights, the environment, and policy toward Third World nations. These topics are linked together by their normative dimensions. They are areas that force us to consider the ethical aspects of U.S international policies. Human rights policy has certain obvious links to moral standards. International environmental policy is supremely important to America due to the moral obligations we owe to current and future generations. The environment has economic and security impacts as well,[7] but by including environmental politics in part III, the authors hope to stress (albeit indirectly) the moral dimensions of sound environmental policy.

U.S. relations with the less-developed countries (LDCs) of the Third World are closely related to environmental politics. The Third World is often overlooked by students of U.S. policy because it has limited economic importance for American trade and because the end of the Cold War greatly reduced perceptions of the Third World's importance to U.S. security. The United States became engaged in relations with the Third World after the Cold War mainly due to its moral obligations to promote development in LDCs (this is a topic discussed in more detail in the introduction to part III).

Part III opens with a review of two theories linking morality to U.S. foreign policy. Chapter 10 also presents a history of human rights policies. Part III then proceeds to a history of U.S. relations with the Third World, focusing on environmental politics between the north and the south. Chapter 12 by Richard Sylves wraps up part III. Sylves's areas of expertise at the University of Delaware include global environmental politics.[8]

The conclusion to this text considers both continuity and changes in American foreign policy (for all of the previously mentioned areas) under the administration of President George W. Bush (who was well into his second year in office at the time of this writing).

This preface must end with two caveats regarding what this book is not about. This book will not use "theories" of American foreign policy to structure each chapter. Use of abstract theory is a common approach to foreign policy used in other textbooks,[9] but not here. Nor will the primary focus of this text be on the processes involved in making American foreign policy. This is another common approach used in other literatures for the study of U.S policy.[10] These methods (theory and policy making) are important and instructive, but they cannot substitute for good historical research on American foreign policy.

One must always be very careful when making theoretical claims as they apply to the social sciences. This is especially true in the study of foreign policy. Each case is highly unique. Therefore, to try to generalize across cases is hazardous at best. One simply cannot generalize across cases for most aspects of foreign policy. Because generalizations are not possible in most cases, the historical approach is even more necessary and justified. "Theory building" via higher and higher levels of abstraction and generalization is problematic for studies of foreign policy. By contrast, it is certainly possible (and even necessary) to understand how one policy approach evolves over time into subsequent policies.[11] For example, many post–Cold War foreign policies cannot be fully understood until after certain Cold War historical facts have been mastered. But the history of Cold War politics needs to be told in such a way as to make it as relevant as possible to current and future policy.

Likewise, the making of foreign policy is a topic that is separate and distinct (in some ways) from the history of the policies themselves. In this text, the focus must be on the latter. Policy-making approaches focus on process. Here the focus will be on policy outputs.

It is not possible in a single text to adequately cover (a) foreign policy "theory," (b) foreign policy making, and (c) the evolutionary history of a wide range of specific foreign policies. In the collective view of these seven authors, the last of these three areas is, indeed, a prerequisite to studies regarding the first two areas. This text can be seen as providing a necessary first step for students who plan to go on to broader or more in-depth studies of American foreign policy.

With these caveats in mind, we hasten to add that theories of foreign policy will not be ignored in this text. Each subsection has its own introduction. Each introduction will lay out the basic theoretical debates relevant to a given area of foreign policy. Theories of national security, of international political economy, and of international norms have given us the conceptual frameworks and the terminology often employed in (descriptive) historical analyses. The introduction to part I begins our study with a brief summary of theories relevant to U.S. defense policy.

William H. Meyer
University of Delaware

PART I

WAR

INTRODUCTION TO PART I

Security policy has been the most extensively studied realm of American foreign policy. Theoretical approaches to defense policy have been remarkably consistent from the Cold War into the post–Cold War era. These theories of international politics and foreign policy tend to cluster into a handful of views. Before proceeding to in-depth studies of past and present American policy, a brief review of these theories would be useful.

The dominant approach to American foreign policy during both the Cold War and the post–Cold War periods has been realism. Realism has occupied the mainstream in debates over the proper way to conceptualize foreign policies. Realism posits the nation-state as the dominant actor in world politics and assumes that nation-states are driven to act by their national interests. The primary means to protect and promote these national interests is power, especially military power. Human nature is characterized as antagonistic (even inherently evil) by most realists.[1] Realists also stress the anarchic nature of global politics. Because there is no world government to restrict the actions of nations (especially the most powerful nations), analysis of foreign policy must realize that states will normally pursue self-help strategies operating in a context of uncertainty and danger. International politics tend to be conflictual according to this view, and therefore a realist's principal policy recommendations are to expand national power while balancing (or otherwise counteracting) the power of enemies and potential enemies. A realist seeks safety for the nation via military power and recommends balance-of-power strategies as the best way to promote international stability.

Realist approaches to foreign policy have been influenced by a long intellectual history in Western civilization. Realists find some of their earliest influences in the works of Thucydides, the classical Greek historian. Realists can also trace their roots back to early modern thinkers such as Machiavelli,

Hobbes, and Rousseau.[2] Twentieth century realism was developed by such notables as Carr, Morgenthau, Kennan, and Kissinger.[3] More recent extensions of this perspective are referred to as "neorealism." Neorealists such as Waltz and Gilpin focus their attention on the anarchic international system itself as a prime determinant of trends in foreign policies.[4] Neorealists argue that the "international system" is an "actor" in its own right and that the system helps to determine foreign policy outcomes (e.g., the existence of war, or the tendency for balances of power to arise and be replicated around the globe).[5]

The primary challenge to realist analysis, but also a mainstream view, has been labeled as "liberalism" or "idealism." Liberalism as a theoretical approach to international politics and foreign policy challenges some of the basic assumptions of realism. Liberalism tends to stress the human capacity for cooperation, at both the individual and the national levels. Advocates for liberalism in U.S. policy, such as Woodrow Wilson, have argued that most nations share a number of common interests. National interests do not necessarily have to conflict. Foreign policies that seek cooperation through international organizations can often be more effective than foreign policies that rely on unilateral military power. Therefore, liberals are more likely than realists to stress the importance of actors other than national governments. Liberalism posits international organizations, nongovernmental organizations, and interest groups (in addition to the federal government) as actors that must be studied for an adequate understanding of American foreign policy.

Liberalism, like realism, finds its antecedents in the works of a long line of thinkers, stretching back over hundreds of years. During the early modern period, philosophers such as Grotius, Montesquieu, and Kant developed the basic premises upon which liberalism is based.[6] In the twentieth century, liberalism was popularized and defended in the works of Wilson, Keohane, Nye, and Fukuyama.[7] As with realism, many of these thinkers have played a direct role in shaping U.S. policy, both through their academic writings and as members of the State Department. Today, this view is often referred to as "neoliberal institutionalism," due to its stress on the importance of international institutions (such as economic regimes).[8]

Other approaches to foreign policy tend to go to other "levels" of analysis. Foreign policy is a very complex area of study, and different theorists tend to stress different causal factors. Some prefer to analyze the impact of public opinion or interest groups on foreign policy.[9] Others find the key factors for explaining particular foreign policy decisions in the operations of government bureaucracies that carry out American policy. A seminal work from this school of thought is Allison's study of the 1962 Cuban missile crisis.[10] Allison's work has shown how specific policy decisions, both in times of crisis and in times of business as usual, are often the result of standard operating procedures or "bureaucratic politics" in Washington, D.C. Yet another approach to foreign policy builds on social psychology and employs psychohistories of great leaders to explain the actions of such men and women.[11]

All of the previously mentioned theories find their home within the mainstream. Moving beyond the mainstream, one can also find useful insights in various "critical" approaches to foreign policy and global politics. The one thing that these minority views have in common is their critical stance regarding both realism and liberalism. Critical theorists (who often are very critical of one another) all support the critique that mainstream approaches leave out too many important dimensions of foreign policy. Some of the oldest critical views focus on economic classes and capitalism as key explanatory variables.[12] More recent critical theories take a decidedly postmodern approach to foreign policy by trying to "deconstruct" both mainstream foreign policy theory and everyday foreign policy making.[13] Feminist theory of politics and diplomacy, and theories of social constructivism, are additional critical approaches that give us insights into foreign policy that cannot be found by using traditional, mainstream views.[14]

Rather than getting too bogged down within the many interstices of these theoretical debates, this text will approach foreign policy from a more interpretive (or historical) stance. One view shared by the authors of this book is that theory is useful only insofar as it helps us to understand real-world problems. The problem we have set for ourselves in this text is to help students understand contemporary foreign policy by reviewing the trends that have spawned current policies. Therefore, theory will be brought into the discussion only when it is deemed useful for describing actual policies. Too many theorists prefer to argue about theory for theory's sake, sometimes forgetting that these theories were initially developed for specific purposes. Those purposes have included trying to understand where we are now, how we got here, and where we are likely to go from here.

There are important lessons to be drawn, however, from even a cursory summary of foreign policy theory such as the one presented here. Students of foreign policy need to keep in mind that any description or recommendation regarding foreign policy harbors analytical assumptions about how the world operates and about which approach to policy is best. Often these assumptions are not made explicit by those who write about foreign policy. Students should always be on their guard. They should always do a skeptical reading of any descriptive or prescriptive account of American foreign policy. That includes their reading of this text. Theoretical assumptions can be hidden. Because such assumptions always carry with them hidden ethical standards, students should never take any account of foreign policy at face value.

An awareness of the range of these theoretical stances helps to facilitate a critical reading of any text, hence the theory-based introductions to each subsection of this book. Another thing that helps to develop critical faculties is gaining as much information from as many different sources as possible. Toward that end, each subsection will also present (in its introduction) a range of websites relevant to the topics covered in that part of the book. The first listing of websites follows.

Internet Resources For Part I

Center for the Study of Terrorism and Political Violence (University of St. Andrews)
    www.st-andrews.ac.uk/academic/intrel/research/cstpv

Center for Strategic and International Studies
    www.csis.org

Central Intelligence Agency
    www.cia.gov

Department of Defense
    www.defenselink.mil

Humanitarianism and War Project (Brown University)
    http://hwproject.tufts.edu

Inter-University Center for Terrorism Studies (George Washington University)
    www.gwu.edu/~terror/intunctr.html

Journal of Studies in Conflict and Terrorism
    www.tandf.co.uk/journals/tf/1057610x.html

Journal of Terrorism and Political Violence
    www.frankcass.com/jnls.tpv.htm

Middle East Research and Information Project
    www.merip.org

National Security Council
    www.whitehouse.gov/nsc/index.html

North Atlantic Treaty Organization
    www.nato.int

Senate Foreign Relations Committee
    www.senate.gov/~foreign

State Department
    www.state.gov

State Department Bureau of Near Eastern Affairs
    www.state.gov/p/nea/

Stockholm International Peace Research Institute
    www.sipri.se

UN Peacekeeping Operations
www.un.org/depts/dpko

U.S. Institute for Peace
www.usip.org

The White House
www.whitehouse.gov

Chapter 1

SECURITY POLICY, FROM YALTA TO VIETNAM

1945: A NEW WORLD ORDER?

On three separate occasions in the twentieth century, the United States had an opportunity to remake the face of international relations.[1] The first opportunity came after World War I. At that time, President Woodrow Wilson tried and failed to establish new ground rules for interaction between states under the League of Nations.[2] The third and most recent occasion followed the collapse of the Soviet Union (USSR). After the USSR broke apart and the Cold War ended, American foreign policy had another opportunity to reshape international politics. The jury is still out on whether post–Cold War foreign policy will be successful or if it even has a clear direction.[3] The only clear-cut success for U.S. policy during such a time of reckoning was on the second occasion, following World War II. Containment policies during the Cold War achieved remarkable long-term success. What has often been overlooked, however, is the fact that the United States developed an elaborate and integrated design for the post–World War II world *prior to* the emergence of the Cold War. To understand America's policies of Cold War containment, as well as American policy after the end of the Cold War, one must first go back to U.S. intentions immediately following the defeat of Germany and Japan. American leaders envisioned a post–World War II order that was to grow out of the anti-fascist alliance forged during the war.

Using the terminology invoked by President George Bush immediately after the Cold War, one could say that the United States desired a "new world order" in 1945.[4] The term *new world order* is often used to refer to little more than the international balance of power. In a larger sense, however, one might think of a new world order (NWO) as a time during which new "rules" are established for the global "game" of international relations. After World War II and prior to the hostility that characterized the Cold War, American leaders conceptualized a NWO that was to exist on two levels. First, peace at the global level would be ensured by the UN Security Council. Second, a lower-level and supplemental order would be based on a system of regional dominance.

Part I of the 1945 New World Order: M.I.P.S. by the Security Council

In late 1945, the United States looked out on a world that was very different from what had just preceded it. America's most deadly enemies of the day, Germany and Japan, had been defeated. Each was forced into an unconditional surrender. Both were occupied by the victorious powers. All other major military powers in the world at that time were allies of the United States The United Nations (UN) was created by the Allied powers in hopes that the cooperation used to defeat fascist dictatorships would carry over into the postwar era. A privileged position for the "big five" victors (the USA, the USSR, Great Britain, France, and China) was institutionalized within the UN.[5] Each was given a permanent seat and a veto at the UN Security Council.

The Security Council has the power under the UN Charter to use force, if necessary, to maintain international peace and security. Maintenance of international peace and security (M.I.P.S.) was one of the founding purposes of the UN.[6] Because the Security Council has direct control over M.I.P.S., and because each permanent member of the Security Council has a veto, unanimity by the big five became a prerequisite for the use of force by the UN. This was part of America's grand design. Big five cooperation at the Security Council, it was assumed, would prevent future wars. The Security Council would safeguard M.I.P.S. at the global level. Each of the big five would also have a regional domain where they would be responsible for local matters of peace and stability.

Part II of the 1945 New World Order: A System of Regional Dominance

As a supplement to M.I.P.S. by the Security Council at the global level, America's NWO for 1945 included a regional dimension. Each of the big five would be expected to keep order and stability within its own bailiwick. The United States would be responsible for security in the Western Hemisphere. This was consistent with American foreign policy going back at least as far as the Monroe Doctrine of 1823.[7] Great Britain would manage things inside its empire, which was converted after World War II into the Commonwealth of Nations. France was to be rearmed and made dominant within continental Europe. France could thereby keep Germany in check. China, still a noncommunist power and an American ally, would be rebuilt and rearmed to be the top power in east Asia. China would stand guard as the local watchdog to prevent a resurgent militarism in Japan. In this system of regional "policemen,"[8] however, the USSR was the odd man out.

The extent of Soviet political and military hegemony after 1945 was something that Russian and American leaders could never agree upon. Soviet dictator Joseph Stalin clearly hoped to control all of Eastern Europe. Presidents Roosevelt and Truman just as clearly did not want to concede that part of the world to the Soviets. Roosevelt met with Stalin and British Prime Minister Winston Churchill at Yalta (on the Soviet Crimean peninsula) in February 1945. They established a political architecture for postwar Europe that was to follow Germany's surrender. There was a lot of wishful thinking at Yalta in 1945. However, there was no long-term meeting of the minds regarding the proper Soviet presence in Eastern Europe.

Stalin's primary concern at the Yalta meetings was to eliminate the possibility of another invasion into Russia from central Europe. He wanted guarantees that the Red Army would never have to face another onslaught like the one inflicted by Hitler's fighting machine, the *Wermacht*. Stalin proposed the dismemberment of Germany. Stalin also demanded that nations freed from Nazi occupation must maintain "friendly" relations with the USSR. To stack the deck in his favor, Stalin drove his forces as far as he could into central Europe. His final attack crushed the remaining German forces stationed on the eastern front. Roosevelt and Churchill both felt that, given Stalin's well-known paranoia, his demand for friendly states along the Soviet frontier was a legitimate concern. As a way to placate Soviet fears, both Roosevelt and Churchill believed that Stalin's wishes should be granted in this key area.

The final agreements from Yalta were contained in the "Protocol of Proceedings of the Crimea Conference."[9] The outlines of the soon-to-be-created Security Council (including veto powers) were defined. Stalin was promised "friendly" buffer states on his borders in exchange for a Soviet declaration of war against Japan. Under the terms of Yalta, all anti-Nazi parties that resisted German occupation during the war were to take part in the new governments formed in Eastern Europe after the war. Stalin and the Red Army did allow coalition governments to form in some of these states (e.g., Czechoslovakia) immediately after the war. Communist and noncommunist partisans shared power, as was stipulated in the Yalta Protocol. However, Stalin would soon see to it that communist, one-party dictatorships replaced these coalitions.

Failure by Stalin to carry out the terms of Yalta in accordance with Western expectations was just one of many sources of tension between the erstwhile allies. The new order that the United States had hoped to create in 1945 was not to be. The global dimension of M.I.P.S. by the Security Council never materialized in a manner consistent with American plans. The system of regional dominance never worked either. Stalin moved quickly to expand the still undefined Soviet sphere of influence. The United States for its part, found that it had to assume unilateral leadership for defense of Western interests not only in the Western hemisphere but also in Western Europe, in east Asia, and in the remnants of the British and French empires as well.

Hopes for postwar cooperation by the big five within the UN were dashed by the competition, even outright confrontation, that characterized the inaugural meetings of the Security Council. Lack of cooperation between the Americans and the Soviets meant that the UN would be largely ineffective in preventing war. Designs for a NWO after 1945 were replaced by the early Cold War.

ORIGINS OF THE COLD WAR

For more than fifty years, scholars and diplomats have debated the causes of the Cold War. Did Stalin start the Cold War with his duplicity at Yalta and subsequent repression of Eastern Europe? Or did the United States back Stalin into a corner with its policies of mistrust, thereby "forcing" him into a hostile, but defensive, posture? Recent analyses go so far as to claim that American foreign policy "constructed" Stalin as our enemy (presumably implying that, as an alternative, we could have "constructed" him as something other than an enemy).[10] The debate over who started the Cold War will not be settled here. Regardless of one's view about who started the Cold War (doubtless both sides shared some of the blame), it is undeniable that particular flashpoints and global hot spots carried the postwar superpowers into a Cold War situation.

Instead of the cooperation that Americans hoped for under the NWO of 1945, competition and conflict emerged as early as 1946. The roots of the Cold War go back even farther, however. Although the United States and Russia were allies against Germany during both world wars, the two nations had always been suspicious of one another. Russians have never really trusted the United States (a sentiment that persists to this day). Communists, led by Lenin, came to power in Moscow in the midst of World War I. After the war, the United States sent 10,000 troops into Russia between 1918 and 1920.[11] U.S. forces gave half-hearted support to a counterrevolution that tried, unsuccessfully, to unseat the communist regime. This intervention, to which the British and French also contributed forces, served to feed fears of "capitalist encirclement" held by Stalin and others in Russia. Stalin's paranoia and his doctrinaire Marxism led him to believe that the West would destroy communist Russia if it ever had the chance.

Americans have never really trusted the Russians either. After Lenin and the Bolshevik party came to power, they abandoned their World War I alliance with the United States. Lenin argued that World War I was a bourgeois war, one fought by capitalists on both sides, and a war in which no proletarian army should participate. Even more significant, Stalin signed a nonaggression pact with Hitler in 1939 in hopes of keeping the Soviet Union out of World War II (a treaty that Hitler later voided with his invasion of Russia).[12] In the context of this long history of mistrust, the United States and the USSR faced off over several crises shortly after World War II. The potential for direct military confrontation between the former allies was very high in many of these cases.

The first crisis centered around the Azerbaijan region in Iran.[13] (See Figure 1.1.) The United States, Britain, and the USSR all had troops in Iran when World War II ended. U.S. and British troops withdrew after the war, but Stalin kept his forces in the Azerbaijan province (northwest Iran) seeking oil concessions from the Iranian government. The Soviets went so far as to support a revolt of the locals and sought to establish a puppet regime in the Azerbaijan province that would grant them access to Iranian oil. The United States demanded that Stalin withdraw from Iran and took its case to the newly created Security Council. At its very first meeting in 1946, the Security Council had to deal with a situation that threatened to explode into war between two of the permanent members. This was a far cry from the cooperative model that America had envisioned for the postwar world order. The U.S. secretary of state threatened the Soviets with force, and Stalin eventually decided to withdraw his army from Iran.

At roughly the same time, a second crisis emerged in Turkey. After World War II, Stalin revived a centuries-old Russian demand that Turkey share access to the Black Sea. The Black Sea has always been a key strategic area for Russian and Soviet navies. Specifically, Stalin wanted the Turks to give up control of one side of the Dardanelles, a narrow choke point at the entrance to the Black Sea. This transfer of territory would have required revision of the 1936 International Straits agreement.[14] To show how serious he was, Stalin amassed troops along the Soviet border with Turkey. Once again, U.S. leaders reacted with alarm. A naval carrier group was mobilized, and American Marines were also dispatched into the area. Once again, after the United States threatened force, Stalin eventually dropped his demands.

American leaders also suspected that Stalin was behind the communist uprising that led to civil war in Greece (1947–49). By 1947, the United States simply assumed that the Greek communists must have been getting their external military supplies directly or indirectly from Stalin. Actually, most of their support was coming from Yugoslavia, not from the Soviets. President Truman felt so strongly about the need for U.S. military aid to the Greek government that he went to Congress in March 1947 and gave the now-famous Truman Doctrine speech. Truman asked Congress to approve $400 million in aid for Greece and Turkey (the Truman Doctrine will be described in greater detail later).

Perhaps these events did not have to lead to a full-blown Cold War. If superpower competition had ended with Iran, Greece, and Turkey, the Cold War might have been avoided. Events in Eastern Europe, however, took both sides beyond the point of no return.

FIGURE 1.1

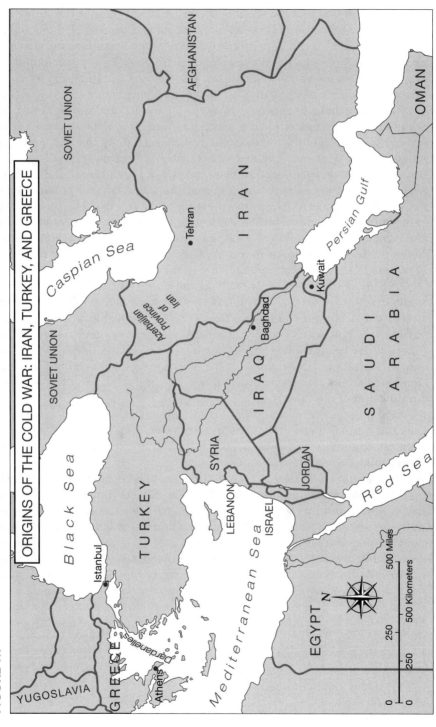

ORIGINS OF THE COLD WAR: IRAN, TURKEY, AND GREECE

One of the earliest disagreements over territories east of the Rhine concerned Poland. The postwar situation in Poland had been singled out and addressed at length in the Yalta protocols. The United States believed that Yalta required the Soviets (as the occupying power) to allow the noncommunist Polish government-in-exile to return from London and participate in a postwar coalition. Stalin, however, had other plans. The government of national unity that was to include "democratic leaders . . . from Poles abroad" was never formed. The "free and unfettered" elections specified by Yalta never took place. Instead, a 1947 election was conducted by the Soviets that exhibited "every conceivable electoral abuse."[15] Similar events took place in Czechoslovakia.

A coalition government had been formed in Czechoslovakia after World War II.[16] For a time, communists and noncommunists shared political power (in keeping with the Western interpretation of Yalta). By 1948, however, the noncommunist parties had been stripped of their independent status and forced into a single political amalgamation controlled by the communists. Stalin massed troops and tanks on the Czech border as leaders of the Czech communists eliminated all independent parties.[17]

The most important standoff, and the event that took the world irreversibly into the Cold War, was the Berlin blockade of 1948–49. Indeed, the precise date when the Cold War officially began is arguable. Perhaps it was as early as the Iranian crisis of 1946, perhaps not. However, under any interpretation of the historical record, Stalin's imposition of the Berlin blockade in June 1948 and the U.S. response to the blockade signaled that both sides had developed a Cold War mentality. This text, therefore, will use 1948 as its date for the onset of the Cold War.[18]

Berlin became the focal point of U.S. foreign policy in the early days of the Cold War. Located in the heart of eastern Germany, Berlin is an important political, cultural, and economic center for all of Germany. Due to the terms of the four-power occupation of Germany, the Soviet occupation zone surrounded Berlin on all sides. The city of Berlin, like Germany itself, was divided into occupation zones for the victors. The Soviets controlled the eastern half of the city (and country). The United States Britain, and France stationed troops in western Berlin. By 1948, Stalin was determined to expel the Western powers from West Berlin.

On June 24, 1948, the Soviet army cut all road, rail, and water routes linking West Berlin to western Germany. Food, energy supplies, and other necessities that had been supplied to West Berlin from the Soviet sector were also cut off. Stalin was hoping to force the West out of Berlin altogether. The United States, Britain, and France considered sending an armed convoy to force open the roads between Berlin and Western Germany. This option was rejected, however, in favor of a massive airlift. For nearly a year, food, fuel, and other goods were flown from western Germany into West Berlin. (See Figure 1.2.)

President Truman raised the stakes during the Berlin crisis by deploying B-29 bombers to Europe as part of the airlift strategy. In 1948, the United

FIGURE 1.2

ORIGINS OF THE COLD WAR: DIVISION OF
EUROPE AND THE BERLIN BLOCKADE

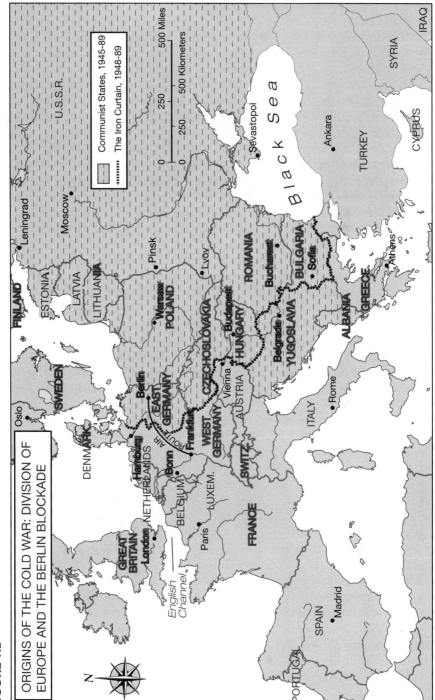

States was still the only nation with atomic weapons. The B-29 had been designed specifically to carry atomic bombs. Truman, who had ordered the atomic bombing of Japan toward the end of World War II, made it clear that he would not hesitate to use the "A Bomb" if war were to erupt over Berlin. America's monopoly on atomic weapons was still Truman's ace in the hole. Few doubted that he would use them again. Due to Stalin's aggression and Truman's reaction, the world stood on the brink of World War III in 1948.

Given America's atomic weapons monopoly, Stalin had little choice but to back down yet again. In May 1949, he lifted the blockade in return for a promise by the Western powers for an international conference on Berlin. That conference was later held in Paris, but nothing significant came out of it. West Berlin remained firmly under Western control, and the Soviets continued to bluster about the need for all of Berlin to be placed in their hands. Although West Berlin continued to be a trip wire for East–West confrontations (e.g., during Khrushchev's 1958 "ultimatum" and during the 1962 Cuban missile crisis), it never fell to the communists.

By 1949, Western leaders in general and President Truman in particular came to the conclusion that events from Iran (1946) to Berlin (1948) were part of a larger pattern. Communism was seen as a monolithic bloc. All communist activities around the globe must be controlled by Stalin, and all communist aggression was traceable back to the Kremlin. China's noncommunist government was overthrown by Mao Zedong's communist party in 1949, and Mao reinforced America's image of a unified global communist conspiracy. Mao spoke of the USSR and of Stalin in glowing terms during the early 1950s. The Soviets also exploded their first atomic weapon in 1949, adding to American fears.

In Eastern Europe, there seemed to be a specific pattern to Soviet domination. Yalta had provided coalitions in some cases. But the Soviet Red Army also occupied most of this region. The Soviets used their control over transportation and communication links in Eastern Europe and their police powers to favor local communist parties. In those states where coalitions had been formed, the Czech model of takeover was followed. Communist party leaders would move quickly to secure control of the interior ministry. Stalin would then transfer police powers and authority over law and order to them. Noncommuinsts would be coerced into a single-party national front, dominated by the communists. Finally, non-Marxists within the national front would be stripped of their power, and all other parties would be outlawed.

By the end of the 1940s, the Cold War dominated world politics and American foreign policy. The United States was forced to abandon all hopes for a NWO based on cooperation between the superpowers. Leaders were forced to develop new strategies to fight the Cold War. The key elements of early Cold War policy were the Marshall Plan, the Truman Doctrine, and the creation of NATO. There was a brief debate, however, regarding the wisdom of fighting the Cold War. The two sides of this debate advocated either the policy of containment or an approach known as "Fortress America."

THE EARLY COLD WAR ERA

Containment versus Fortress America

While the Cold War emerged, leaders in Washington argued over the best way to respond to these new threats. Former president Herbert Hoover and the conservative wing of the Republican Party favored an approach that they dubbed "Fortress America." Fortress America was little more than a new name for isolationism. Isolationism had been the preferred approach to America's role in the world since the end of the Revolutionary War. It had also been a policy that worked well for U.S. interests prior to the two world wars.

The hallmark of isolationism had always been a refusal by America to enter into any permanent military alliances. From the end of the revolutionary period to the beginning of the Second World War, the United States entered into no permanent military alliances. The United States also eschewed all military alliances when it faced no direct, violent hostilities.[19] The Cold War would soon change all that. Hoover and the Fortress America camp, however, believed that a return to isolationism was the wisest course of action. According to this view, the United States would stay out of Europe and away from the Orient. Fortress America was based on policies that would defend only North and South America. This faction believed that enough resources existed in the Western Hemisphere to keep the U.S. economy strong and robust. As had been the case after World War I, America would cut military ties to its European allies. According to diplomatic historians, the majority of American public opinion was pro-isolationism until as late as 1947.[20]

The other side of this debate, and the view that would eventually win out, was containment. Early policies of containment were developed by George Kennan. Writing in the journal *Foreign Affairs* in 1947 under the pseudonym "Mr. X," Kennan laid out the basic logic of containment. U.S. policy had to contain the spread of Soviet power and influence. Kennan's view was based, in part, on the belief that the Soviets would expand only in situations where they perceived their risks to be low. Stalin was more conservative and less of a risk taker than it might seem, Kennan argued.[21] The USSR, therefore, would not attempt to expand when it was met by strong resistance. If the United States opposed Soviet adventurism forcefully enough, Stalin would back down. Events in Iran, Turkey, and Berlin seemed to support Kennan's claims. The Soviets may try to expand their hegemony gradually and cautiously, but there would be no high-risk adventures and no attempt at a global takeover (i.e., no support from Stalin for worldwide revolution).

Kennan's policy recommendation was for constant vigilance. The United States would have to keep watch over all areas vital to its national interests. If the Soviets threatened American interests in any vital region, quick and decisive action must be taken to show them that nothing would come easily or at a low cost. Until 1948, containment was a hard sell for Kennan and Truman. Before 1948 most Americans favored isolationism. The Berlin crisis was the event that finally tipped the scales in favor of the Mr. X formula for containment.[22] Because of the Berlin blockade, a majority of U.S. public opinion shifted away from isolationism toward support for containment.

Containment won the day, and isolationism was eliminated as the preferred American foreign policy. The victorious camp developed its initial methods of containment by means of the Truman Doctrine, the Marshall Plan, and NATO.

The Truman Doctrine, the Marshall Plan, and NATO

The events that brought the United States and the USSR into the Cold War also led to the first American policies on how to fight the Cold War. The Truman Doctrine was originally devised as a way to inhibit the spread of Soviet influence in Western Europe. It later expanded to become the primary vehicle for containment at a global level. The particular cases that first produced the declaration of the Truman Doctrine were the postwar crises in Greece and Turkey. The Greek government was trying to put down an internal communist uprising. The Turks needed assistance to resist pressure from Stalin on their borders. Prior to World War II, Greece and Turkey had received most of their aid from Great Britain. In the late 1940s they once again turned to Britain for support, but the English government was unable to respond. Britain had been economically devastated by two world wars and was struggling to rebuild. When the British began to retreat from their overseas commitments, especially in the Mediterranean and the Middle East, the United States had to step in to pick up the slack.

President Truman offered Greece and Turkey $400 million, but he did not stop there. Truman generalized from these two cases. In 1947, Truman told Congress that he wanted the authority to help any nation that was fighting against internal communist subversion or external communist pressure. In practice, the Truman Doctrine pledged economic aid, military assistance, and even U.S. troops to do the fighting if necessary.

The Truman Doctrine was a form of military containment. The Marshall Plan was an economic approach to containment that supplemented Truman's military doctrine. Announced in the same year as the Truman Doctrine, the Marshall Plan provided more than $16 billion during a four-year period to help rebuild Western Europe.[23] America's postwar economic health required trade with Western Europe. When Stalin took control of Eastern Europe, he halted almost all trade between East and West. Communist control over Western Europe would allow Stalin to cut off that part of the world from the United States as well. Free trade with Europe would remain possible only if the democratic governments in the West were protected from Soviet domination.

There was also good reason in the 1940s to fear the rise of indigenous communist parties in Western Europe. In those days, the local communist party in France was receiving as much as twenty-five percent of the popular vote in national elections. At the same time, local communist parties in Italy were being voted into power at the municipal level. American ideology ascribed these electoral gains by communists in the West to the economic problems brought on by World War II. Western European nations first tried to rebuild after the war on an individual basis. Unemployment was high, the industrial base was devastated by wartime destruction, and national reconstruction efforts failed. The United States stepped in to offer aid to rebuild under the Marshall Plan, but the money came with strings attached. In order to qualify for Marshall Plan assistance, all nations had to integrate their rebuilding efforts and present to the United States a single, coordinated reconstruction plan.

The ultimate goal of the Marshall Plan was containment. U.S. leaders believed that if the economic devastation in Europe could be overcome, then the Marshall Plan would indirectly diminish the threat of indigenous communist parties attracting votes. People would be put back to work, and communist party propaganda would become less persuasive for working-class voters. The Marshall Plan was a rousing success in at least two senses. First of all, the rebuilding of Western Europe succeeded well beyond anyone's expectations. Second, once economic growth took off in Europe, communist parties in the West lost much of their popularity at the ballot box.

Communist governments in Eastern Europe, including the USSR, were also invited to participate in the Marshall Plan. However, the Soviets refused to integrate their economic planning with Western Europe as the Marshall Plan required. In effect, the preconditions laid down by the United States required recipients to open their books and allow American oversight of their development strategies. Stalin would never agree to such terms. Indeed, it would appear that the United States imposed these conditions on Marshall Plan funding as a way to guarantee Soviet nonparticipation.[24]

The third dimension of early Cold War containment was the creation of the North Atlantic Treaty Organization (NATO). NATO was established in 1949 with twelve founding members: the United States, Belgium, Britain, Canada, Denmark, France, Iceland, Italy, Luxembourg, the Netherlands, Norway, and Portugal. Greece and Turkey joined in 1952 to strengthen the alliance's southeastern flank. West Germany became a member in 1955, and Spain joined in 1982. When the two Germanys were reunited in 1990, the unified state remained within NATO. Post–Cold War international agreements stipulate that NATO's non-German troops and nuclear weapons cannot be deployed into the territory that was once communist East Germany. After the end of the Cold War, NATO also expanded into Eastern Europe. Its newest members were added in 1999: the Czech Republic, Hungary, and Poland. Each of the new members was once a communist satellite of the USSR.

During the Cold War, NATO had two founding purposes. First and foremost was to create a military alliance that would deter a Soviet invasion of Western Europe. Under Article 5 of the NATO charter, an attack against any one nation in the alliance is considered to be "an attack against them all."[25]

The creation of NATO directly tied the United States to the defense of all NATO's other members. It is a permanent military alliance, the first significant alliance that the United States ever entered into *in advance* of hostilities. The creation of NATO in 1949 ended isolationism in American foreign policy for all time.

A secondary purpose for NATO, and one that remains relevant even in a post–Cold War world, was to create an external check on German military power. Germany is prohibited by treaties signed after World War II from possessing its own nuclear weapons. However, as long as NATO exists, America's nuclear arsenal is the last line of defense for all of its European allies, obviating any need for Germany to create an independent nuclear force. Hence, because the Cold War ended and NATO no longer needs to worry about a Russian invasion, the existence of NATO serves the cause of peace and security in Europe by maintaining that external check on any possible resurgent German militarism.

The end of the Cold War has also brought about a new "mission" for NATO. NATO forces have become an indispensable element for peacekeeping and peace enforcing in places such as Bosnia and Kosovo (see chapter 5). Such out-of-area military operations were not envisioned when NATO was established. However, as we shall see in chapter 5, only NATO has been able to muster the power and the will to stop ethnic cleansing and genocide in southeastern Europe. Despite this, some have questioned the need for the continued existence of NATO now that the Cold War is over. Germany's place in NATO is one obvious answer to such questions. As long as NATO exists, neither Germany nor Russia shall ever again pose a threat to their neighbors. Concurrently, NATO's actions in the Balkans have been the subject of much controversy. How can NATO justify such activity under the terms of its own treaty? This is because, in the phrase used by Secretary of State Madeleine Albright, "Non-Article 5 threats can become Article 5 threats if they are not addressed early."[26] NATO's supporters believe that genocide in any part of Europe represents a long-term threat to international peace and security. Therefore, genocide in the Balkans, if left unchecked, threatens the peace of all NATO members.

The debate over the continued need and the proper actions for NATO in a post–Cold War world will be addressed in greater detail later in this text. However, it is important to note at this point that one cannot separate the events of the Cold War (such as the creation of NATO) from the subsequent political and military crises of the post–Cold War era. NATO was established first and foremost for purposes of containment. So too were the Truman Doctrine and the Marshall Plan created in 1947. NATO remains relevant to today's world and will no doubt face many new challenges in the future.

The Truman Doctrine faced its own tests during the Cold War. The first great test of putting the Truman Doctrine into practice was the Korean conflict of 1950–53.

THE KOREAN WAR

Prelude to War

Containment was designed by Kennan as a Eurocentric policy. Kennan believed that few areas other than Europe were vital to U.S. interests. Other decision makers, however, took Kennan's ideas of containment and expanded them to a global scale. Containment became a global policy after 1950, primarily due to events in Asia.

When World War II ended, the Soviet Red Army occupied the northern half of the Korean peninsula, and American troops occupied the south. Nationwide elections, which would have created a single government for all of Korea were proposed. The United Nations (UN) agreed to supervise these elections. All indications at that time pointed to an electoral victory for noncommunist political parties. Therefore, the USSR would not allow UN election observers into northern Korea. Instead, the Soviets established a communist government for North Korea under the dictatorship of Kim Il-Sung.

Free elections were held in South Korea in 1948. A noncommunist regime was elected, headed by Syngman Rhee. Shortly thereafter, Mao came to power in China, and the United States used its veto to keep Mao's government (the People's Republic of China, or PRC) out of the UN. Until the 1970s, the United States saw to it that China's seat in the UN, including its permanent seat on the Security Council, was occupied by the government of Nationalist China (Taiwan). Because of American actions to deny the PRC a place on the Security Council, the Soviets began a boycott of Security Council meetings in January 1950. The Soviet boycott became an important factor during the subsequent Korean conflict.

Ironically, in 1948 the United States started to send signals that an independent South Korea was not all that important to perceived American interests. Syngman Rhee was an anticommunist, but he was also brutally antidemocratic. Press censorship and arrests of Rhee's local political opponents were common in the Republic of South Korea (ROK). These actions were an embarrassment to Truman, who wanted to distance himself from the repression in the ROK. Truman began pulling some troops out of South Korea to demonstrate his displeasure. In an even more forceful show of American disengagement, Secretary of State Dean Acheson gave a speech to the National Press Club in Washington in January 1950 that seemed to deny the ROK military protection by the United States.

In his now infamous Press Club address, Acheson declared a "defensive perimeter" on the Pacific rim. The United States would fight to defend only those territories to the east of this defensive perimeter. The line drawn by Acheson ran from the Aleutian Islands off Alaska, down to Japan, to the Ryukyus south of Japan, and on to the Philippines. Acheson's defensive line explicitly *excluded* South Korea from America's defensive zone. In the same speech he said that "no one can guarantee" the independence of South Korea.[27]

At the same time that the United States was distancing itself from the ROK, unbeknownst to American leaders, North Korea was preparing an invasion of the South. In early 1950, Kim Il-Sung traveled to Moscow to discuss the invasion with Stalin. Although we have no way of knowing exactly what was said between the two, it is clear that Stalin did not veto Kim's plans. Stalin promised Kim military supplies but no Soviet troops. Both dictators probably saw an invasion of the South as a relatively safe move. The United States seemed to be abandoning the South to fend for itself. The exact timing of the initial invasion remains a mystery, however. Why would Stalin allow the North to invade the South at a time when the Soviets were boycotting the Security Council? Perhaps Stalin never anticipated Truman's policy of working through the Security Council to oppose this aggression. Apparently, the exact date on which Kim planned to launch his attack was unknown even to Stalin.[28]

The Korean Conflict

North Korea invaded South Korea on June 24, 1950. By September 15, the North had almost completely overrun the South. North Korea made its furthest penetration when it reached the outskirts of Pusan in the southeast corner of the peninsula. (See Figure 1.3.) Truman was terrified. No one in the United States was certain about what to make of this aggression by the North. Was it merely an attempt to unify all of Korea? Did the communist nations have more ambitious hopes beyond the conquest of the South? Truman feared that an easy victory for the North would be tantamount to appeasement.[29]

Truman's worst-case scenario envisioned the war in Korea as the first battle of World War III. He feared that the Korean invasion could be a diversionary tactic to take U.S. attention away from Europe. Under this scenario, Stalin had given the North orders to invade the South. Then, after U.S. forces became bogged down in a land war in Asia, the Red Army would attack what was thought to be the communist bloc's true objective: Berlin and the rest of West Germany. The Berlin blockade was still fresh in Truman's mind. Fighting in Korea seemed to raise the specter of atomic warfare in Europe once again. Even worse, if the United States did have to use the Bomb to defend Western Europe, there was a possibility that the Soviets would respond in kind, for now they too had atomic weapons.

If one sees the world in these terms, containment necessarily becomes a complex web. One must fight communists anywhere to protect U.S. interests everywhere. The fear that Korea could be a diversionary tactic and a prelude to atomic warfare in Europe brought together defense of those two parts of the world. Not to fight in Korea would be equal to appeasement, which could lead to a larger war in the future, according to Truman.[30]

Truman felt that a quick and decisive response was necessary. This approach was in tune with the thrust of Kennan's "Mr. X" article. The communist

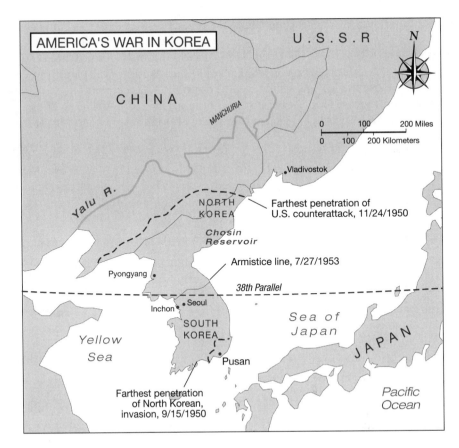

FIGURE 1.3

bloc had to be shown that such aggression would carry enormous costs. American troops that had been withdrawn to demonstrate displeasure with Syngman Rhee's regime were quickly sent back to Korea. Truman went to the Security Council and had North Korea labeled as the "aggressor" in this conflict. This was possible because the Soviets were not at the Security Council to veto the resolution. Designating North Korea as an aggressor opened the door for UN approval of troops. Fifteen members of the UN contributed forces, but the vast majority came from the United States and the ROK. Americans and South Koreans accounted for 85% of the ground forces. Nearly all of the naval and air forces were American.

By December 1950, U.S. troops had pushed their counteroffensive almost to the Yalu River. The Yalu separates Korea from the PRC. Advancing the war to China's doorstep brought the PRC into the conflict. Three hundred thousand so-called volunteers from the People's Liberation Army (PLA) joined the fight to assist North Korea.[31] U.S. forces were once again pushed back, this time to below the 38th parallel (which had been the original dividing line between

North and South). General Douglas MacArthur, an American hero in the Pacific theater during World War II and commander of U.S. forces in Korea, wanted approval from Truman to attack air bases and supply depots inside China. Truman feared that direct attacks on China could start World War III and refused to grant MacArthur's requests to expand the war. Disagreement between the general and the president became so acrimonious and so public that Truman had to remove MacArthur from his position as supreme commander in Korea in 1951.

The remainder of the Korean War (1951–53) consisted of a long stalemate, fought back and forth but never far from the 38th parallel. In 1953, a cease-fire was finally negotiated, but there was no peace treaty between North and South Korea. Technically, the two nations remain at war with one another to this day.

U.S.-Korean Relations after the War

Throughout the Cold War, South Korea remained a client state of the United States, and North Korea remained a client state of the USSR. For more than fifty years, the United States has maintained more than 35,000 troops in the ROK. This remains the case even after the end of the Cold War. When the Berlin Wall fell and the two Germanys were reunited, there were brief hopes that the conflict in Korea might also be replaced with reunification. However, these hopes were very short-lived, as tensions reemerged on the peninsula in 1993. This time, an international crisis in Korea erupted due to nuclear politics.

In 1993, the North Korean government announced that it was "temporarily" withdrawing from the Nonproliferation Treaty (NPT). The NPT prohibits the spread of nuclear weapons. The provisions of the NPT (see chapter 3) oblige nations without nuclear weapons to forgo acquisition or development of such weapons. The NPT also requires states to allow the International Atomic Energy Agency (IAEA) full inspection powers to guarantee compliance with the terms of this agreement.[32] Although it had once been a party to the NPT, North Korea denied the IAEA access to any of its nuclear facilities beginning in 1993. It was clear to American leaders that North Korea had taken this action in order to hide a newly acquired nuclear weapons capability.[33]

President Clinton responded to North Korea's action with the threat of a naval blockade in 1994. Under international law, a naval blockade is considered an act of war. In 1994 it appeared that the United States and North Korea were once again on the verge of war. At the eleventh hour (and prior to the imposition of the naval blockade), former president Jimmy Carter negotiated an agreement that avoided war. The 1994 "Agreed Framework" between the United States and North Korea required the North to freeze all of its nuclear programs. The North also promised to dismantle the nuclear power plants that were producing weapons-grade plutonium. Finally, North Korea agreed to allow eventual resumption of inspections of its nuclear facilities.[34]

The United States promised in return to supply North Korea with 500,000 tons of oil and to provide $3–4 billion in aid for the creation of a new generation of nuclear power plants. The oil would provide a short-term alternative energy supply as the old reactors were shut down. The new reactors would be a long-term solution and are based on a technology that cannot yield weapons-grade plutonium. The Agreed Framework did not directly address the two or more nuclear bombs that North Korea may be concealing.

As things stand after the turn of the century, however, these matters remain largely unresolved. There is still no peace treaty between the two Koreas, and none is likely in the foreseeable future. The United States still has more than 35,000 troops deployed in Korea. North Korea, meanwhile, has teetered on the verge of economic collapse. One of the most unstable regimes in the world, North Korea has suffered from repeated agricultural failures for nearly a decade. Its people are starving in mass numbers. The 1994 Agreed Framework has also been unsuccessful. The Clinton administration began the process of providing moneys for the new reactors, only to see the program suspended by a Congress that suspected North Korea of not holding up its end of the bargain. For their part, the North Koreans have not allowed the independent inspections that the 1994 agreement called for. Add to these troubling developments the fact that North Korea quickly advanced during the 1990s in its ballistic missile testing, and you have a very unstable situation indeed.

Here we have another case in which Cold War security policy has left a legacy that cannot be escaped in the post–Cold War era. U.S soldiers are stationed in Korea to this day because one of the most important campaigns of the Cold War was fought there. The United States shoulders the burden of reigning in North Korea's nuclear capabilities, just as it shoulders the burdens of NATO operations in the Balkans, because of the long-term results of early Cold War policy. Americans now stand guard in Korea and Kosovo in large part due to military policies whose origins reach back into the Cold War.

A final case of Cold War intervention had an even greater impact on U.S. military policy. That case was American involvement in Vietnam.

THE WAR IN VIETNAM

Prelude to American Involvement

The Korean War expanded the focus of containment. Kennan had developed containment as a policy centered on Western Europe. Korea elevated containment to a global level. Truman's fears that the Korean conflict was merely a diversionary tactic cemented a relationship between the defense of Europe and wars in Asia. The United States also became convinced that it had to fight communist aggression in Asia to prove its commitment to defend Europe. America's credibility was at stake in Asia, or so U.S. presidents argued. If the United States did not stand up to communist aggression in Asia, then its NATO allies might question America's resolve for defending them. Credibility also became a key issue in Vietnam.[35] The war in Korea and the global containment mentality that it created set the stage for U.S. involvement in Vietnam.

Events in Korea forced the United States to rethink all of its policies in east Asia. After the North's invasion of the South, the navy's Seventh Fleet was redeployed into the Straits of Formosa to protect Nationalists on Taiwan from the PRC. More important, the United States shifted from a policy of passive acceptance of French imperialism in Indochina to a position of active support for the French. During the Korean War, the United States gave France more than $1 billion to help finance a French campaign against communists in Vietnam. By the time the French decided to withdraw its forces from Vietnam, the United States was paying seventy-five percent of the costs for French military operations there.[36]

Vietnam had been a French colony since the 1880s. In World War II, Japan wrested control of Vietnam from the French. After the war, the French moved to reestablish their control over Vietnam. After much fighting, the French suffered a massive defeat at Dien Bien Phu, in northern Vietnam. Communist forces surrounded and laid siege to the French base in Dien Bien Phu for more than two months in 1954. The French suffered 14,000 casualties during this long battle. Defeat by communist forces at Dien Bien Phu broke the French will to fight in Vietnam. After their defeat, the French started a gradual withdrawal of their forces. As the French withdrew, the United States slowly and gradually stepped in to take over France's role as the Western power fighting against communism in Southeast Asia.

The French withdrawal led to independence for their other colonies in Southeast Asia (Laos and Cambodia). Peace talks at Geneva in 1954 also produced a treaty under which the French agreed to nationwide elections in Vietnam that would create a single independent government. The elections were scheduled to take place in 1956, and all indications pointed to a victory for Ho Chi Minh and the communists.[37] Ho Chi Minh had been the most popular leader of the resistance to Japanese occupation during World War II. He was also the most popular leader among the Vietnamese people after World War II, when their campaign for liberation shifted from a war against Japanese imperialism to a war against French imperialism.

The United States pressured the French to renege on their promise for elections in Vietnam. Unlike the case in 1940s Korea, communists could have been voted into power in Vietnam. Therefore, the United States adopted an antidemocratic stance in regard to nationwide elections in Vietnam during the 1950s. Fearing defeat at the ballot box for the anticommunists, the United States saw to it that such elections did not take place in Vietnam.[38] When American troops entered the war in the 1960s, Vietnam was divided. North Vietnam was under the control of Ho Chi Minh and the communists. South Vietnam was governed by a series of puppet regimes that were created first by the French and later by the United States.[39]

To President Kennedy, the war in Vietnam was essentially an internal conflict. Soviet and PRC aid was clearly coming in to support Ho Chi Minh and the communists, but Kennedy said many times that the war was one that the South Vietnamese had to win or lose for themselves.[40] Kennedy was willing to send in U.S. military advisors, but he believed that the army of South Vietnam had to do the actual fighting. By the time of Kennedy's assassination in 1963, these American "advisors" in Vietnam numbered 20,000.

There are indications that Kennedy had planned to pull all U.S. forces out of Vietnam after his anticipated reelection in 1964.[41] However, despite a wealth of conspiracy theories about linkage between Kennedy's plans for withdrawal and his death, these arguments are largely moot.[42]

America's War in Vietnam

After Kennedy was assassinated, President Johnson approved plans in early 1964 for the U.S. Air Force to supply limited air support for the South Vietnamese army (the Army of the Republic of Vietnam, or ARVN). These air operations went on for about five months before the Tonkin Gulf incident.

In July 1964, ARVN forces were engaged in attacks on islands off the coast of North Vietnam. (See Figure 1.4.) U.S. warships were nearby in international waters in order to provide cover for the ARVN operations. U.S. naval operations to support the ARVN attacks on North Vietnamese territory were kept secret by the Johnson administration.[43] A U.S. destroyer was hit by fire from Northern forces. A second attack on U.S. vessels was also reported but was unconfirmed.

Due to what President Johnson called "unprovoked" attacks on U.S. naval vessels, Congress passed the Gulf of Tonkin Resolution on August 7, 1964. The Tonkin Gulf Resolution gave Johnson and his successor (Nixon) a free hand in conducting the war in Vietnam. They could send in as many troops as they deemed necessary and use these troops as they saw fit. All of this was justified, according to President Johnson, by the allegedly unprovoked nature of the North's attacks on American warships. However, we now know that Johnson lied to the American people when he described the events of the Tonkin Gulf incident.[44] American ships were involved in a military operation in conjunction with the ARVN, making the North's attacks on U.S. ships anything but unprovoked.[45]

Johnson also stepped up bombing of the North in response to the Tonkin Gulf incident. Increased military pressure by the United States, however, only increased the North's resolve and strengthened their commitment to fight. To the communists, the United States was just one more in a long line of foreign imperialist powers that they had to fight against to free their nation from external domination. Increased air strikes by the United States had little or no impact on the North's will to fight.

During the presidential election campaign of 1964, Johnson ran as a "peace" candidate. At the same time, his Republican opponent, Senator Goldwater was calling for the introduction of tactical nuclear weapons into Vietnam as a way to bring a quick end to the fighting. Democrats painted Goldwater as a loose canon who would take the United States into a nuclear confrontation. Johnson, by comparison, was promising that he would not introduce American ground forces into the war. Johnson won in a landslide, but

FIGURE 1.4

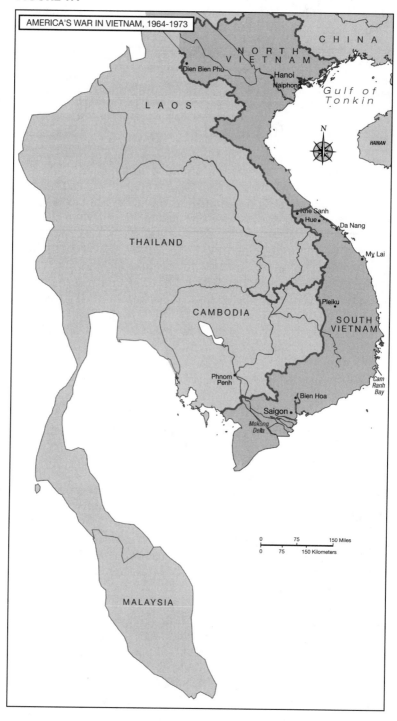

his victory did not lead to peace. Instead, he embarked upon a major escalation of the conflict.

In the spring of 1965, Johnson approved plans for Operation Rolling Thunder. Rolling Thunder called for massive, sustained bombing of the North. In March 1965, Johnson dispatched the first Marine contingents into the war. At first, these ground forces were sent in only to protect airbases used for the bombing campaigns. But that action put the United States on a slippery slope toward total involvement. Marines could not just secure a perimeter around the airstrips and thereby guarantee the safety of the bombers. Communist snipers near the bases would shoot at Americans and then escape back into the jungles. Therefore, the Americans decided that they had to go in hot pursuit of the snipers. Soon the United States would take over the fighting of the ground war altogether.

By 1966, U.S. forces in Vietnam numbered 400,000. The commander of these forces, General Westmoreland, devised tactics that he felt were especially well suited for fighting in a jungle war against a guerilla army. One tactic was called "search-and-destroy." U.S forces would go into the jungles to search out and destroy as many of the guerillas as possible. However, because it was so hard in Vietnam to distinguish between communist guerillas and noncombatants, search-and-destroy missions killed more innocent bystanders than revolutionaries.[46] Estimates are that the kill ratio of noncombatants to guerillas ran as high as 6:1. In other words, perhaps as many as six innocent noncombatants were killed for every one guerilla eliminated by means of search-and-destroy.[47]

Another tactic employed by Westmoreland was called "strategic hamlets." Strategic hamlets were adapted from prior British campaigns against a communist uprising in Malaysia. Noncombatants and "friendlies" among the peasants were moved into designated hamlets or villages. The United States would then lay waste to the surrounding countryside and jungle cover with defoliants such as Agent Orange.[48] This policy was supposed to deny the things that all guerilla armies need from civilian populations in order to succeed: food, shelter, and information. Strategic hamlets had worked well for the British in Malaysia as a way to deny communist guerillas support from the general population. In Malaysia, it was comparatively easy to distinguish communists and their supporters from noncommunists. Most Marxist revolutionaries in Malaysia were people of Chinese descent. Noncommunists, by contrast, tended to be indigenous Malays. There are physical differences that distinguish Chinese from Malays. No such ethnic differences separated communists from noncommunists in Vietnam. Therefore, although this tactic had worked for the British in Malaysia, creation of strategic hamlets did not work for the United States in Vietnam.[49]

Strategic hamlets and search-and-destroy were both unsuccessful tactics. Sustained bombing also failed to produce victory for America in Vietnam. Bombing campaigns, like the search-and-destroy missions, killed more innocents than guerillas. The kill ratio of civilians to communists from strategic bombing has been estimated at 2:1—two civilians were probably killed for every one guerilla eliminated by American bombing.[50] When military tactics kill more innocents than enemies, these tactics create more enemies among the families and friends of those noncombatants who died.

Communist forces countered these U.S. tactics with standard guerilla warfare (ambushes, hit-and-run, etc.). The communists relied on the fact that American troops were not very mobile. American GIs could not move around as efficiently as the guerillas. U.S. soldiers carried so much gear that they quickly became bogged down when they tried to fight in the jungles. Ho Chi Minh and his supporters were content to wait out the U.S. forces. This war of national liberation had been going on long before the Americans had arrived. Communist guerillas were willing to pay the price required in terms of lives lost and other casualties to wear down the U.S. will to fight.

The ground war peaked in Vietnam with the communist Tet offensive of early 1968. By this time U.S. forces had reached 525,000 (a number roughly equivalent to the contingent that America sent into the 1991 Gulf War against Iraq many years later). Eighty thousand communist troops staged a widespread attack on 100 cities and villages throughout South Vietnam during their offensive.[51] Six thousand Marines in Khe Sahn suffered through a long siege that evoked memories of the French defeat at Dien Bien Phu.[52] The U.S. embassy in Saigon (the city now known as Ho Chi Minh City) was overrun and occupied by guerillas, and American casualties reached 500 per week.[53] After the Tet offensive ended, U.S. soldiers discovered communist bases only twenty miles outside of Saigon, indicating that the enemy was almost omnipresent throughout the countryside. General Westmoreland requested an increase of 200,000 more troops during the Tet offensive, but his requests were denied.[54] Westmoreland's mistaken tactics were becoming obvious by 1968. He had tried to use strategic bombing and a war of attrition to defeat a peasant-based army. The guerillas and the peasants that supported them, however, were willing to endure as long as it took to force foreign troops out of their homeland.

1968 was also the year during which bipartisan support for containment and popular support for military interventions disintegrated in Washington. Both major political parties polarized into "hawks" that supported the war versus "doves" who opposed it. Antiwar demonstrations on college campuses and at the national conventions for both parties were widespread and massive. Richard Nixon was elected president in 1968 by promising to bring the United States out of the war. Nixon spoke of his "secret" plan to end the war that would provide "peace with honor." Before ending American involvement, however, Nixon escalated the war yet again.

Nixon increased the bombing of Vietnam. The North was bombed night and day. Nixon expanded the bombing to include communist camps and supply lines in Cambodia. The bombing of Cambodia was an action that Nixon tried to keep secret. After information about the secret bombing of Cambodia was leaked to the *New York Times,* Nixon's White House created a "plumbers" unit, led by former CIA agents, to stop such leaks. Actions by the plumbers would later lead to Nixon's political downfall when they broke into Democratic Party offices at the Watergate Hotel and precipitated the Watergate scandal.

Nixon's policy of peace with honor turned out to be a strategy of escalating the war, while negotiating for a cease-fire. Peace talks in Paris headed by Henry Kissinger produced a deal whereby Ho Chi Minh and the communists would halt the fighting in 1973. After the fighting was suspended, U.S. troops could withdraw "with honor," or at least at a time when it did not appear that they were abandoning their positions while under hostile fire. American troops came home in 1973, and the fighting was turned over to the ARVN (see chapter 2). In 1975, ARVN forces deserted in droves when the communists mounted their final offensive. Since 1975, all of Vietnam has been united under the communist government.

The Korean War had reinforced containment and made containment a global policy. The Vietnam War created the first major reassessment of containment tactics. The results of Vietnam reduced the global reach of containment. After its traumatic experience in Vietnam, the United States sought to reduce its commitment to containment in many parts of the world. The United States won every major battle in Vietnam, and it managed to repel the Tet offensive, but it lost the war.

American Intervention Tactics after Vietnam

As a result of Vietnam, especially due to the widespread domestic opposition against using American troops, the United States was forced to devise a new set of intervention policies.[55] In 1970, Congress repealed the Tonkin Gulf Resolution. During his first term, Nixon announced the Nixon Doctrine. The Nixon Doctrine can be loosely thought of as an amendment to the Truman Doctrine. Under the Nixon Doctrine, the United States supplied economic aid and military hardware to oppose communist aggression, but allies were expected to provide their own troops. Nixon "Vietnamized" the war in Vietnam by turning the fighting over to ARVN forces in 1973.

In 1973, Congress passed the War Powers Act, which was at first vetoed by Nixon. Congress, however, overrode Nixon's veto. Under the War Powers Act, a president must report to Congress within forty-eight hours of sending troops into any area where they might face "imminent hostilities." Congress then has sixty days during which to debate this use of military forces.[56] If Congress votes to withdraw the troops, the president then has another thirty days to bring the forces home. The War Powers Act was designed to prevent another war like Vietnam: a long-drawn conflict during which Congress has little or no control over the initial decision to go to war. (Post-Vietnam intervention tactics are discussed in more detail in chapter 5.)

Perhaps the most significant change to post-Vietnam intervention policies is the Weinberger Doctrine, first announced in 1984 by Secretary of Defense

Casper Weinberger (during the Reagan administration). The Weinberger Doctrine requires, first and foremost, that leaders specify a clear and limited objective for the use of military forces *prior to* deployment of troops. Second, there must be a limited time frame and a limited commitment of forces. Intervention must be structured so that the forces can get in, achieve their objectives, and then get out as quickly as possible. Finally, Weinberger insisted that the government must be sure of domestic political support for intervention in advance of hostilities.[57] Obviously, none of these guidelines were employed prior to or during American involvement in Vietnam.

In a larger sense, Vietnam also forced American leaders to look for means of containment that reduced reliance on military options and increased the range of nonmilitary alternatives to direct intervention. President Nixon was the first to make a concerted effort in this regard. Nixon's nonmilitary policies of containment will be the first topic of the next chapter. The term that Nixon and Kissinger coined for these policies was *détente*.

Chapter 2

SECURITY POLICY FROM DÉTENTE TO THE END OF THE COLD WAR AND BEYOND

The Korean War reinforced containment as the central focus of post–World War II defense policy. America's involvement in the Korean conflict also expanded the scope of containment to a global scale. The war in Vietnam caused the first serious reevaluation of containment policies. Military force as the primary means of ensuring containment lost domestic support in the United States. The antiwar movements of the 1960s and 1970s, especially on college campuses, forced policy makers to respond. In Washington both parties became polarized over the war. There were sizable factions of "doves" (opponents of the war) in both the Democratic and the Republican parties. The doves challenged the wisdom of pro-war policies promoted by their party leaders, the "hawks" (supporters of the war). Opposition to the war in Vietnam forced changes in American foreign policies of containment. Presidents and diplomats turned to other means (nonmilitary means) as a way to contain Soviet power. These new strategies relied on economic incentives and international treaties as new modes of containment. The term used by President Nixon and Secretary of State Kissinger for these new tactics was *détente.*

Détente is a French term that refers to the relaxation of tensions. Under the détente approach, both superpowers sought to establish a form of peaceful coexistence. However, the era of détente was relatively short-lived. It died with the Soviet invasion of Afghanistan in 1979. Peaceful coexistence under détente was replaced by the "new" Cold War of the 1980s. Throughout most of the 1980s, Presidents Carter and Reagan reverted to military means for fighting the renewed Cold War. On the other hand, détente policies of the 1970s also left a lasting imprint on superpower relations. The long-term impact of détente did not become evident until after the rise to power of Soviet President Gorbachev. By 1989, both the United States and the USSR had reverted to a type of neo-détente in their foreign polices. Neo-détente in the late 1980s and early 1990s helped to bring about the final end of the Cold

War. This chapter opens with a summary of détente policies, proceeds to a description of the new Cold War of the 1980s, and concludes with an explanation of how the end of the Cold War came about. Post–Cold War policies will also be reviewed.

FOUR ELEMENTS OF NIXON'S DÉTENTE

In the opinions of Nixon and Kissinger, Soviet behavior could be altered via methods other than military force. They looked to diplomacy and the use of economic incentives as ways to reduce America's reliance on military options. Détente was still very much based on the assumption that the United States had to contain Soviet power and stand guard against Soviet aggression. However, due to domestic opposition to Vietnam, they had to employ foreign policy techniques that were markedly different from those used to fight the wars in Korea and Vietnam. In fact, the first key element of Nixon's détente was designed to get America out of Vietnam. Nixon's four-part strategy of détente sought 1) an end to the war, 2) nuclear arms control, 3) a settlement in Europe, and 4) increased trade with the Soviets. Each of these elements will be described in more detail.

Peace with Honor

To get U.S. forces out of Vietnam, Nixon and Kissinger needed diplomatic assistance from the Soviet Union. Nixon had promised Americans that he had a "secret plan" to achieve "peace with honor" in Vietnam.[1] Peace with honor required, at the very least, a cease-fire agreement with Ho Chi Minh's government in North Vietnam. A cease-fire would allow American forces to withdraw without giving the impression that the United States had been forced out of Vietnam due to pressure from a superior fighting machine. Nixon did not want to give the appearance that American troops had been chased out of Vietnam. He needed the Soviets to put pressure on Ho Chi Minh to stop the fighting.

This first key goal of détente required Kissinger to play a global game of balance of power politics. A first step was to begin normalizing relations with the People's Republic of China (PRC). America had yet to accord diplomatic recognition to Mao Zedong's communist government in the PRC. Due to Cold War ideology, the United States had maintained that the only "legitimate" government for China was the noncommunist regime headed by the Nationalists on the island of Taiwan. The Nationalists had lost the civil war in China that brought Mao Zedong's communist party into power in 1949. Nationalists fled to Taiwan in 1949, where they remain to this day. Prior to Nixon, the official position of every presidential administration was to deny diplomatic recognition (and deny a seat on the UN Security Council) to the PRC.

Nixon and Kissinger set out to change all that. They normalized relations with the PRC as a way to pressure the Soviets. This strategy worked remarkably well.

In the early days of America's involvement in Vietnam, the Soviets looked with glee on the political and military difficulties that this conflict created for America. Nixon's trips to China, however, raised grave concerns for Soviet leaders. By the time of Nixon's first visit to China in 1972, the communist leaders of the PRC and the USSR were themselves on very bad terms. Disagreements over foreign aid, communist ideology, and border wars between the PRC and the Soviet Union had strained their ties with each other beyond the breaking point. Now, Nixon's overtures to the Chinese (orchestrated by Kissinger) looked like a possible entente between the United States and the PRC that Soviet leaders viewed with alarm. By "playing the China card" (i.e., normalizing relations) Nixon and Kissinger put indirect pressure on the Soviets to seek strategic cooperation with the Americans. In part due to their desires to maintain a wedge between the United States and China, the Soviets began to develop détente strategies of their own. One of the first Soviet policies of détente was to cooperate with the United States to bring about peace talks in Paris designed to stop the fighting in Vietnam.

During the Paris peace talks, the USSR put pressure on Ho Chi Minh's government to stop the fighting. The Soviets had considerable leverage because they were North Vietnam's principal benefactor. Once a peace treaty was signed that included a cease-fire (in 1973), the United States was able to withdraw its forces in a manner that was consistent with Nixon's desire for peace with honor.

Nuclear Arms Control

Diplomatic cooperation with Brezhnev's regime in the USSR was also necessary to achieve Nixon's second goal for détente. By the 1970s, both the United States and the USSR wanted to stop the unconstrained escalation of the nuclear arms race. America's one-time monopoly over atomic weapons had changed into a strategic balance of nuclear capability by 1970.[2] Once parity had been reached and both sides had a roughly equivalent nuclear strike force, it was in the interests of both nuclear superpowers to put some limits on the arms race.[3] Arms control negotiations by Nixon and Kissinger culminated in the Strategic Arms Limitation Treaty of 1972 (now known as SALT I). This is perhaps the best example of détente strategies that relied on diplomacy and treaty commitments as a way to constrain Soviet power. The SALT I treaty of 1972, as well as the other key treaties relating to strategic arms control, will be discussed in more detail in the next chapter. At this point, however, a brief summary of SALT I is needed to understand the overall strategy of détente.

SALT I consists of two parts. First of all, SALT I contains a formal treaty limiting antiballistic missiles (ABMs). ABMs are missiles used to shoot down other missiles. By 1972, both sides had achieved a rudimentary ABM capability. The easiest way to overcome any so-called defensive system (such as an array of ABMs) is to throw so many targets (missiles and warheads) at it that the ABM system cannot hope to shoot down all the incoming weapons. Hence, development of any ABM system evokes an almost certain reaction on the part of one's potential enemies. They will increase their offensive might beyond the ABM system's capabilities. In the 1970s, deployment of ABM systems by both sides led them to increase their arsenal of offensive nuclear missiles as well. An offensive-defensive spiral thus held out the possibility of an all-out and endless arms race.

To avoid such an arms race, SALT I restricted both sides to only one ABM system.[4] Russia still has a single ABM system; it is outside of Moscow. The United States used to have one ABM system around a missile base in North Dakota, but it was closed down long ago. The 1972 ABM Treaty was also very clear about restrictions on new generations of ABM technology. Research and development of new ABM systems were allowed under the terms of SALT I, but deployment of any new nationwide ABM system was explicitly prohibited.[5] The possibility of deploying a new generation of national missile defense (NMD) in the twenty-first century brought about intense debate over the ABM treaty during the administration of George W. Bush. The second President Bush has been so firmly committed to developing a new NMD capability that he decided in 2002 to scrap the ABM treaty altogether (see chapter 3 and the conclusion to this text for more detailed discussions of these matters).

The second part of SALT I has also left a lasting impact on nuclear politics. In the protocol attached to the SALT I treaty, both sides agreed to a cap on long-range nuclear missiles. This cap on strategic nuclear missiles was above the number of weapons each side had in 1972. Each nation could continue to build up their arsenals under the terms of SALT I until they reached their respective cap (set at 1,600 for the USSR and 1,054 for the United States). SALT I set a higher limit for the USSR than for the United States because, at that time, the United States had a technological edge in fitting more than one nuclear warhead on each missile. In other words, SALT I allowed the Soviets to have more nuclear missiles, but because no restrictions were placed on the number of warheads that each missile could carry, and because the United States had a distinct advantage in multiple warheads (or MIRVs), the United States retained a superiority in deliverable warheads. Neither side exceeded their SALT I cap on missiles during the Cold War. Both sides have moved well below these 1972 limits now that the Cold War is over (see chapter 3).

A Settlement in Europe

A third element of 1970s détente, and one that was prized by both the United States and the USSR, was a settlement of a broad range of political issues involving Europe. Many of these unresolved issues dated back to the outcome of

World War II. The détente settlement on Europe was formalized in the Helsinki Accords of 1975. Thirty-five nations met at Helsinki, Finland, to sign these agreements. All NATO members and all communist countries in Europe (with the exception of Albania) participated. The Helsinki Accords were too broad and extensive to be fully summarized here. However, two key parts of these agreements (e.g., borders in Europe and human rights issues) spoke to issues of détente. Helsinki represented a trade-off between the Russians and the Americans. The United States and its NATO allies agreed at Helsinki to recognize the de facto borders in Europe.[6] By recognizing the existing borders in Europe in 1975, NATO accepted the division of Germany, the partition of Berlin, and (implicitly) Soviet hegemony over Eastern Europe. This agreement on the division of Europe into two separate spheres of influence was one that the Soviets had been pursuing for thirty years prior to Helsinki. The Helsinki Accords also did away with the likelihood of any more blockades or ultimatums designed to force American troops out of West Berlin. In return, the USSR made promises to respect human rights within its borders.[7] Soviet leader Brezhnev probably never intended to abide by his promises at Helsinki to guarantee respect for civil and political rights inside the USSR. The Soviet state was notorious during the Cold War for denying basic freedoms of speech and suppressing democracy both at home and in its satellites. However, the human rights elements of the Helsinki Accords were a Western proposal that Soviet leaders had to accept in order to secure NATO's agreement on the issue of borders. The Helsinki Accords led to the "Helsinki process," a series of follow-up conferences. These subsequent meetings were used by the West to focus increased international attention on human rights violations within the Soviet bloc.

These meetings were held under the auspices of the newly created Conference on Security and Cooperation in Europe (CSCE). The CSCE itself was a product of détente. After the end of the Cold War, the CSCE evolved into the Organization on Security and Cooperation in Europe (OSCE). The existence of the OSCE is a Cold War legacy that has had an important impact on European politics by promoting peace and democracy in such war-torn areas as Bosnia and Kosovo (see chapter 5).

Helsinki also led to the creation of "Helsinki watch committees" in both communist and noncommunist nations. Helsinki watch groups sought to monitor human rights conditions and draw attention to human rights abuses. Under the terms of the Helsinki Accords, these watch committees were supposed to be free and independent of government control. Helsinki watch groups were allowed to form, even inside the USSR, but the Soviet government then viciously suppressed them. Many of the same watch groups survived this Cold War repression, however, and eventually led the movements that contributed to the downfall of communist dictatorships in Poland, Czechoslovakia, and the USSR.

Trade and Détente

A final element of détente as developed by Nixon and Kissinger was the offer of new trade incentives for the USSR. Offering better trade relations was the carrot by which Nixon hoped to induce Soviet cooperation in the other areas of détente (ending the war in Vietnam, arms control, and human rights). America can provide many things that Russia has never been very good at producing on its own. First and foremost among them are advanced technology and abundant investment capital. During the Cold War, and even more so now that the Cold War is over, Russian leaders have sought to boost their economy with inputs of American high-tech goods and American investment. For more than three decades, Russian leaders have also needed imports of grain and other foodstuffs in order to feed their population. The once-productive Russian agricultural sector succumbed long ago to inefficiencies and waste associated with Stalinist centralization of production.

Kissinger favored linking offers of increased trade to Soviet cooperation over arms control. Once the SALT I negotiations culminated in the first treaty to limit nuclear weapons, Kissinger thought it was important to reward the Soviets for their compliant behavior. The reward that the Nixon administration proposed was to grant the USSR most favored nation (MFN) trade status. MFN trade status is accorded to almost all of America's major trading partners. It gives foreign nations nondiscriminatory access to U.S. markets (see chapter 7 for a full description of MFN). However, on this point, the White House and Congress disagreed. Nixon and Kissinger wanted to increase trade with the USSR via MFN and believed that the Soviets had already done enough to deserve MFN. Congress, on the other hand, wanted more.

Under the Jackson-Vanik Amendment of 1974, Congress attached human rights conditions to MFN status for the Soviet Union. This amendment required that the USSR give Soviet Jews a right to free emigration. Anti-Semitism has had a long and violent history in Russia. Under Soviet rule, Jews were persecuted in numerous ways. To improve human rights for Jews living in communist nations, Congress required the right for Jews to leave a communist dictatorship before that government could be accorded MFN status. Nixon and Kissinger were opposed to this policy but could not dissuade Congress. Brezhnev refused to abide by the terms of the Jackson-Vanik Amendment. Therefore, the USSR never got what they wanted most out of 1970s détente. The Soviets never received MFN in the 1970s and did not acquire the economic advantages that they expected from peaceful coexistence. The dispute over MFN status was just one of several sources of tension that eventually led to the collapse of détente in late 1979. The Soviets launched a military invasion into Afghanistan that killed détente in December 1979. The invasion of Afghanistan brought out an underlying disagreement over the nature of détente that had remained hidden. The invasion of Afghanistan revealed that the USA and the USSR had distinctively different conceptions of détente.

AMERICAN VERSUS SOVIET VIEWS OF DÉTENTE

As it turned out, there never was a true meeting of the minds between U.S. and Soviet leaders regarding the essential nature of détente. The two nations shared some common interests during the 1970s. Both sides wanted an agreement to limit the nuclear arms race. Both sides were also interested in the possibility of increased trade. However, their expectations regarding other important areas of détente were diametrically opposed. Conflicting views over the heart of détente did not emerge until the USSR sent troops into Afghanistan.

For the United States détente meant that an implicit agreement existed between the two sides. For American leaders, peaceful coexistence required that the superpowers not provoke one another. The United States believed that détente was based on a "gentlemen's agreement" containing the (largely unspoken) assumption that both countries would avoid provocative actions. American leaders thought that the Soviets had pledged to uphold this principal on nonprovocative foreign policies. This U.S. misperception was based largely on its understanding of the Basic Political Agreement (BPA) of 1972. The BPA was a broad and loosely worded statement of détente sentiments. It was not a treaty as such and hence had no binding legal force. The BPA was also vague enough to allow for any number of interpretations. It said, in part: "Both sides recognize that efforts to obtain *unilateral advantages* at the expense of the other . . . are inconsistent with [the] objectives [of détente]." The objectives of détente are specified in the BPA to include peaceful coexistence, avoiding military confrontations, and preventing nuclear war. The BPA goes on to say: "The U.S.A. and the U.S.S.R. . . . [will] do everything in their power so that conflicts or situations will not arise which would serve to increase international tensions."[8]

Based on its understanding of the BPA, the United States thought that the spirit of détente required both sides to employ only nonprovocative foreign policies. Clearly the Soviets (in their view) had never agreed to this.

For the USSR détente meant arms control and the hope for increased trade with the United States. On that much, both sides agreed. However, for the Soviets, the other key element of détente, and the heart of peaceful coexistence, was an agreement that each superpower would have its own sphere of influence. Russians have always wanted to be thought of as peers, as equals to any other nation. They have always desired the honor and respect that they see accorded to the great powers of Western civilization. They feel that they have never been given such commensurate respect. The Soviets probably believed that this was what détente should provide them. They wanted their own sphere of influence. Furthermore, they wanted the United States and NATO to stay out of the Soviet sphere. In the view of Russian leaders, détente was an implicit agreement between the superpowers to stay out of each other's way and to give each other free rein within their own sphere. The Soviets probably thought that NATO had agreed to separate spheres of influence under the terms of the Helsinki Accords. Clearly, the United States (in its view) had agreed to no such thing.

The Soviet invasion of Afghanistan brought all of this disagreement over the spirit of détente out into the open. The Soviets sent troops into Afghanistan for the first time in late 1979. Soviet power was used to remove one leader from power and replace him with another. President Carter was outraged. Soviet troops had never occupied Afghanistan before. To Carter, this was clearly an act of overt military aggression. Most of the rest of the world agreed with Carter, including not just NATO allies but most Third World governments as well. The Soviet invasion was roundly condemned by nearly all nonaligned nations. The United States had been under the mistaken impression that the Soviets had pledged not to do such things. The BPA indicated to American leaders that détente prohibited such actions.

In response to the Soviet invasion, Carter boycotted the 1980 Olympics in Moscow, which was a huge blow to Soviet prestige. Carter also embargoed the sales of American grain to Russia that had been set up as part of détente trade policy. He also withdrew the second SALT treaty of 1979 from Senate consideration (see chapter 3 for more on SALT II).

The Soviets were bewildered and angered by Carter's reaction. In the Soviet view, what they did in Afghanistan was none of America's concern. Afghanistan was clearly within their sphere of influence, and they felt that events there were none of America's business. Afghanistan had a communist government before the Soviets invaded. The Soviets intervened initially to remove one communist dictator from power and replace him with another communist dictator that was more to Moscow's liking.[9] Afghanistan was a client state of the USSR following World War II, receiving the bulk of its economic and military aid from Moscow. Because Afghanistan was so clearly within their hegemonic sphere, and because the USSR thought that détente was based on a principle of the two superpowers staying out of each other's way, Soviet leaders felt that the spirit of détente justified their actions. They thought that they had every right to act as they did in Afghanistan, and the United States should have nothing to say about the matter.

Other tensions had grown in the 1970s to contribute to the end of détente, but the invasion of Afghanistan was the event that killed it. Soviet support for Marxist regimes in Angola, Cambodia, and Ethiopia during the 1970s had strained the goodwill established during the early days of détente. Invading Afghanistan ended détente and brought the superpowers back into an era of Cold War hostility. The USSR never got what it wanted most out of détente: the trade it desired due to the Jackson-Vanik Amendment and the uncritical freedom of movement within its own sphere that Soviets thought they deserved. Likewise, the United States never got what it wanted most out of détente; it never secured a less aggressive and less militaristic foreign policy on the part of the USSR. The invasion of Afghanistan was proof that the Soviets had not changed their aggressive ways. Because of these harsh feelings, superpower relations and U.S. security policy abandoned the détente of the 1970s for the new Cold War of the 1980s.

THE NEW COLD WAR
FOR CARTER AND REAGAN

Throughout most of the 1980s, a "new" Cold War raged between the two superpowers. Also referred to by some as the "second" Cold War, this was an era of increased hostilities, harsh rhetoric, and militarism in foreign policy. To call it the new Cold War, or the second Cold War, is to stress the marked change between the détente of the 1970s and the belligerence of the 1980s. These terms also highlight the way that foreign policy in the 1980s reflected the policy of the 1950s, that prior age being the heyday of the "old" Cold War (or the "first" Cold War).

During the new Cold War, there was a return to military modes of containment. There was also a resurgence of militarism in both the United States and the USSR. This was an age that witnessed a massive arms buildup and a new arms race, especially with regard to nuclear weapons. Arms control was ignored, or (at best) put on hold. Détente-style efforts to cultivate better economic ties and peaceful coexistence were abandoned.

The new Cold War of the 1980s is commonly associated with the presidency of Ronald Reagan, but it actually began during President Carter's last year in office. Jimmy Carter had been elected in 1976 as a pro-détente president. During his first three years in the White House, Carter's foreign policy stressed building on the prior successes of a détente approach. Carter negotiated the SALT II treaty (1979) as a follow-up to SALT I. Cyrus Vance, Secretary of State and principal foreign policy advisor during the first three years of the Carter administration, was also pro-détente. Vance stressed the need for arms control and adopted a conciliatory approach toward the USSR in order to promote negotiations. Vance was also more interested in international human rights than military budgets (see chapter 10). So great was his opposition to military options that Vance resigned in 1980, the first year of the new Cold War, when Carter sent a military expedition on a (failed) rescue mission to free Americans held hostage at the U.S. Embassy in Iran.

Vance was replaced as Carter's top foreign policy advisor by Zbigniew Brzezinski. Brzezinski was very much a political realist and a cold warrior. An intellectual and academic rival to Kissinger, Brzezinski was also anti-détente. Brzezinski scrapped Vance's conciliatory approach and took a hard line against the Soviets. Under Brzezinski's tutelage and in response to the invasion of Afghanistan, Carter began a significant military buildup in 1980. Military spending, which had been allowed to slip during détente, now grew at a pace that was five percent above the rate of inflation. Carter reestablished a requirement that young men register for the military draft.[10] Carter also escalated the nuclear arms race. He agreed to deployment of new intermediate-range nuclear forces (INF) missiles in Europe.[11] And he approved plans to deploy a new generation of long-range strategic nuclear missiles (the MX).

The most significant new policy adopted by Carter in response to the invasion of Afghanistan was the Carter Doctrine. Still a key element of American foreign policy to this day, the Carter Doctrine declares that the United States will go to war if necessary to protect the oil fields in the Middle East. Carter and Brzezinski's worst fear was that the invasion of Afghanistan might be a first step toward a more wide-scale Soviet invasion of the Middle East. Afghanistan sits on the eastern doorstep to the Middle East. It borders Iran (which was in the midst of its own revolution and turmoil in 1979–80). Afghanistan is also just a few hundred miles from the Persian Gulf. The Gulf region is the source of most of the Middle East's oil reserves.

Carter created a new military unit to enforce his doctrine, the Rapid Deployment Force (RDF). An RDF is made up of smaller military divisions that are lightly armored and highly mobile. Deployment strategies for the RDF require extensive airlift and sealift capabilities. The United States had no permanent military bases in the Middle East. Therefore, the RDF had to employ an out-of-area force posture, but also be ready to mobilize and project its power into the Middle East on short notice and in record time. Carter negotiated agreements with Egypt and Saudi Arabia to allow the United States to pre-position supplies in their countries. The same nations allowed the United States to construct airstrips, bunkers, and troop housing that would be ready and waiting should the United States ever need them. All of this was done consistent with a Cold War mentality that viewed the USSR as the likely threat to Western interests. As we shall see in chapter 4, all of the planning, military units, and facilities that were established under the Carter Doctrine were later used to fight a war in the Middle East. That war was not against the USSR, however, it was the war fought to expel Iraq from Kuwait in 1991.

Ronald Reagan defeated Jimmy Carter in the 1980 presidential campaign in part due to his arguments that Carter had not done *enough* to increase the military strength of the United States during this time of international troubles. These arguments were very popular with the voters. Reagan charged that Carter had hurt America's friends and helped America's enemies by being too soft on the Soviets and other U.S. adversaries. The Soviets had invaded Afghanistan, and Americans were taken hostage in Iran, all on Jimmy Carter's watch. Therefore, Reagan ascribed the blame for these problems to Carter.

The new Cold War of the 1980s peaked during Reagan's first term in office. American foreign policy during this time paralleled the strategies used during the old Cold War. First, President Reagan unleashed some of the harshest rhetoric against the Soviets since the Truman administration. Reagan referred to the Soviet bloc as an "evil empire." Reagan characterized the USSR as the ultimate source of all political instability in the world, especially terrorism and Third World revolutions. In a typical campaign speech during

June 1980, Reagan said: "Let's not delude ourselves. The Soviet Union under-lies all the unrest that is going on. If they weren't engaged in this game of dominoes, there wouldn't be any hot spots in the world."[12]

By blaming the Soviets for all hot spots and global instability, Reagan was also laying out a very simple policy response. U.S. foreign policy would oppose the Soviets at every turn. Reagan's supporters (and even many of his detrac-tors) had to admire his ability to distill the often chaotic world of internation-al relations into such an oversimplified political calculus. Reagan's policies were designed to attack what he saw as the root cause of global instability (i.e., the Soviet Union).[13]

Reagan's second policy for fighting the new Cold War was to replace détente-style offers of increased trade with anti-détente economic sanctions. During his first term in office, President Reagan had no interest in promoting economic interaction as a way to enhance peaceful coexistence. Instead his policy was designed to "tighten all screws" and to deny the USSR any econom-ic advantage that he could. The Reagan administration sought to put as much economic pressure on the communist bloc as was politically feasible.[14] Two prime examples were the pipeline sanctions imposed against Russia and the economic embargo of Poland.

In 1981 and 1982, Reagan tried his best to stop the building of a natural gas pipeline between the Soviet Union and West Germany. Reagan did not want Germany, a key NATO ally, to become dependent on the Eastern bloc for its energy supplies. He ordered U.S. firms based in America not to work on the pipeline. He also tried, unsuccessfully, to persuade the rest of NATO to embargo the pipeline's construction. Reagan tried to stop U.S.-owned sub-sidiaries in Europe from participating in the building of the pipeline. How-ever, the European NATO governments opposed Reagan's efforts. They ordered their own corporations and American-owned subsidiaries in Europe to honor their contracts for pipeline construction and maintenance. Even British Prime Minister Margaret Thatcher, who usually saw eye-to-eye with Reagan on Cold War issues, thwarted Reagan's efforts by requiring American corporations located in England to continue working on the pipeline.[15]

Reagan was more successful in applying sanctions against Poland. When Poland's communist regime outlawed the Solidarity labor union in December 1981, Reagan embargoed trade and aid to Poland. Reagan's sanctions against the Polish government remained in effect until after Solidarity was once again allowed to operate freely.

Reagan's primary strategy for fighting the new Cold War was a massive mil-itary buildup. He expanded military spending well beyond anything that Carter had proposed. The defense budget skyrocketed by forty percent during Reagan's first three years in office. During his first five years, Reagan author-ized $1.6 trillion in military expenditures–a level of defense spending unlike anything the United States had experienced before that time. Over a ten-year period, Presidents Reagan and Bush spent $3 trillion on defense, or an average of $300 billion per year for every year from 1982–91. Where did all that money go? It was used to expand U.S. conventional and nuclear capabilities across the board. Badly needed and long-overdue increases for military pay and force "readiness" were among the first of the new expenditures.[16] Conventional forces were upgraded with new tanks and antitank weapons. The Navy expanded to a 600-ship fleet. Two new aircraft carrier groups were established. Four World War II–era battleships were taken out of mothballs and fitted with sea-launched cruise missiles (capable of carrying nuclear warheads).

Strategic nuclear forces were especially favored during this time. All three legs of the nuclear triad were modernized. Reagan revived work on the B-1 bombers that Carter had cancelled and began development of the B-2. New submarine-launched and land-based strategic missiles were developed and deployed. Production of cruise missiles was stepped up.[17] Reagan's military advisors often talked about their willingness to fight a nuclear war against the Soviets and guaranteed that America would "prevail" in such a conflict.[18]

Finally, the Reagan administration developed a new policy for fighting the Cold War on Third World battlefields. This strategy came to be known as the Reagan Doctrine. The focus of the old Cold War in the 1940s had been on Europe. The crises in those early days had been in Greece, Poland, Czechoslovakia, and especially in Berlin. Confrontations between the forces of communism and the clients of Western liberal democracy during the new Cold War were played out in the Third World. Reagan viewed a series of Marxist revolutions in El Salvador, Nicaragua, Grenada, Peru, and the Philippines as traceable to Moscow. He believed that all of these leftist and anti-American movements were either instigated or loosely coordinated by the Soviet Union. In that respect, attacks against U.S. Marines in Lebanon during 1983 were essentially the same as the Marxist regime in Grenada. Hence Reagan's decision to dispatch a single military intervention force to deal with both problems in succession. In the terms often employed by Reagan's secretary of defense, Casper Weinberger, U.S. foreign policy and military strategies had to realign the global "correlation of forces" in a way that was more consistent with American interests.

The Reagan Doctrine promised military aid to antigovernment forces in communist Third World nations. Under the Reagan Doctrine, containment of the communist bloc was not enough. Reagan was the first American president since the 1950s to speak publicly of "rolling back" communism. He gave aid to many groups trying to overthrow communist governments. Reagan called these groups "freedom fighters." They included the Islamic mujahadeen who were fighting against the Soviet occupation of Afghanistan and the UNITA party led by Jonas Savimbi that has fought for more than twenty-five years in an unsuccessful attempt to unseat the Marxist regime in Angola.[19]

The most famous, even notorious, example of the Reagan Doctrine in practice was aid to the Contras in Nicaragua. The Contras began as a loosely allied array of groups that sought to unseat Nicaragua's government, at that time controlled by the Marxist-led Sandinista Party.[20] The Contras were precisely the kind of group that Reagan wanted to support. Aid to the Contras, however, devolved into the biggest scandal of the Reagan presidency. Evidence emerged that the White House had sold weapons to Iran and then diverted profits from those arms sales to Contra bank accounts. The Iran-Contra scandal led to long congressional investigations that were, at the very least, a major embarrassment to the Reagan administration.[21]

AMERICAN AND SOVIET POLICIES THAT ENDED THE COLD WAR

Why did the Cold War end? This simple question requires a complex answer. The end of the Cold War was "overdetermined;" which is to say that many causal factors contributed to this event. The end itself stretched from the fall of the Berlin Wall in 1989 to the collapse and breakup of the USSR in 1991. To understand the end of the Cold War, one must study the foreign policies of both superpowers.

A popular answer as to why the Cold War ended points to the massive defense expenditures of Presidents Reagan and Bush. According to this view, the $3 trillion that America spent on defense between 1982 and 1991 bankrupted the Soviet economy when Soviet leaders tried to keep up. Therefore, Reagan "won" the Cold War through his policies to fight the new Cold War of the 1980s. There is a kernel of truth in this explanation, but the causes for the end of the Cold War go beyond U.S. military spending.

A second contributing factor that helps us to understand the end of the Cold War is stressed in the work of Peter Stavrakis.[22] According to Stavrakis, Mikhail Gorbachev had his own reasons for ending the Cold War, reasons that were largely independent of U.S. policy. Gorbachev very much wanted to "return" to Europe by integrating the economies of the eastern and western halves of the continent. One of Gorbachev's favorite metaphors characterized all of Europe as a single "house" and its many nations as simply different "rooms" in that shared house. If the Soviet Union was but one room in the European house, then it made sense for countries on both sides of the Iron Curtain to more fully integrate with each other. At the same time that Gorbachev was promoting East-West integration, the members of Western Europe's European Union (EU) were making rapid steps forward in merging their economies. In 1986, the EU adopted the Single European Act (SEA). The SEA promised to drop almost all remaining barriers to trade within the EU by 1992. In 1991, the EU adopted the Maastricht treaty that called for monetary union (an integrated banking system and a single currency) within the EU.

Stavrakis stresses plans for the rapid economic integration of the EU as one of the most important motivating factors for Gorbachev's overhaul of Soviet foreign policy (see following discussion). According to Stavrakis, if Gorbachev did not revive the moribund Soviet economy and catch up with Western Europe before 1992, then he knew that the USSR would never be able to catch up after 1992. Stavrakis's analysis is useful for understanding the end of the Cold War for several reasons. First, it takes our attention beyond monocausal explanations that rely on military budgets alone to account for this sea change in global politics. Stavrakis instructs us to consider economic factors as well. Second, Stavrakis shows us causes for the end of the Cold War that operated independently of U.S. foreign policy. Finally, Stavrakis emphasizes Soviet policy, not U.S. policy, as a key to understanding the end of the Cold War. But there is at least one more level of analysis that must be incorporated into any adequate description of the end of the Cold War. This is the systemic level of international economic trends in the late twentieth century.

Economic prosperity in the West during the latter half of the twentieth century increased the gap between living standards on the two sides of the Iron Curtain. As economic output expanded in Western Europe and North America, the USSR command economy stagnated in the 1970s and then fell into negative growth by the 1980s. Compare this situation to the 1950s when, at times, Soviet growth rates exceeded those of the United States. At one time (in the 1950s), Soviet leaders such as Khrushchev sincerely believed that the USSR would one day overtake and surpass the United States in total economic output. By the 1980s, however, it became clear that such hopes would never materialize.

Soviet leaders such as Gorbachev were well aware of these facts. Gorbachev is widely traveled and, like most Russians, he is well educated. Gorbachev was the first Russian leader to publicly admit what most average Russians realized all too well: the Soviet economy was on the verge of collapse. The long-term inefficiencies inherent in any centrally planned and government-owned economy were destroying the Soviet economic system. Mr. Gorbachev made a remarkable speech before the UN General Assembly in 1988 during which he conceded defeat in the Cold War. Gorbachev threw in the towel because he knew that the USSR had to adopt some degree of capitalism if it was to survive. However, by moving toward capitalism, Gorbachev was also sealing the fate of his communist dictatorship. Without realizing it, and without intending to, Gorbachev doomed the Soviet empire to extinction when he started down a slippery slope toward free markets and democracy. A closer look at specific U.S. and Soviet policies that contributed to the end of the Cold War must be added to the larger explanatory factors of defense budgets, EU integration, and the victory of capitalism.

U.S. Policy and the End of the Cold War

Many American foreign policies helped to hasten the end of the Cold War. A remarkable turnaround in U.S policy took place under President Reagan. It has often been said that "only Nixon could go to China." Only someone with Nixon's anticommunist credentials could have been trusted by conservative Americans to normalize relations with the PRC.[23] Likewise, only Reagan could go to Moscow after the outbreak of the new Cold War in the 1980s. Reagan had come into office promising to vigorously pursue the Cold War and to make life difficult for communists around the globe. During his first term in office, he eagerly engaged in confrontations with America's potential enemies. However, during his second term, Reagan quickly warmed to the idea of a new form of détente between the United States and the USSR. The differences between his first term policies and his second term can be attributed to the arrival of Mr. Gorbachev.

Gorbachev came to power as the head of the Soviet political system in 1985. Reagan and Gorbachev quickly hit it off. Unlike any Soviet leader before him, Gorbachev was willing to agree to deep cuts in his own military might in order to revive détente. By agreeing to specific arms reductions, Gorbachev gained the trust of President Reagan. The two men also genuinely liked each other as individuals. Their personal friendship served to hasten a significant reversal of prior Cold War hostilities.

Once a good working relationship had been established, Reagan made policy changes that moved the United States into a neo-détente mode. In 1987, a key breakthrough in arms reductions came about as a result of a Reagan proposal. The first treaty to ever require reductions in nuclear arsenals was established by the 1987 Intermediate Nuclear Forces agreement. The INF treaty required that the United States and the USSR eliminate all intermediate-range missiles in Europe. Reagan also contributed to a sustained policy of peaceful coexistence and rapprochement with his broader pro-Gorbachev attitude.

Policies of neo-détente were maintained and expanded by the first President Bush. He too was "pro-Gorby," and like Reagan before him, Bush reestablished policies that were throwbacks to 1970s-style détente. Bush pushed for nuclear arms agreements. He negotiated and signed both Strategic Arms Reductions Treaties (START I of 1991 and START II of 1993). These treaties were the first agreements to require cuts in long-range nuclear arsenals. START I was signed by Gorbachev, and START II was signed by President Yeltsin of Russia after the breakup of the USSR (see the next chapter for details on these agreements).

During the 1990s, Bush became the first U.S. president to extend foreign aid to Russia in order to subsidize nuclear disarmament and the spread of democracy. Such aid to Russia continued under President Clinton.

The revival of détente by American leaders helped to speed up the end of the Cold War. In relative terms, however, the man who did the most to end the Cold War (and unintentionally to cause the collapse of the USSR) was Gorbachev.

Soviet Policy and the End of the Cold War

One cannot fully understand the end of the Cold War if one does not understand Gorbachev's reforms. Mr. Gorbachev came to power when he was named General Secretary (GenSec) of the Communist Party in 1985. As GenSec,

Gorbachev ruled the Party. The Party, in turn, ruled the USSR. Gorbachev followed a long line of Stalinist dictators who had wanted, above all else, absolute
rule by the Party. Gorbachev, on the other hand, was decidedly not a Stalinist.
He was willing to sacrifice some degree of the Party's political monopoly in exchange for needed economic reforms. Gorbachev's number one goal was to revive the dying Soviet economy. In order to restart his economy, Gorbachev
needed help from the West, especially from the United States. In order to get
help from the United States he had to end the new Cold War of the 1980s and
revive détente. In order to establish trust, Gorbachev embarked on a series of
foreign policies that he referred to collectively as the "New Thinking." The
New Thinking in Soviet foreign policy had five key elements: 1) arms control
and arms reductions, 2) trade with the United States, 3) military withdrawals,
4) an end to Soviet domination of Eastern Europe, and 5) an end to Russian
domination of the non-Russian Soviet republics. Each of these elements will be
described in greater detail.

The arms reduction aspects of Gorbachev's New Thinking involved
sweeping new proposals. At one time, Gorbachev went so far as to propose the
complete elimination of all U.S. and Soviet nuclear weapons.[24] President Reagan would not go along with this most ambitious of Gorbachev's proposals because it would have required an end to U.S. "Star Wars" strategic defense
systems. But the very fact that Gorbachev would even make such a proposal
helped to lead to a new round of nuclear treaties (INF, START I, and START
II). In 1988, Gorbachev announced ten percent unilateral cuts in his troop
strength and tanks corps, while asking for no U.S. reductions in return. A ten
percent cut in the Red Army in 1988 was equal to about 500,000 troops.

Like Brezhnev before him, Gorbachev hoped his polices of détente would
lead to MFN trade status for the USSR. Unlike Brezhnev, however, Gorbachev
agreed to the terms of the Jackson-Vanik Amendment and allowed Jewish emigration from the USSR. Gorbachev also improved human rights conditions in
the USSR in many ways beyond the right for Jews to leave. He was the first Soviet leader to allow foreign nongovernmental human rights organizations
(e.g., Amnesty International, Human Rights Watch) to come into the USSR
and monitor conditions there. As a reward for his human rights reforms, the
Soviet Union was granted MFN status in 1990.

Gorbachev's policies of arms control and seeking MFN were cut from the
same cloth as 1970s détente. Other parts of the New Thinking, however, went
well beyond old-style détente. He pulled Soviet troops out of Afghanistan in
1988. Recall that the invasion of Afghanistan in 1979 had killed the earlier era
of détente. Gorbachev also withdrew most of his forces from Eastern Europe.
Soviet troops that had dominated Eastern Europe as a result of Yalta came
home to the USSR. Recall that Soviet domination of Eastern Europe had
sparked the old Cold War of the 1940s. For economic and political reasons,
Gorbachev also ended Soviet aid to revolutionary regimes in the Third World.
In all these ways, Gorbachev sought to remove the underlying tensions that

fed superpower hostilities during the many phases of the Cold War. His biggest gamble, however, was his tolerance for democracy within the communist bloc.

The New Thinking allowed democracies to replace communist dictatorships in Eastern Europe. In Poland during 1989, Solidarity formed the first noncommunist government in the Soviet bloc via peaceful, constitutional means. Gorbachev allowed the Solidarity government to be voted into power. In the same year, Hungary was the first communist government to open its borders to the West. Perhaps most significant was the fall of the Berlin Wall in 1989 and the reunification of the two Germanys in 1990. Gorbachev did what no Soviet leader before him would have done. He stood by and allowed all of these reversals of Cold War communist doctrine to take place. He even agreed to allow the reunited Germany to become a member of NATO. At the same time, he presided over the dissolution of the Warsaw Treaty Organization. The Warsaw Treaty Organization had been the eastern counterpart to NATO. Gorbachev no longer saw any need for this alliance between the USSR and its former satellites in Eastern Europe.

When democracy began to sweep across Eastern Europe in 1989, Gorbachev said publicly that such changes were fine for other communist countries. However, he also claimed that liberalization of the Soviet political system was unnecessary. He was, after all, the leader of the Communist Party. He sincerely believed that this myriad of political and economic changes could proceed apace outside of the USSR, while his hold on domestic power and the continued existence of the Soviet state would remain unthreatened. He was badly mistaken. Gorbachev's New Thinking eventually forced him to propose a loosening of the ties that held the USSR together. Once he started to loosen those restraints, events quickly spun beyond his control, leading to the collapse of the USSR and the final end of the Cold War.

Inside the USSR, the New Thinking led to demands by non-Russian republics for independence. The New Thinking ended a long history of Russian domination over the non-Russian peoples of the USSR. Russians had always controlled the USSR through their control of the Party. There is, however, an even longer history of mistrust (in some cases even hatred) of Russians by their non-Russian neighbors. The New Thinking allowed increased local autonomy for all republics. Gorbachev tolerated free speech and multiparty elections for the first time in Soviet history. These political reforms eventually led to complete independence for all Soviet republics (including the Russian Republic headed by Boris Yeltsin), although that was not Gorbachev's intention.

According to the Soviet constitution, the USSR had always been made up of fifteen separate republics. The individual republics even had, on paper, the nominal right to secede from the USSR. No leader before Gorbachev took the "independent" constitutional status of the republics seriously. In fact, any effort to assert autonomous rights in the republics had always resulted in severe repression from the central authorities (prior to Gorbachev).

The Baltic republics were especially strident in their demands for independence during the 1990s. Latvia, Lithuania, and Estonia had been independent countries between the two World Wars, only to be forcibly annexed into the USSR by Stalin in the early days of World War II. Local leaders in these Baltic republics looked on events in Eastern Europe during 1989 and then demanded the same kind of democratic rights for their own peoples. When the Baltic republics took steps toward declaring independence, Gorbachev was unable to use force to stop them. Because of his desires for trade and détente with the West, Gorbachev had effectively tied his own hands. A widespread invasion of the Baltic republics, or any other massive show of force by the Red Army, would have killed all of the goodwill that he had built up with the United States. The age of neo-détente would have ended. The USSR would have been denied MFN trade status again, and Gorbachev's top priority (economic rebirth via foreign economic assistance) would have suffered a deathblow.

The rise of democracy and demands for independence in the republics were an unavoidable outcome of Gorbachev's New Thinking. In a desperate attempt to hold the USSR together, Gorbachev proposed a limited transfer of political power from the central Soviet government to the republics. Under his proposed Union Treaty of 1991, the republics would have obtained increased autonomy, but the central Soviet government would retain control over defense and a common currency. The Soviet Red Army would maintain defense, and the Soviet central bank would still control fiscal policy. A grand ceremony for signing the Union Treaty was scheduled. Leaders from the republics traveled to Moscow for the event. One day prior to the scheduled signing of the Union Treaty, however, hard-liners in the Party, the KGB, and the Red Army staged a coup against Gorbachev to prevent this devolution of power to the republics. For four days in August 1991, the coup's conspirators controlled the Soviet government in Moscow. Yeltsin rallied the people in popular resistance to the coup while Gorbachev was under house arrest. The coup failed, and the failure of the 1991 coup discredited the Communist Party in a manner from which it has never recovered.

As a result of the coup, the Union Treaty was never signed, and all fifteen republics declared full independence. A popular backlash led Yeltsin to outlaw the Communist Party in Russia for a time. Gorbachev himself resigned from the Party but also made one last-ditch attempt to hold the USSR together in the fall of 1991. By that time, however, the end was inevitable. Gorbachev resigned as the last president of the USSR on Christmas Day 1991. At that moment (if not before) the USSR simply ceased to exist. All former Soviet republics have been independent nation-states since late 1991.

With no more USSR, there is no more Cold War. With the end of the Cold War came the end of American policies of containment. A few communist nations remain scattered throughout the world, but containment had always been a policy designed to stop the spread of Soviet power. The central focus and the unifying theme in American foreign policy for more than forty years had become obsolete. Nothing has come along in the post–Cold War era to replace containment as a guiding light for U.S. policy. Post–Cold War foreign policy has been cast adrift; it is still in search of a purpose.

POST–COLD WAR FOREIGN POLICY

Clinton was the first president elected into the White House after the end of the Cold War. As such, he was also the first leader to have to come into office with some conception of what a post–Cold War foreign policy should be. A key Clinton advisor, Anthony Lake, suggested "enlargement" as a logical substitute for prior policies of containment. Enlargement would seek to expand the global presence of democratic governments and capitalist economies.[25] Presumably, now that the Soviet state was no longer a viable alternative to the American model of free markets and liberal democracy, enlarging the sphere of U.S. politico-economic values would be relatively easy. Enlargement, however, never caught on as a unifying theme for post–Cold War foreign policy. Politicians and diplomats have advanced other alternatives, but they have met with a similar fate. Although there is no overriding or unifying theme for post–Cold War policy, it is possible to summarize Clinton's thinking on foreign policy by looking at the assumptions and priorities on which his policies were based.

Early in the 1990s, the Clinton administration outlined four key assumptions and six priorities for its foreign policy. Throughout two terms in office, President Clinton generally acted in keeping with his assumptions and his declared foreign policy priorities. The first assumption was that threats to U.S. interests have become increasingly nonmilitary in nature since the end of the Cold War.[26] Economic competition and environmental degradation, for the Clinton administration, had to be considered threats to U.S. interests; threats that at times were more salient than the old dangers associated with military confrontations. The second assumption asserted that there are no military solutions for what are essentially political problems. For example, only negotiations and compromise (rather than military aggression) can solve the political differences that lie at the heart of the Arab-Israeli disputes.

Assumption number three for Clinton's foreign policy posited a need for increased multilateral action and less reliance on unilateral American international policy. The final assumption, consistent with Lake's concept of enlargement, was that the United States needed to spread democracy and promote human rights throughout the world.

The six priorities of Clinton's post–Cold War international policies were always listed by members of the administration in order of decreasing importance.[27] Topping the list were America's economic interests. During his 1992 presidential campaign, Clinton's staff used the slogan "it's the economy, stupid" as a reminder that pocketbook issues would determine the outcome of future presidential elections. Economic issues also rose to the top of America's foreign policy priorities. Clinton often spoke of how international trade needed to be reconceptualized as a national security issue after the Cold War faded. Making America a stronger economic power and protecting the economic interests of U.S. citizens and U.S. businesses became the number one concern regarding the welfare and security of the nation. In essence, this required a redefinition of what constitutes "national security" after the collapse of the USSR and after the demise of containment. Policies had to address the various connections between trade relations and national defense (see the beginning of chapter 7). In addition, the entire concept of "security" had to be expanded to include nonmilitary threats to the national wellbeing. Clinton's initial foreign policy emphasis on economic matters was reflected in his early foreign policy successes, such as the completion of the North America Free Trade Agreement (NAFTA) free trade area and securing Congressional approval for U.S membership in the World Trade Organization (WTO; see chapter 7).

The number two priority for Clinton's foreign policy was relations with Russia (and the other former Soviet republics). This had always been the number one concern for U.S. policy during Cold War containment. In effect, American concerns about Russia were "demoted" from first to second place by Clinton in regard to foreign policy and national interests. In this region, the primary concern is still Russia's enormous nuclear arsenal. President George Bush and President Clinton both provided aid programs that have funded as much as seventy-five percent of the costs of reducing the Russian nuclear stockpile. Clinton also institutionalized a set of foreign aid programs that provided funding for promotion of democracy and free markets in the former Soviet republics.

The third foreign policy priority for Clinton was relations with Europe and the maintenance of NATO. Contrary to those who argued that NATO was a Cold War alliance that had outlived its utility in a post–Cold War era, Clinton sought to reaffirm the U.S. commitment to a robust Atlantic alliance. In fact, Clinton took the lead in policies to expand NATO. At first, the Partnership for Peace program was created to ease the transition to NATO membership for former communist nations such as the Czech Republic, Hungary, and Poland. This aspect of NATO policy culminated in 1999 with the admission of these three states into full NATO membership. NATO has also moved, under American leadership, to expand the mandate of its operations beyond the mutual defense of its neighbors to include the new tasks of peacekeeping and peace enforcement, especially in the Balkans (see chapter 5). Much of the expansion of NATO's theater of operations was due to the forceful leadership provided by Clinton's last secretary of state, Madeline Albright.

Beyond defense policy, relations with Western Europe have also figured prominently into U.S. trade policy, especially trade disputes. From the Uruguay Round battles over agricultural subsidies to the subsequent "banana wars" at the WTO dispute panels (see chapters 7 and 9), American economic confrontations with EU nations have tended to dominate the nation's foreign policy energies for long periods of time.

A fourth international priority for Clinton was increased attention to Asia. Trade disputes with Japan and China, the first steps toward creating a free trade area for all Pacific nations (e.g., the APEC meetings), U.S. policy to facilitate China's membership into the WTO, and a series of economic/monetary crises in the east Asian region required sustained and onerous efforts to mold new American policy responses.[28] As we already saw in chapter 1, Asia has also become an area of utmost concern when it comes to proliferation of nuclear weapons, including the possibility of a nuclear attack on the United States by the "rogue state" in North Korea. The threat of North Korean intercontinental nuclear missiles (whether real or imagined) has led to the biggest new debate over nuclear policy in the twenty-first century: Should the United States develop a NMD system to counter these perceived threats? The debate over NMD is another topic to be addressed in the following chapter.

The fifth priority for Clinton's foreign polices was the Middle East. At least during his first term, Clinton put military operations and peace efforts regarding the Middle East on a back burner compared to his other international initiatives. The United States did participate in two significant steps forward for the peace process when it acted as one of the arbitrators (along with Norway) for a mutual recognition treaty between Israel and the Palestinian Liberation Organization (PLO) in 1993 and for a peace treaty between Israel and Jordan in 1994. During his second term, Clinton escalated military operations against Iraq designed to punish Saddam Hussein's refusal to comply with UN Security Council requirements for weapons inspections. During his last year in the White House, Clinton convened a second Camp David summit with the United States, the PLO, and Israel in attendance. Camp David II sought to repeat some of the successes enjoyed by President Carter's Camp David I summit in 1978. (See chapter 4 for a description of Camp David I.) The declared goal of Camp David II in 2000 was to set the outlines for a final settlement regarding the most contentious issues still separating the Palestinians and the Israelis (i.e., statehood for a Palestinian homeland, the borders of that state, the status of Jerusalem, Israeli settlements on the West Bank, and the return of millions of Palestinian refugees). The failure of Camp David II, along with Clinton's limited success regarding other policies in the Middle East, will be discussed in chapter 4.

The sixth and final priority for Clinton's foreign policies was a mixed bag of "global issues." This residual category of foreign policy interests included issues as diverse as the global environment (see chapter 12), international human rights (see chapter 10), Third World debt crises (see chapter 11), proliferation of weapons of mass destruction (see chapter 3), and participation in UN and NATO peacekeeping efforts (see chapter 5). Subsequent chapters in this text will cover post–Cold War American foreign policies in each of these areas.

AMERICAN SECURITY POLICY
IN THE NEW MILLENNIUM

At the time of this writing, George W. Bush was still new in office as America's forty-third president. Initial indications are that American security policy will undergo some significant (but not seismic) changes under his administration.

<P>Candidate Bush spoke often during the 2000 election campaign about the need to base U.S. foreign policy on a realistic understanding of America's national interests. He implied that his administration would be less likely than his predecessor to sponsor humanitarian interventions and the use of force for peacekeeping or "nation-building." Secretary of State Colin Powell, however, tempered the rhetoric of the new administration by noting that the United States has "an interest in every place on this Earth."[29] Secretary Powell was also slightly less enthusiastic than the new president about a NMD. Finally, both President George W. Bush and Secretary Powell promised a more vigorous campaign against Saddam Hussein in Iraq. These three areas—NMD, policy toward Iraq, and peacekeeping forces—are among the topics addressed in chapters 3–5.[30]

Chapter 3

NUCLEAR DETERRENCE AND ARMS CONTROL

INTRODUCTION: BIRTH OF THE ATOMIC AGE

During the Cold War, American foreign policy was dominated by security concerns. Fears of Soviet nuclear weapons sat at the top of a list of perceived threats to the United States. Now that the Cold War is over, fears of nuclear war have receded significantly, but the nuclear superpowers still retain vast arsenals of these weapons of mass destruction. Furthermore, nuclear weapons are spreading to other major powers, and chemical and biological weapons are also proliferating. Although policy attention to chemical, biological, and nuclear weapons (CBNs) was relatively greater during the Cold War, American policy on CBNs remains a top priority to this day. To understand the present situation regarding the possible use and proliferation of nuclear weapons, one must first understand their evolution during the Cold War. This chapter will present a history of U.S. policy on nuclear weapons and a review of arms control efforts for CBNs to date. Like so many of the structural aspects of the Cold War and the post–Cold War era, the atomic age was itself born during World War II.

Early Atomic Policy and the Baruch Plan

America developed the first atomic bombs under the Manhattan Project of World War II. When President Truman ordered the bombing of Hiroshima and Nagasaki, the United States had a monopoly on this technology. However, American leaders were already concerned about the possibility that the USSR would also acquire such weapons. One reason the A-bomb was used to end the war against Japan was to demonstrate to the Russians America's atomic capabilities.[1] Scientific and intelligence experts in the United States estimated in 1945 that it would take the Soviets at least eight more years to develop their own atomic weapons. Therefore, not only did the United States have a monopoly on the Bomb, but it also assumed that this strategic superiority would last for some time to come.

At first, the United States developed no unique military policies for use of atomic weapons. Atomic bombs would be used like conventional (nonnuclear) bombs. They would be loaded onto a long-range bomber and dropped on population centers (cities) to cause as much destruction and loss of life as possible. In other words, at the dawn of the atomic age, there was no immediate recognition by military leaders of the difference *in kind* that these new weapons represented. Military decision makers understood that atomic weapons could deliver a much greater charge than any conventional weapon, but early planning for the use of the Bomb was simply an extension of existing military strategy. There was one exception to this lack of unique policies for atomic weapons. That was the U.S. proposal before the UN to create an international body to supervise and control all atomic technology throughout the world. In 1946, the United States proposed the Baruch Plan.

The Baruch Plan would have created a new organ of the UN to control all phases of atomic research.[2] The Baruch Plan fell through due to Soviet opposition, and the proposed Atomic Development Authority (ADA) never came into being. The U.S. proposal would have given the ADA complete control over research and development of atomic technology in all parts of the globe, starting with the mining of uranium (the raw material for atomic bombs). The ADA would have had authority over mining and enriching the uranium and control over peaceful uses of atomic technology, including control of all electrical power plants. The United States proposed that the ADA construct and operate atomic power plants throughout the world based on a system of geographic equity (i.e., all members of the UN would share the electricity generated by atomic plants). The ADA would also have had authority over all atomic weapons. The United States proposed the Baruch Plan (1946) at a time when it still had a monopoly on these weapons. Part of the U.S. proposal included an offer to destroy all of its atomic bombs under certain conditions.

Before the United States would eliminate its atomic arsenal, all other members of the UN would have to put themselves under the authority of the ADA. The ADA would be managed by its members, with no country having a veto. Once all other nations were under the ADA and each had given up the option of independent development of atomic technology, then the United States would destroy its atomic bombs at a time of America's choosing.

The USSR rejected the Baruch Plan for a number of reasons. First, the Soviets objected to the lack of ADA veto powers. The Soviets had few allies in the newly created UN. A majority of members at that time were allies or friends of the United States. Recall that most of the Third World was still held as colonies in 1946. Communist dictatorships had yet to spread to Eastern Europe and Asia. Therefore, without a bloc of supporters to rely on, the Soviets insisted on retaining a veto (similar to the Security Council) if the ADA was to be established. Americans insisted on no veto for ADA members. The Soviets also objected to the proposed timetable for the creation of the ADA and the subsequent elimination of America's atomic weapons. The Russians wanted the United States to destroy its arsenal *prior to* creation of the ADA as a guarantee that America's atomic monopoly would not survive. American leaders rejected both the veto in the ADA and Russian insistence that the United States eliminate atomic bombs as a precondition for enacting the remainder of the Baruch Plan.

As a result, the Soviets rejected the Baruch Plan as proposed. American leaders insisted that the plan was an all-or-nothing deal. Therefore, the Baruch Plan was never adopted, and each of the major powers was left free to develop their own atomic technologies.

The Soviets exploded their first atomic device in 1949, at least three years ahead of American expectations.[3] China fell to communism in 1949. These events spurred the "Red Scare" and McCarthyism in the 1950s. With the onset of the Korean War, both superpowers became locked into a Cold War mentality, and all hopes for the prevention of atomic proliferation were dashed. Once Russia developed an atomic bomb, President Truman gave the go-ahead to develop the hydrogen bomb, or the H-bomb. Known in those days as the "superbomb" (or simply the Super), hydrogen weapons are even more powerful than atomic weapons.

Atomic bombs use the principle of nuclear fission to split atoms apart in an uncontrolled chain reaction. This was the type of weapon used against Japan in World War II. Hydrogen weapons use the principle of nuclear fusion to force atoms together under intense heat and pressure. Also known as thermonuclear devices, or simply "nuclear" weapons, H-bombs represented another quantum leap forward in the early postwar arms race. In fact, it takes a small fission device to trigger most nuclear (fusion) weapons.[4] Most of the U.S. and Russian arsenals for mass destruction now consist of nuclear weapons. The largest nuclear weapons deliver an explosive yield that can be thousands of times more powerful than the atomic weapons dropped on Japan in 1945.[5]

President Eisenhower favored development of nuclear weapons like the H-bomb. During the 1950s, one slogan guiding U.S. deterrence policy was "more bang for the buck." By developing the H-bomb, the United States could produce more powerful nuclear weapons for roughly the same costs needed to build A-bombs. The United States exploded its first hydrogen weapon in 1952. Ike and his secretary of state, John Foster Dulles, also developed the first deterrence strategy devised specifically for the use of nuclear weapons. Dulles called his strategy "massive retaliation." Massive retaliation itself was one form of what has come to be known as "minimum deterrence."

MINIMUM DETERRENCE OR MAD

Massive retaliation was a product of the early Cold War. It was a policy that reflected American thinking during the Korean War era. The communist bloc always had an advantage at the level of conventional forces. The USSR had a much larger army and more battle tanks. The United States came to rely on its nuclear arsenal to offset the superior numbers of troops and armor that the Soviet bloc could muster. Massive retaliation was a threat to use America's nuclear superiority against Moscow and other cities in the Eastern bloc. If the communists sought to expand their sphere of influence through a series of conventional wars (as in Korea), Dulles warned that the United States would not restrict itself to countering such aggression with purely conventional means. Massive retaliation reserved the option of striking back at what the United States saw as the ultimate source of communist aggression—Moscow and Beijing. More wars like that in Korea, according to Dulles, might cause the United States to launch a nuclear strike against the capitals of the communist powers.

Massive retaliation was a specific instance of a more general approach to nuclear deterrence. The generic term for this approach is minimum deterrence. Minimum deterrence is the oldest form of nuclear deterrence. It is defined by its targeting strategies and by the relative size of the nuclear arsenal needed for a minimum deterrence force posture. Minimum deterrence employs a relatively small arsenal of weapons aimed at cities. Massive retaliation relied on long-range bombers to threaten population centers in the USSR and China. Because it targets cites, minimum deterrence was also referred to as a "countercity" or a "countervalue" strategy. By roughly 1960, massive retaliation had given way to a better known form of minimum deterrence: mutual assured destruction, or MAD.

MAD is a form of minimum deterrence, like massive retaliation, because it targets cities. Pentagon strategists used a MAD approach to calculate the minimum amount of potential nuclear destruction that would be necessary to deter communist aggression. The rule of thumb for MAD was that the United States needed a large enough nuclear arsenal to ensure the deaths of one-quarter of the enemy's population plus the destruction of two-thirds of their industrial base. Destruction of the 200 largest cities in the USSR would have guaranteed the catastrophic loses needed for MAD. If the United States could guarantee these losses, then it had achieved "assured destruction," or AD. Both the USSR and the United States developed an AD capability in the 1960s.

During the late 1950s and most of the 1960s, the United States employed a minimum deterrence approach based on the assumptions of MAD. MAD planning further required that the United States take into account the possibility of a Soviet first strike. If the USSR were to launch a "bolt out of the blue," or a sneak attack with their nuclear arsenal, then the United States would still want to be able to inflict a level of AD in response. This meant that the United States would have to retain enough weapons *after* it had been attacked to destroy one-quarter of the Soviet population and two-thirds of its industry. Therefore, MAD relied on a second-strike capability.

Massive retaliation and MAD were two types of minimum deterrence. Both strategies targeted cities. Both approaches assumed that nuclear war would necessarily escalate to all-out city busting. By relying on minimum deterrence, an all-out strike against the heart of one's enemy is the only nuclear option. Because of its relatively limited options, minimum deterrence came under criticism almost as soon as it was introduced.

Problems with MAD: The Kissinger Critique

The best-known critic of minimum deterrence is Henry Kissinger. In his 1957 text *Nuclear Weapons and Foreign Policy*, Kissinger advanced three fundamental critiques of the MAD approach. First, according to Kissinger, minimum deterrence was an all-or-nothing strategy. A president would be faced with engaging in all-out nuclear war against cities, or capitulation. Kissinger believed that it did not make sense to stockpile weapons that one was afraid to use in battle. Because minimum deterrence would almost certainly bring about the complete destruction of all major cities on *both* sides, going to the nuclear level to counter conventional Soviet aggression would mean mutual suicide. Therefore, Kissinger viewed MAD as a mistaken military policy. It did not give decision makers enough options. It was also largely an empty threat, according to Kissinger, after the Soviets developed their own hydrogen weapons in 1953.

A second Kissinger critique of minimum deterrence is closely related to the first. Kissinger argued that MAD was a mistake because it would not allow the United States to limit the escalation of war during a nuclear confrontation. If the Soviets used their conventional advantage or if they launched a limited nuclear attack against NATO military installations, the United States would have little alternative but to strike back against Russian cities, once again taking the world into all-out nuclear war. Any strike against Soviet cities would almost certainly bring about an all-out attack on American cities as well. Kissinger argued that the West needed to develop nuclear weapons that would be more discriminating, weapons that could be used in less than an all-out nuclear war. Kissinger favored the strategy of "limited" nuclear war.[6]

Kissinger's third critique followed from the other two. Kissinger argued that, due to its inherent reliance on all-out war as the only nuclear option, minimum deterrence was not credible.[7] Kissinger warned that America's enemies might not take the threat of massive retaliation seriously. Even worse, America's allies might start to question America's commitment to their defense if its only strategic option was an all-out nuclear war. Charles de Gaulle, president of France in the late 1950s and early 1960s, lent some credence to Kissinger's fears about the credibility of MAD. De Gaulle was fond of saying things such as: "The U.S. will not trade Washington for Paris." By that, de Gaulle meant that (in his opinion) the United States could not be counted on in all circumstances to come to the defense of Western Europe, especially if protecting European allies would guarantee a nuclear strike against North America. In other words, de Gaulle was unsure if the United States would "trade" an attack on Washington in exchange for American actions to protect Paris (or London or West Berlin, etc.) from the Red Army. De Gaulle used this logic to argue in favor of an independent nuclear capability for France. Under his leadership, the French developed their own nuclear weapons in the 1960s. Kissinger used the alleged lack of credibility for minimum deterrence to argue for an alternative U.S. strategy. This approach favored by Kissinger and other critics of MAD came to be known as "flexible deterrence."

FLEXIBLE DETERRENCE OR NUTS

Kissinger's critique of MAD, combined with allies' fears that the United States might abandon them rather than risk a nuclear attack on the United States, lead the United States slowly away from the MAD approach of minimum deterrence. As a first step, the United States began to miniaturize its nuclear weapons in the late 1950s. To create short-range "tactical" weapons (also known as "battlefield" or "theater" weapons), the United States made nuclear devices smaller and smaller. Some were small enough to be shot out of a conventional artillery cannon. Deployment of tactical nuclear devices gave the United States more options for its deterrence strategy. Short-range and lower-yield tactical weapons could be used as a first line of defense on the battlefields of Europe or Asia, with massive retaliation or MAD as a fallback position. MAD would be the West's last line of defense, but nuclear war would not have to begin and end with MAD. The Soviets responded by developing their own tactical nuclear weapons.

Both sides also began to develop new types of long-range weapons in the 1950s and 1960s. The most dangerous are the (land-based) intercontinental ballistic missiles, or ICBMs. An ICBM is a virtually unstoppable weapon. It is a ballistic missile with a range greater than 3,000 miles. When the USSR successfully launched the first man-made satellite, Sputnik, in 1957 they demonstrated the capability to deploy ICBMs. An ICBM can carry a nuclear device as its warhead. They travel on a ballistic trajectory that takes the warhead into outer space and then back into the atmosphere en route to the enemy's territory. Fears of a possible Soviet ICBM advantage after the launching of Sputnik (the so-called missile gap of the 1950s) led the United States to begin a crash program to develop and deploy its own ICBMs in the 1960s. The 1960s also witnessed the deployment of submarine launched ballistic missiles (SLBMs) by both sides. SLBMs are very similar to ICBMs, although they tend to be smaller than their land-based counterparts.

Development of tactical weapons, combined with the advent of ICBMs and SLBMs, led to the first nuclear arms race of the Cold War. When combined with the existing stockpiles of nuclear bombs and long-range bombers, this expansion of the nuclear arsenals on both sides led to a new type of deterrence policy: flexible deterrence.

Flexible deterrence, or flexible response, became official NATO policy in 1967. Flexible deterrence sought to overcome the alleged deficiencies in minimum deterrence that were pointed out by Kissinger and others. Flexible deterrence relied, in part, on the types of weapons needed to fight "limited" nuclear wars. Flexible deterrence required a wide range of many different types of weapons. Flexible deterrence also required a much larger arsenal of nuclear devices than did MAD or minimum deterrence. The primary purpose of possessing nuclear weapons under the MAD approach was to deter the other side, in hopes that these weapons would never be used. Advocates of flexible deterrence such as Kissinger believed that the United States had to have the kinds of weapons that could be used to fight, and win, nuclear wars. Flexible deterrence weapons were designed primarily to be *used* and were not deployed as a deterrent alone (as were MAD weapons). Hence the strategies of flexible deterrence came to be known as nuclear utilization theories or NUTS.[8]

Flexible deterrence, or NUTS, relied on a "ladder of escalation." At the lowest rung of this ladder was conventional military forces of the types used in World War II, Korea, and Vietnam. All levels above the conventional rung were reached by crossing the "nuclear threshold" or the "nuclear firebreak." All of the higher rungs were levels or stages of a nuclear war. The first nuclear rung was the tactical level, employing short range, battlefield nuclear devices such as the "neutron bomb."[9] The next level contained intermediate-range nuclear forces (or INF weapons). The highest level of the ladder would be all-out strategic war, employing the nuclear triad of ICBMs, SLBMs, and long-range bombers (or LRBs).

The basic logic of NUTS was to meet any attack against the United States or its key allies at a given level. If an enemy attacked a member of NATO with conventional weapons, the initial response would also be conventional. However, under the doctrine of flexible response, NATO always reserved the right to escalate to the next rung of the ladder if an attack could not be repelled at the lower level. In other words, inherent in the NUTS approach to Cold War deterrence was a "first use" policy. Because the Soviet bloc always had an advantage at the conventional level, NATO (and the United States) publicly declared during the Cold War that it would be the first to introduce nuclear weapons into a conflict if necessary to avoid defeat. The USSR always maintained publicly that they had a "no first use" policy. The USSR claimed that it would never be the first to introduce nuclear weapons into a conflict. Of course, their conventional advantage made it much easier for the Soviets to declare a no first use policy. In any event, the United States and its NATO allies never gave much credence to the Soviets' alleged no first use policy. NATO always assumed that the Soviets had a *declared* policy of no first use but that their actual policy relied on the possibility of a Soviet first use of nuclear weapons.

If NATO's conventional forces could not stop Soviet tanks that were rolling across West Germany, then NATO pledged to escalate to the tactical nuclear level. If that was not sufficient to stop the invasion, then NUTS doctrine would move to the INF level. The last line of defense for NATO allies, both during and after the Cold War, has always been the American strategic arsenal. NUTS doctrine promised to fight limited nuclear war in defense of American allies and American interests. But NUTS also held the possibility that, if limited wars did not suffice, then America's total nuclear arsenal would be called into use.

NUTS relied on a much wider range of weapons and a much larger stockpile of weapons than did MAD. NUTS also used "counterforce" targeting. Counterforce targeting aimed some of the NUTS arsenal at the opponent's nuclear forces. NUTS targeted not just the enemy's cities but also their weapons. This form of targeting required the United States to develop and deploy "hard-target" or "first-strike" weapons. A hard-target weapon is a nuclear missile that is so powerful and so accurate that it can destroy an enemy ICBM while that land-based missile is still in the ground in its launching silo, protected by concrete and steel. Both sides moved to a NUTS or flexible deterrence approach in the late 1960s and into the 1970s. In the 1970s and 1980s, both sides developed and deployed new hard-target, first-strike, land-based weapons (such as the U.S. MX or the Soviet SS-18). America also developed and deployed hard-target weapons for its submarines. These newer and deadlier strategic weapons were supplemented on both sides by deployment of new INF missiles in Europe.

Advantages and Disadvantages of NUTS

In the terms laid out by Kissinger's critique of minimum deterrence, NUTS overcame some of the drawbacks of MAD. Kissinger and others had criticized MAD as an all-or-nothing strategy. They said it lacked sufficient options to make it effective. NUTS, on the other hand, provided the United States with a wealth of nuclear options. Tactical weapons and INF missiles might be used to avoid or delay the escalation of a conflict to the level of an all-out nuclear war. NUTS offered more options for the use of nuclear weapons, and advocates of NUTS argued that it would also help to limit escalation once a nuclear confrontation erupted. Because of the enhanced options and alleged ability to limit escalation, supporters of NUTS maintained that it was more credible. If U.S. cities could be spared from direct nuclear attack, according to the logic of NUTS, then there was an increased likelihood that the United States would employ its nuclear arsenal. The ability to fight a limited nuclear war is supposed to make it more likely that the United States would be able to accept the otherwise "unthinkable" prospect of engaging in nuclear battles.

On the other hand, the evolution of deterrence from MAD to NUTS brought with it new strategic dangers that were unique to flexible deterrence. First, the costs of NUTS were enormous. Because NUTS required such a huge arsenal (much larger than was needed for minimum deterrence), and because NUTS must rely on many more types of weapons, its costs were far superior to that of a MAD force posture. Furthermore, the hard-target weapons needed for counterforce targeting were much more costly on a per-unit basis.

Hard-target weapons must have greater power and incredible accuracy. That means they must have more sophisticated (hence more costly) guidance systems than weapons used for MAD's countercity targeting.

Second, the development of all these new generations of nuclear weapons led to a renewed arms race between the United States and the USSR in the 1970s and 1980s. Critics of NUTS and defenders of MAD argued that arms races were inherently destabilizing. The development of so many weapons would make the United States *less secure* rather than more secure. Carl Sagan likened the late twentieth-century arms race to giving more matches to two antagonists who are already locked in a room together and up to their knees in gasoline. Giving one or both of the combatants an increased supply of matches only serves to place both of them in greater danger. If Sagan's analogy is valid, then introducing more nuclear weapons into the volatile Cold War situation only served to make both nuclear superpowers less safe.[10]

Most troubling are the dangers of NUTS that Theodore Draper highlighted by his term *nuclear temptations*. Draper argued that NUTS is more dangerous than MAD because NUTS increased the nuclear "temptations" to go to war.[11] NUTS increased temptations by reducing the *psychological* barriers to fighting a nuclear war. NUTS theory believed that nuclear weapons were made to be used (under certain restricted circumstances). They were not just for deterrence, or even primarily for deterrence. Kissinger had long argued that the United States must develop the necessary weapons and the will to fight limited nuclear wars. Kissinger's 1957 text criticized minimum deterrence for stockpiling the kinds of weapons that any leader would be deathly afraid to use. NUTS theorists like Kissinger believed that the United States could fight, and must win, limited nuclear wars. In the 1980s, there was much talk by the Reagan administration of limited nuclear war. The Reagan Pentagon also was fond of the term *prevail*. It was often said during the 1980s that the United States must necessarily prevail in any nuclear exchange with the Soviets.

Critics of NUTS believed that this sort of talk is inherently dangerous. Draper, for one, argued that talk of limited nuclear war, and belief that the United States could win a nuclear war, made such a war more likely to occur. NUTS rhetoric and beliefs about the possibility of limited war could increase the temptations to go to nuclear war during a crisis. If one or both sides believed that nuclear war could be limited or if either side thought it could win a nuclear war, then there would be fewer psychological inhibitions against engaging in a nuclear war. Critics of NUTS pointed out that, in a nuclear war, there could be no "winners." Both sides would suffer hundreds of thousands, even millions, of deaths and perhaps the end of their social-political-economic orders. How, under any definition of the term *win*, could that be considered a victory?

Furthermore, critics of NUTS argued that the term "limited nuclear war" was an oxymoron. No nuclear war could be accurately described by the term *limited*, and all nuclear war would most likely quickly escalate to all-out city busting. NUTS did not remove the threat of mutual annihilation. At best, the layers of deterrence added by the NUTS strategy would only temporarily delay the eventual unleashing of the full nuclear arsenal by both sides. Once nuclear war starts, all bets are off. It is hard to imagine any circumstances under which total war could be avoided. This is because MAD remained as an inherent part of NUTS. NUTS employed weapons that did not exist in the early days of MAD, but "NUTS has not offered us an escape from the MAD world."[12] According to Spurgeon Keeny and Wolfgang Panofsky, we are forever "fated to live in a MAD world" for at least three reasons. First, the tremendous power of any nuclear device must carry with it enormous collateral damage. Second, the technical limitations of strategic defense make building an invulnerable shield against nuclear missiles impossible (see the following discussion for more on missile defense). Third, the unavoidable uncertainties involved in efforts to control the escalation of nuclear war are based on human nature not technology, and human nature is unlikely to change.[13]

Draper made a similar valid point when he pointed to counterforce targeting as the most dangerous of all nuclear temptations. It was the most dangerous temptation because it falsely promised "to take much of the horror out of nuclear war."[14] Advocates of NUTS liked to use misleading terms such as "limited war" and "surgical strikes." A limited war or a surgical strike was said to be possible by attacking only an opponent's nuclear weapons. Counterforce targeting was supposed to spare the populations of both sides from the nuclear holocaust. What NUTS theorists didn't like to talk about, however, were the deaths that would follow from *any* so-called surgical strike. The *lowest* estimate from credible sources for deaths from a counterforce attack on U.S. nuclear weapons is between 800,000 and one million lives lost. The same studies show that even more people would die from a U.S. counterforce attack on Russia.[15] NUTS theorists wanted us to believe that presidents in the United States and/or Russia, when faced with the loss of a million lives due to a surgical counterforce attack, would not strike back in response with everything they had in their nuclear arsenal. That possibility seems highly unlikely.

A final problem with NUTS was one that it shared with minimum deterrence. That was the problem of vulnerability. MAD weapons were also vulnerable to attack from the USSR. However the problem of vulnerability was especially relevant to NUTS strategies. NUTS relied in part on the ability to launch a counterforce first strike. This was one of the key differences between MAD and NUTS. MAD was essentially a second-strike strategy. Because NUTS depended on a first-strike capability, the weapons needed for this dimension of NUTS required enhanced survivability. Otherwise an MX missile (a NUTS counterforce weapon) that replaced an aging Minuteman ICBM (a prior MAD second-strike weapon) was simply a more costly target for Soviet strategic rockets. For NUTS to have the enhanced credibility that Kissinger and others ascribe to it, its weapons had to be less vulnerable than the prior MAD arsenal.

Policy Fixes for the Problems with NUTS?

American decision makers were well aware of these new problems raised by switching from MAD to NUTS. In the 1980s and 1990s, a number of new policies were adopted to ameliorate the problems created by NUTS. First, to enhance survivability and reduce the vulnerability of the nuclear arsenal, a number of proposals were advanced. President Carter was the first to propose making the weapons mobile and hence less easy for the Soviets to target. These mobility proposals all fell through due to inherent drawbacks. One idea was to make the weapons smaller and then launch them from a truck-and-trailer platform. A more ambitious idea was to build a system of aboveground launching sites linked by hundreds of miles of railroad tracks. The missiles would have been fired from a railroad car that could be moved from one covered launch site to another. The Soviets would never be sure of which of the many possible positions to target for each American weapon. The dangers of moving weapons around the country by truck or train, combined with opposition to the environmental impact of building the large-scale railroad "shell game," made these approaches to enhanced survivability politically unfeasible.

The most persistent proposal for making nuclear weapons survivable has been to create some sort of missile defense. In 1983, President Reagan proposed a "strategic defense initiative," or SDI, that would make nuclear weapons "impotent and obsolete." The popular term for what Reagan called SDI quickly became "Star Wars." Reagan hoped that Star Wars would create an invulnerable shield capable of stopping all incoming nuclear warheads. SALT I specifically prohibits deployment of a new, nationwide antiballistic missile (ABM) system. Therefore, deployment of Star Wars defenses would require the United States to renegotiate or abrogate the SALT I treaty. This debate remains a key element of American foreign policy to this day. At the beginning of the twenty-first century, one of the key questions facing American presidents is whether or not to deploy a new national missile defense (NMD) system. Missile defense is another area of foreign policy that first became relevant during the Cold War but has carried over into the new millennium. A discussion of the current debate over NMD will follow this chapter's review of arms control (which follows).

A second area of concern raised by the switch to NUTS was the destabilizing nature of this approach. The vast nuclear arsenals developed by both sides to make NUTS possible raised fears of a less stable nuclear environment. To attenuate the destabilizing nature of NUTS, American and Soviet leaders agreed to a series of confidence-building measures. A 1987 agreement created two new "risk reduction centers." One was built in Washington, D.C., and manned by the American military. A second center was created in the USSR and manned by the Soviets. A "hot line" of communication linked the two centers. The risk reduction centers have been used to funnel information from one side to the other regarding nuclear testing, ballistic missile tests, false alarms,[16] and reassurances during times of international tensions. More recently, due to fears of the Y2K problem, Russian leaders were invited to the headquarters of the U.S. strategic command in Cheyenne Mountain, Colorado. On New Year's Eve in 1999, Russian military leaders were present at the heart of America's nuclear command as a way to prevent any false alarms that might have been caused by a Y2K computer glitch.[17]

Finally, new policy innovations became necessary to address the enormous costs of NUTS. These policy innovations were needed to halt the arms race stimulated by the switch from MAD to NUTS. These new diplomatic initiatives revived the arms control strategies of 1970s détente. Arms control and nuclear arms reductions have been a central focus of American foreign policy from 1987 to the present. Three treaties are especially relevant in this regard. They are the INF treaty of 1987 and the two Strategic Arms Reduction Treaties (START) of 1991 and 1993. INF, START I, and START II represent nuclear arms agreements of a new age. The new approach has been to reduce the number of nuclear weapons, not to simply put caps on the buildup of nuclear arsenals (as was the case for the 1970s Strategic Arms Limitation Treaties [SALT]). In that sense, nuclear arms control is directly connected to deterrence strategies. Arms reductions since 1987 can be viewed as a partial answer to the enhanced dangers and escalating costs inherent in flexible deterrence. These recent treaties will be reviewed in the remainder of this chapter. A broader perspective on arms control is required, however, if one is to understand how these particular agreements came to be. Therefore, the presentation of arms control that follows will review the overall history of efforts to control nuclear weapons and other weapons of mass destruction.[18]

ARMS CONTROL: WEAPONS OF MASS DESTRUCTION

Nuclear weapons are a necessary element of U.S. strategic defense. Nuclear deterrence will remain a central part of defense policy for the foreseeable future. However, there are other policies that enhance America's strategic security. Possession of nuclear weapons is not the only means, and not always the most efficient means, for countering potential threats to American interests. Equally important in the post–Cold War era are diplomatic efforts to limit the development, possession, and transfer of all weapons of mass destruction. Furthermore, to understand arms control in the new millennium one must put current and future policy into its proper historical context. Cold War arms control developed methods and agreements that are still relied on to this day.

The remainder of this chapter will summarize the progress in arms control to date for CBNs. CBNs are weapons of mass destruction that represent potential dangers to all nations. Because of America's unique role in the world, however, CBN threats and efforts to control CBNs have been especially important to the United States. The presentation of arms control that follows will begin with nuclear weapons and then move on to chemical and biological weapons. Related issues regarding missile defenses will also be addressed. Nuclear arms control can be divided into three areas: nuclear testing, nuclear proliferation, and limits on nuclear weapons.

Nuclear Testing and Nuclear Proliferation

One of the best ways to stop production of nuclear weapons is to stop nuclear testing. A freeze on nuclear testing is especially important for preventing all nations from creating new generations of nuclear devices. Limits to testing date back to the Partial Test Ban Treaty (PTB) of 1963. Nuclear tests conducted in the atmosphere before 1963 led to radioactive fallout entering the food chain. Due to fears of such fallout, the PTB prohibits nuclear tests in the atmosphere, under water, or in outer space. Only underground testing is allowed under the PTB. The United States was one of the first countries to ratify the PTB. Advocates of bans on testing worked hard after 1963 to prevent all testing. Their efforts culminated in the Comprehensive Test Ban treaty (CTB) of 1996.

The CTB bans all nuclear testing, including underground tests. By 1997, both the United States and Russia had adopted their own voluntary moratoriums on nuclear testing. This led advocates of the CTB to hope that the two nuclear superpowers would follow through with ratification of the total ban treaty. President Clinton signed the CTB, but opposition in the Senate, led by Jesse Helms of North Carolina, doomed the treaty in Congress. In October 1999 the Senate voted 51 to 48 against ratification of the CTB. (A two-thirds vote of the Senate is required to ratify any international treaty.) Of the acknowledged nuclear powers, America, Russia, China, Britain, and France have all signed the treaty. (India and Pakistan possess nuclear weapons, but they have not signed the CTB.) To date, however, only Britain and France (of the acknowledged nuclear powers) have ratified the document.

Opponents of the CTB (including George W. Bush) have advanced three arguments to justify rejecting this treaty. First, there may be no way to detect very small nuclear tests; hence the CTB could be unverifiable at these very low levels. Second, nations now seeking a nuclear capability, such as Iraq and Libya, will probably never accept the CTB. Finally, the CTB does not contain sanctions for violation of its total ban on nuclear testing.[19]

Advocates of the CTB, including Clinton, countered, first, that the United States has stopped all nuclear testing. Why not ratify a treaty that prohibits something that the United States does not do anyway? Second, it is possible to detect any nuclear test that is large enough to have military or strategic importance, even if microblasts may be undetectable.[20] Finally, ratification of the CTB would be a way for the United States to increase international pressure on other states to sign (India, Pakistan) and to ratify (Russia, China) this treaty. The CTB has already been signed by more than 150 nations but ratified by only two.

Preventing proliferation of nuclear weapons to new states is another area of arms control that has carried over from the Cold War into the new millennium. This was the area of nuclear policy in which there was the greatest cooperation between the USSR and the United States during the Cold War. It was in the Cold War interests of both superpowers to keep these weapons out of the hands of third parties. Under the Nonproliferation Treaty (NPT) of 1968, ratified by more than 140 nations, nuclear powers pledge not to transfer weapons technology to nonnuclear powers. Likewise, nonnuclear powers pledge not to acquire nuclear weapons technology. All parties to the treaty have to put themselves under the inspection regime created by the NPT to enforce its ban on nonproliferation. The NPT imposes "fullscope safeguards" on all parties through the International Atomic Energy Agency (IAEA, a UN body). The IAEA is given full access at all times to any nuclear facilities within a state that is party to the treaty. A refusal by North Korea to allow such inspections was the event that precipitated the crisis between the United States and North Korea in the 1990s (previously discussed in chapter 2).

Post–Cold War events have forced American policy makers to take action on several occasions to sanction nations that defy the NPT regime. North Korea was a case in point, in addition to Iraq and Pakistan. The United States went to great lengths after the Gulf War to see that Iraq's nuclear programs were destroyed (see chapter 4). American economic and diplomatic sanctions were also imposed, to a much lesser degree, on its ally Pakistan when the Pakistani government conducted its first nuclear weapons tests in 1998. The Pakistani tests were a response to similar tests by India during the same year. Nonnuclear powers and rising regional powers such as India and Pakistan often consider acquisition of nuclear weapons as proof that they are becoming global powers—equal to the Americans and the Russians in at least this one crucial respect. Nonnuclear powers also point to the alleged hypocrisy that they perceive in American foreign policy when the United States, the only nation ever to use atomic weapons during a war, declares that no states should be allowed to become new members of the "nuclear club." Robert Frost anticipated these views in his classic poem "U.S. 1946 King's X":

> Having invented a new Holocaust
> And been the first with it to win a war,
> How they make haste to cry with fingers crossed,
> King's X—no fair to use it anymore![21]

Limits to Strategic Nuclear Weapons: SALT I and SALT II

Nuclear arms control was discussed in chapter 2 as one element of 1970s détente. The most important agreements of that era were the two SALT treaties. SALT I of 1972 and SALT II of 1979 put caps on the long-range nuclear arsenals of both superpowers. These limits were *above* what each side had when the treaties were signed. The SALT agreements were important not only for the limits they contained, but also because they provided momentum toward more recent treaties that required *cuts* in American and Russian nuclear arsenals (see following discussion). A brief look at the details of the SALT treaties will help to put more recent arms control agreements into historical perspective.

The impetus toward SALT I was provided largely by the arms race of the 1960s. The United States enjoyed a nuclear advantage in the early 1960s. After the Cuban missile crisis of 1962,[22] the Soviets created their own crash program to deploy long-range nuclear missiles. Soviet efforts resulted in nuclear parity between the two sides by 1970.[23] A second dimension of the 1960s arms race was the development of ABMs. ABMs are missiles that shoot down other missiles. Both sides developed rudimentary ABM capabilities in the late 1960s and early 1970s. Possession of ABM technology by both sides compelled each to escalate their offensive capabilities as well.[24] This included development of missiles that carry more than one warhead each, or MIRVs.[25] The existence of both ABMs and MIRVs, combined with a rough balance of power (i.e., nuclear parity), made it in the best interests of both sides to seek limits to the arms race.

SALT I contained two parts. The first was a formal ABM treaty. This agreement limits each side to only one ABM system.[26] The second part of SALT I was a protocol that placed limits on the total number of strategic missiles for each side.[27] Again, these limits were above what each side possessed in May 1972 when SALT I was signed. Both sides were allowed to continue building up until they reached their respective caps. The United States was limited to 1,054 ICBMs (land-based missiles) plus 656 SLBMs (sea-launched missiles) for a total of 1,710 strategic missiles.[28] The Soviets were limited to 1,409 ICBMs and 950 SLBMs for a grand total of 2,359 long-range missiles. America agreed to a lower limit for its weapons because, at that time, the United States had far more MIRVs than did the Soviets—the USSR may have had more missiles under the terms of SALT I, but the United States still had more deliverable nuclear warheads. MIRVs themselves were not included in the SALT I limitations, but the American advantage in MIRV technology made possible the deal that became SALT I.

SALT II was the last arms agreement of 1970s détente. It was completed before the USSR invaded Afghanistan (in December 1979), which killed détente. President Carter signed SALT II in 1979 but withdrew it from Senate consideration after the invasion of Afghanistan. Although the U.S. Senate never ratified SALT II (hence it was not legally binding to the United States), America stayed within the limits set by SALT II throughout the remainder of the Cold War.[29] SALT II was a more detailed agreement than SALT I. It put limits on strategic missiles plus LRBs. LRBs had not been included in SALT I caps. SALT II also had a sublimit on MIRVed missiles (another area omitted from SALT I).

The SALT II cap on all strategic delivery vehicles (ICBMs + SLBMs + LRBs) was 2,504 for each side.[30] The sublimit on MIRVs restricted each to

1,320 total missiles with multiple warheads. No single missile could carry more than ten warheads under the terms of SALT II. President Reagan was openly opposed to the SALT II treaty, which had been negotiated and signed by his predecessors. The Reagan administration argued that SALT II was fatally flawed because it did not limit the "throw weight" (or payload) that an ICBM could carry, and because there were no provisions in SALT II (or in SALT I for that matter) to allow on-site verification of the treaty. On-site verification would require that each side permit the other to make visits to their military installations and nuclear weapons production facilities to ensure that their antagonists were abiding by the terms of the treaty. On-site verification of nuclear agreements did not come until much later (see following discussion), and Reagan did not trust the Soviets without this provision. His motto in this regard was: "trust, but verify." Because the Soviets had an advantage in throw weight, especially via their mammoth ICBMs known as SS-18s, this was another area of utmost concern to Reagan.[31]

Reagan was so strident in his opposition to SALT II, and so suspicious of all Soviet leaders before Gorbachev, that he had little or no interest in any type of arms control during his first term in office. After Gorbachev came to power, however, Reagan developed a keen interest in reducing nuclear weapons during his second term. Cooperation between Reagan and Gorbachev led to some important breakthroughs, contained in the INF and START treaties.

Nuclear Arms Reductions: INF and START

The INF and START treaties were mentioned in chapter 2 within the context of a discussion of the end of the Cold War. These were important agreements because they helped to end the new Cold War of the mid-1980s and because they contained several great leaps forward to reduce arms. These were compromises that helped to revive détente, beginning with the INF treaty. Although the military significance of INF was minimal, the political significance of this treaty can hardly be overstated.

An INF missile is a weapon with a range between 300 and 3,000 miles (less than the range of a strategic weapon). The United States deployed INF missiles into Western Europe to counter a perceived threat from similar Soviet missiles that had already been deployed to the east. The NATO arrangement for INF deployment called for a "dual-track" strategy. U.S. INF missiles would be deployed to balance the Soviet weapons, but the United States also promised its European allies that it would follow a second track in its foreign policy; it would seek to negotiate removal of INF weapons on both sides. The dual-track policy led Reagan to propose to Gorbachev a complete elimination of land-based INF by both sides. Gorbachev, for reasons discussed in chapter 2, had his own agenda that required significant and rapid cuts in arms on both sides. Gorbachev agreed to Reagan's proposal. Indeed, Gorbachev agreed to many things that no Soviet leader before him would have accepted, including unbalanced cuts at the expense of the Soviet military and on-site verification of nuclear treaties.

The INF treaty was the first agreement on nuclear weapons that required *reductions* in nuclear arsenals. The Soviets accepted larger cuts than those required of the United States. The INF treaty forced the Soviets to scrap 1,752 missiles, whereas the United States had to eliminate only 859 missiles. This represented the total land-based INF arsenal for each side. INF was also the first nuclear treaty to provide on-site verification.[32] Military and political leaders from both sides watched the destruction of delivery vehicles. The INF rockets were destroyed over a three-year period. The INF treaty also provided for a ten-year follow-up period during which on-site visits to U.S. and Russian production facilities had to be allowed. This guaranteed that the destroyed weapons could not be replaced by new production.

The military reductions brought about by INF were minimal. The weapons that were eliminated represented less than two percent of the total nuclear arsenal on each side. However, the diplomatic breakthroughs contained in INF were landmark achievements. INF required the first cuts in nuclear weapons. Russian leaders accepted larger cuts in their arsenals to get the treaty completed. Finally, on-site verification was included in a nuclear treaty for the first time. All of these elements helped give momentum to parallel negotiations on reducing strategic weapons via the START talks.

President Bush and Soviet President Gorbachev signed the first START treaty in 1991 (prior to the collapse of the USSR). START II was signed in 1993 by Bush and Russian President Boris Yeltsin (after the breakup of the USSR). START picked up where INF left off, requiring arms reductions for long-range weapons. The START treaties required cuts in the most powerful and most dangerous nuclear arms. INF also served as a model for the START agreements. Like INF, START required reductions that are verified through on-site visits. START I imposed a greater relative reduction on the Russians (see Table 3.1). The START treaties are also superior to the SALT process because START imposed its reductions on warheads, whereas SALT only imposed limits on delivery vehicles (and not the warheads themselves).

START I represents a cut in American strategic warheads of nearly one-third (thirty-two percent), whereas the Russian arsenal was reduced by more than forty percent. START I also included sublimits on different types of delivery vehicles. Russia's "heavy" missiles (e.g., the SS-18) had to be reduced by fifty percent.[33] START I was signed shortly before the final collapse and breakup of the USSR. Subsequent negotiations made possible the transfer back to Russia of all former Soviet nuclear weapons out of the non-Russian republics. Belarus, Kazakhstan, and Ukraine all had to give up nuclear weapons that were within their borders when the USSR collapsed. Russia is today the last remaining post-Soviet republic with a nuclear capability.

TABLE 3.1: Strategic Arms Control

	USA	USSR/RUSSIA
TREATY	*Limits*	*Limits*
SALT I (1972)	1,710 ICBMs + SLBMs [no limit on MIRVs]	2,359 ICBMs + SLBMs [no limit on MIRVs]
SALT II (1979)	2,504 ICBMs + SLBMs + LRBs [1,320 MIRVs]	2,504 ICBMs + SLBMs + LRBs [1,320 MIRVs]
START I (1991)	8,556 warheads [reduced from 12,646]	6,163 warheads [down from 11,012]
START II (1993)	3,000–3,500 warheads + bombs [0 MIRVs]	3,000–3,500 warheads + bombs [0 MIRVs]
START III (Treaty of Moscow, 2002)	1,700–2,200 warheads	1,700–2,200 warheads

START II, negotiated and signed by Bush and Yeltsin, makes further cuts below START I levels. Under START II, both sides are limited to a range of 3,000–3,500 strategic warheads and nuclear bombs. In this case, the United States is making the larger cuts, because it was left with a larger arsenal after START I. Like START I, START II is subject to on-site verification. START II is significant also because it bans all MIRVs. Both sides agreed to convert to only single-warhead missiles. Both sides had to give up some of their most cherished assets under START II. Heavy Russian SS-18 ICBMs are eliminated altogether, and U.S. SLBMs (America's greatest strategic advantage) were cut in half.[34]

START II was signed in 1993, and the U.S. Senate ratified the treaty in 1996. The lower house of the Russian parliament, known as the Duma, refused to ratify START II until 2000. Russia's ratification of START II was conditioned on a further stipulation. The Russians declared that they would not proceed with the actual reductions required under START II until the United States agrees to preserve intact the 1972 ABM treaty. American leaders proposed renegotiating the SALT I ABM agreement to allow the United States to deploy a new generation of missile defenses. Such new deployments were prohibited under the "Agreed Interpretations and Statements D and E" that were attached to the ABM treaty and agreed upon by both sides in 1972.[35] The Duma, the Russian people, and even many of America's allies expressed opposition to U.S. plans to deploy a new $60 billion missile defense system. Advocates of the new system in the United States favored renegotiation of the ABM treaty. Some advocates of the new missile defense went so far as to favor scrapping the ABM treaty and START II in order to deploy the new generation of missile defenses (see following discussion). We shall return to this matter after a summary of efforts to ban chemical and biological weapons (see next section).

Once the Duma ratified START II, talks began on a START III treaty. The target for the third START agreement was to reduce strategic warheads on each side to no more than 2,200 total (and perhaps even lower). START III was completed in 2002 and is now officially known as the Treaty of Moscow (discussion follows).

Chemical and Biological Weapons

As post–Cold War efforts toward nuclear disarmament progress, the existence of chemical and biological weapons around the world becomes ever more salient. Chemical and biological weapons are sometimes referred to as the "poor man's nuclear bomb" because they are relatively cheap and easy to acquire. Chemical and biological weapons are similar to nuclear devices in that they are weapons of mass destruction. They have the potential to kill thousands, even millions, of people, if used on a wide scale. Efforts to ban these weapons began during the Cold War and have carried over into the new millennium. A look at the Chemical Weapons Convention (CWC) of 1993 and the Biological Weapons Convention (BWC) of 1972 informs an understanding of arms control in the twenty-first century.

The CWC imposes a total ban on all chemical weapons. These weapons of mass destruction were first used on a wide scale during World War I. American troops have been exposed to chemical weapons as recently as the Gulf War in 1991.[36] The CWC seeks to end production, possession, and use of all chemical weapons. The CWC also bans transfer of these weapons between nations. Perhaps most important, the CWC bans all precursors (chemical agents used to make chemical weapons) as well.

The CWC requires routine, on-site inspections and authorizes unannounced inspections on demand. One state that is a party to the CWC can demand inspection of another state under the terms of this treaty. All parties to the treaty pledge to provide full access (or "full-scope" inspection) to their military facilities, storage sites, and chemical plants (including pesticide and pharmaceutical manufacturers).

To manage this inspection regime, the CWC creates its own enforcement and inspection agency under the terms of the treaty. The Organization for the Prohibition of Chemical Weapons (OPCW) was created by the CWC. Inspections to enforce the CWC bans are conducted by the Technical Secretariat of the OPCW. By the year 2000, more than 100 states had ratified the CWC. The U.S. Senate voted to ratify the CWC in 1997.

Nations that possess chemical weapons must destroy their entire stockpiles under the terms of the CWC. The treaty establishes a ten-to-fifteen year timeframe for carrying out the disposal of chemical weapons. Only the United States and Russia publicly admit to possession of chemical weapons. The

United States declared its intentions to destroy its chemical stockpile even before the existence of the CWC. Due to environmental concerns, however, the burning of these chemical agents has proceeded very slowly. As recently as December 2000, previously uncovered nerve gas bombs were still being discovered on U.S. military bases.[37] Russia is also committed to destroying its stockpile, but it needs aid and expertise from the United States to make this possible. Special efforts were made after the Gulf War to locate and destroy the Iraqi chemical arsenal, but Saddam Hussein successfully thwarted those efforts (see chapter 4). Iraq is not a party to the CWC. Efforts to destroy Iraq's weapons of mass destruction were part of the Security Council sanctions imposed on Iraq as a result of the Gulf War.

At least nine other countries are suspected of having chemical weapons, although they do not admit to this publicly. Of those nine, only Iran, South Africa, and South Korea have ratified the CWC. The remaining six nations–Egypt, Israel, Libya, North Korea, Syria, and Taiwan–are suspected of having chemical weapons, but they are not parties to the CWC and are thus not subject to OPCW inspections. As many as thirty other nations may have both the precursor chemicals needed to make these weapons plus the technical know-how to do the job. The dangers of chemical weapons, therefore, will persist well into the twenty-first century. The same could be said for biological weapons.

The BWC predates the CWC, but its ban on biological weapons is much weaker and almost unenforceable. The BWC is similar to the CWC in some respects, but it does not have the necessary procedures to enforce its ban on biological weapons. In fact, there has been almost no enforcement of the BWC for more than thirty years, and it contains a loophole in its ban on biological weapons that weakens the treaty to a debilitating extent.

In theory, the BWC bans all production, stockpiling, or use of biological weapons. It also bans possession or transfer of the agents used to make biological weapons, and it requires parties to the treaty to destroy all of their biological weapons. Because more than 140 nations have ratified the BWC, this treaty is almost universal in its scope. But the BWC is fundamentally flawed in two respects. First, there is no agency comparable to the OPCW to enforce the BWC's ban. No independent agency exists to inspect states and guarantee that they are not hiding biological weapons. Talks have been going on since 1993 to try to strengthen the BWC. The most important new element needed to enforce the BWC would be an independent agency with inspection powers comparable to those of the OPCW. The international talks in this regard are moving at a snail's pace. American foreign policy is partially to blame in this regard. The United States has not been proactive in pushing for a new inspection regime under a revised and amended BWC. Lack of U.S. leadership in this regard is directly connected to the second fundamental flaw in the BWC: its loophole on "dual use" technology.

The BWC loophole allows the development of biological agents and toxins for "peaceful" purposes. Given that it was a product of Cold War détente (in 1972), perhaps the this loophole in the BWC was the best that could have been expected at that time. However, today, this huge loophole needs to be closed. Opposition to eliminating the BWC loophole on dual use agents comes primarily from the private sector, especially from U.S. biotechnology firms.

Almost all biological agents have dual use applications. For example, anthrax is one of the most common agents used to make biological weapons. In its less virulent forms, however, anthrax is used to inoculate cattle and prevent bovine disease. Because the BWC allows such peaceful research, development, and use of biological toxins, its ban on military uses of the same agents is almost useless. In the 1980s, prior to its differences with Iraq over Kuwait, the United States allowed at least seventy shipments of anthrax to be exported from the United States to Iraq. This was supposed to go to peaceful uses but was instead diverted into weapons development.

The enforcement procedures of the BWC are so weak that they are never used. Enforcement is left to the Security Council, where one state can request inspection of another state. It is remotely possible that a complaint filed before the Security Council could lead to BWC inspections of a sovereign state, but the Security Council must order those inspections, and that was never done before 1991. After 1991, Iraq was forced to allow inspections in search of its biological weapons, but those inspections were imposed as a result of Iraq's defeat in Kuwait, and not due to the BWC. Saddam Hussein halted those inspections in late 1998, before the UN could locate and destroy his biological arsenal (see chapter 4).

What is needed is a new protocol to the BWC, one that has an agency akin to the OPCW to carry out inspections, and one that closes the dual use loophole. U.S. private firms are lobbying the government not to seek an end to the peaceful purposes loophole in order to guard their corporate secrets and to protect their profits. Domestic U.S. drug and biotechnology firms oppose inspections that would prohibit dual use technology. They don't want international inspectors in their plants, fearing the loss of proprietary secrets. They also do not want international regulation of peaceful biological agents. Development of biological weapons by Iraq from peaceful shipments of anthrax is proof that the current BWC system is inadequate. There have also been more recent incidents in which private individuals have tried (in some cases successfully) to acquire anthrax or botulism spores over the Internet. With a stolen lab identification number from a legitimate biotech business, almost anyone could acquire a rudimentary biological weapons capability. New millennium terrorists are no doubt at work right now trying to do just that. A revised and strengthened BWC that includes mandatory inspection powers and that outlaws dual use technology is needed to guard against such post–Cold War security threats. American foreign policy should be more concerned about such threats and less concerned about protecting corporate profits in this area.

President George W. Bush came into office opposed to new agreements that would make the BWC enforceable. In December 2001, only three months after September 11 and only weeks after anthrax attacks through the U.S. mail system killed five people, the second Bush administration proposed ending all UN efforts to add new enforcement procedures to the BWC. By this time, the ad hoc group set up by the UN to draft a protocol on enforcing the BWC had almost completed its years of work. A 210-page document was ready for the 144 nations that are parties to BWC. During the 2001 BWC meetings in Geneva, the Bush administration proposed dissolving the ad hoc group, ending its mandate, and suspending efforts to create a system of inspections to enforce the BWC.[38] America's allies were "upset . . . shocked . . . stunned" by the Bush proposal, and all efforts to make the BWC enforceable were sent into disarray by this U.S. action.[39]

CONCLUSION—NUCLEAR ARMS REDUCTIONS AND MISSILE DEFENSE: A STRATEGIC POLICY BEYOND MAD VERSUS NUTS?

Significant cuts in nuclear arsenals began with the INF treaty and continued under the START process. These arms reductions represent movement toward a more stable nuclear "balance of terror." Lowering the number of strategic weapons for the two nuclear superpowers is a good thing. In an ideal world, arms reductions would continue until we achieved total nuclear disarmament. Unfortunately, this will never be the case. Complete nuclear disarmament is not possible. Since the days of the Manhattan Project of World War II, the world has had the knowledge required to produce weapons of mass destruction based on power from the subatomic level. It is not possible to "unlearn" this knowledge. No one can put the nuclear genie back into his bottle.[40] As long as the ability to create these weapons exists, at least a few nations will have them. Complete disarmament is an admirable but unrealistic goal. Short of that, all parties should continue efforts to reduce nuclear stockpiles to the lowest possible levels.

As nuclear arsenals are cut, strategic defense systems become even more controversial. Plans by either side to unilaterally deploy a new generation of ballistic missile defenses could threaten to ignite a new global arms race, affecting not just the United States or Russia, but other nuclear powers as well. "Our own intelligence services [the CIA] estimate that moving forward with national missile defense could trigger a tenfold increase in China's expansion of its nuclear capability."[41] To understand how the deployment of new missile defense systems is related to America's strategic deterrence doctrines, one must compare the process of nuclear arms reductions to the theories of MAD and NUTS.

Cuts in nuclear arms under the INF and START treaties are, in one sense, a big step back from NUTS. Cuts in nuclear stockpiles move the world back in the direction of a minimum deterrence posture. One of the defining features of the NUTS policy was its much larger and more diverse array of weapons. Cuts under START I, START II, and the Treaty of Moscow will remove roughly ninety percent of the Cold War era strategic arsenals. That would be an obvious step toward enhanced global stability. On the other hand, recent policy changes enacted by George W. Bush recall theories of "usable" nuclear weapons that were once closely associated with NUTS doctrines. To understand current nuclear policy and how it relates to the prior approaches of MAD versus NUTS, one must look at recent developments regarding missile defenses and the creation of "earth-penetrating weapons."

National Missile Defense (NMD) and Other Recent Developments

The attraction of missile defense is powerful and simple. Missile defense advocates pose a simple question: If the United States has the technology to stop at least some incoming nuclear weapons, then why would we not want to deploy such a system? Advocates of NMD also tend to stress the changes in nuclear affairs that have occurred since the end of the Cold War. First and foremost, weapons of mass destruction are proliferating at an alarming rate, as is ballistic missile technology. Second, the ABM treaty is less relevant now to global politics than it was during the Cold War. There is also strong support from the White House and a clear majority in the American Congress in favor of deploying a new NMD system. Finally, new technologies now give the United States potential ABM capabilities that did not exist during the Cold War.[42]

In contrast, opponents of NMD tend to stress the strategic similarities that typify both the Cold War and the post–Cold War eras. First, both the United States and Russia still have thousands of strategic weapons. Russia may be an economic basket case, but it remains a nuclear superpower. This continues to be the single most important factor in the global balance of power. Political instability inside Russia and nuclear proliferation around the world ensure the continued possibility of nuclear threats. Contrary to popular belief, the importance of nuclear deterrence for international security has not decreased during the post–Cold War era.[43]

A second consistent factor (despite the end of the Cold War) is the fact that missile defense remains enormously expensive. The United States has already spent more than $50 billion since Reagan's 1983 Star Wars speech on failed efforts to develop NMD. A report by the nonpartisan Congressional Budget Office estimates the cost for the new generation of NMD to be an additional $60 billion.[44] Third, the technology needed for a robust NMD system has yet to be found. Fourth, even if existing or proposed technology could give the United States a reliable NMD, there are cheaper and easier-to-develop countermeasures available to America's adversaries that "would doom any national missile defense." This is a fact that "NMD proponents tend to ignore."[45]

In all these respects, the essential facts about NMD remain unchanged (as compared to the Cold War era).

When the Russian Duma ratified START II in 2000, it attached an anti-NMD protocol to that act of ratification. Russian President Putin took the same position when proposing deeper cuts in nuclear weapons under a possible START III treaty. Putin suggested that limits under START III (the Treaty of Moscow) could be as low as 1,500 warheads for each side, but only if the United States would forego its plans for NMD.[46] The Russian position at that time was clear. They were not willing to make any cuts under START II (or any subsequent treaty) until the United States agreed to preserve the 1972 ABM treaty.

Advocates of the new antiballistic missile project most commonly cite so-called rogue states such as North Korea and Iran when justifying the need for the new system. However, although the proliferation of CBNs and ballistic missiles is undeniable, and even though proliferation creates threats to the United States that did not exist during the Cold War, it would still be "folly to deploy NMD in such a way as to damage the US-Russian strategic balance."[47] Therefore, Russian cooperation, or at least their acquiescence, became a necessary condition for creating an American NMD system that would not destabilize the nuclear balance of power.

Ironically, the events of September 11 and the subsequent global war against terrorism led Russian leaders to drop their adamant opposition to America's plans for an NMD system. After September 11, America and Russia found themselves in an entirely new strategic relationship. They no longer thought of each other primarily as former enemies, with all the mistrust and suspicion that can accompany residual hostilities left over from the defunct Cold War. Now they saw themselves mainly as allies in a war against a common enemy—the enemy of radical Islamic fundamentalism in the form of terror. Long before September 11, Russia had been fighting Islamic terrorists from Chechnya, some of them allegedly trained by Osama bin Laden in Afghanistan. Russia gave support to the initial U.S. invasion of Afghanistan and offered no objections when former Soviet republics in central Asia provided bases and logistical support to the American war effort.

On a new footing as allies, President Putin set aside all Russian objections to George W. Bush's intentions to scrap the ABM treaty. In fact, the Russians agreed to combine an end to the ban on new NMD systems with cooperation regarding deep cuts in offensive weapons. The Bush administration unexpectedly found that it could have the best of both worlds: effective in June 2002, the United States formally withdrew from the 1972 ABM treaty as a step toward deploying NMD, and in May 2002, the United States and Russia signed the Treaty of Moscow, which cut each side's nuclear arsenal to about two-thirds below START II levels.

America and Russia, along with all NATO allies, institutionalized this new rapprochement by establishing the NATO–Russia Council less than a week after the Treaty of Moscow was signed. Although stopping short of giving Russia a formal vote within NATO, the new NATO–Russia Council accords the Russians a voice on how to confront the common foe represented by international terrorism. The council also pledged to pursue joint efforts to deal with arms control, nonproliferation of CBNs, and expansion of NATO to include some former Soviet Republics (e.g., Latvia and Lithuania). Speaking in Rome on the occasion of the council's creation, Putin said: "What unites us is far more serious than what divides us."[48]

The Treaty of Moscow was the culmination of negotiations for what had been referred to as START III. The third major bilateral treaty for strategic arms reductions is a brief (only three pages) and vaguely worded document that contains several important compromises between the U.S. and Russian positions. The Moscow Treaty has no verification provisions (as did START I and II), contrary to what the Russians had wanted. Putin did not get an agreement from George W. Bush to allow for on-site verification, nor did the Americans promise to destroy the decommissioned nuclear warheads (as Putin had hoped). Instead, Bush agreed only to put the U.S. warheads into storage. But Putin did get Bush to put all of these promises into a formal treaty that creates legally binding obligations. Prior to 2002, the Bush administration had proposed that the cuts be made via an informal agreement between the two heads of state. The Treaty of Moscow limits each side to total strategic warheads in the range of 1,700–2,200. These reductions are supposed to be completed by the year 2012.

Ending the 1972 ABM treaty and enacting further nuclear reductions under the Treaty of Moscow were major changes in U.S. nuclear policy created by George W. Bush's administration. A third major development has been Bush's advocacy for a new generation of "usable" nuclear weapons. In 2002, Bush authorized the Pentagon to provide Congress with a nuclear policy review calling for new nuclear devices that can destroy underground targets, including storage facilities for chemical and biological arms, or bunkers of the type used by Saddam Hussein and Osama bin Laden. The energy department began work in April 2002 to develop "earth-penetrating weapons" that could reach America's enemies who hide deep underground.[49] Experts sometimes refer to these new nuclear weapons as "bunker-busters." Bush's nuclear policy review also speaks of possible nuclear attacks against nonnuclear enemies, thereby abandoning a Cold War–era promise that the United States would never use nuclear weapons against nations that made no efforts to acquire their own nuclear arsenal.[50]

The Bush administration also presented several possible scenarios under which they believe nuclear weapons might be required. These include a future Arab–Israeli crisis, a military confrontation with China over the status of Taiwan, a North Korean attack on South Korea, or an Iraqi assault on its neighbors.[51] Critics immediately charged that the Bush approach was seeking to lower the nuclear threshold and blur the distinction between nuclear versus conventional war. Much like the criticisms advanced against NUTS theories twenty years earlier, opponents of Bush's nuclear policy review warned that by making the "unthinkable thinkable," that is, by making nuclear war more imaginable, the new policy also serves to make nuclear war more likely.[52] Although the president himself argued that defense policy must move beyond Cold War ideas of nuclear deterrence, his rhetoric regarding the need for a new generation of smaller nuclear weapons that can be employed in warfighting scenarios in fact demonstrates the need to understand current strategic policy by means of a firm grasp of the history of MAD versus NUTS.

The strategic defense policy of the second Bush administration recalls some elements of NUTS, and other aspects of MAD. Even after the cuts under the Moscow treaty have been completed, the United States will retain some hard-target, first-strike weapons. Existence of such weapons continues the "use-it-or-lose-it" problems associated with NUTS whenever there is a false alarm or if there should be an accidental nuclear launch. Continued existence of first-strike weapons means that some of the nuclear temptations associated with the NUTS approach of counterforce targeting remain. Likewise, creating a new generation of usable bunker-busters reduces the nuclear threshold and increases the nuclear temptation to launch a first strike, another destabilizing factor long associated with NUTS.

On the other hand, the world must also continue to deal with another problem that reflects a defining feature of MAD. Even after the Moscow Treaty reductions in nuclear arsenals have been carried out, the United States and Russia will still have thousands of nuclear weapons. These smaller arsenals, although preferable to the larger stockpiles of today, are still big enough (when used) to create a nuclear winter that could destroy almost all life on the planet.[53] Mutual destruction could still result from the smaller arsenals allowed under the Treaty of Moscow. Experts estimate that nuclear winter (a black cloud of smoke and soot that chokes all life on Earth) could be triggered by as few as 400 strategic warheads.[54]

Therefore, as we move further into the twenty-first century, significant nuclear reductions bode well for the future. But the task is far from complete. A top priority for U.S. nuclear policy must be to maintain the momentum provided by past agreements as a way to achieve even deeper reductions. Even though total nuclear disarmament is probably impossible to achieve, Americans must push for further cuts in nuclear weapons, at least until all combined arsenals are below the level that could trigger a nuclear winter.

Chapter 4

WAR, PEACE, AND THE EVOLUTION OF U.S. POLICY IN THE MIDDLE EAST

Bahram Rajaee

U.S. interests in the Middle East appear obvious to most observers today. They include securing access to oil, ensuring the security of Israel, broadening the zone of Arab–Israeli peace, opposing potential regional challengers such as Iran, combating terrorism, and preventing the proliferation of weapons of mass destruction. Underlying this set of issues is the conviction that the United States must be proactive in regional affairs to protect its interests, and a belief that adopting a passive role, or dependence upon others, will not be sufficient to accomplish these tasks. As a result, the United States is now more intimately involved in Middle Eastern affairs than at any other point in history.[1] It has erected a political and military network of alliances, bases, and client states that provide it with strategic depth and support for its own direct actions in the region. Allies such as Egypt, Israel, Jordan, Turkey (a NATO member), and Saudi Arabia (and by extension the other Persian Gulf Arab members of the Gulf Cooperation Council, or GCC) participate to varying degrees in that network. Furthermore, unilateral U.S. action is made possible by the ongoing presence of approximately twenty thousand troops that are now based in Saudi Arabia, Bahrain, and Turkey, as well as on a large naval force in the Persian Gulf. Other forces are now deployed in Afghanistan, Georgia, and the former Soviet republics in central Asia as part of Operation Enduring Freedom.

As policy makers, students, and scholars analyze U.S. foreign policy toward the Middle East in a post-September 11 context, it is important to keep in mind that the interests and policies of the United States in that part of the world have changed dramatically over the course of the last fifty years. More specifically, the evolution of U.S. policy in the Middle East has reflected the rise of the United States as a global power since 1945. This process has been shaped by several distinct factors, including changes in U.S. perceptions of the international system (from isolationism to greater involvement), shifts in the structure of that system (such as the decline of European powers, the rise and fall of the USSR, and the establishment of Israel), the emergence of oil as a critical economic resource, and the terrorist attacks of September 11, 2001.

THE UNITED STATES IN THE MIDDLE EAST PRIOR TO 1947

Until the early 1930s, U.S. foreign policy toward the Middle East was dominated by two main principles: the Monroe Doctrine and economic expansionism. The Monroe Doctrine, which aimed to keep European powers out of the Western Hemisphere, also committed the United States to staying out of European politics and intrigues. Regions recognized at that time to be part of the European sphere of influence—such as the Middle East—were also included in this policy of noninterference. As a result, until the 1920s the United States adopted a largely passive role in the Middle East. This passivity was best reflected by the long time that passed before the United States established a diplomatic presence throughout the region, despite the fact that large numbers of American missionaries had been operating there for almost half a century.

Under the auspices of religious organizations, many Protestant missionaries were sent to the region beginning in the 1830s. They were engaged in teaching, providing medical services, and preaching. They often operated in highly unstable and dangerous areas and therefore needed periodic aid and official protection. The lack of legal and diplomatic services afforded to these missionaries caused them to place significant pressure on the U.S. government to expand its direct regional presence. Along with growing trade interests, this lobbying spurred the spread of U.S. diplomatic missions and embassies in the Middle East. Before official U.S. missions were in place, the missionaries and their families were often forced to rely on British protection. By 1900, however, the State Department had established a network of treaties and corps of diplomatic agents throughout the region.

The second main principle of early U.S. foreign policy was economic expansion. The United States opposed threats to its trading interests because it wanted to gain as much access for U.S. businesses to international markets as possible. The early importance of trade for U.S. policy in the Middle East was demonstrated by the fact that the first official contacts between the newly established United States and Middle Eastern states occurred during disputes over shipping. In 1784, Congress established a commission composed of Benjamin Franklin, John Adams, and Thomas Jefferson to negotiate treaties with the local rulers of the Ottoman provinces of North Africa (Morocco, Algiers, Tunis, and Tripoli)—the so-called Barbary States. The rulers of those provinces were supporting pirates that operated against European and American shipping in the Mediterranean Sea. Due to the efforts of the commission and the deployment of U.S. military forces these rulers signed treaties with the United States and the raids eventually ceased. In due course, the United States also signed treaties of trade and friendship with the Ottoman Empire itself (1830), and with Iran (1856). However, it was not until after World War I and the discovery of oil by American firms that economic interests began to guide U.S. policy into a more assertive regional stance vis-à-vis the European powers. Even then, the mandate system adopted by the League of Nations after World War I had firmly established British and French political control over the Arab territories of the former Ottoman Empire. As a result, direct treaties were signed with only Egypt (1929, 1930), Saudi Arabia (1933), and Iraq (1934, 1938), and only after European influence began to erode. The establishment of diplomatic relations with Syria, Lebanon, Palestine, and the other Persian Gulf Arab states occurred only after World War II drew to a close.

The 1920s and 1930s saw the rise of oil as a powerful new factor in U.S. Middle Eastern policy. Much of the current importance ascribed to the Middle East is due to that region's position as the major supplier of oil to the international economy. Persian Gulf oil producers currently account for approximately sixty percent of the world's proven oil reserves. However, as late as the 1920s, the United States itself dominated the global oil market, producing more than seventy percent of the world's supply. After World War I, the U.S. government came under increasing domestic pressure from U.S. companies to advance their interests in the face of European efforts to maintain exclusive control over oil production areas in the Middle East. That lobbying by oil interests resulted in a more active U.S. policy on their behalf—much as the missionaries were able to invigorate the government several decades before. The U.S. government itself was also worried about the possible depletion of global oil resources after World War I, due to rapidly rising levels of domestic and military oil consumption.

Oil production in the Middle East prior to the 1930s was concentrated in two areas: the Azerbaijan region of the USSR and Iran. The United States and the USSR had yet to establish official diplomatic relations, and Iran's oil was controlled by the British, who also controlled much of the rest of Middle Eastern oil supplies. As a result, during the 1920s U.S. companies had to painstakingly negotiate entry into British-controlled areas or gamble on bids to develop less promising oil reserves in the region. In the end, with U.S. government support, they did both.

A real breakthrough came when Standard Oil of California (SOCAL) found oil in the Persian Gulf island state of Bahrain in 1932. This marked the beginning of a large-scale presence of American oil companies in the region. The rest of the 1930s witnessed a steady increase in the pace and scope of the operation of American oil firms. In 1938, American firms explored for and discovered the world's largest oil reserves in Saudi Arabia. They also struck oil in a joint venture with British firms in Kuwait that same year. By the eve of World War II, American companies had successfully challenged British domination of Middle Eastern oil ownership, and they controlled huge reserves on the Arabian peninsula and in the Persian Gulf. U.S. foreign policy in the Middle East adjusted to reflect this changing reality and consequently became more active. This trend toward greater U.S. involvement was exacerbated by World War II, a true watershed in the evolution of U.S. policy in the region. World War II shattered the prewar American conviction that noninterference, per the Monroe Doctrine, was an appropriate foundation for U.S. policy.

The Second World War

Between 1941 and 1943, Lend-Lease programs of military assistance were extended to Iran, Saudi Arabia, and Turkey. By the end of the war, U.S. assistance to these Middle Eastern states had risen from a nonexistent factor to become an important consideration in their bilateral relations. U.S. forces also were deployed in Iran to assist in the delivery of badly needed military supplies for the Soviet Union.[2] In 1942, the U.S. Army formed the Persian Gulf Service Command (PGSC) and assumed full control over the Iranian supply corridor on behalf of the Allies. Ultimately, more than thirty thousand U.S. troops were based in Iran during the 1942–45 period. In addition to Lend-Lease and the PGSC, the United States also became committed to the independence of Turkey and Iran. As discussed in chapter 1, crises in Turkey and Iran directly led to a reformulation of U.S. policy, paving the way for the crucial Truman Doctrine. In both countries (as well as in Greece), the United States took a leading role in fending off Soviet pressure and preventing the expansion of Soviet influence.

The emergence of the Cold War with the USSR combined with the growing influence of the oil lobby to take U.S. regional involvement to unprecedented levels. Other U.S. commitments also slowly developed with the creation of Israel in 1948. By the late 1970s, those commitments had firmly bound Israel's survival—and the Arab–Israeli peace process—to U.S. interests. The end of the Cold War in 1991 left the United States as the dominant power in the Middle East, as reflected by its central role in orchestrating the ejection of Iraqi forces from Kuwait during the 1990–91 Gulf War. The twentieth century, therefore, saw U.S. interests in the Middle East evolve from those of a disinterested, marginal power to those of a global power immersed in the intricacies of regional affairs. The remainder of this chapter will broadly chart the course of that evolution, as reflected in the various foreign policy doctrines of U.S. presidents since World War II.

KEY DOCTRINES IN U.S. MIDDLE EASTERN POLICY, 1947-73

Even as U.S. interest in the Middle East was growing due to wartime commitments, the rapidly declining British capacity to maintain its regional influence pushed American policy makers to fill the emerging vacuum. In 1947, financially drained from the war and unable to maintain its overseas colonial commitments, Great Britain made three significant decisions: first, to withdraw from India by June 1948 (later moved up to August 1947); second, to refer the "Palestine Question" over the creation of a Jewish state in Palestine to the UN for resolution; and third, to terminate its aid to the governments of Greece and Turkey—which were both resisting communist insurgencies— in March 1947. From the perspective of the United States, the termination of aid was equivalent to a British abdication from the Middle East. As a result, the United States was left as the only power that could give Greece and Turkey the political, military, and economic support necessary to prevent them from being overwhelmed by Soviet influence. The U.S. response, in the form of the 1947 Truman Doctrine, was nothing less than its first commitment to a direct role in regional affairs.

The Truman Doctrine

On March 12, 1947, President Truman addressed a special joint session of Congress. In his speech he described the deteriorating situation in Greece and Turkey and called for the extension of U.S. aid to both countries in the amount of $400 million, along with military advisors. Notably, he couched his appeal in terms of a global struggle between freedom and totalitarianism in which the goals of U.S. policy should be to "support free peoples who are resisting attempted subjugation by armed minorities or outside pressures.[3] Congress approved Truman's request for aid. Through the Truman Doctrine, the Marshall Plan, and support for international institutions (such as the UN, the International Monetary Fund (IMF), and the World Bank), the United States equated its own security with the maintenance of global peace and security. This was the most drastic change in U.S. foreign policy since the Monroe Doctrine.

The Truman Doctrine was further reinforced by the National Security Act (NSA) of 1947 and by National Security Council Memorandum 68 (NSC-68) in 1950.[4] These two documents significantly altered the manner in which U.S. foreign policy was formulated and carried out in the Middle East (and elsewhere). The NSA established a new National Security Council (NSC). The NSC immediately determined that the security of the Middle East was vital to the United States. In August 1948, the joint chiefs of staff also reported to the president that the importance of the Middle East to British and U.S. interests made the region critical in the global military strategy of the United States. Three months after the announcement of the Truman Doctrine, the United States promised $25 million in military aid to Iran. In 1950, President Truman also established the Point Four program of technical and economic aid to underdeveloped countries in order to use "technical information already tested and proved in the United States . . . [to help prevent] the expansion of Communism . . . by helping to ensure the proper development of those countries."[5] Arab states, Iran, and Israel received $2.1 million out of the initial

$26.9 million appropriated for the program; of that total, Iran received two-thirds. In 1951, U.S. assistance programs in the region were further expanded through the Mutual Security Program. Through this program, more than $415 million in new military aid was provided to Greece, Turkey, and Iran. By 1959, the United States had supplied nearly $3 billion in military aid to Middle Eastern countries.

The Palestine Question and the Founding of Israel

In the nineteenth century, Jews in Western Europe began to organize a movement dedicated to the establishment of a Jewish state. In 1897, the first World Zionist Conference was held, and Palestine was selected as the location for a proposed Jewish state. Throughout the early 1900s, Zionist leaders lobbied European powers for support and encouraged Jewish immigration into Palestine. In November 1917, the British government—which seized control of Palestine from the Ottoman Empire during World War—issued the Balfour Declaration pledging its support for the creation of a "national home" for the Jewish people in Palestine. In 1922, the League of Nations incorporated the Balfour Declaration into the terms of the Palestine Mandate, which had been awarded to Great Britain after World War.

In 1947, the UN proposed dividing Palestine between the Jews and Arabs. Jewish leaders accepted the proposal, as it would have given six hundred thousand Jews fifty-five percent of Palestine. However, the Palestinian Arabs—numbering 1.3 million—rejected the partition resolution as unfair. After the partition plan fell through, fighting quickly broke out between Jewish forces and Palestinian Arabs, who were supported by the armies of Arab neighbors such as Egypt, Jordan, Syria, and Transjordan. On May 15, 1948, the Jewish leadership unilaterally declared the independent state of Israel. After defeating subsequent Arab attacks during 1948–49, Israel negotiated an end to the fighting with its Arab neighbors in 1949. Between December 1947 and September 1949, Israeli forces expelled seven hundred thousand Palestinian refugees from their land. Another one hundred fifty-thousand Arabs remained within the borders of the new Jewish state. By the time the fighting ended, Israel controlled eighty percent of the original mandate of Palestine. By 1952, another seven hundred thousand Jewish immigrants had arrived in Israel, further shifting the balance between Arabs and Jews. The Truman administration supported the creation of Israel due to its sympathy for the Jewish experience during the Holocaust, and the United States was one of the first states to extend diplomatic recognition to it. However, private support and empathy aside, U.S. policy was more concerned with countering Soviet actions and maintaining regional stability; the Arab–Israeli conflict was therefore seen as a potentially destabilizing situation, the consequences of which had to be managed. It was not until the late 1960s that the United States embarked on the path of deepening and strengthening its strategic relationship with Israel to the level that exists today.

The Eisenhower Doctrine

The Eisenhower administration pursued an even more aggressive global strategy, notably through the increased use of undercover operations to destabilize unfriendly governments. The Central Intelligence Agency (CIA) sponsored the 1953 overthrow of a democratically elected regime in Iran that was perceived to be vulnerable to Soviet influence, replacing it with the increasingly authoritarian rule of the Shah (king). By 1954, the Eisenhower administration had also transformed its strategic approach in the Middle East to emphasize the so-called Northern Tier concept. This approach focused on the security of Turkey, Iran, Iraq, and Pakistan—a northern tier of countries that could guard the Persian Gulf from Soviet encroachment (see Figure 4.1). The Northern Tier strategy was implemented with the signing of a Turkish–Pakistani mutual security treaty in April 1954 (a pact secured through U.S. diplomacy and promises of U.S. aid to both countries), the extension of U.S. military aid to Iraq, and the accession of Iraq in the so-called Baghdad Pact in 1955. That same year, Great Britain and Iran also joined the Baghdad Pact, which eventually was renamed the Central Treaty Organization (CENTO). The United States did not formally join CENTO, but supported it indirectly. Along with the North Atlantic Treaty Organization (NATO), CENTO became an important link in the global chain of alliances the United States created during the Cold War in order to contain the USSR.

In July 1952, the Egyptian monarchy was overthrown by a coup led by army officers. Two years later, one of the officers, Gamal Abdel Nasser, seized power; he ruled Egypt for the next eighteen years. Nasser advocated nonalignment with the superpowers but slowly began to increase his ties to the Soviet bloc. He also refused to join the Baghdad Pact. In 1956, the United States withdrew an offer to help Egypt build the crucial Aswan dam project and was replaced in that role by the Soviet Union. More significantly, in 1956 Nasser nationalized the Suez Canal Company, which controlled that strategic waterway. Great Britain, the former colonial ruler of Egypt and owner of the canal, responded by coordinating an invasion of Egypt with the French and Israelis in October 1956 in a bid to reimpose its control. The crisis rapidly threatened to destabilize the region when Israeli forces captured the entire Sinai peninsula from Egypt. As a result, the conflict threatened to draw in the two superpowers as well. In a move that reflected its preoccupation with maintaining a strategic balance against the USSR, the United States applied heavy economic and diplomatic pressure to force the withdrawal of British, French, and Israeli troops from Egypt, causing significant tensions with its allies. Due to heavy U.S. pressure, all forces were withdrawn from Egyptian territory by March 1957, and a UN peacekeeping force was deployed to the area. In exchange for the withdrawal, the United States guaranteed Israel the right of access to the Strait of Tiran and the Gulf of Aqaba on the Red Sea.

After the Suez crisis, President Eisenhower announced the Eisenhower Doctrine, aimed at limiting the expansion of Soviet influence. This doctrine

FIGURE 4.1

had three main points. First, the United States would help develop the economic strength of Middle Eastern countries. Second, increased programs of military and economic assistance to the region would be implemented toward that end. Third, the United States would deploy troops to Middle Eastern countries that requested such aid in the face of communist aggression. This marked the first time the United States formally committed itself to troops in the region if needed. In doing so, Eisenhower went well beyond the Truman Doctrine.

The initial proving grounds for the new doctrine was Lebanon. After receiving a request for assistance from the Lebanese government, fourteen thousand U.S. Marines were deployed to that country in July 1958 to prevent what was thought to be an imminent Soviet takeover. In June 1957, the United States had already extended $10 million in aid to Jordan. By 1958, this amount was increased to $40 million annually in order to compensate for the loss of British assistance. Moreover, after a 1959 coup overthrew the pro-Western Iraqi monarchy, the United States signed identical agreements with remaining CENTO members Iran, Pakistan, and Turkey, formally extending the military protection of the Eisenhower Doctrine to them. By the 1960s, therefore, the United States was firmly committed to supporting its regional allies through a variety of means—including the deployment of troops—to prevent Soviet gains in the Middle East.

The Nixon Doctrine

The 1960s, for the most part, saw few changes in the strategic framework of U.S. regional policy. The major exception was the increasingly close nature of U.S.–Israeli ties after the Arab–Israeli war of 1967. U.S. policy took a clear turn in a pro-Israeli direction after the 1967 war, establishing a consistent theme that has endured ever since. U.S. military assistance to Israel rose from $25 million in 1968 to $307.5 million in 1973. The United States became Israel's largest supplier of arms. Israel also received the highest amount of per capita U.S. aid of any country. By the early 1980s, average annual aid to Israel was close to $3 billion; from 1949 to 1996, official U.S. aid to Israel totaled approximately $78 billion.

In May 1967, Egyptian President Nasser deployed troops to the Sinai and requested the withdrawal of UN peacekeeping forces from the peninsula. Soon afterward, he also closed the Gulf of Aqaba to Israeli shipping—thus sparking the 1967 Six Day War. Once again, Israel faced the combined forces of Egypt, Syria, and Jordan and defeated them handily. By the time the fighting stopped, Israel had recaptured the entire Sinai peninsula from Egypt, seized the Golan Heights from Syria, and also taken control of the remainder of the original Palestine Mandate, including the Gaza Strip, the West Bank, and East Jerusalem—collectively known as the Occupied Territories (see Figure 4.2). An additional two hundred thousand Palestinians fled to neighboring

FIGURE 4.2

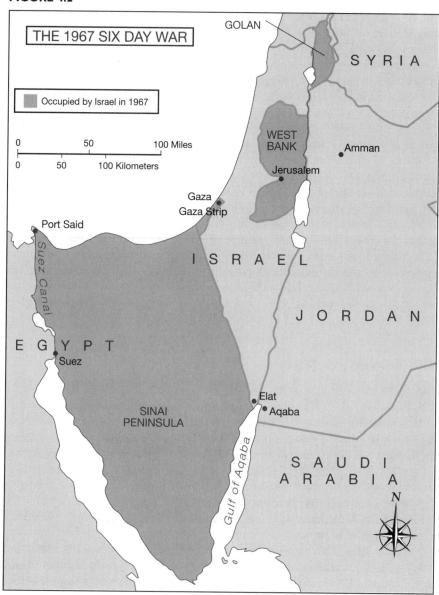

Arab countries, adding to the already massive Palestinian refugee problem in the region. Israel also formally annexed Jerusalem and encouraged Jewish settlements in the Occupied Territories, expropriating nearly half of the West Bank between 1967 and 1997.

Following the war, the UN Security Council adopted Resolution 242, which became the basis for resolving the Arab–Israeli conflict for the next several decades. Resolution 242 called for the withdrawal of Israeli forces from the territories seized during the 1967 conflict as well as a resolution of the refugee issue. The long-term significance of Resolution 242 was that it legitimized the concept of "land-for-peace," a precedent that was later adopted in the Camp David and Oslo negotiations in the 1970s and 1990s, respectively. Land-for-peace also served as the basis for a regional peace proposal advanced by the Saudi government in 2002. From Camp David to the more recent Saudi initiative, all peace efforts in the Middle East have followed the precedent set following the 1967 war by Security Council Resolution 242.

In January 1968, the British government announced its intention to withdraw its remaining forces from the Persian Gulf, completing the process of reducing costly overseas commitments that it had begun in 1947. With the Vietnam conflict at its peak, the United States was unwilling to assume the burden of additional defense commitments at that time. It was not until well into the Nixon administration that a solution to the Persian Gulf situation emerged. In order to justify the gradual removal of U.S. forces from Vietnam, President Nixon adopted a new strategic approach. In 1970, he officially stated the three central principles of the Nixon Doctrine. First, the United States would keep all of its treaty commitments to allies. Second, the United States would provide a nuclear shield for allies whose survival was vital to U.S. security. Third, in cases of nonnuclear aggression, the United States would provide military and economic assistance but would not assume the primary responsibility of providing military manpower in such a conflict. The Nixon Doctrine was announced during America's war with Vietnam, but this policy also had direct implications for the U.S. role in the Middle East.

The Twin Pillar Policy

Although the main objective of the Nixon Doctrine was to provide a rationale for the administration's policy in Southeast Asia, it was also applicable to the Middle East. The question of who would fill the vacuum left by Britain's post–World War II withdrawal from the region was resolved through the adoption of the "twin pillar" corollary to the Nixon Doctrine. The twin pillar policy asserted that the United States would support Iran and Saudi Arabia as regional protectors of U.S. interests. Given Iran's greater population, strength, and more strategic location, the United States came to depend primarily on that country in the 1970s. This led some to dub the policy as a "one-and-a-half pillar" approach instead. In May 1972, President Nixon agreed to increase the number of uniformed U.S. advisors in Iran and to guarantee the Shah of Iran access to the most sophisticated nonnuclear technology in the U.S. military arsenal. In return, the Shah assumed the lead role in protecting Western interests in the Persian Gulf. Examples of Iran's increased regional role during this time were its intervention in Oman throughout the 1970s in support of the Omani government's fight against communist rebels and its collaboration with the United States to support Kurdish rebels in pro-Soviet Iraq. The Nixon Doctrine also led to massive increases in U.S. arms sales to Iran, amounting to $16.2 billion between 1972 and 1977 alone. Military sales to Saudi Arabia increased at similar rates and also began on a smaller scale to the other Persian Gulf states in 1973.

However, these new U.S. doctrines also had negative consequences. They led to a corresponding rise in the military expenditures of Iran's neighbor, Iraq, whose leadership viewed growing Iranian power with alarm. As a result, Iraq turned to the USSR to provide it with the means to rival Iran's military strength. Moreover, U.S. options in the region were reduced by relying too much on Iran as a proxy. When the Shah's regime was overthrown by a popular revolution in February 1979 and replaced by an Islamic Republic, the United States lost its safety net for Persian Gulf policy. The Iranian revolution also brought an end to the Northern Tier strategy, something that the United States had relied on for nearly three decades. The new Iranian regime immediately withdrew from CENTO. Turkey and Pakistan followed suit in March 1979, effectively ending the alliance.

THE YOM KIPPUR WAR

U.S. policy continued to be shaped by Arab–Israeli conflicts in the 1970s. In September 1970, Jordan's King Hussein ordered the expulsion of Palestinian guerrilla fighters—who increasingly acted beyond the control of Jordan's government—from Jordanian refugee camps. Most Palestinian fighters were under the command of the Palestine Liberation Organization (PLO), which subsequently established new bases in Lebanon. From there, the PLO continued its operations against Israel until the Israeli invasion of Lebanon in 1982 forced their evacuation to Tunisia. Moreover, in 1973 the fourth war between Israel and its Arab neighbors broke out, following the death of Egyptian President Nasser in 1970. The so-called Yom Kippur War began on October 6, 1973, when Egyptian and Syrian forces launched a surprise invasion of Israel in a bid to recapture territories lost during the 1967 war. Over time the Israeli armed forces were able to stop, then reverse, the Arab gains—although heavy losses suffered by Israel in 1973 put an end to the myth of Israeli military invincibility.

Both superpowers also became directly involved in supporting their client states. The United States began direct wartime shipment of arms to Israel for the first time, while the Soviet Union was heavily arming Egypt and Syria. As a result, the Arab members of the Organization of Petroleum Exporting Countries (OPEC) expressed their anger at growing U.S. support for Israel by announcing an embargo on oil exports to the United States and other Western countries. Given this escalating situation, the two superpowers negotiated a cease-fire on October 22 that was subsequently ratified by the UN as Resolution

338 and also accepted by the warring parties. Nevertheless, continuing advances by the Israeli army threatened to bring about direct Soviet action, which was averted only by last minute diplomatic efforts that led to the passage of UN Resolution 340. This resolution, which finally ended the fighting, called for a return to October 22 borders, an immediate cease-fire, the dispatch of a UN peacekeeping force, and the implementation of Resolution 338.

OIL IS STRENGTHENED AS A REGIONAL FACTOR

By the early 1970s the dynamics of the international oil market were shifting from favoring the buyers to favoring the suppliers. This was largely due to rapidly rising demand among industrialized countries. The United States led the way in higher oil consumption. From 1970 to 1973 alone, U.S. imports of oil jumped from 3.2 million barrels per day to 6.2 million.[6] Underscoring the importance of this growing dependence on the Middle East was the fact that Middle Eastern members of OPEC controlled more than two-thirds of global oil reserves. Since 1955, eighty percent of all new oil discoveries had occurred in the Middle East. Saudi Arabia alone provided twenty-one percent of global oil production by 1973. The "oil weapon" was potentially a powerful tool.

The imposition of the Arab oil embargo on Western countries during the Yom Kippur War made that potential a reality. Between 1970 and 1973, oil prices rose from $1.40 per barrel to $17.00 per barrel, leading to the first "oil shock" of the 1970s. The revenues of oil exporters increased from $23 billion in 1972 to $140 billion in 1977. Another important consequence of the 1973 oil embargo was the linking of events in the Arab–Israeli conflict with those in the Persian Gulf (where many of the large OPEC producers are located) in U.S. policy. By the late 1970s, this linkage had become a key foundation of U.S. policy in the Middle East. For example, in justifying its high profile in the Arab–Israeli peace process, the Carter administration stated that Arab–Israeli peace was "intimately tied in with the Persian Gulf['s] stability" and with "energy supplies for our country."[7] The importance of oil for the international economy was brought home yet again when the Iranian revolution and subsequent Iran–Iraq War led to disruptions of oil exports from the Persian Gulf, causing a second oil shock and severe increases in oil prices in the early 1980s. This pattern of high oil prices during a regional crisis was also briefly repeated during the initial phases of the 1990–91 Gulf War.

THE CAMP DAVID ACCORDS

After the 1973 war, an uneasy truce existed between Israel and Egypt. Throughout the 1970s, the United States attempted to negotiate a withdrawal of Israeli forces from the Sinai peninsula while continuing to improve its ties with Israel. In 1975, the United States and Israel signed a Memorandum of

Agreement (MOA) that "obliged the United States to be 'responsive' to Israel's economic and energy needs" and to guarantee it adequate supplies of oil. Another MOA in 1979 allowed Israeli firms to compete with U.S. firms for Pentagon contracts.[8] For the first time, the United States also became a direct partner in efforts to bring about an end to the Arab–Israeli conflict through step-by-step negotiations. This commitment to the "peace process" has since become a hallmark of U.S. policy in the Middle East. Although unable to bring about a comprehensive peace, by the mid-1970s the United States had successfully mediated the peaceful disengagement of Egyptian and Israeli forces in the Sinai peninsula as well as the disengagement of Israeli and Syrian forces in the Golan Heights. President Nasser's successor, Anwar Sadat (who was himself assassinated and replaced by Hosni Mubarak in 1981), became supportive of improved U.S.–Egyptian relations after Egypt's defeat in 1973. This gave the incoming Carter administration a unique opportunity to advance the peace process.

In September 1978, President Carter hosted the leaders of Israel and Egypt at the presidential retreat at Camp David, Maryland, for an intensive round of negotiations that led to a tentative agreement—known as the Camp David Accords. The Accords resolved the outstanding territorial issues between Egypt and Israel in the Sinai and also established a framework for ongoing discussions regarding autonomous Palestinian self-government in the West Bank and Gaza Strip. An Egyptian–Israeli peace treaty to that effect was signed on March 26, 1979. Israeli forces were to be withdrawn from the Sinai in stages (finally completed in 1982), Egypt and Israel established normal diplomatic relations, and both countries made a commitment to further support the peace process regarding Palestinian autonomy. The treaty was cemented by the extension of a $4.8 billion package of loans and grants by the United States to Egypt and Israel in 1978—an element of U.S. Middle East policy that remains in place to this day. The Accords arguably represented the Carter administration's greatest success in its Middle East policy; they were also a product of the most high-profile U.S. role in the Arab–Israeli conflict to date.

THE CARTER DOCTRINE

During the late 1970s, major challenges to U.S. interests emerged that ultimately led to a deepening of U.S. commitments in the Middle East during the 1980s and 1990s. The most dramatic event was the Iranian Revolution and the establishment in that country of an Islamic Republic dominated by Muslim clerics who embraced anti-Americanism as the cornerstone of Iran's new foreign policy.[9] As a result, the main pillar of the two-pillar policy from the 1970s crumbled. In addition, Soviet activity in and around the region had increased notably since the late 1960s. This included a growing naval presence in the Indian Ocean and treaties of friendship or trade with Iran, Iraq, and Yemen.

In the late 1970s, Soviet activity became even more aggressive, culminating with the 1979 Soviet invasion of Afghanistan.

President Carter's response to these Soviet actions was to create a rapid deployment combat command capable of intervening in a regional crisis. Through Presidential Directive 18 (PD-18), he ordered the creation of a force of light divisions with strategic mobility that was not dependent on overseas bases. By the time of the Soviet invasion of Afghanistan, planning for this force, initially known as the Rapid Deployment Force (RDF), was well underway. The Carter Doctrine was formally announced by President Carter during his state of the union address in January 1980, in which he revealed the creation of a Rapid Deployment Joint Task Force (RDJTF) and warned the Soviets that

> an attempt by any outside force to gain control of the Persian Gulf region will be regarded as an assault on the vital interests of the United States of America and such an assault will be repelled by any means necessary, including military force.[10]

The Carter Doctrine formally elevated the security of the Persian Gulf to a vital national security interest of the United States. It was the culmination of presidential doctrines dating back to 1947. The Middle East/Persian Gulf region had now become the "third central strategic zone" of U.S. foreign policy, along with Western Europe and the Far East. In keeping with this new commitment, for fiscal year 1981 the Carter administration requested $157 billion in military expenditures, nearly $20 billion more than in 1980.[11] The announcement of the Carter Doctrine also built on the Camp David Accords, which had reincorporated Egypt into the pro-Western camp after decades of mutual hostility.

THE REAGAN COROLLARY: IMPLEMENTING THE CARTER DOCTRINE

Throughout the 1980s and early 1990s, the Reagan and Bush administrations adopted and refined the Carter Doctrine. The Reagan administration's approach to the Middle East, in particular, reflected its perception that Soviet gains during the 1970s were part of a grand design for world domination. Soviet aggression had to be rolled back wherever possible. This was especially true in areas that were considered to be vital to U.S. interests, such as the Middle East and the Persian Gulf. The first three defense budgets submitted by the Reagan administration were fifty-two-percent higher than the last budget submitted by President Carter in 1980; under the first President Bush, they reached a level of $446 billion in 1989. A conventional military buildup that began under President Carter was expanded. This buildup revolved around enhancing the U.S. military's ability to intervene effectively around the world—especially the Middle East. This involved upgrading strategic mobility (airlift, sealift, pre-positioning, and amphibious lift capacity). It also involved the development of new weapons systems, increases in the size of the U.S. Navy, and efforts to establish new regional bases and improve existing ones. By the mid-1980s, the United States could deploy combat units in the Persian Gulf in a matter of days—as compared to several weeks during 1980. In addition, strategic airlift and sealift capabilities nearly doubled between 1980 and 1987.

In January 1983, the Reagan administration formally converted the RDF from an ad hoc force into a permanent military command known as the U.S. Central Command (CENTCOM).[12] CENTCOM was assigned responsibility for all U.S. military activity in the Middle East and in parts of Africa; its central mission was to ensure continued access to Persian Gulf oil and to prevent the USSR from acquiring control of the region. By the 1990s, CENTCOM could call upon four hundred thousand troops—as compared with the one hundred thousand troops envisaged in the original RDF established by PD-18 during the Carter administration. The establishment of CENTCOM symbolized the willingness of the United States to act unilaterally in the region. Reliance on Great Britain, CENTO, and the twin-pillar policy had finally given way to the realization that the United States may have to do the job itself. However, in addition to the Soviet threat to the Persian Gulf, there were several other pressing issues that faced the United States in the 1980s.

President Reagan made the removal of Soviet troops from Afghanistan a high priority. To achieve this goal, the United States gave large amounts of aid to the Afghan resistance (the mujahedin), this aid rose from $122 million in 1984 to $280 million in 1985. The United States also provided massive quantities of weapons that steadily increased in quality and quantity throughout the decade, and it began diplomatic efforts to enlist sympathetic states such as Pakistan and Saudi Arabia to aid the resistance. When combined with the ferocity of the local resistance and changing Soviet policies after the assumption of power by Mikhail Gorbachev, these efforts led to a negotiated withdrawal of Soviet forces from Afghanistan in 1989.

President Reagan came into office viewing Israel as an important asset in his campaign against the Soviet Union. In November 1981, the United States and Israel signed an agreement that represented a high point in U.S.–Israeli relations. Known as the Strategic Cooperation Agreement, it built on mutual security interests and recognized the need to "deter all threats from the Soviet Union to the region."[13] The 1981 agreement provided for joint military exercises, the use of Israeli ports by the U.S. Sixth Fleet; the pre-positioning of U.S. military supplies on Israeli soil, a $425 million annual increase in U.S. aid to Israel (for a total of more than $3 billion), and the conclusion of a trade agreement that gave Israeli firms preferential treatment in U.S. markets.[14] The agreement did not bind the United States directly to the defense of Israel, but it did represent a significant American step forward in support of Israel.

In June 1982, Israel invaded Lebanon in pursuit of PLO guerrillas based in southern Lebanon. The subsequent deployment of a multinational force composed of U.S., French, and Italian marines in September was intended to mediate the conflict, help to re-establish the authority of the Lebanese government, and protect Palestinian refugees. It also marked the first landing of U.S. troops in the eastern Mediterranean since 1958. Following the PLO's departure from Lebanon due to a cease-fire agreement, the multinational force was withdrawn. It returned after massacres of Palestinians and Lebanese Shi'a's by Israeli-backed Christian factions in Beirut area refugee camps. This time, however, the multinational force itself was perceived by Lebanese Muslims as being pro-Israeli and became the target of subsequent attacks. On April 18, 1983, a U.S. Marines barracks was destroyed by a Shi'a Muslim suicide bomber, resulting in the death of 241 U.S. personnel. This event resulted in the withdrawal of U.S. forces from Lebanon and a general lowering of the U.S. profile in the Arab–Israeli dispute. Thus, when the Occupied Territories erupted in violence in 1987 against Israeli rule, the United States supported Israel but remained largely on the sidelines. This popular Palestinian uprising, known as the first "Intifada," endured until 1990. The United States gradually began to reenter the picture in late 1988, when official contacts with the PLO were authorized following the PLO's recognition of Israel's right to exist and rejection of terrorism (despite their unsettled disputes with the Jewish state).[15]

THE IRAN–IRAQ WAR

On September 22, 1980, Iraq invaded Iran in hopes of exploiting the chaos that followed the fall of the Shah. Iraq's initial surprise attacks and rapid gains were soon blunted. Iraqi forces were largely evicted from Iranian territory by 1982, after which Iran embarked on a series of offensives into Iraqi territory in a bid to overthrow the Iraqi regime. Ultimately, however, Iraq's steadily increasing superiority in the quantity and quality of its weaponry—based on the large amounts of external assistance that it received during the war—allowed it to fend off the Iranian offensives. A bloody stalemate ensued until 1988.

From the beginning of this conflict, the United States adopted a policy that emphasized five points: a balance between the two countries to prevent an outright victory by either, a containment of the conflict itself, the prevention of the exploitation of the conflict by the USSR, the survival of the conservative Persian Gulf Arab monarchies, and the continued free flow of oil from the Persian Gulf. The United States also took direct steps to protect its interests and reassure its allies in the region. For example, in September 1980 President Carter's secretary of state, Edmund Muskie, pressed for and received a pledge of neutrality from the Soviets. In October 1980, the Carter administration also approved the deployment of four additional AWACS aircraft (along with 300 U.S. personnel) to Saudi Arabia. In the same month, more than thirty U.S. warships were deployed to the western Indian Ocean.[16]

The Reagan administration strengthened these efforts, most notably by pursuing more cooperation with the Persian Gulf Arab states. In February 1981, the United States and Oman signed an agreement granting the United States access to military facilities in Oman, and later that year the United States agreed to sell AWACS aircraft to Saudi Arabia to bolster its air defenses. The AWACS sale was actually part of a larger, secret agreement in which the Saudis agreed to build advanced "networks of command, naval, and defense facilities large enough for a massive deployment of U.S. forces."[17] This top-secret project cost nearly $200 billion, and by 1990 these Saudi facilities rivaled those of NATO. In October 1981, President Reagan also declared that "Saudi Arabia we won't permit to be another Iran."[18] Known as the "Reagan Corollary" to the Carter Doctrine, this was widely interpreted to mean that the United States would not allow an unfriendly government to take over Saudi Arabia—thus extending a U.S. commitment to the security of that country.

In May 1981, Saudi Arabia, Kuwait, Oman, Qatar, the United Arab Emirates, and Bahrain founded the GCC. The GCC was a way to coordinate policies and promote their common security. The GCC clearly could not match either Iran or Iraq in military power, but its existence did help to increase the stability of those states during the 1980s. It was also a way for the Saudis to assume a greater regional role—making subsequent U.S. interventions in the region that much easier. Over time, the GCC's military weakness pushed its members toward greater security cooperation with the United States.

Beginning in 1982, a thaw in U.S.–Iraqi relations emerged. That year, the United States temporarily removed Iraq from the official list of states that sponsor terrorism, sold Iraq nonmilitary transport planes, and also extended loans to that country. In return, Iraq announced in August 1982 its acceptance of Israel's right to exist—an important symbolic gesture from one of the most anti-Israeli of Arab states. As Iraq's fortunes in the war with Iran began to plummet, U.S.–Iraqi relations improved even further. In May 1984, the United States publicly blamed Iran for the first time for the continuation of the war. Nearly $1 billion in agricultural credits were subsequently made available to Iraq, Export-Import Bank guarantees for critical Iraqi oil projects were also provided, and finally, diplomatic ties between the United States and Iraq— broken off after the 1967 Arab–Israeli war—were reestablished in 1984. The U.S. "tilt" toward Iraq during the Iran–Iraq war was in full swing by the late 1980s. It was facilitated by the increasing spillover of the war into the rest of the Persian Gulf and the dismal failure of a U.S. initiative aimed at improving U.S.–Iranian relations.

During 1985–86, the United States and Iran were involved in secret negotiations (mainly through Israel as an intermediary). Iran sought U.S. weapons and spare parts for its war effort in return for the use of its influence to arrange the release of American hostages held by pro-Iranian Shi'a groups in Lebanon. The United States wanted to improve relations with Iran in order to stabilize the region and prevent Soviet gains and to secure the release of the hostages.[19] This strategic initiative, which came to be known as the Iran–Contra scandal, collapsed in 1986 after its exposure by the media and due to the illegal use of its proceeds to finance arms sales to Nicaraguan guerillas (the Contras). The public and humiliating end of the Iran–Contra scandal dealt an enduring blow to President Reagan's prestige and popularity. It also hardened the administration's stance regarding Iran, paving the way for even better ties with Iraq.

THE KUWAITI REFLAGGING OPERATION

By late 1986, Iranian efforts to cripple Iraq and its supporters (which ironically included Kuwait) escalated through missile attacks on shipping and the mining of shipping lanes in the Gulf. In December 1986, Kuwait requested that the United States and USSR reflag and escort its shipping; on May 19, 1987, the United States officially agreed to do so.[20] Throughout 1987, a multinational force of more than sixty ships (approximately thirty U.S. and an equal amount of European ones) patrolled the Persian Gulf's shipping lanes. Although few major incidents occurred, beginning in early 1988 the United States became less passive in its operations in order to pressure Iran into ceasing its attacks on Gulf shipping. This resulted in several encounters between U.S. and Iranian forces that inflicted heavy losses on the Iranian navy. Increased U.S. military pressure combined with a series of dramatic Iraqi victories to push Iran into seeking a cease-fire. The most immediate cause of that decision was the accidental shooting down of an Iranian passenger airliner on July 3, 1988, by the U.S.S. *Vincennes*, a missile cruiser that was engaged in heated surface action with Iranian forces at the time (it was later revealed that the cruiser was operating in Iranian territorial waters). All 290 passengers on board lost their lives. This event, and the lack of international support for Iran in its aftermath, underscored the extent of Iran's isolation. On July 18, Iran officially accepted the terms of UN Resolution 598, finally ending the war. The reflagging operation was "yet another step in the development of progressively deepening American interests and involvement [in the Persian Gulf]."[21] The displacement of Great Britain by the United States as the "guardian of the Gulf" was now complete.

THE FIRST BUSH ADMINISTRATION: OPERATIONALIZING THE REAGAN LEGACY

By the late 1980s, the Cold War was in its final stages. Under the leadership of Mikhail Gorbachev, the USSR was increasingly concerned with internal reform and less willing to involve itself in conflicts with the United States or to expend large amounts of resources propping up its allies. When President Bush took office in January 1989, prospects for U.S. policy and interests in the

Middle East appeared to be encouraging. The end of the Iran–Iraq war had removed a major source of regional instability, and the increasing flexibility of the PLO heralded an era of greater progress in the Arab–Israeli peace process. The decline of the USSR's capacity to threaten U.S. allies and interests removed the most dominant threat to the United States. The network of U.S. allies in the region was intact and strong, anchored by Saudi Arabia, Israel, the Gulf Arab states, Jordan, Egypt, and Turkey. Syria was hostile to U.S. interests and to Israel, but it was also bogged down by its own military occupation of much of Lebanon and plagued by a weak economy. Iran, although still defiantly anti-American, was isolated and exhausted from its long war with Iraq. In 1989, Iran embarked on a program of domestic reconstruction that would absorb much of its energies for the next decade.

For its part, Iraq sought to improve its relations with the United States.[22] Although there were tensions in the U.S.–Iraqi relationship based on Iraq's poor human rights record and its drive to acquire weapons of mass destruction, the first Bush administration continued on the path of cultivating a beneficial relationship with Iraq. A review of U.S. policy by the Bush administration was completed in October 1989, concluding that

> normal relations between the U.S. and Iraq would serve our longer-term interests in both the Gulf and the Middle East. The U.S. government should propose economic and political incentives for Iraq to moderate its behavior and to increase our influence with Iraq.[23]

This seemingly calm atmosphere belied very unstable dynamics rooted in Iraq's postwar situation that would soon cause the next regional crisis.

Given that Iraq is significantly smaller than Iran, the war had taken a larger toll on Iraq. It emerged from the Iran–Iraq war with greater regional political influence, but was left as an economic cripple. Although Iraq had foreign exchange reserves of $35 billion in 1980, at the end of the war it was left with an $80 billion foreign debt and had suffered an estimated $230 billion in infrastructure damage.[24] In addition, Iraq continued to maintain more than one million men in arms despite the large drain of resources that entailed and the tensions it caused in the region. Iraq reached its breaking point in 1990. With annual oil revenues of $13 billion barely covering the military budget, it was faced with hard currency outflows of more than $23 billion, requiring an extra $10 billion per year to rectify its balance of payments—all this before any rebuilding could even be considered.

As a result, Iraq began to pressure its Arab neighbors (most notably, Kuwait) to meet its demands on a variety of issues. Iraq's pressing need for hard currency led it to push OPEC to increase the price of oil to $25 a barrel in 1989. By doing so, it came into conflict with Kuwait. Kuwait had used the disruption of Iraqi oil production during the war to expand its own exports and was in favor of keeping prices down in order to maintain its share of production. Iraqi President Saddam Hussein also began to publicly criticize U.S. policy in the region and called for the withdrawal of U.S. forces. Moreover,

Iraq accused the other Arab oil producers of colluding with the United States to hold down the price of oil. It denounced Kuwait for stealing oil from an oil field that straddled the Iraq–Kuwait border, claimed $2.4 billion in compensation, and demanded that the GCC states forgive Iraq's $30 billion debt to them.[25] Iraq also persistently pressed Kuwait to grant it some form of control over the strategic islands of Warba and Bubiyan in order to improve its access to the Persian Gulf.

The U.S. reaction to the mounting level of Iraqi agitation was tepid and largely disinterested. U.S. decision makers were too caught up in the end of the Cold War and the dramatic events of 1989 and 1990 that accompanied the fall of communist regimes throughout Eastern Europe. President Bush even sent a now infamous letter to Hussein expressing American neutrality regarding tensions in the Middle East. In late July 1990, just days prior to the invasion of Kuwait, America's ambassador to Iraq (April Glaspie) met with Hussein. She hand delivered Bush's letter, which stated that the United States would take no position in Arab-versus-Arab disputes. At the same time, and unbeknownst to the United States, Hussein was preparing his invasion. To Hussein, Bush's statement of neutrality in his disputes with Kuwait must have looked like an invitation to take the small, oil-rich nation. At the very least, Hussein probably assumed that his invasion of Kuwait would leave the United States watching from the sidelines.

THE 1991 GULF WAR

On August 2, 1990, Iraq invaded and occupied Kuwait (see Figure 4.3). Despite improved U.S. relations with Iraq, CENTCOM's planning for a crisis had been revised to emphasize the growing Iraqi threat to regional stability. Its response plan, known as Plan 1002-90, had even been developed to the point at which, as late as June 1990, exercises had been carried out with the goal of dealing with an Iraqi military challenge. As a result, once the appropriate political decisions were taken, the American military response was firm and effective.

On August 3, the U.S. National Security Council declared that the invasion was an act of unprovoked aggression in an area vital to U.S. interests. On August 4, U.S. military commanders determined that to fully implement Plan 1002-90, two hundred fifty thousand troops and seventeen weeks would be required; by August 6, Saudi King Fahd had agreed to host the forces necessary for the expulsion of Iraq from Kuwait. The very next day, five days after the invasion, U.S. forces began deploying to implement Operation Desert Shield aimed at protecting Saudi Arabia. By mid-September, nearly 700 aircraft and a core defensive force of forty thousand troops were in place. With more than one hundred thousand troops deployed by the end of September 1990 and more arriving daily, Saudi Arabia was effectively protected from an Iraqi attack without incident. In October, the administration shifted into planning for an

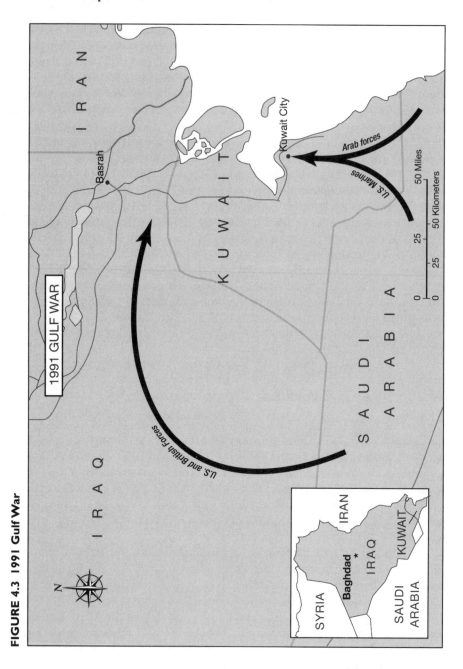

FIGURE 4.3 1991 Gulf War

offensive, requiring a doubling of Operation Desert Shield's two hundred thousand troops. On October 30, President Bush approved CENTCOM's plans for an offensive ground campaign called Operation Desert Storm, ordering a further buildup that would ultimately include 527,000 U.S. troops in a larger multilateral alliance. The critical element in this massive movement of troops and materiel to the Persian Gulf was the Carter- and Reagan-era expansion of strategic lift capabilities.

More than thirty countries eventually joined the coalition that ejected Iraqi forces from Kuwait. Great Britain, France, Egypt, Syria, Pakistan, and the GCC all contributed substantial ground, naval, and air forces. Italy, Belgium, the Netherlands, Denmark, Norway, Spain, Portugal, and others provided naval and air assets that were devoted mainly to the enforcement of a UN-sponsored trade embargo against Iraq.[26] Other countries limited their participation to the provision of financial assistance: Germany ($6.5 billion) and Japan ($10.7 billion) contributed more than $17 billion toward the war's total cost of $54 billion.

This massive buildup of coalition forces culminated with Iraq's comprehensive military defeat between January 17 (the beginning of a thirty-eight-day air campaign) and February 25, 1991, (the end of a 100-hour ground war). For Iraq, the war resulted in the indefinite imposition of international economic sanctions, a weapons of mass destruction (WMD) inspection regime implemented by the UN, and the creation of two "no-fly" zones inside Iraq patrolled by coalition aircraft to protect the Kurds in the north and the Shi'as in the south. Other consequences of the war to date have included the immiseration and pauperization of the Iraqi people and the severe erosion of Iraq's regional and international standing. It also set the stage for the renewed importance of Iran. Finally, the war brought about a permanent U.S. regional presence that surpasses even the Kuwaiti reflagging operation in size and scope.

The establishment of the no-fly zones necessitated the continuous monitoring of Iraqi airspace by U.S. and coalition forces via assets based in Saudi Arabia, Turkey, and the Persian Gulf. In addition, the United States strongly supported efforts to establish a regional collective security system. The most notable effort took place under the Damascus Declaration of March 6, 1991, which envisaged strategic collaboration between the six GCC states, Egypt, and Syria. In exchange for the permanent stationing of Egyptian and Syrian forces in the Persian Gulf, the smaller, wealthier GCC states were to provide those two countries with economic assistance. Eventually, the initiative collapsed due to disagreements over the quantity and quality of the security and aid needed. Egyptian and Syrian forces withdrew from Saudi Arabia by May 1991.

The United States however, persisted with plans to enhance its unilateral regional influence and position. The U.S.–Kuwait Defense Cooperation Agreement was signed in September 1991 and provided for U.S. access to Kuwaiti military facilities, the pre-positioning of supplies for U.S. forces, joint exercises, and training. The United States also upgraded its facilities access agreement with Oman and concluded new security accords with Qatar and Bahrain. In October 1991, Bahrain also renewed its previous access and pre-positioning agreement with the United States. In addition, in June 1992 the United States and Qatar signed a twenty-year defense cooperation agreement.

For its part, Saudi Arabia provided more port access to the U.S. Navy and more ground support for U.S. Air Force contingents already in its territory. The combined effect of these new agreements and the ongoing deployment of substantial U.S. forces to the Middle East and Persian Gulf was to firmly install the United States as the region's preeminent military and political power.

The Madrid Conference

The first Bush administration moved quickly to capitalize on its strong hand following the 1991 Gulf War. The impact of the Gulf War increased U.S. attention to the Middle East in general, and to the Arab–Israeli dispute in particular. In October 1991, the United States and a weakened USSR jointly hosted a landmark Middle East peace conference in Madrid, Spain. The conference was attended by Israel, Syria, Lebanon, a joint Jordanian-Palestinian delegation, and representatives of Saudi Arabia, the UN, and the European community. For the first time, representatives of the PLO were invited to such a forum, marking a symbolic breakthrough in the peace process that built on the resumption of official contacts that had taken place in 1988. Unlike the Carter administration, however, the Bush administration did not seek to play an active role in the negotiations. Rather, it chose to act as a facilitator and brought the parties together for face-to-face negotiations eight times over the course of the next year. Although President Bush was defeated in the 1992 presidential election by Bill Clinton, the groundwork for much of the progress in the peace process during the 1990s was attributable to prior steps taken by the first Bush administration.

THE CLINTON DOCTRINE OF ENLARGEMENT

The Clinton administration came into office in January 1993 beset by a number of pressing foreign policy issues, including crises in Haiti, Somalia, and Bosnia (see chapter 5). The rapidly changing international context led Clinton to reevaluate U.S. security interests through initiatives such as the Bottom-Up-Review (BUR). A BUR examines the defense posture of the United States by using budget constraints as a starting point. Clinton's BUR recommended that the United States shift away from existing strategy aimed at fighting and winning two regional wars simultaneously toward a strategy to fight and win two regional wars in overlapping stages—a "win-hold-win" strategy. The BUR's concept of a post–Cold War U.S. military therefore envisioned an even greater role for pre-positioned equipment, effective airlift capacity, and technological superiority.

In September 1993, National Security Advisor Anthony Lake floated the policy doctrine of "enlargement." The Clinton Doctrine of Enlargement formally emerged in a policy paper in July 1994 as the president's *National Security Strategy of Engagement and Enlargement.* The doctrine included four main points. First, that the United States should strive to strengthen the international community of market democracies. Second, that it should foster new market democracies wherever possible. Third, the United States should counter aggression and support the liberalization of states hostile to democracy. Fourth, it should aid market democracies that were taking root in regions of greatest humanitarian concern.

A corollary to the Clinton Doctrine of Enlargement served as the basis of U.S. policy in the Persian Gulf during the 1990s. This was the notion that so-called rogue states would be dealt with firmly if they tried to undermine the new order. According to National Security Advisor Lake, this "backlash corollary" meant that that "our policy must face the reality of recalcitrant and outlaw states that not only choose to remain outside the family [of nations] but also assault its basic values."[27] The states accused by Lake of being in this category included Cuba, Iran, Libya, North Korea, and especially Iraq. These states were characterized as oppressive, radical, irrational, paranoid, and dangerous. It would fall to the United States to neutralize and contain the risks they posed to the international community. Moreover, the backlash corollary created the logic for applying pressure to states that were beyond the scope of enlargement. In the Middle East, this strategic framework was given substance by the policy of dual containment.

DUAL CONTAINMENT

In May 1993, the United States embarked on an important shift in its Middle Eastern policy. Known as "dual containment," the new policy elevated both Iran and Iraq to the front rank of rogue states that were to become targets for increased U.S. pressure under the Clinton Doctrine.

> Dual containment derives from an assessment that the current Iraqi and Iranian regimes are both hostile to American interests in the region. . . . As long as we are able to maintain our military presence in the region; as long as we succeed in restricting the military ambitions of both Iraq and Iran; and as long as we can rely on our regional allies—Egypt, Israel, Saudi Arabia and the GCC, and Turkey—to preserve the balance of power in our favor in the wider Middle East region, we will have the means to counter both the Iraqi and Iranian regimes.[28]

Dual containment is based on beneficial changes that the Clinton administration believed had been denied to previous administrations. These included the lack of a Soviet threat, a militarily weakened Iran and Iraq due to wars since 1980, a functioning Arab–Israeli peace process, and a robust U.S. military presence bolstered by the new willingness of the GCC states to enter into security arrangements with America. As a result, the Clinton administration felt that the United States no longer needed to pursue its traditional policy of balancing Iran and Iraq against one another, as it had done for decades. It could now contain both states.

Dual containment did try to differentiate between Iran and Iraq, despite placing both in the same category of rogue states. Given the existing UN sanctions regime against Iraq, it was relatively easy for the United States to gather international support for a harder line against Iraq in order to bring about its full compliance with Security Council resolutions. Iran, on the other hand, was seen by the administration as less aggressive than Iraq and as a state with which normal relations could be established in the future—if its objectionable behavior moderated over time.[29] The essence of the dual containment policy toward Iran has been to bring about—or more accurately, to force—its moderation through an accumulating process of political and economic pressure orchestrated by Washington. Unlike the case of Iraq, however, the United States had no international consensus or sanctions to work with, forcing it to take what amounted to unilateral steps against Iran. In 1995, the Clinton administration announced a unilateral trade embargo against Iran; in 1996, it signed into law an extraterritorial measure designed to prevent international investment in Iran's oil industry. The law, known as the Iran–Libya Sanctions Act (ILSA), committed the United States to punishing companies from third countries that invested more than $20 million in Iran's oil industry. These steps gradually placed the U.S. relationship with its allies, especially the countries of the European Union (EU), under great pressure due to differences over the proper approach to Iran.

Although most Europeans shared U.S. concerns regarding Iraq, they disagreed with the United States about Iran. Instead, they pursued a policy of "critical dialogue." Collectively implemented through the auspices of the EU, critical dialogue shared dual containment's goal of encouraging moderation in Iran—but it did so through dialogue rather than pressure. By 1997, U.S.–European relations had deteriorated markedly over their differences regarding relations with Iran. ILSA's passage in 1996 represented the high-water mark of the most hyperactive phase of the dual containment policy. Yet, the inability of the United States to enforce the law became increasingly apparent over time, as did growing differences with the EU. ILSA's threat to place sanctions on European firms investing in Iran was met with a barrage of hostility and criticism by European officials.

In November 1997, the EU lodged a formal complaint against the United States at the World Trade Organization (WTO), challenging the validity of ILSA's extraterritoriality. The complaint revolved around a consortium of European, Russian, and Malaysian companies that was formed to develop an Iranian oil field. The consortium's ability to implement this contract became the first major test case for the United States's capacity to enforce ILSA. After it was granted the contract by the Iranian government, the companies were immediately threatened by Washington with economic sanctions should they proceed with their planned investment. Details of the contract were also closely scrutinized by U.S. officials for evidence of a violation. By the spring of 1998, the consortium was still determined to proceed and was also backed by the full support of the EU and the Russian and Malaysian governments. In May 1998, the United States finally backed down and reached a compromise on ILSA's implementation in order to avoid sparking a trade war with the EU. The United States agreed to waive sanctions against the consortium and also indicated that other European companies making similar investments in Iran could expect this waiver as well.

The election of reformist Iranian President Muhammad Khatami in June 1997 provided supporters of a more moderate policy toward Iran with ammunition to criticize an increasingly inflexible and obsolete U.S. approach to Iran. As a result, there is even less willingness on the part of the Europeans and other Middle Eastern states to support U.S. efforts to isolate Iran. Since 1997, there has been a flurry of diplomatic activity and an increasing number of high level links between Iran, the EU, and GCC countries. The reformist trend in Iran has been strengthened even further with additional landslide victories by Iranian liberals in 1999 municipal elections and in parliamentary elections in February 2000. For Europe, the changes in Iran

> are taken as proof that, despite all setbacks, a policy of keeping up lines of communication and not isolating Iran is perhaps more than ever the appropriate one. . . . The obvious power struggle in Iran has verified the working hypothesis of European policy.[30]

As a result of these changes, U.S. policy toward Iran has also moderated somewhat. Beginning in 1998, visits by athletes, scholars, and private citizens between the two countries have been encouraged by their respective governments. In June 1998, the U.S. government officially expressed its desire to begin a process of reconciliation with Iran as prelude to the eventual normalization of ties. In 1999, the Clinton administration lifted sanctions on food and medicine exports to Iran. It lifted bans on the import of Iranian goods such as carpets, fruit, and caviar in March 2000. Nevertheless, the fundamental premise of dual containment—that of a significant "Iranian threat" in addition to the Iraqi threat—remained in place. It has been fueled by concerns over Iranian ties to extremist Islamic terrorist groups after September 11 and by the inability of Iranian reformists to wrest control of the government from conservatives in nonelected positions of (religious and political) power.

THE OSLO ACCORDS AND THE ARAB-ISRAELI PEACE PROCESS

Beginning in January 1993 and utilizing the momentum generated by the Madrid Conference, the Israeli government and the PLO held secret bilateral negotiations in Oslo, Norway. These talks resulted in the signing of a Declaration of Principles on the White House lawn in September 1993. In a historic ceremony reminiscent of the signing of the Camp David Accords, Israeli

Prime Minister Yizhak Rabin shook hands with PLO Chairman Yasser Arafat. The declaration, also known as the Oslo Accords, committed the Israelis and Palestinians to the pursuit of peaceful coexistence and the implementation of preexisting UN resolutions. It called for the creation of a Palestinian Interim Self-Government Authority (with a police force and elected legislature) to take control over parts of the Occupied Territories. It also deferred highly problematic issues, such as the future of Jerusalem and the fate of Palestinian refugees, to final status talks to be held later. In May 1994, an interim agreement was signed giving the Palestinian Authority control over Jericho in the West Bank and most of the Gaza Strip. That September a more comprehensive agreement known as Oslo II was also signed. It laid out the specific stages by which the Palestinian Authority would gain total or partial control over parts of the West Bank. Under Oslo II's complex framework, the West Bank was divided into three areas. The Palestinian Authority was to gain degrees of control within parts of all three areas over a period of years. The accords also broke the logjam between Israel and the larger Arab world. In October 1994, Jordan became the second Arab state (after Egypt) to sign a peace treaty with Israel; other Arab states such as Tunisia, Morocco, and Qatar also established normal ties with the Jewish state. Negotiations with Syria were also resumed regarding the status of the Golan Heights, which remain occupied by Israel. Although the talks eventually foundered in 1996, the death of hard-line Syrian leader Hafez al Assad in June 2000 has fed new hope regarding the so-called Syrian track of the peace process.

The success of the Oslo process depended directly on the continued goodwill of Arab and Israeli leaders. With the assassination of Yitzhak Rabin by a right-wing Israeli extremist in 1996, the peace process stalled; the liberal Labor Party was also subsequently voted out of power in favor of the conservative Likud Party. Likud's prime minister, Benjamin Netanyahu, was far less committed to trading land for peace than Rabin had been. He was also more insistent on retaining Israeli control over the West Bank and encouraging new Jewish settlements. In addition, he was adamantly opposed to the creation of a Palestinian state or the return of Palestinian refugees to their former homes. At the same time, the PLO was also increasingly challenged by Islamist Palestinian groups (such as Hamas) that are less tolerant of compromise with Israel and critical of the Palestinian Authority's corruption.

From 1996 to 2000, the peace process was undermined by a growing cycle of mutual suspicion, growing extremism, and recrimination. For most of 1997 and 1998, the Israelis and Palestinians did not meet at all—until they were invited to Wye River, Maryland, in October 1998 by President Clinton. The 1998 Wye River Memorandum was yet another interim agreement intended to demonstrate the commitment of the two parties to the original Oslo Accords. It stipulated the withdrawal of Israel from another thirteen percent of the West Bank in exchange for additional security guarantees by the Palestinian Authority. Nevertheless, progress was exceedingly slow. It was only after the election of the more progressive Ehud Barak as prime minister in 2000 that the peace process temporarily showed renewed signs of life.

Under Barak, Israeli forces withdrew from their positions in southern Lebanon in May 2000 (where they had maintained a security zone since 1982), and the new government's rhetoric indicated a renewed Israeli commitment to negotiations with the Palestinians and the notion of land-for-peace. However, President Clinton's efforts to achieve a breakthrough during a second Israeli–PLO summit at Camp David in the summer of 2000 failed. Arafat did not agree to the final terms offered by the Israelis, which included total Palestinian control over the Gaza Strip and near total control over the West Bank. Yet, issues such as the right of return of the millions of Palestinian refugees to their original homes in Israel proper and the future of Jerusalem (both parties wanted it as their capital) remained intractable. Despite intensive last-minute efforts at reaching an agreement by President Clinton prior to his departure from office in January 2002, what was a clear window of opportunity to move the Oslo process along to its final stages ultimately foundered on these issues after a decade of progress.

The Second Intifada

The election of Ariel Sharon as prime minister of Israel in 2001 marked a significant turning point in the Arab–Israeli conflict. Before the 2001 election, Sharon had made a high-profile visit to the Temple Mount in Jerusalem during September 2000, sparking an eruption of violence by Palestinians, who protested his visit to the site. Temple Mount has several Jewish religious shrines and also houses the Al-Aqsa Mosque, one of Islam's holiest shrines. Sharon's visit was widely seen as an indication that, if elected, he would support the removal of the Palestinian administration over the complex.

Sharon's visit to the Temple Mount was also viewed by many as a bid to gain the support of conservative Israeli voters in his campaign to become prime minister. Instability and violence resulted from this incident. A mounting cycle of conflict between Israel and the Palestinians came to be known as Intifada II. Sharon's visit to Temple Mount was the event that sparked the second intifada. The second intifada, in turn, propelled Sharon to victory in the election based on his platform of increased security and a tougher line toward the Palestinians.[31] Following the election of George W. Bush as president of the United States in 2000, the United States at first adopted a hands-off approach to the Arab–Israeli issue—largely in reaction to the experience of the Clinton administration, which was widely viewed by Republicans as having overreached its responsibility in the Camp David talks the previous summer.

Throughout 2001–02, the conflict intensified. The progress and goodwill generated by the 1990's Oslo peace process unraveled in the midst of increasing bloodshed caused by both sides. Palestinian groups—some controlled by Yasser Arafat's Palestinian Authority and others that were not, such as Hamas and Islamic Jihad—began targeting civilians in Israel proper—instead of military targets in the occupied West Bank and Gaza Strip. As attacks by suicide bombers against Israeli buses, malls, and cafes began to escalate, the Israeli government's reaction under Sharon became increasingly harsh and similarly indiscriminate. Israel began a campaign of targeting the infrastructure and offices of the Palestinian Authority, as well as those of suspected terrorist groups, and employed the full force of its military including tanks, jets, and helicopter gunships in civilian areas.

In March 2002, Sharon ordered Arafat's isolation. The Palestinian leader was not allowed to travel outside the town of Ramallah on the West Bank, where the Palestinian Authority headquarters are located. By April 2002, Sharon had declared Arafat an enemy of the Israeli people. Israeli forces laid siege to the Palestinian Authority compound itself as part of Operation Defensive Wall, a massive deployment of forces to the West Bank and Gaza Strip. This operation involved the largest call-up of Israeli forces since the 1982 invasion of Lebanon, it included more than twenty thousand troops, raising tensions in the region to the brink of war. A new peace proposal advanced by the Saudi crown prince at about this same time—a proposal offering peace between all Arab nations and Israel in exchange for an end to Israeli control of all of the Occupied Territories—was given almost no serious attention due to the widespread chaos and violence.

POSTSCRIPT: SEPTEMBER 11, 2001, AND ITS AFTERMATH

U.S. foreign policy was transformed by the events of September 11, 2001. On that morning, four airliners were hijacked by members of the Al-Qaida terrorist organization led by Osama bin Laden, son of a wealthy Saudi Arabian family. In the 1990s, Al-Qaida ("The Base") had grown into a worldwide network of organized cells, supported by bin Laden's personal wealth and donations from sympathizers in Muslim countries. Al-Qaida was dedicated to forcing changes in U.S. policy, deposing its client regimes in the Middle East, and forcing the withdrawal of U.S. forces from the region. A synchronized attack resulted in the deaths of more than three thousand people from more than sixty countries. Two airliners were piloted by the hijackers into the World Trade Center towers in New York, and a third was flown into the Pentagon. In the days and weeks immediately following these horrific events, the Bush administration reacted with a clear and forceful response: terrorism, in all its forms—but in particular the extremist Islamic, anti-American version nurtured by bin Laden and his allies—would henceforth be the main target of U.S. foreign policy. America would actively seek out its supporters and eliminate them. No longer would the United States look the other way as states, groups, or even individuals such as bin Laden fostered extreme anti-American sentiments and gathered the resources to accomplish their goals.

The Bush administration's response came swiftly once the evidence pointed toward bin Laden. Since the early 1990s, the Clinton administration had been closely monitoring Al-Qaida and bin Laden, following a string of terrorist attacks on U.S. citizens and assets. These included the 1993 bombing of the World Trade Center, bombings on the U.S. embassies in Tanzania and Kenya in 1996, and an attack upon the destroyer U.S.S. *Cole* in Yemen during 2000. The United States intelligence community and military was therefore well aware of the close links established between bin Laden and the Taliban regime in Afghanistan, which had taken over control of most of that country following an internal power struggle after the withdrawal of Soviet forces in the early 1990s. During their resistance to the Soviet occupation of Afghanistan in the 1980s, the Taliban had also received significant assistance from the United States via the CIA, as well as from the Pakistani Inter-Services Intelligence (ISI) agency. Once the war against the Soviets ended, however, the United States largely withdrew its assistance, whereas the Pakistani government continued it in a bid to have a friendly regime on its northern border.

The Taliban, led by Mullah Mohammad Omar, was a grouping comprised largely of ethnic Pashtuns. The Taliban favored a strict and highly conservative interpretation of Sunni Islam, the dominant branch of the religion.[32] Indeed, the word *Taliban* is derived from the Arabic word *taleb*, or student, reflecting the heavy influence of the religious schools in Pakistan and southern Afghanistan where their power base originated. Since the late 1990s, Mullah Omar had accepted bin Laden and Al-Qaida into Taliban-controlled areas in Afghanistan and provided them with shelter and support. The Taliban's domestic opposition, known as the Northern Alliance, was supported by Iran and Russia, but controlled only ten percent of the country prior to September 11. Once the links between Al-Qaida and the September 11 attacks became clear, the Bush administration focused on three main goals: (1) convincing the Taliban to turn over bin Laden and his Al-Qaida forces, (2) waging a campaign to overthrow the Taliban regime and take custody of bin Laden and his supporters if the Taliban proved uncooperative, and (3) engaging in a global campaign to eradicate the bases of support for Al-Qaida around the world. The Taliban rejected all U.S. requests for the extradition of bin Laden and expulsion of Al-Qaida from Afghanistan following September 11. As a result, in October 2001 the United States began a military campaign entitled Operation Enduring Freedom designed to overthrow the Taliban regime and dismantle the supportive infrastructure that Al-Qaida had established there over the years. The campaign consisted of three main elements: direct military and political support to the opposition (non-Pashtun) Northern Alliance and other anti-Taliban forces in Afghanistan; the use of U.S. air power to complement their attacks on the Taliban; and the selective deployment of U.S. intelligence agents and special forces to work with the Northern Alliance forces on the ground.

Conventional military success was remarkably quick. By December 2001, the Taliban had been driven from urban strongholds such as Mazar-i-Sharif,

Kabul (the capital city), and their original power base in Kandahar. With assistance from Afghan allies and an international coalition, the United States then shifted its focus to defeating the remaining organized Taliban resistance—based in cave and tunnel complexes located in the rugged terrain of Afghanistan's southeastern mountains. By January 2002, due to a massive bombing campaign and subsequent ground assault, the Taliban had been militarily defeated and driven from power. A coalition government comprised of the Northern Alliance and other opposition groups—headed by interim leader Hamid Karzai, (an anti-Taliban Pashtun leader)—was installed in Afghanistan with U.S. and international support. Nevertheless, periodic fighting persisted in the southern and eastern mountainous regions bordering Pakistan. At the time of this writing, sporadic fighting continued in those areas, and the Taliban and Al-Qaida leadership remained at large.

Nevertheless, the military objectives of the United States had largely been met by April 2002, but this success in Afghanistan has only led to larger questions regarding the strategic direction and consequences of U.S. foreign policy after September 11, in particular in the Middle Eastern region.

In response to the rapidly deteriorating situation between Israel and the Palestinians and the potential implications for the larger U.S. war on terrorism, the second Bush administration was forced to adopt a more hands-on role in mediating the Israeli–Palestinian conflict. The more hawkish elements in the Bush administration began to press for immediate action against Iraq following the defeat of the Taliban. However, it became abundantly clear that the Arab world—whose support or acquiescence for such action was required —would not support the United States against Iraq unless the Arab–Israeli conflict was resolved. In January 2002, President Bush used his state of the union speech to identify Iran, Iraq, and North Korea as an "axis of evil" that posed the greatest single long-term threat to U.S. security. Although the axis of evil comment attracted near unanimous criticism from the rest of the world (including U.S. allies), the Bush administration insisted that the U.S. campaign obligated it to put state sponsors of terrorism on notice. Bush argued that these three rogue states had made significant progress in developing WMD along with the means to deliver them, such as long-range missiles. The most immediate concern to the United States was Iraq, where the regime of Hussein continued to defy U.S. efforts to isolate it.

As a result of these factors, by the spring of 2002—despite the Bush administration's initial reluctance to do so—the United States was deeply involved in mediating the Arab–Israeli conflict while simultaneously engaging in a global war on terrorism. In the midst of Intifada II, President Bush sent Secretary of State Colin Powell to the region in April 2002 in response to Israel's launching of Operation Defensive Wall, which threatened to widen the war dramatically and destabilize the entire region. The administration hoped that it could build on the Saudi proposal for peace: the complete withdrawal of Israeli forces and settlements from the West Bank and Gaza Strip in return for full recognition by the Arab world and normalized relations. The United States could then turn its attention to dealing with Hussein in its next step in its war against terrorism. However, it became increasingly clear that Arab leaders were not willing to co-operate with the United States until the Israeli–Palestinian conflict was re-solved—in particular, the Israeli reoccupation of much of the West Bank and Gaza Strip.

As this book was going to press, Bush advanced a new peace proposal for the Arab–Israeli conflict. The Bush plan requires the Palestinian Authority to replace Arafat with a new leadership, draft a new constitution with broader democratic elements, end all terrorism (especially suicide bombings) against Israel, and adopt more transparent and more accountable financial practices. In return for these massive reforms, the United States would advocate a "pro-visional" Palestinian state that would be replaced (after several years) by a permanent, independent Palestinian state.[33] The Bush plan also called on Is-rael to withdraw from territories occupied during its most recent attacks on Arafat and the Palestinian Authority, lift the ban against movement by Pales-tinian civilians in and out of the Occupied Territories, cease all building of settlements within the Occupied Territories, negotiate the status of Jerusalem and the right of return for Palestinian refugees, and ultimately pull all of its troops back to the dividing lines that existed before the 1967 Six-Day War.[34]

U.S. POLICY AND STRATEGY
IN THE MIDDLE EAST TODAY

The Middle East was a region of the world that had been formally declared to be vital to U.S. national security interests even prior to the events of Septem-ber 11. By the late 1990s, it was viewed as a critical theater that required a "sub-stantial, capable, and ready military force in the Persian Gulf region."[35] Following September 11 and the deterioration of Palestinian–Israeli relations, this perspective on the region has only been reinforced, but the overall evol-ution is fully consistent with the evolution of U.S. policy since the Carter Doc-trine. Following steady cuts in U.S. military spending from $368 billion in 1990 to $262.3 billion in 1997, the second Bush administration dramatically increased defense spending following the terrorist attacks of September 2001 to $396 billion for FY2003.[36] Although some argue that these levels are inade-quate given the campaign against terrorism, current U.S. spending is still twenty-six times that of the top seven countries regularly identified as its prin-ciple threats, and the U.S. military budget exceeds the total defense spending of the next twenty-five countries combined. President George W. Bush also maintained the policy of (renewed) direct military pressure on Iraq that was established by Clinton in 1998.

Hussein declared in late 1998 that he would allow no more UN weapons inspections inside Iraq, a direct violation of the terms of peace imposed on his regime by the Security Council after the second Gulf War. He also declared in early 1999 that Iraq would no longer recognize the no-fly zones. President

Clinton responded with regular air strikes against Iraq for the remainder of his administration. Those weekly air strikes continued into the second Bush administration. George W. Bush's first use of military force was his order to attack Iraqi air defenses outside of the no-fly zones (near Baghdad) in early 2001. These frequent military confrontations continued on a regular basis, culminating with the war of "Operation Iraqi Freedom" to overthrow Saddam Hussein in 2003.

U.S. Policy in the Middle East and the End of the Cold War

The fall of the USSR had important consequences—in addition to the removal of the Soviet threat and the end of assistance to its client states—the salience of which emerged with dramatic clarity after September 11. One such consequence has been the increased importance of Islamic fundamentalist political movements across the region. The United States claims that states such as Iran are the principal sponsors of such movements. Yet, there is much evidence to suggest that in Egypt (the Muslim Brotherhood), Lebanon (Hezbollah), the Occupied Territories (Hamas, Islamic Jihad), Afghanistan (the Taliban), and Turkey (the Virtue Party), domestic social and political unrest is providing the necessary conditions for their growth. As a non-Arab country with limited economic means, Iran's influence in the Arab world is significantly less than is generally assumed in the United States. Iranians are also staunch adherents to the Shi'a minority branch of Islam—a fact that also prevents Iran from exercising any significant form of leadership over most Islamist political movements in the region. Clearly, the revival of Islamic political activism is a phenomenon that surpasses Iran's capability to nurture and control; U.S. policy must come to grips with that reality. It must also develop practical options that can be used in the event that another U.S. ally, such as Egypt or Saudi Arabia, is plunged into a revolution similar to Iran's in 1979.

A second consequence of the end of the superpower competition has been the proliferation of WMD and conventional arms throughout the Middle East. Iran, Israel, and Syria are developing deadly arsenals in their bid to enhance security and deter aggressors. Much of the proliferation within these states since 1991 has been facilitated by greater access to Russian scientific and technical know-how after the fall of the USSR. At the same time, their shared and enduring sense of insecurity is perhaps the most important impetus of their weapons programs. Such instability would be best resolved through an inclusive regional security system. However, the United States continues to be the largest provider of arms to the region. U.S. policy also continues to give preferential treatment to Israel, the only regional state that possesses nuclear weapons, by not pressuring it to join international regulatory regimes such as the nuclear Nonproliferation Treaty (NPT).

A third consequence has been the independence of the eight former Soviet Republics (FSRs) of Transcaucasia and Central Asia.[37] Historically, these areas were well-integrated parts of Middle Eastern affairs. Today, given their century-long separation from the Middle East during Soviet control, a re-creation of historical ties between the FSRs and the Middle East would not be welcomed by the West. This problem is particularly acute in Washington, because the United States emerged as a global power at a time when the separation of the FSRs from the Middle East was already complete. The importance of the FSRs for U.S. policy in the Middle East is reflected, for example, in their direct role for circumventing U.S. efforts to isolate Iran by establishing good relations with the latter. It is also reflected in a historical, but potentially disruptive, rivalry between Iran, Turkey, and Russia for dominance over the FSRs that has colored much of the interaction between these three key states since 1991. For its part, the United States has supported its NATO ally, Turkey, in this triangular competition. However, the larger context of regional reintegration that is clearly underway has not effectively been addressed by the United States. The most notable exception has been efforts to extend the dual containment policy regarding Iran to the Caspian Sea region. Since 1995, the United States has been attempting to discourage the FSRs from establishing normal relations with Iran. These efforts have met with little success to date, mainly due to the fact that the FSRs need good relations with Iran to fend off Russia's efforts to restore its control over them. The fact that U.S. policy has not integrated this basic regional dynamic is reflective of the degree to which American decision makers remain mired in the legacy of the Cold War.

The maintenance of U.S. interests in the Middle East in the twenty-first century requires more than the mere recycling of obsolete policies, or a headlong rush into an open-ended military campaign against Islamic extremists all around the world (with little attention paid to the pernicious consequences of such a campaign). Yet, the fundamental premises of current U.S. policy in the Persian Gulf remain the Carter Doctrine and dual containment. That policy was crafted over a twenty year period and designed to counter threats that no longer exist—in a region that is no longer the same. What has taken place since 1991 is nothing less than a tectonic shift in international and regional dynamics that has made many of the assumptions upon which U.S. policy rested effectively out-of-date. This is especially true in regard to the Middle East. The United States, as the dominant global and regional power, must respond to these changes appropriately in order to protect its interests in this new and different environment. It must craft a Middle Eastern policy for the new millennium that demonstrates a proactive commitment to constructive leadership, given its longstanding regional interests. Understanding the evolution of U.S. policy, and the forces that have shaped it, is the first step of that process.

Chapter 5

U.S. INTERVENTION POLICY AFTER THE COLD WAR

Robert DiPrizio

INTRODUCTION

To what end and for which goals should a major power use its political-military influence in international relations? This is a perennial question powerful states face. After World War II, the United States focused its efforts on containing the global influence of the Soviet Union (USSR). In so doing, it often faced the possibility of direct, cataclysmic conflict with the USSR. In the post–Cold War era, however, the United States is largely free to intervene where it chooses and without fears of provoking a global war. Determining where and when to employ military force in the post–Cold War era has become one of the most vexing issues in American foreign policy.

The first major use of American military force after the Cold War was in the 1991 Gulf War. In that case, traditional national security interests (stability of a geostrategic region) were clearly at risk. But since then, U.S. military operations have more often than not been in response to humanitarian crises. In the past, traditional civilian relief organizations were capable of responding effectively to humanitarian crises around the world. Unfortunately, more recent humanitarian crises have tended to result from violent internal conflicts and civil wars. Such conflicts produce environments that are so unstable and so violent that private relief organizations are unable to operate effectively. Humanitarian nongovernmental organizations (NGOs) are unable to reach their target populations—either because the victims are too remote or because warring factions prohibit access. Moreover, diplomatic efforts have consistently failed to resolve the underlying causes for conflicts that spawn humanitarian emergencies. Under such circumstances, it is not surprising that many see military forces as the only actors capable of responding quickly and forcefully enough to ensure the delivery of aid or to put a stop to the violence. With no end in sight to the emergence of humanitarian crises that cry out for international attention, the United States will have many opportunities and face many pressures to intervene in the future.

THE WEINBERGER-POWELL DOCTRINE AND PDD25

U.S. policy toward humanitarian interventions has developed in stages. During the Reagan-Bush era, the Weinberger Doctrine was supposed to guide U.S. decisions on the use of military force. This doctrine was first announced by Secretary of Defense Casper Weinberger in 1984. It set forth six "tests" for guiding when and how the United States would commit combat troops in the future: (1) vital national interests must be at stake, (2) overwhelming force must be employed to ensure victory, (3) political and military objectives must be clearly defined, (4) force structures and dispositions must be adjusted as events on the ground dictate, (5) there must be "some reasonable assurance" of public and Congressional support, and (6) force must be the last resort. Years later, Chairman of the Joint Chiefs of Staff General Colin Powell, who once served as Weinberger's military advisor, reiterated the main themes of the doctrine by emphasizing the need for an "exit strategy." This policy has since become known as the Weinberger-Powell Doctrine (W-P). Clearly, the aim of the doctrine was to restrict U.S. interventions in the future and, until the end of the 1991 Gulf War, it seemed to have the desired effect.

Since the 1991 Gulf War, the United States has faced many complex emergencies that have not threatened vital national interests and that were not amenable to the type of overwhelming use of force envisioned by the W-P. Although George Bush refused to intervene in Bosnia and Haiti (ostensibly because U.S. vital interests were not at stake), he did order interventions into northern Iraq and Somalia—neither of which clearly met all the conditions of the W-P doctrine.

Bush left office soon after he ordered the intervention into Somalia, leaving President Clinton to devise new policies that could manage the challenges of humanitarian intervention. As soon as he took power, Clinton ordered his staff to carry out a comprehensive review of U.S. peace operations and to create new policy guidelines for future interventions. Initially, it was expected that these new guidelines would reflect Clinton's "assertive multilateralism"—a phrase meant to capture the new administration's strong support for, and participation in, increased UN operations. But as the policy-making process proceeded, Congress grew increasingly uncomfortable with peace operations in general and with the Somalia intervention in particular. When eighteen U.S. soldiers died in a 1993 ambush in Mogadishu, Congressional opinion soured on U.S. participation in such operations. Clinton, always primarily concerned with domestic politics, grew increasingly weary of risking his domestic political capital on this issue. When Presidential Decision Directive 25 (PDD25) was finally completed, it turned out to be a public retreat from "assertive multilateralism." (See annex 1.) The new guidelines placed so many contingencies on U.S. participation in UN peace operations that it was clearly an attempt to reduce, not increase, U.S. involvement in international peace operations. (See the following discussion of Rwanda for more details on PDD25.) PDD25 seems to have been more of a politically expedient sop to Congress than it was an articulation of the principles that would truly guide Clinton's humanitarian intervention decisions. PDD25 was cited as the rationale for keeping the United States out of Rwanda. However, the Clinton administration's later interventions in Haiti, Bosnia, and Kosovo are equally difficult to justify if one follows PDD25 criteria.

In short, neither W-P nor PDD25 tell us much about the true motivations for U.S. humanitarian intervention in the post–Cold War era. Although there are substantial differences between the two doctrines, both are open to wide-ranging interpretations of whether or not national interests are at stake, if a proposed operation has clear objectives, if an acceptable exit strategy exists, or if popular support can be ensured. Moreover, a close look at each of six cases—northern Iraq, Somalia, Rwanda, Haiti, Bosnia, and Kosovo—will show that the factors driving American intervention are not easily accounted for by either W-P or PDD25. The remainder of this chapter will review how and why President George Bush and the Clinton administration responded to all six humanitarian crises.

NORTHERN IRAQ

U.S.-led intervention into northern Iraq, known as Operation Provide Comfort (OPC), sparked the greatest amount of debate over armed humanitarian intervention. For some, OPC offered much optimism for a "new world order" in which humanitarian issues would be a central concern of international relations. Many saw OPC as a precedent for similar interventions in the future, although the Somalia operation would soon temper such enthusiasm. By most accounts, OPC was a great success. In just three months, more than twenty thousand U.S. and allied soldiers entered western Turkey and northern Iraq, providing emergency aid and repatriating nearly a million Iraqi Kurdish refugees. But unlike the 1991 Gulf War, President Bush was initially hesitant to intervene in northern Iraq.

The first Bush administration decided to end the Gulf War on February 28, 1991, without completely destroying Iraq's military capability or removing Saddam Hussein from power. To do either would have unnecessarily risked the lives of coalition soldiers and split the coalition against Hussein. Moreover, overthrowing Hussein would have required either a U.S. occupation of Iraq or Iraq's dismemberment. The latter option would have left no local counterweight to America's other regional threat—Iran. President Bush and his advisors were also concerned with the "undesirable public and political baggage with all those scenes of carnage."[1] Still, Bush wanted Hussein removed from power and made a number of public calls in the 1990s for the Iraqi people to overthrow him.[2] The preferred method was a military coup, which was more likely to leave in power a strong government capable of keeping the country together. But in the weeks that followed, the only evident threats to Hussein's position were uprisings by Shiite Muslims in southern Iraq and Kurds in the north.

Despite verbally encouraging rebellion, Bush was resolute not to offer any tangible assistance. He was determined to excise the ghost of Vietnam from the American psyche with an unambiguous victory in the Gulf. He wanted a "clean end" to his war. He was determined to bring U.S. soldiers back home as soon as possible.[3] Bush was not going to taint America's overwhelming victory by getting involved in a civil conflict that could lead to a "Vietnam-style quagmire." Furthermore, the first Bush administration never really wanted the rebels to succeed, for this could lead to Iraq's disintegration and regional instability. Encouraging Kurdish separatism in northern Iraq might promote similar efforts among Kurds in Turkey, Syria, and Iran. The administration would then be in the awkward position of being forced to choose between support for regional stability or support for the self-determination of an oppressed minority. Regional stability was of the utmost importance to Bush, and anything likely to threaten that stability had to be avoided.

In the first weeks of March 1991, Kurdish guerrillas (or *peshmerga*) rebelled against Hussein's authority in northern Iraq and secured control of much of the region. Although much of Hussein's army was devastated during the Gulf War, he was able to reconstitute his vaunted Republican Guard. The rifles and pistols of the *peshmerga* proved to be no match for the tanks, artillery, and helicopter gunships of the Guard. As Iraqi troops retook the region, some two million Kurds fled toward Turkey and Iran. Most of those that fled eastward found asylum in Iran. Turkey, however, was reluctant to accept the refugees because it was struggling to control its own Kurdish minority. By April 9, the UN estimated nearly three hundred thousand Kurds made it into Turkey, whereas just as many were stranded in the snow-covered mountain region after the Turkish government closed off its border. Food, shelter, health care, and security became problematic. A humanitarian disaster loomed. Media coverage brought the plight of the Kurds to the attention of the West, while Turkey and Iran lobbied the international community for assistance.[4]

By this time, the weak Kurdish uprising was no longer a threat to regional stability: the Kurdish rebellion had been routed. The resulting humanitarian crises demanded the attention of those Western powers that had encouraged the Kurds, especially the United States. Maintaining a hands-off policy in the face of such massive human misery was morally and politically untenable. The administration emphasized the humanitarian motivation when it decided to launch OPC. The scope, methods, and duration of the operation that followed matched its humanitarian rhetoric.

But humanitarian concerns alone did not drive Bush's policy. The single most important motivating factor was the administration's concern for Turkey's well-being. A longtime American ally and NATO member, Turkey, lies at the crossroads of Europe and the Middle East. As such it is well positioned to influence events in the entire region. From an American point of view, Turkey serves as a counterweight to anti-Israeli, Russian, Iraqi, and Iranian influences in the area. During the 1991 Gulf War, Turkey allowed the United States to fly thousands of sorties from its air base in Incirlik, even though leaders feared retaliation from Iraq. Moreover, in support of the UN embargo against Iraq, Turkey cut off oil flows from Iraq costing Turkey an estimated $9 billion in oil revenues.[5]

The massive Kurdish exodus posed a humanitarian challenge that Turkey was incapable of managing alone. It also presented Turkey with a potential security threat. Fighting against its own Kurdish uprising for many years, and still caring for upwards of thirty thousand Iraqi Kurds who were victims of Husseins 1988 gassing campaign,[6] the Turkish government had no interest in hosting another million refugees. The immediate humanitarian needs of the Kurds had to be met without delay, but they also had to be repatriated as soon as possible.

President Bush shared these concerns. During the Kurdish uprising in Iraq, the administration repeatedly justified its refusal to offer material support by arguing that a Kurdish victory would lead to a number of destabilizing effects, including Kurdish secessionist movements in Turkey. It comes as no surprise then that the Bush administration was also concerned with the destabilizing effects of a massive influx of Iraqi Kurds into Turkish Kurdistan.[7] As one observer bluntly put it, "Keeping Iraqi Kurds in Iraq was the biggest reason America joined the fray."[8] When Iraqi Kurds began trekking to the Turkish border in April 1991, Turkey requested international assistance to stem the flow. Turkey's President Ozal made public calls for help. He appealed directly to President Bush. Obviously, assisting a loyal and important ally when possible is good diplomacy.

International pressure to address the growing humanitarian crisis in northern Iraq and eastern Turkey came also from America's closest allies, most notably Britain and France. The irony of President Bush's hesitant response to the growing humanitarian crisis so soon after his "finest hour" during the Gulf War prompted one commentator to write, "Six month ago, it was the United States that was trying to lead France, Turkey, the Germans, and a number of others who ultimately began to make up the Coalition, into a moral crusade. And now, curiously enough, it is those self-same countries that seem to be in a position of trying to lead a reluctant United States."[9]

Humanitarian concerns, geostrategic interests, and international pressure convinced Bush to act. On April 5, the UN Security Council passed Resolution 688, which called upon Iraq to cease its attacks on the Kurds and to allow humanitarian relief actors immediate access. The Security Council also appealed to member states and international aid organizations to contribute to the needed relief effort. On the same day, President Bush ordered the U.S. military to begin immediate airdrops of aid to Kurdish refugees in the Turkey-Iraq border regions. Britain, France, Germany, Spain, and Italy joined in the effort, and OPC was soon underway.

This U.S.-led multinational operation of nearly twenty-two thousand soldiers quickly responded to the growing humanitarian crises.[10] Beginning with airdrops of emergency food aid on April 7, 1991, military personnel (in coordination with a few civilian humanitarian relief organizations) fed, sheltered, treated, and protected the Kurdish refugees. Food and medical aid was flown in from around the world to makeshift camps that had developed along the Turkey-Iraq border. By mid-April, coalition relief efforts managed to stabilize conditions in the mountains, but the overall situation was still precarious. Aid deliveries to the mountain camps were cumbersome, inefficient, and could not be maintained indefinitely. It was apparent that the refugees would have to be coaxed out of the mountains and into more serviceable camps.

Turkey did not relish the thought of hosting hundreds of thousands of Iraqi Kurds in refugee camps that could become semipermanent. And the Kurds understandably considered returning home unsafe so long as Hussein's troops controlled the region. Turkey President Ozal first suggested the possibility of establishing "safe havens" inside Iraq for the Kurds so they could return home. British Prime Minister John Major picked up on the idea, which was quickly supported by his European Union (EU) colleagues. The Bush administration initially resisted, fearing a "Vietnam-style quagmire" and Iraq's disintegration. But as the logic of the situation on the ground became clear, and as he faced continued pressure by his counterparts in Europe and Turkey, Bush relented. On April 16, 1991, the president announced U.S. forces, along with allied troops, would enter northern Iraq and set up refugee camps: "I am announcing an expanded, a greatly expanded and more ambitious relief effort. This approach is quite simple: if we cannot get adequate food, medicine, clothing, and shelter to the Kurds living in the mountains along the Turkish-Iraqi border, we must encourage the Kurds to move to areas in northern Iraq where the geography facilitates, rather than frustrates, such a large-scale relief effort."[11]

The first troops entered northern Iraq on April 19, and in a matter of weeks the security zone stretched thirty miles into Iraq covering much of Iraqi Kurdistan. A no-fly zone that stretched from the 36th parallel to the north provided a greater measure of protection for the Kurds than OPC ground troops alone could guarantee. As OPC soldiers crept into the region, they gave Iraqi forces fair warning—retreat or be forced out. Usually a verbal warning was enough. But on occasion, when Iraqi troops would hesitate, American forces would rattle their sabers and the Yankee-shy Iraqis would flee. In the end, OPC faced no armed resistance.

As OPC troops cleansed the region of Iraqi troops, they also built transition camps to facilitate the repatriation of the Kurdish refugees. Once convinced it was safe to come back, the vast majority of Kurds came down from the mountains and returned to their homes. By early June, responsibility for the transition camps was transferred to the UN, the mountain camps were almost emptied, and OPC forces began pulling out. By July 15, 1991, all allied forces withdrew, save a small contingent of U.S. officers in Turkey monitoring Iraqi actions and a few hundred lightly armed UN guards backed up by a rapid re-action standby force stationed in Turkey. The no-fly zone in northern Iraq was enforced by allied planes flying out of Turkey until 2003.

SOMALIA

Nearly a year after the success of OPC in northern Iraq, and just after his loss in the 1992 elections, lame-duck President Bush initiated an armed interven-tion into Somalia. His expressed purpose was the delivery of humanitarian aid. America's Operation Restore Hope joined with a multinational force to create the United Task Force (or UNITAF). Humanitarian intervention into Somalia succeeded in meeting its stated objectives in a short period of time and with minimal loss of life. Its "success," however, was largely overshadowed by subsequent events. The second UN Operation in Somalia (UNISOM II) followed UNITAF. It was charged with a vastly more ambitious mission but was afforded far fewer capabilities. UNISOM II has come to be seen by most as a failure, unfairly tainting subsequent humanitarian relief efforts that took place in the face of complex emergencies. Although blame for the "failure" of UNISOM II is shared by many, the U.S. decision to limit UNITAF's mission had much to do with it. The United States participated in UNISOM II, though its vastly reduced troop contributions were limited to logistical support and a small quick reaction force which, contrary to popular belief, was under U.S., not UN, operational control. In any event, our primary concern in this dis-cussion is UNITAF.

In 1991, Somalia was in the throes of a civil war. Siad Barre, the longtime dictator of Somalia, was forced from power by a "coalition" of clan-based op-position forces in January. Soon, the factions began fighting amongst them-selves to fill the power vacuum. The fighting killed tens of thousands, forced hundreds of thousands of people from their homes, and disrupted political, economic, and social structures to such an extent that one could rightfully de-scribe Somalia in the 1990s as a "failed state." The combination of internecine fighting and an ongoing drought created a famine (especially in the southern parts of the country), which in turn contributed to the creation of a massive humanitarian crisis.

With continuous warfare for six months, the entire agricultural system was destroyed: from the fields themselves to the production, distribution, and market systems. A million people were displaced during this period, seeking refuge in Kenya, Ethiopia, and Somalia's major cities. The capital, Mogadishu, became separated between the forces of Ali Mahdi Mohamed in the north and General Mohammed Farah Aidid in the south. From November 1991 to

March 1992, it is estimated that fighting between these two camps led to the deaths of fifty thousand noncombatants and "nearly completed the destruction of the city."[12]

As clans warred with each other and famine grew, food became scarce. With no state apparatus to speak of, the Somali people were left to their own devices to manage the growing crisis. Unfortunately, their normal coping strategies for dealing with food scarcity were insufficient, and civilian international relief efforts were largely ineffective.[13] The anarchy that spread throughout Somalia led to an insecure environment for humanitarian relief organizations (HROs). "With the growth of the famine, whoever had food had power. With no economy to speak of and an environment where one had to carry a gun for both survival and income, the looting and/or extortion of NGO shipments of food became routine."[14] Relief agents resorted to hiring armed Somali gunmen for protection. Still, large quantities of aid were looted or diverted. HROs were thus faced with a moral dilemma: "accept 50% food losses and the fact that the food itself, if not the hiring of gunmen, was exacerbating the situation or continue to feed the needy."[15] Many HROs deemed the region too dangerous, but others stayed. By the fall of 1992, some were calling for greater involvement on the part of the United States and UN to ensure aid deliveries.

Despite UN diplomatic and humanitarian efforts throughout 1991–92, the situation continued to deteriorate. In August 1992, the United States initiated Operation Provide Relief (OPR). Operating out of Mombassa, Kenya, and lasting until mid-December, OPR airlifted some twenty-eight thousand metric tons of aid to southern Somalia, but this also proved insufficient to stem the humanitarian crisis. Without access to safe ground transportation, aid could not get to those most in need. At the time, however, there was little interest among Western governments to do more. Secretary General Boutros-Ghali admonished the Security Council, charging that it was concentrating too much on the "rich man's war" in the (white European) Balkans while paying little attention to tragedy in poor (black African) Somalia.[16] Throughout the fall, the secretary general made it known he wanted greater involvement from the United States and held numerous informal talks with midlevel U.S. officials about increased American involvement.[17] There was also significant, but sporadic, media coverage. In mid-November 1992, just days after losing the presidential election to Bill Clinton, President Bush gathered his security team and demanded options for ending the starvation in Somalia. A week later, the president had settled on the most ambitious option presented to him.

As one midlevel administration official wrote, "The authoritative explanation for this US decision to lead a major humanitarian intervention into a failed state where the United States had no important political or strategic interests will probably have to await the publication of George Bush's memoirs or release of his papers. What seems clear is that it was truly his personal decision, based in large measure on his growing feelings of concern as the humanitarian disaster continued to unfold relentlessly despite the half measures being undertaken by the international community."[18] Prior to November 1992, the Bush administration had managed to resist pressures to intervene into Bosnia and Somalia. Bush decided to intervene in Somalia only after he lost his bid for reelection. This suggests that he was not pushed into his decision by political forces. Thus, a lame-duck president under reduced political pressure authorized a massive armed intervention into a country where the United States had no vital national interests for the expressed purpose of feeding people.

On November 25, 1992, President Bush proposed to the UN secretary general a UN-sponsored intervention that would secure the immediate delivery of humanitarian aid. By December 9, U.S. Marines were being broadcast live on CNN as they landed on Somali beaches under the cover of darkness (or, more accurately, the shine of camera lights). Pictures of armed soldiers securing the delivery of aid to starving Somalis soon filled television screens around the world. Operation Provide Relief involved twenty-six thousand U.S. troops, which combined with ten thousand more from twenty other nations to form the multinational coalition known as UNITAF. UNITAF's area of operation covered about 21,000 square miles of southern Somalia. It was authorized by Security Council Resolution 794 (December 3, 1992) to employ "all necessary means to establish as soon as possible a secure environment for humanitarian relief operations in Somalia."

This intervention went through four phases. The first was the initial deployment of forces and the securing of harbor and airport sites around Mogadishu from which the operation could be managed. The second phase was to expand the security zone into the surrounding area of southern Somalia. A permissive environment and encouragement from NGOs enabled UNITAF forces to complete the second phase weeks ahead of schedule. The third phase included a further geographic expansion of operations and the maintenance of secure land routes for the delivery of relief supplies throughout the area of operation (AOR). The final phase was a transition to UN control of the operation and eventual withdrawal of U.S. forces.

In a matter of five months, UNITAF completed its stated objectives and sought to turn the operation over to a reluctant UN. There is little debate over the effectiveness of UNITAF in meeting its goals—the region was secured, which allowed a more effective and efficient delivery of aid by HROs. In addition, UNITAF assisted in delivering aid, promoted coordination with and among the NGOs, and built or improved Somali infrastructure including schools, roads, bridges, airports, harbor facilities, and sanitation. UNITAF even assisted in restoring the justice system. It began recruiting and training a local police force and carried out limited disarming efforts. Though there is debate over how many people were actually saved or how much suffering was actually alleviated, most believe the intervention saved hundreds of thousands of lives. Moreover, the initial operation experienced few fatalities—seventeen

UNITAF soldiers (including eight Americans) and about 100 Somalis died. Estimates are that UNITAF operations cost upward of $2 billion.[19]

Thus, UNITAF is properly viewed as a successful short-term humanitarian intervention. Its success, however, was in no small part a function of its limited scope. The American decision to limit UNITAF's operational objectives to the protection of HROs allowed it to avoid tackling the more complicated issues of conflict resolution and nation building. As early as December 8, 1992, Secretary General Boutros-Ghali insisted that UNITAF expand its mandate to help ensure the success of a UN follow-up mission. Among other things, the secretary general wanted UNITAF to extend its operations across all of Somalia (not just the southern part), help establish a cease-fire, create and train a new national police force, and most importantly, take control of all heavy weapons and disarm the warring factions. The UN, he argued, was not experienced with, or equipped for, peacemaking operations. The UN might be able to carry out a peacekeeping mission and humanitarian effort in combination with reconciliation and reconstruction efforts, but only in a permissive environment.

American policy makers refused to engage in extensive disarmament of the Somali factions, though the United States did try to control weapons within its AOR. UNITAF also confiscated some light arms and ammunition, but it refused to attempt a general disarmament, which most experts and practitioners saw "as essential, not peripheral, to the realization of the objective [the creation and maintenance of a secure environment]."[20]

Despite continued controversy, UNITAF refused to act on the secretary general's more ambitious requests. After some foot dragging on the UN's part in planning for the follow-up mission, UNISOM II officially took over from UNITAF on May 4, 1993. UNISOM II, established by Security Council Resolution 814, was authorized under Chapter VII of the UN Charter. Thus, it could use force to implement its many missions, which included monitoring cease-fires, preventing violence, establishing a secure environment throughout all of Somalia,[21] disarming the Somali clans and cantoning heavy weapons, protecting humanitarian relief agencies, protecting ports and airfields for humanitarian relief deliveries, de-mining, assisting in the repatriation of refugees, and rehabilitating Somalia's politico-economic institutions.[22] It should be noted here that the primary author of Resolution 814 was the United States: "In a virtually unprecedented development for the United Nations, the first drafts of UN Security Council Resolution 794 (December 3, 1993), authorizing UNITAF, and later Security Council Resolution 814 (March 26, 1993), authorizing the expanded mission of UNISOM II, were written in the Pentagon. There were several modifications during Security Council debates on the resolutions, but the essential substance of the resolutions was designed to satisfy the concerns of [the U.S. Central Command]."[23] In short, the United States expanded the UN follow-up mission to include the very actions it refused to accept as part of UNITAF. Moreover, it offered important but insufficient material support to the new UN operation, which would end up a far less capable and far less skilled military force than UNITAF. Thus, the United States pushed the UN to do more with less, thereby courting disaster.

UNISOM II lasted from May 1993 to March 1995 and eventually included twenty thousand troops and eight thousand logistical and civilian staffers from more than twenty-seven countries. The United States contributed 3,000 troops for logistical support, and another 1,200 soldiers from the U.S. quick reaction force, which would operate under U.S., not UN, operational control. Despite promising agreements made in Addis Ababa by the combatants to form a national government, UNISOM II quickly came into conflict with the warlord Mohammed Farah Aidid, who viewed the UN operation as a threat to his political ambitions. On June 5, twenty-four Pakistani soldiers were killed following an inspection of an Aidid radio station. The Security Council responded with Resolution 837 (June 6/7), which called for Aidid's arrest. On June 12, 1993, U.S. forces operating under U.S. tactical command bombed Aidid's headquarters killing dozens (perhaps hundreds) including elders who were discussing possibilities for reconciliation. Aidid was unharmed in the attack. The UN/U.S. manhunt for the warlord led to the disastrous events of October 3, 1993, when eighteen U.S. soldiers and more than 200 Somalis were killed in a daylong firefight between Aidid supporters and American forces.[24] The Clinton administration responded by announcing a withdrawal of troops (phased in over the next six months) and called off the manhunt.[25] By the end of March 1994, all U.S. soldiers were out of Somalia. The UN followed suit a year later.

RWANDA

In mid-1994, Hutu extremists attempted to eradicate the minority Tutsi population in Rwanda. The violence lasted three months and left nearly one million dead. The U.S. response to this genocide was lackluster to say the least. Initially, the United States sought a complete withdrawal of the UN Assistance Mission in Rwanda (UNAMIR) but settled for a reduction in UNAMIR's authorized size from 2,500 to 270. After much foot dragging and under intense international pressure seeking to "shame the council into action,"[26] the United States supported a modest response to the genocide by expanding UNAMIR's mandate and force level, but then impeded its deployment. UNAMIR didn't reach full deployment until six months after the violence began and well after the genocide had ended. Still, the limited UNAMIR forces can be credited with saving tens of thousands of lives and mitigating the suffering of many others.[27] And although Washington "was the primary obstacle"[28] to a more vigorous international response that could have saved hundreds of thousands of lives, the Clinton administration did carry out a two-month humanitarian relief operation that contributed to the post-genocide international aid effort.

The Crisis

During the age of imperialism, the Tutsi ethnic minority in Rwanda collaborated with Belgium's colonial governors and ruled over the Hutu ethnic majority. Following independence from Belgium in 1962, the Hutu majority reversed centuries of Tutsi minority rule. Widespread violence between Hutus and Tutsis followed independence, resulting in the first of many waves of Tutsi refugees streaming into Uganda, Burundi, and Zaire. By 1963, there were more than two hundred thousand Tutsis living in exile. This diaspora became a breeding ground for rebel armies seeking to reverse their fortunes in Rwanda.[29] Periodic ethnic violence in Rwanda (especially in 1963, 1966, 1973, and 1990–93) resulted in many massacres of Tutsis and large outflows of even more refugees. In Uganda alone, the number of Tutsi refugees grew to more than two hundred thousand. It was largely based on this group that the Rwandan Patriot Front (RPF) was founded.

Formed during the 1980s, the RPF sought reintegration into Rwanda, through force if necessary. From its bases in Uganda, it launched an invasion into Rwanda during October 1990. RPF forces quickly advanced to within 20 miles of the capital, Kigali, before they were pushed back by the Rwandan Armed Forces (RAF). Thousands died, famine racked the Rwandan countryside, and large numbers of displaced persons were Hutu extremists who stoked the flames of ethnic tensions. Thousands of Tutsis and moderate Hutus were detained by the authorities in Kigali. Many others were massacred.

Because neither side could achieve a clear victory during the fighting, the Organization of African Unity (OAU) was able to broker a cease-fire between Rwanda's Hutu government and the Tutsi RPF. It was signed on July 12, 1992, in Arusha, Tanzania. A multiphased negotiation process culminated one year later in what became known as the Arusha Accords.[30] The Arusha Accords called for new power-sharing arrangements between Hutus and Tutsis, repatriation of refugees, and the integration of the RPF and RAF. The accords were never implemented, however, due in large part to Hutu extremists that refused to share power with the Tutsis.

On April 6, 1994, while returning from a meeting in Tanzania aimed at salvaging the failing Arusha Accords, a plane carrying the Rwanda's Hutu president was shot down by two ground-to-air rockets. The rockets were launched from territory near the Rwandan airport that was controlled by the Hutu presidential guard. Those responsible for the attack were never identified. Many suspect the Rwandan presidential guard of assassinating their own leader for agreeing to terms with the Tutsis.[31] The downing of the plane triggered civil war and genocide.

Although there had been several massacres in Rwanda since 1959, the scale of the violence between April and July 1994 was unprecedented. Up to one million Tutsis and moderate Hutus were massacred in what was clearly a campaign of genocide.[32] Moreover, the evidence clearly indicates that these efforts were not spontaneous. Just hours after the assassination, "selected and pre-planned murders of Tutsis and moderate Hutus began."[33] The targets of these political murders included the prime minister, the speaker of the national assembly, the president of the supreme court, and leaders of opposition parties.[34] Presidential guards set up roadblocks around Kigali, searching out and killing political opponents and ethnic Tutsis. The orgy of murder centered around Kigali at first but quickly spread to the countryside. A UN commission of experts concluded: "Overwhelming evidence indicates that the extermination of Tutsis by Hutus had been planned months in advance of its actual execution. The mass exterminations of Tutsis were carried out primarily by Hutu elements in a concerted, planned, systematic and methodical way and were motivated out of ethnic hatred. The mass exterminations were clearly 'committed with intent to destroy, in whole or in part, a national, ethnic, racial, or religious group, as such' within the meaning of article II of the Convention on the Prevention and Punishment of the Crime of Genocide."[35]

It is clear that the genocide was organized prior to April 1994 and that its execution depended on the participation of a large portion of the Hutu population. Though elements of the Rwandan Armed Forces participated in the killings, the bulk of the murders were committed by Hutu extremist militias—the *interahamwe* and the *impuzamugambi*. With upwards of fifty thousand members, both groups "did the bidding of government authorities, though without accountability to them."[36] A large number of nonmilitia Hutu civilians participated as well. Much of Rwanda's Hutu population had blood on its hands, making it extremely difficult to ever ensure accountability.[37] Government radio broadcasts spewing anti-Tutsi rhetoric and inciting Hutus spurred on the massacres.[38]

As soon as the killings started in April, the RPF launched another attempt to overthrow the Rwandan government. From its strongholds in northern Rwanda near the Uganda border and around Kigali (secured in the fighting prior to the Arusha Accords), the RPF quickly advanced southward, overrunning government positions with relative ease. By mid-July, the RPF had taken complete control of Rwanda, except for the southwestern region where French forces had set up a safe haven for their Hutu allies and clients. Victorious, the RPF declared a unilateral cease-fire on July 18, 1994, effectively ending the civil war and bringing a halt to the genocide.

U.S. Operation Support Hope

As the RPF conquered more and more territory, millions of Hutus fled to government-controlled areas or to neighboring countries, especially Tanzania and Zaire. At the same time, hundreds of thousands of Tutsis sought refuge in RPF-controlled regions. By September 1994, there were more than two million Rwandan refugees (mostly Hutu) in neighboring countries and nearly two million more internally displaced. Add to these totals the hundreds of thousands of genocide victims, and the result is that more than two-thirds of Rwandan's population had been displaced or murdered. Over a two-day period in late April, upwards of five hundred thousand Rwandans fled into Tanzania. In the wake of the RPF victory in July, even larger numbers of refugees fled Rwanda. More than a million (mostly Hutu) Rwandans fled to Goma, Zaire, during July 14–15.[39]

Following weeks of media coverage of the desperate plight of Rwandan refugees, President Clinton authorized Operation Support Hope (OSH) on July 23, 1994. As part of OSH, 3,000 American troops gave assistance to HROs in the region and provided direct relief to the refugees. OSH activities included water purification and distribution, improving airfields, and managing aid distribution. OSH was conceived and implemented as a strictly humanitarian operation, with no security responsibilities (other than self-defense). It was the largest of the stand-alone operations in response to the Rwandan crisis operating under American command and control, though it did work closely with UN actors. In short, OSH contributed tremendous logistical support to relief actors in the region and provided much needed immediate assistance in Goma and Kigali.

Critics raised objections to OSH in regard to inadequate planning, inappropriate operational strategies, and cost-effectiveness problems. However, OSH was clearly a success in terms of its narrowly defined mission. As Minear and Guillot put it, "The balance sheet on Operation Support Hope is, within its own term of reference, largely positive. It did most of the heavy lifting at a scale and pace well beyond the capabilities of civilian agencies at the time. Supporting UN and NGO aid organizations in Goma and Kigali and also UNAMIR, it made a significant difference in what they were able to accomplish. Its own direct relief activities in Goma were also important, helping to achieve the overall objective of stopping the dying which it shared with others."[40] Still, the operation wasn't initiated until *after* the RPF ended the genocide. The United States took *no* action to stop the genocide while it was occurring. The United States also prevented *other* members of the Security Council from acting to stop the genocide. And OSH had no mandate to carry out any security functions. Thus, enthusiasm for the limited benefits of OSH must be tempered with disgust for the lack of earlier, more forceful intervention during the three months of unparalleled slaughter.

Clinton's Refusal to Stop the Genocide

Soon after the genocide in Rwanda began, the Clinton administration indicated it had no intention to take forceful action to stop the violence.[41] It actively sought the removal of UNAMIR, though it had to settle for a stark reduction in troop size. It also impeded later efforts to initiate more vigorous UN responses. It blocked all attempts to mobilize a response to the genocide by means of the Security Council. In short, the Clinton policy toward Rwanda during the genocide was nonintervention and in this sense was "successful." But why this policy? The official explanation was quite clear: Rwanda was not of sufficient national interest to justify the risks and costs associated with an American or UN intervention. Despite Clinton's prior rhetoric supporting an activist UN and "assertive multilateralism," when the Rwanda crisis struck, his administration simply lacked the political will necessary to risk intervention. Why? The short answer is Somalia.

The Clinton administration came into office advocating increased U.S. participation in international peace operations—what UN Ambassador Madeleine Albright called "assertive multilateralism." Upon taking office, President Clinton ordered a comprehensive review of international peace operations and the U.S. role in them. Although early drafts of what would become PDD25 emphasized the "rapid expansion" of UN peacekeeping operations and a strengthened political, economic, and military commitment by the United States, the final draft was highly restrictive. This was in large part due to events in Somalia and the eighteen U.S. soldiers killed in the 1993 firefight in Mogadishu. The Mogadishu debacle soured executive, congressional, military, and public opinion on humanitarian interventions. Although opposition existed in some of these quarters even prior to the Somalia operation, the killings in Mogadishu galvanized opinion against intervention, thus ensuring America's inaction and sealing Rwanda's fate.

The PDD25 guidelines on U.S. support for peace operations were announced at the height of the Rwandan crisis. They were offered as the explanation for not acting. Each set of guidelines was to be applied in succession, so that an increasing number of conditions had to be met as the United States considered moving from politically supporting a UN mission to actually participating in it to contributing combat troops. PDD25 lays down nineteen preconditions. These conditions required that any operation must be a response to a threat to international peace and security, to serve U.S. interests, and to have an international consensus regarding the proper response. For the United States to participate, an operation would need to have clear objectives, and it must pose "acceptable" risks to U.S. troops. Contributing American combat troops would be considered only if the proposed plan had a sufficient number of troops dedicated to clearly defined goals, if they were prepared to use decisive force, and if the command and control arrangements were acceptable to the United States. (See annex 1.)

In short, the new guidelines placed so many conditions on U.S./UN peace missions (with each condition open to a wide range of interpretations) that it served as a very public retreat from "assertive multilateralism."[42] PDD25 made it clear that peacekeeping operations would not be central to the new administration's policy on the use of force. As National Security Advisor Anthony Lake put it, "Let us be clear: peacekeeping is not at the center of our foreign or defense policy. Our armed forces' primary mission is not to conduct peace operations but to win wars."[43] The many conditions of PDD25 require a cautious approach and, when applied to the Rwanda crisis, they clearly served as an official excuse for America's inaction.

A Clintonian "Apology"

During a tour of Africa in March 1998, President Clinton managed a brief stop in Kigali, Rwanda.[44] In a speech to a crowd that included survivors of the genocide, the president delivered what is widely regarded as an apology:

> The international community, together with nations in Africa, must bear its share of responsibility for this tragedy as well. We did not act quickly enough after the killings began. We should not have allowed the refugee camps to become safe havens for the killers. We did not immediately call these crimes by their rightful name: genocide. . . . It may seem strange to you here, especially the many of you who lost members of your family, but all over the world, there were people like me sitting in offices, day after day after day, who did not fully appreciate the depth and the speed with which you were being engulfed by this unimaginable horror.[45]

Clinton's pseudo-apology implied that he did not act because he did not know what was happening. This was disingenuous. Numerous accounts have documented the plethora of information that officials in Washington were privy to, both before and during the massacres. Early reports from NGOs and the CIA warned of possible widespread violence. The most infamous piece of intelligence ignored by Washington was a fax from the UNAMIR commander, General Dalliere, to the UN Department of Peacekeeping Operations (UNDPO). Based on information supplied by a Hutu militia leader, the fax detailed plans for a coup, for driving out the UN force, and for genocide. The informant claimed to have a hit list and the capacity to kill 1,000 Tutsis in twenty minutes. UNAMIR personnel investigated. After corroborating this evidence, Dalliere requested authorization to seize the weapons that were to be used in the killings. The UNDPO, headed at the time by Kofi Annan, refused his request. Due to U.S. obstruction, the Security Council was bound to block any actions that smacked of disarmament. All of General Dalliere's information was shared with U.S., French, and Belgian officials.[46]

It is difficult to believe that the Clinton administration did not know what was happening during this crisis. As one critic writes, "The truth is not that 'people like' President Clinton failed to act to stop the massacres and 'the international community' merely 'failed to act quickly enough.' The truth is that President Clinton, with full knowledge of what was happening in Rwanda, directed his administration to block repeated attempts by the United Nations to send military force to stop the slaughter."[47]

Aware of the ongoing events in Rwanda, but determined to stay out, the Clinton administration made a conscious effort not to call the killings "genocide." They feared that use of this term would take public opinion in a direction that they did not want it to go. Over the following months, U.S. officials were instructed not to use the word *genocide*. Instead, they were to use only the term "acts of genocide." Attempts at implementing such verbal gymnastics led to some surreal public statements by administration officials,: including this pathetic performance by State Department spokeswoman Christine Shelly during a June 10 briefing:

> REPORTER: How many acts of genocide does it take to make genocide?
> SHELLY: That's just not a question that I'm in a position to answer.
> REPORTER: Well, is it true that you have specific guidance not to use the word "genocide" in isolation, but always to preface it with these words "acts of"?
> SHELLY: I have guidance which I try to use as best as I can. There are formulations that we are using that we are trying to be consistent in our use of. I don't have an absolute categorical prescription [*sic*] against anything, but I have the definitions. I have phraseology which has been carefully examined and arrived at as best as we can apply to exactly the situation and the actions which have taken place.[48]

Having signed the 1948 Convention on the Prevention and Punishment of the Crime of Genocide, the United States is legally obligated to seek to halt and punish genocide whenever and wherever it occurs. To apply the term "genocide" to the violence in Rwanda would have placed increased pressure on the United States (and all signatories of the Convention) to act more forcefully, which Clinton was determined not to do. It was not until the middle of June that the Clinton administration dropped the charade and admitted that what had happened in Rwanda amounted to genocide. But by this time, events had largely run their course. UNAMIR II was on its way, and the RPF would soon halt the genocide by force of arms. A Hutu refugee flow of biblical proportions was soon to capture the international conscience, instantly changing the crisis from politically-difficult-to-respond-to genocide to a more familiar and politically-easy-to-respond-to humanitarian crisis.

Clinton's decision to initiate OSH was a welcome response to the growing humanitarian disaster in the autumn of 1994. But again, any praise must be tempered by the even greater criticism of U.S. inaction during the preceding genocide. It was only after the genocide was ended by the RPF's victory that Clinton sent in the military. As Weiss points out, "There are fewer risks for politicians from humanitarian assistance, however costly and inefficient, than from early preventative action by military forces with possible casualties or the potential for protracted involvement in a civil war."[49]

In any event, the basic facts are inescapable. The U.S. government is the most influential actor on the Security Council and within the international humanitarian relief system. As a signatory to the genocide convention, it was faced with large-scale violence in Rwanda that it knew to be genocide. However, President Clinton chose a policy of nonintervention and obstruction, the Clinton administration concluded that Rwanda was not important enough to risk another debacle like Somalia. Other domestic and international issues were more important to the administration. Rwanda was simply too peripheral and the crisis happened too soon after Somalia. Would the Clinton administration have been more assertive if Somalia had been seen as a success rather than a failure? One can hope. Could the administration have overcome congressional, military, public, and UN reticence to act if it had chosen to lead the charge against genocide? Probably. Did the international community fail miserably to act in the face of genocide? Undoubtedly. Although there is plenty of blame to be shared by the UN Secretariat and Security Council, the Clinton administration must accept a greater share of the responsibility for it has a disproportionate amount of political, economic, and military influence in the UN and in the broader international community. Only the U.S. government could have overcome the numerous obstacles to more forceful engagement. As one disgusted observer put it, "US leaders shamed themselves and degraded the highest ideals of our human race by their inaction during Rwanda's genocide."[50]

HAITI

In December 1990, Jean-Bertrand Aristide was elected president of Haiti in that country's first free and fair democratic election. When he took office in February 1991, Aristide carried with him the hopes and dreams of the majority of Haiti's poor for "an end to decades of abusive authoritarian rule and the beginning of a new era founded on the principles of democracy and social justice."[51] But this optimism was short-lived. Seven months later, Aristide was overthrown by the Haitian military and exiled from the country. The Organization of American States (OAS), the UN, and the United States responded with economic and political sanctions in an effort to reverse the military coup and return Aristide to power. During this period, large waves of Haitians fled to the United States in an effort to escape their desperate political and economic situation. Both the Bush and Clinton administrations struggled to manage the refugee flow. After three years of unsuccessful attempts to reverse the military coup, and with the political and humanitarian situation deteriorating, the Clinton administration opted for a military intervention (with UN authorization) to remove the military regime and return Aristide to power. Hours before the intervention was scheduled to begin, the coup leaders agreed to step down and allow Aristide to return. The U.S.-led multinational force faced no organized resistance when it landed on September 19, 1994. Within a few weeks, Aristide returned to power and all economic and political sanctions were lifted. Although U.S. soldiers were not required to fight or to provide extensive humanitarian services, it was America's belated decision to use its military might that forced an end to the illegal regime in Haiti and allowed for improvement of the humanitarian situation.

The Crisis

When General Raul Cedras led his military forces in a violent overthrow of the newly elected government of Haiti in September 1991, President Aristide fled to the United States where he would spend the next three years campaigning for international assistance to return him to power. The coup led to widespread political repression, unprecedented human rights violations, large numbers of internally and externally displaced persons, and economic sanctions that made conditions worse for the poor and displaced. During the following thirty-six months, more than three hundred thousand Haitians were internally displaced, and more than one hundred thousand attempted to flee the country (though nearly half of all refugees were forcefully repatriated).

The military overthrow of Haiti's first democratically elected leader led to numerous international economic sanctions and diplomatic initiatives. The most promising chance at a negotiated solution came in late June 1993, when the UN's special envoy to Haiti, Dante Caputo, mediated negotiations between Cedras and Aristide on Governors Island in New York. An agreement was reached that provided for Aristide's return, amnesty for the coup leaders, and a UN peacekeeping force. Though there were some positive signs early on that Cedras would live up to the agreement, opponents to Aristide's return escalated their violence. When the USS *Harlan County* arrived off Port-au-Prince on October 11, 1993, with 220 American and Canadian lightly armed military engineers, a Haitian mob demonstrated on the port and armed thugs threatened journalists and diplomats. With the recent loss of U.S. soldiers in Somalia still fresh in the minds of most Americans, President Clinton ordered the ship to return home the next day. Though warned that sanctions would be intensified if he reneged on the agreement, Cedras was apparently unwilling to quell the violent minority opposed to Aristide's return. Thus, another proposed diplomatic solution failed, and the UN responded by reinstating sanctions (lifted in July as part of the Governor's agreement). A naval blockade was imposed to tighten enforcement of the sanctions.

Following the failure of the Governors Island agreement, Washington began to change its policy toward Haiti. In 1991, the Bush administration quickly condemned the Cedras coup, called for Aristide's return, and supported OAS economic sanctions. Immediately following the overthrow, and periodically for the next couple of years, tens of thousands of Haitians fled in small boats and rafts to America. In accordance with existing procedure, prospective refugees were sent to detention camps at the U.S. naval base in Guantanamo, Cuba, to await interviews by immigration officers. The Bush administration insisted that most were fleeing economic conditions, not political persecution, and thus were not eligible for asylum (though up to one-third were awarded asylum in the early stages of the crisis). In early 1992, Bush ordered the forced repatriation of Haitians who arrived after the coup. This provoked widespread criticism by human rights groups, and the policy was temporarily suspended by a federal court. The Supreme Court, however, upheld the Bush policy and on May 24, in response to the continued flow of Haitians and reports of more to come, Bush ordered the U.S. Coast Guard to interdict refugee boats leaving Haiti and return them.[52] Between thirty thousand and fifty thousand people were returned to Haiti during the crisis period. As part of Bush's policy, refugee-processing centers were opened in Haiti where people could apply for asylum. Many Haitians were too frightened to apply in view of Haitian government and paramilitary "security" forces, casting doubt on the effectiveness of these centers as substitutes for out-of-country processing.

Among the critics of the Bush administration's policy was presidential candidate Bill Clinton. Once in power, however, President Clinton continued Bush's repatriation policy. The failure of the Governors Island agreement was followed by increased violence against Aristide supporters. Renewed UN and U.S. economic sanctions contributed to a decline in humanitarian conditions in Haiti. This led to increased pressure on Clinton from Aristide, the Congressional Black Caucus, and activists such as Randall Robinson.[53] Clinton was urged to change his interdiction and return policy and to get tougher on Haiti's ruling junta. In May 1994, President Clinton announced that prospective refugees would be processed out of country. They would be sent to ships off the Jamaican coast to be interviewed by U.S. immigration officials. But the flood of Haitians that followed quickly overwhelmed the process. Washington then announced a "safe haven" policy by which those awarded asylum status would not go to the United States but instead to "safe havens" in participating Caribbean countries and, later, to the U.S. military base in Guantanamo, Cuba. The U.S. government also intensified its economic and political sanctions on Haiti.

But the pressures driving Haitians to the sea would only grow worse as humanitarian conditions deteriorated in the face of continued political oppression and economic sanctions. The refugees would not stop coming until the junta was removed from power and a more legitimate government was installed. Under the circumstances, returning Aristide to power was the only tenable solution. The continuing refugee crisis, the deteriorating political and humanitarian situation in Haiti, and continued domestic pressure for more effective action preceded Clinton's decision to employ military intervention into Haiti. Contrary to administration explanations, however, it is clear that Clinton's decision was driven more "by naked political fear—the fear of domestic fallout over continued flows of Haitian refugees and of the righteous wrath of the U.S. community that supported President Aristide"[54] than by any principled concern for democracy or human rights. In short, the Haitian crisis was undermining Clinton's domestic political capital and threatening his congressional agenda. Without the support of the Congressional Black Caucus, Clinton had no chance of getting his health-care programs, welfare reform, and crime bills through Congress. By the summer of 1994, Clinton and his advisors determined that it was essential to "put an end to the refugee flow and get Haiti off Washington's political agenda."[55]

On July 31, 1994, the UN Security Council (at America's insistence) passed Resolution 940. Under Chapter VII of the UN Charter, the resolution authorized a U.S.-led Multinational Force (MNF) to use "all necessary means to facilitate the departure from Haiti of the military leadership, . . . the prompt return of the legitimately elected President and the restoration of the legitimate authorities, . . . and to establish and maintain a secure and stable environment that will permit implementation of the Governors Island Agreement."[56] Though many Latin and Caribbean states first opposed any intervention, Aristide's public support for the option and American pressure convinced most to support the effort. Though led and largely manned by American troops, the twenty-two thousand MNF personnel came from twenty-eight countries.

On the eve of the invasion, Clinton sent a negotiating team in a last-ditch effort to avoid armed conflict. Former president Jimmy Carter and former chairman of the joint chiefs of staff Colin Powell offered Cedras one last chance to abdicate power. Only hours before the invasion was to begin, and faced with certain defeat, Haiti's military rulers opted to cut and run. On September 19–20, 1994, MNF troops landed in Haiti. Instead of armed resistance, they encountered crowds of cheering Haitians. Aristide was soon restored to power and all economic sanctions were lifted. Humanitarian actors and human rights organizations were again afforded the space necessary to operate effectively. The humanitarian situation quickly improved and the outflow of Haitians largely ceased. Facing no organized opposition, the MNF concentrated mostly on policing, disarming, and various nation-building activities (reforming police and judicial systems; rebuilding infrastructure, health, and sanitation projects).

BOSNIA

Unlike its interventions into northern Iraq, Somalia, and Haiti, the United States refused to send troops into Bosnia until after a "peace" was established. The war in Bosnia raged from April 1992 to December 1995, but the administrations of both George Bush and Bill Clinton were loath to place American soldiers in harm's way within the Balkans. Prior to 1995, American military units did participate in an important airlift to Sarajevo, helped to enforce a no-fly zone over Bosnia, and enforced an arms embargo. But it was only after parties to the conflict had signed the 1995 Dayton Accords that President Clinton sent ground troops to Bosnia.

Beginning in early 1992, the UN, with American political and financial support, fielded a peacekeeping force in Bosnia—UNPROFOR (the UN Protection Force). It was made up largely of NATO troops, and although its mandate and composition expanded over the years, its primary mission was to help ensure the success of the UN High Commissioner for Refugees (UNHCR)-led humanitarian relief effort in Bosnia. UNPROFOR made numerous important contributions to the humanitarian effort, but it would be stretching the truth to label UNPROFOR a success.[57] Though many factors contributed to this poor performance, not the least of them was "a collective spinelessness"[58] on the part of the international community as a whole. At the heart of the international community's failure to adequately address the Bosnian crisis was a collective lack of will on the part of Western leaders, especially Americans, to make the hard choices to intervene with force.[59]It was not until the summer of 1995 that the Clinton administration took on a clear leadership role and facilitated a negotiated agreement (however flawed and precarious) among the warring parties. Conflict on the Balkan peninsula has had a long and complicated history. The remainder of this chapter will outline the key events in Bosnia and in Kosovo, including Clinton's policies on intervention in both cases.

Yugoslavia Dissolves

Bosnia was once part of Yugoslavia. During the Cold War, Yugoslavia was made up of six republics that were held together by the charismatic leadership of its communist head of state, Josep Broz Tito. After Tito died in 1980, Yugoslavia faced increasing economic, political, and ethnic tensions that the leaders of the six Yugoslav republics were unable to resolve. In the first meaningful postcommunist elections held throughout Yugoslavia during 1990, nationalist leaders gained control in five of the six republics.[60] When the newly elected leaders failed to come to an agreement on the structure for a federal constitution,[61] Slobodan Milosevic, the communist-turned-nationalist president of the Serbian republic, instigated a constitutional crisis by not allowing the representative from Croatia to assume the chairmanship of the collective federal presidency. The republics of Croatia and Slovenia, increasingly disturbed by growing Serbian nationalist belligerency, declared independence from Yugoslavia on June 25, 1991 (see Figure 5.1).[62]

Milosevic's response to Slovenia's declaration of independence was immediate military action. The fighting lasted only two weeks, however, and the Yugoslav National Army (JNA) pulled out. Serbia's defeat in Slovenia can be explained by Slovenia's preparedness and its geographic location (hundreds of miles from Serbia, with Croatia in between). But maybe just as important was the lack of a large Serb minority or any prior Serbian claim to Slovenian territory. In any event, Slovenia escaped the wars of Yugoslavian disintegration relatively unscathed.

This was not the case for Croatia. The JNA combined forces with ethnic Serbs living in several parts of Croatia and, by the end of 1991, they took control of one-third of Croatia. A cease-fire was agreed to in early 1992, and the UN sent fourteen thousand peacekeepers into Croatia to monitor the agreement.[63] (UNPROFOR would later expand its area of operation into Bosnia,

FIGURE 5.1

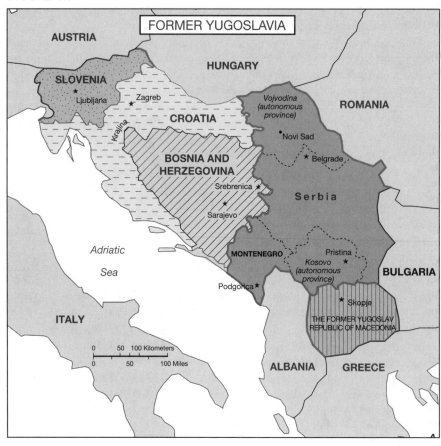

where it would meet with a far more difficult set of circumstances.) Although the first round of fighting in Croatia was relatively short-lived, it included the shelling of some major Croatian cities and led to as many as ten thousand deaths and three hundred fifty thousand displaced Serbs and Croats. Still, the death and destruction war in Croatia pales by comparison to that which would soon visit Bosnia.

Conflict Spreads to Bosnia

In 1991, Bosnia-Herzegovina had a population of about four million. It was ethnically mixed, both demographically (forty-four percent Muslim, thirty-one percent Serb, and seventeen percent Croat) and geographically. All three groups were intermixed throughout Bosnia's many villages and cities. Like the Croatians and the Slovenes, Bosnian Muslims and ethnic Croats in Bosnia feared living under a Serbian-dominated Yugoslavia. Ethnic Serbs in Bosnia, on the other hand, feared living under the rule of the local Muslim majority, who (Serbs feared) might create an Islamic state. In October 1991, the Muslim-Croat majority in the Bosnian Republican assembly voted for independence from Yugoslavia. The Serbian contingent in Bosnia's parliament walked out, created its own assembly, and declared the Serbian community in Bosnia to be autonomous.

In order to receive EU diplomatic recognition, the Bosnian government had to hold a popular referendum on independence, which passed by a large margin on February 29, 1991. Ethnic Serbs in Bosnia boycotted the vote. On March 3, President Izetbegovic (a Muslim) declared Bosnia to be independent. Days later, the EU and the United States extended formal diplomatic recognition. Ethnic Serbs in Bosnia responded with their own declaration of independence from the new state, and war broke out in Bosnia.

The fighting quickly took on a triangular pattern with Serbs, Croats, and Muslims fighting each other. Serb forces initiated the fighting by attacking vulnerable Muslim and Croat positions throughout Bosnia. At a minimum, Bosnian Serb leaders sought to clear the territory they declared as "Republica Serpska" of all non-Serbs. They also sought control over an additional swath of Bosnian territory that was to become part of a "Greater Serbia."[64] When widespread fighting began, Serb paramilitary forces were joined by the JNA. By the summer of 1992, they had gained control of seventy percent of Bosnia.[65]

During the early stages of the war, Bosnian Croat and government (Muslim) forces maintained an uneasy alliance. But the Croat fighters were unreliable allies for the Muslims. Bosnian Croats were supplied by and allied to Croatian President Tudjman in Zagreb, and their ultimate goal was unification with Croatia. In the spring of 1993, Croat forces turned on the Muslims in an attempt to carve out an ethnically pure zone for themselves. By February 1994, after weeks of American pressure, the Bosnian Croats and government forces agreed to join into a loose confederation. Fighting between these two parties dissipated, allowing both to concentrate their efforts on defeating the Serbs.

Ethnic Cleansing

The conflict in Bosnia was characterized by numerous atrocities including mass murders, rape, concentration camps, and siege warfare. All sides participated in these horrible acts to some degree. All sides targeted civilians and impeded the transport of humanitarian aid at one time or another. The preponderance of evidence, however, has led most observers to view the Serb forces as being by far the worst culprits. The Muslim population was the most victimized. Serb forces were the first to employ a strategy that they called "ethnic cleansing." Ethnic cleansing is "a euphemism to describe removing representatives of the 'wrong' ethnic group from an area to gain numerical, political, and military control by employing whatever tools are most effective—incentives, forced movement, threats, rape, or death."[66] The out-manned Serbs avoided direct confrontation as much as possible. They had two primary tactics. The first involved "the besieging and stand-off bombardments of areas occupied by Muslims, or under the control of the Bosnian Government, using heavy artillery." The second "involved the use of 'shock troops' . . . to enter smaller, more vulnerable towns and carry out a series of demonstrative atrocities: mutilation, murder and rape. The intention again was not to capture the area through direct combat but to induce capitulation and flight."[67] It was these Serb tactics (perpetrated so close to the heart of Europe), more than anything else, that spawned the massive humanitarian emergency and international indignation.

The International Response

The international response, however, was largely ineffectual. Because none of the major powers in the West were willing to exert the political, economic, and military effort necessary to end the fighting, the strategy of choice became conflict containment. As Yugoslavia dissolved in 1991–92 and conflict spread to Bosnia, the Bush administration refused to take forceful action. It quickly determined that American interests in Bosnia were insufficient to justify risking a political and military quagmire. "The Bush team, according to one individual involved, had taken a good look at the problems of Yugoslavia and judged from the outset that it was too difficult, that there was nothing which could usefully be done to avoid a violent break-up, and that there was no reason strong enough to justify an armed intervention."[68] Secretary of State Baker put it more succinctly in his famous quip "we don't have a dog in that fight."

Instead, the Bush administration encouraged the Europeans to take the lead. Anxious to demonstrate European political unity and diplomatic acumen, EU representatives, in cooperation with the UN, sought various negotiated solutions, but all failed, mostly because of Serb, Croat, or Muslim intransigence, but also due to lukewarm U.S. support. Beyond diplomatic negotiations, the international response also included a controversial arms embargo (which clearly benefited Bosnian Serbs and Croats at the expense of Muslims) and a "peacekeeping" mission known as UNPROFOR (the United Nations Protection Force). UNPROFOR's mandate and force level grew over the years, but for the most part, its mission was not to patrol a cease-fire or to impose a peace, but instead to help keep Bosnians (mostly Muslims) alive while the war (and negotiations aimed at ending it) continued.[69] To this end, the UN and NATO maintained a long-term airlift of Sarajevo, escorted humanitarian relief convoys, imposed a no-fly zone over all of Bosnia, declared so-called safe havens that were to provide UN protection to six besieged Muslim cities (Tuzla, Srebrenica, Sarajevo, Zepa, Gorazde, and Bihac), and often threatened to bomb Bosnian Serb targets in response to egregious violations of the safe havens. These efforts enjoyed limited success at best. Undoubtedly,

UN and NATO presence mitigated to some extent the ferocity of the conflict, largely to the benefit of the Bosnian Muslims. But the international community fell well short of conflict resolution or even effectively mitigating the humanitarian crisis.

American Leadership

President Clinton did not take the lead regarding Bosnia until the summer of 1995. This is largely explained by his administration's slow realization that the prolonged conflict was producing unacceptably high political risks and that it could not be resolved without increased U.S. leadership. This determination took a while to develop in part because the president was focused "like a laser" on domestic issues. Upon entering office in January 1993, Clinton was unfamiliar with and disinterested in foreign policy issues. His foreign policy team was supposed to keep things under control and out of the limelight. Clinton did not want to become another Lyndon Johnson, whose domestic agenda was overshadowed and hampered by a foreign war (Vietnam). But Clinton's foreign policy team was uncertain about how to respond to Bosnia. Some wanted a more vigorous response, including using force. Others saw Bosnia as a political and military quagmire. The military, still under Powell's leadership in the early days of the Clinton administration, was dead set against engagement. Congress, the press, and public opinion were split. Support might have been forthcoming for multilateral action to end the conflict, but not for unilateral U.S. action. Indecision and flip-flops plagued the Clinton administration's Bosnia policy. As one observer put it: "Clinton's indecisiveness and inconsistency confused the world, and his statements promised much that his policies could not deliver."[70] The only position the administration consistently maintained was its determination not to send American troops into a nonpermissive environment. In this sense, it reflected the essence of the first Bush administration's policy.

As a presidential candidate, Clinton had criticized President Bush for not doing enough on Bosnia. If elected, Clinton indicated he would adopt a more vigorous policy of "lift and strike," lifting the arms embargo to aid the Muslims and ordering air strikes to punish Serb aggression and ensure aid deliveries. Once in power, however, Clinton backed off the lift-and-strike proposal and then dropped it in the face of NATO opposition. Embarrassed, frustrated, and determined to get Bosnia out of the public eye, the Clinton team then adopted a hands-off policy and abdicated leadership to the EU and the UN. But by early 1994, there seemed to be a growing desire within the White House to get more involved again as tensions with NATO allies grew and as Clinton's credibility on foreign policy continued to be questioned.[71] Events in Sarajevo afforded the United States an opportunity to reengage in Bosnia. However, so long as Clinton was only willing to "lead from behind," he would have difficulty getting NATO to follow.

To compound problems, the Clinton administration's "lead" was usually more reactive to immediate events than strategically oriented to an endgame. Thus, after a brief flirtation with bombing in 1994 (following a Serb shelling of a Sarajevo market that killed sixty-eight people) NATO and the UN reverted to largely ineffective diplomacy. This time, however, the Clinton administration vested itself in negotiating a diplomatic solution to the conflict. United States, Russia, Germany, France, and Great Britain began meeting to attempt to coordinate policy on the Bosnia issue. This five nation "Contact Group," as it came to be known, quickly became central to the international community's efforts to end the Bosnian war. In July 1994, it proposed a "take it or leave it" peace proposal to the warring parties in Bosnia. It called for a fifty-one–forty-nine percent split of the country with the new Muslim-Croat Federation receiving the larger portion and leaving Sarajevo under international control. The Bosnian Serbs, however, refused to sign the peace deal, and the international community could not agree on how to change this situation. (This Contact Group plan would later serve as the basis of the Dayton agreement.)

As diplomatic negotiations faltered and the war continued, the potential political fallout continued to rise for Clinton. Fully engaged, his administration looked impotent, as did NATO and the UN, furthering tensions with allies and undermining the administration's domestic and international credibility. Even more worrying to Clinton by the summer of 1995 was the possibility that UNPROFOR might pull out of Bosnia. The United States was committed to assisting its allies in any such pullout, putting Clinton in the unenviable position of risking American soldiers to implement the last stage of an embarrassing policy failure while on the cusp of his reelection campaign. To top it all off, the likely Republican presidential candidate for the upcoming election (Senator Bob Dole) was leading a drive in Congress to force a unilateral lifting of the arms embargo, which would have precipitated UNPROFOR's withdrawal and left the administration holding the bag. These options were unacceptable. By mid-1995, the Clinton foreign policy team began feverishly to develop an endgame strategy. Serendipitously, these renewed efforts within the Clinton administration coincided with fortuitous events in Bosnia that afforded the administration an opportunity to move NATO toward forceful action and an end to the violence.

In early July 1995, the Muslim town of Srebrenica became the scene of the worst single massacre Europe has seen since World War II. This supposed safe haven, "protected" by only a few hundred Dutch peacekeepers, was overrun by Serb forces. The Dutch troops were taken hostage. Tens of thousands of Muslims fled the onslaught. As many as 8,000 men, women, and children were massacred.[72] Still, international outrage did not translate into forceful action. The Dutch government resisted the use of force until all its soldiers were released and out of Bosnia. Other NATO countries were also concerned about the safety of their troops. The president of France, however, called for America to contribute helicopters to assist France in a daring rescue of the city. There was no support for this in Washington, or in other parts of Europe, and Clinton refused. French officials, echoing earlier statements by the British, Dutch, and Canadian governments, threatened to pull out if there was no will to respond more vigorously to Serbian atrocities.[73] It became increasingly clear after Srebrenica (the safe haven in Zepa would fall a few weeks later) that for Europe to stay in Bosnia much longer, the United States would have to get deeply involved.

In August 1995, Croatia launched a military operation aimed at retaking the Krajina, a part of western Croatia bordering Bosnia and an area that had been captured by Croatian Serbs in 1991. Croat forces routed the Serbs in two days. Milosevic did not come to the rescue of the Krajina Serbs, who were finally on the receiving end of a definitive military defeat. Croatia's victory surprised many, including the intelligence communities in America and Britain. It also shattered the myth of Serb invincibility and gave confidence to their enemies, who would soon inflict another defeat on Serb forces, this time inside of Bosnia.[74]

While Croatia was retaking the Krajina, Clinton and company continued their review of various policy options. The final decision was to send National Security Advisor Anthony Lake to Europe to gain support for a new U.S. position. The Clinton administration was now willing to coerce all the parties to sign an agreement based on the Contact Group plan. A combination of sticks and carrots would be used: a version of lift and strike in the face of Serb intransigence or "lift and leave" in the face of Muslim intransigence; a lifting of sanctions on Yugoslavia and "equip and train" the Muslim-Croat Federation in the wake of an agreement. Lake was to make it clear that European support and participation was strongly desired, however, Clinton would not be dissuaded by European indecision. The United States was now committed and would go it alone if necessary.

Washington's more robust Bosnia policy was seen as long overdue by some. Better late than never, the initiative was welcomed in Europe. A full court press on the warring parties in Bosnia followed, but the negotiations were going nowhere quickly. As the fighting continued, the Bosnian Serbs intensified their assaults on the UN safe havens. On August 28, 1995, a shell exploded in a Sarajevo marketplace, killing thirty-seven people and wounding many more. Although Serb officials again accused the Muslims of bombing themselves to gain international sympathy, the international community assumed Serb culpability. Television pictures of the carnage were again transmitted around the world in a matter of hours. Years of watching similar events from Bosnia led to calls "to do something," calls that tended to ebb and flow in conjunction with events.[75] Although there is little evidence that the CNN effect was ever a key factor in driving policy on Bosnia,[76] the Clinton administration seized upon the shelling to show its new resolve. After some strong encouragement and arm twisting by U.S. officials, NATO launched air strikes against Serbian positions around Sarajevo on August 30.[77]

Coinciding with the NATO air attacks, a loosely coordinated but intense Muslim-Croat offensive was launched against Serb positions throughout Bosnia. Despite the regional arms embargo, the Croats and Muslims were able to build up their arsenals with weapons from Iran and other Middle East countries.[78] Encouraged by the recent Serb defeats in Croatia, Croat and Muslim forces attacked Serb positions in western and central Bosnia. By September 1995, Serbian control of Bosnia's territory dropped from seventy percent to fifty percent.[79]

The combination of NATO bombing and the Croat-Muslim offensive turned the tide on the battlefield and forced Bosnian Serbs to the negotiation table. After a few weeks of tense negotiations, Presidents Izetbegovic (representing Bosnia's Muslims), Tudjman (representing Bosnia's Croats), and Milosevic (representing Bosnia's Serbs) signed the 1995 Dayton Accords.[80]

Consistent with his long-held promise to assist in the implementation of a peace agreement, Clinton contributed twenty thousand American troops to NATO's sixty thousand–person peacekeeping force known as IFOR (Implementation Force). This was the single largest armed contribution. Authorized by UN Security Council Resolution 1031 under Chapter VII of the UN Charter, IFOR began deploying just six days after the Dayton Accords were signed. IFOR had a one-year mandate to "oversee implementation of the military aspects of the peace agreement—bringing about and maintaining an end to hostilities; separating the armed forces of Bosnia's two newly created entities, the Federation of Bosnia and Herzegovina and Republika Srpska; transferring territory between the two entities according to the peace agreement; and moving the parties' forces and heavy weapons into approved storage sites."[81] By the end of 1996, a good measure of stability had been secured. NATO scaled down and renamed its force SFOR (Stabilization Force). Initially, SFOR contained around 32,000 troops, including 8,500 Americans. It maintained IFOR's Chapter VII status and robust rules of engagement, including the use of force not just for self-defense but also to accomplish its mission. Not only did SFOR continue as the guarantor of peace in Bosnia, but it also expanded its support of international civilian organizations charged with humanitarian and nation-building duties. By August 2000, SFOR had been reduced to 20,000 troops, about 4,600 of which are Americans.[82] It is currently engaged in, among other things, repatriation efforts, arms control, reforming the Bosnian military, and occasionally arresting indicted war criminals for transfer to the International Criminal Tribunal for the former Yugoslavia in The Hague. Although there have clearly been improvements in the political and economic relationships among the major ethnic groups in Bosnia, many fear a resumption of violence if NATO were to exit anytime soon. Therefore, American troops remain in Bosnia indefinitely, standing guard to prevent a renewal of the civil war and attendant genocide.

KOSOVO

In February 1999, international diplomatic efforts were underway in France to stave off another Balkan war. Yugoslavia's Serb government and paramilitary forces were on the march against the ethnic Albanian minority population in the Serbian province of Kosovo. Even as negotiations were proceeding, forty thousand Yugoslav government forces were massing in and around the Kosovo region. When Yugoslav President Milosevic refused to sign the proposed Rambouillet agreement in 1999, he did so with the full knowledge of NATO's long-standing threats to respond with force. Given Milosevic's prior aggression against Croatia, and in light of his support for Serb atrocities in Bosnia, NATO feared that this large-scale buildup of forces in and around Kosovo presaged another full-scale Serbian campaign of ethnic cleansing. With NATO's reputation on the line, the United States led a NATO bombing campaign against Yugoslavia that began on March 24, 1999, which lasted for seventy-eight days. Milosevic capitulated in early June. He agreed to end his offensive against ethnic Albanians in Kosovo, withdraw his forces, and allow a NATO-led international peacekeeping force into Kosovo.[83] In the end, NATO achieved its stated goals. To this day, NATO forces are engaged in efforts to stabilize Kosovo and to rebuild the region.

Of course, much controversy still surrounds what President Clinton likes to call the "first ever humanitarian war." Did events in Kosovo justify such a blatant transgression of Yugoslav sovereignty? Was the operation in accordance with international law? Did NATO's tactics (ruling out ground troops, a phased bombing plan launched from the relative safety of 15,000 feet, limiting collateral damage) extend the conflict and cause increased suffering for Kosovar Albanians? How much responsibility does NATO have for causing the massive displacement of Albanians? Did bombing win the war? There is a wide range of opinions regarding the proper answers to these important questions. But our concern here is to understand what the U.S. role in this operation was and why the United States behaved as it did.

The Crisis

Kosovo is a province in southern Serbia. Covering 4000.4 square miles, it borders Montenegro, Albania, and the Former Yugoslav Republic of Macedonia. Fifty years ago, Serbs accounted for close to thirty percent of Kosovo's population. But steady Serb emigration out of Kosovo and a higher birthrate among the ethnic Albanians over the past few decades have considerably altered the demographics. Prior to the 1998–99 violence, ethnic Albanians made up ninety percent of Kosovo's population of 2 million. The remaining two hundred thousand or so Kosovars were mostly Serbs. Kosovo had been part of Serbia's medieval state since the early thirteenth century and was for a time the home of Serbia's Orthodox Church.[84] In 1389, Serbia lost the Battle of Kosovo Polje against the invading Ottoman Empire, marking the beginning of the end of Serbia's medieval state. Although Kosovo was the site of this major defeat for the Serbs, Kosovo's battlefields also gained a mythic place in Serbian folklore as the birthplace of the modern Serbian nation. Serbia finally fell to the Ottoman Turks in 1459. For more than 400 years, the Ottomans ruled Kosovo. By 1912, Serbia had regained control of Kosovo from the collapsing Ottoman Empire.

When Tito established the Yugoslav constitution of 1946, he created six republics (Serbia, Croatia, Slovenia, Bosnia-Herzegovina, Montenegro, and Macedonia) with equal status, equal rights, and formal political powers. Though many ethnic Albanians wanted Kosovo to receive full republic status, it instead became an autonomous province with Serbia. Legally, they enjoyed certain rights and protections, but over the next thirty years, Albanian Kosovars suffered widespread discrimination and oppression at the hands of Yugoslav Serb authorities. At the same time, ethnic Albanians increased their numerical preponderance in the province as more and more Serbs emigrated from Kosovo and more and more Albanians had children. Increasingly, ethnic Albanians pushed for greater political control of Kosovo.

A revised Yugoslav constitution in 1974 awarded Kosovo greater local autonomy, giving the Albanian majority extensive control over their internal affairs. It even gave Kosovo representation in all federal bodies, including the collective presidency. Kosovo now enjoyed a status almost equal to that of the six republics, although it was not afforded the right to secede. Over the next twenty years, Kosovo Albanians reversed much of the economic and political discrimination they had suffered for so long and nurtured their ethnic identity, all to the dismay of most Kosovo Serbs, who continued to emigrate from the region.

When Tito died in 1980, ethnic tensions rose throughout Yugoslavia, including Kosovo. In 1981, student demonstrations at the Albanian-dominated Prishtina University in Kosovo degenerated into riots against Serb and Montenegrin residents and businesses. The students had to be forcefully suppressed. Tensions remained high throughout the decade, occasionally spilling over into violence. In 1987, Milosevic took up the Kosovo issue. When Serbs clashed with Kosovo police in a staged protest during April 1987, Milosevic addressed crowds of Serbs in Kosovo and declared that "no one shall dare beat you again." With this, Milosevic transformed himself from a bland Communist Party apparatcik of little distinction into a nationalist protector of victimized Serbs. By the end of 1987, he captured the presidency of the Serbian Communist Party and quickly solidified his control over Serbian politics. In 1989, Milosevic abolished Kosovo's local autonomy, fully reincorporating it as an administrative region within Serbia. Milosevic even went to the medieval battlefield in Kosovo to announce his renewal of Serbia's domination over Kosovo. This was an obvious attempt to stir Serbian nationalist fervor.

From the time Kosovo lost its autonomous status until 1996, Kosovo's ethnic Albanians pursued largely peaceful forms of resistance and political struggle. Yet many were deeply discouraged when the Dayton Accords, which put an end to the war in Bosnia, failed to address the growing tensions in Kosovo. America's decision to treat Milosevic as a peacemaker for purposes of reaching an agreement on Bosnia sent a clear signal that the West was not likely to push very hard for changes in Kosovo. In 1996, frustrated with continued oppression in Kosovo, some Albanians began resorting to violent opposition against Belgrade. The Kosovo Liberation Army (KLA), which organized in 1995, began a low-level campaign of violence against Serb police and state officials. In early 1998, when Belgrade decided to crack down on the KLA, Yugoslav state-run media reported that nearly 200 Serb policemen and civilians had been killed by the KLA. In February and March, Serb police carried out raids in the Drenica region of Kosovo, burning hundreds of homes, emptying villages, and murdering dozens of ethnic Albanians. Security Council Resolution 1160 condemned Belgrade's excessive use of force in Kosovo and imposed an arms embargo on Yugoslavia. Violence between Yugoslav authorities and Kosovo Albanians increased throughout the summer of 1998, with numerous instances of Serb offensives (including artillery and air operations) against ethnic Albanian villages and KLA reprisals.

When the Kosovo crisis broke onto the international scene, President Clinton and his political aides were consumed with the Monica Lewinsky scandal. Clinton's foreign policy team was concentrating on Russia's economic implosion and the upcoming presidential trips to China and Africa. Domestic politics were never far from his mind and Kosovo was not registering in any opinion polls. However, despite these many distractions, the Clinton administration was quick to lead the international response to Serbian oppression in Kosovo.

When Milosevic began cracking down on Kosovo's Albanian population, Secretary of State Albright led the U.S. government in mobilizing a strong international response. By March 1998, she began a conscious effort "to lead through rhetoric," targeting European allies, U.S. public opinion and her own colleagues. She declared, "We are not going to stand by and watch the Serbian authorities do in Kosovo what they can no longer get away with doing in Bosnia."[85]Albright made it clear that, in her opinion, the United States would consider the use of force in Kosovo. Initially, both her colleagues in the administration and her counterparts in Europe were uneasy with her strong language. With the continued vulnerability of NATO troops in Bosnia, and with President Clinton fighting for his political life against calls for impeachment, ground troops were quickly ruled out. Still, Albright was convinced that diplomacy would work only if it was backed by the credible threat of force. She continued to press her colleagues at home and abroad for support.

In July 1998, after more than sixty Serb policemen were killed in fighting with the KLA, Milosevic ordered an all-out offensive in Kosovo. More than 2,000 ethnic Albanians were killed, and more than 300,000 were displaced. As the violence in Kosovo intensified, Albright continued to push for a vigorous NATO response. As NATO met in Portugal, Secretary General Javier Solana told a closed-door meeting that Serbs were mocking NATO with "a slow-motion offensive aimed at keeping NATO in its torpor." He asserted that one Serb diplomat went so far as to joke that "a village a day keeps NATO away."[86] On September 24, 1998, NATO issued an ultimatum: stop the crackdown in Kosovo or face air strikes.

Despite the bold threats, however, NATO had little desire to bomb Yugoslavia. Washington sent Richard Holbrooke, architect of the Dayton Accords, to Belgrade once again hoping Milosevic would make a deal. Armed with the threat of airstrikes, Holbrooke extracted enough promises from Milosevic to keep NATO jets grounded for a time. This agreement did not last long, however, as Milosevic failed to live up to his promises. The KLA, likely sensing NATO sympathy, began retaking land vacated by Serb forces and even launched some small-scale attacks. Yugoslav forces responded in kind, and on January 16, 1999, Serbian troops murdered forty-five Albanian civilians in Racak.[87]

Capitalizing on the shock value of the Racak massacre, Secretary of State Albright was quick to push her colleagues to support her new plan for Kosovo. NATO would demand that the bulk of Yugoslav troops leave Kosovo, autonomy would be restored to the province, and NATO peacekeepers would be allowed in to monitor the arrangements. The United States, Albright insisted, also had to declare that it would contribute ground troops to the peacekeeping force to convince NATO (and others) of its seriousness. President Clinton approved the plan and proceeded to sell it to his counterparts in Europe.

By the end of January, through the efforts of the president and Albright, NATO agreed to support the plan. On January 27, 1999, Clinton announced the plan to the world and threatened both sides if they did not participate. Belgrade would be hit with air strikes and Kosovo Albanians would face a blockade of Albania's coastline to cut off their source of arms.

France and Britain insisted on cochairing the talks and selected the Rambouillet castle outside of Paris as their site. The talks began in February and dragged on inconclusively for two weeks. Meanwhile, President Clinton was acquitted in the U.S. Senate impeachment trial, and he then turned his attention to Kosovo. Intelligence reports were warning that Yugoslavia was amassing troops above Kosovo in preparation for a large-scale attack. Austrian intelligence even reported to NATO that Belgrade was planning a spring offensive termed Operation Horseshoe aimed at expelling large numbers of Kosovars and destroying the KLA.

Neither side signed the agreement while they were in Rambouillet. But following weeks of intense international pressure, the Kosovo Albanians signed the accord. This left the ball in Belgrade's court, but Milosevic refused to play. On March 22, 1999, Holbrooke made a last-ditch effort to get Milosevic to change his mind. As negotiations bogged down, the U.S. ambassador reportedly asked, "Look, are you absolutely clear in your own mind what will happen when I get up and walk out of this palace that we are now sitting in?" Milosevic's reply was short: "You're going to bomb us."[88] Days earlier, Yugoslav forces had initiated Operation Horseshoe. NATO had to either put up or shut up. On March 24, 1999, NATO began bombing Yugoslavia.

The bombing campaign lasted seventy-eight days, killed thousands of Yugoslavs (Serbs and ethnic Albanians alike), and destroyed much of the country's infrastructure. There remains much controversy over the justification and legality of the NATO intervention, its tactics, and their effects. Unlike America's military intervention into Bosnia, there was no explicit, widely accepted, controlling legal authority (such as an international treaty or a UN Security Council resolution) authorizing the intervention in Kosovo. Nevertheless, a strong case can be made that a combination of recent precedents for "humanitarian intervention," a growing international concern for human rights and humanitarianism, and traditional "just war" rationales legitimized intervention in Kosovo, both morally and legally. Even though NATO can claim it achieved its stated goals, the bombing catalyzed Serbia's offensive, resulting in widespread death and destruction and the temporary displacement of more than a million Kosovo Albanians. The scope of murder and war crimes perpetrated by Serb forces in Kosovo was not discovered until well after the fact.[89] NATO tactics, which placed such a high regard on force security, were not the most effective in bringing the conflict to a quick conclusion and probably increased the short-term suffering of the Kosovo Albanians.

Regardless, after eleven weeks of bombing and with the threat of a NATO ground invasion growing more real, Milosevic caved in to NATO demands, agreeing to withdraw from Kosovo and accept a NATO-led peacekeeping force in the region. NATO's Kosovo Force (KFOR) began entering Kosovo on June 12, 1999, but did not reach its peak deployment of fifty thousand until early in the year 2000. There are still more than forty thousand troops in Kosovo today, with another 7,500 providing rear support in neighboring Macedonia. Although KFOR is led and largely manned by NATO, more than thirty countries have contributed to the force, including nearly 8,000 American soldiers. KFOR's missions in Kosovo are to create and maintain a secure environment, including public safety and order; to monitor, verify, and, when necessary, enforce the demilitarization of the region, including the retreat of Yugoslav forces and disarming of the KLA; and to assist the UN Mission in Kosovo (UNMIK) in its political, economic, and social reconstruction efforts.[90]

Although KFOR has had some success repatriating Kosovo Albanian refugees, it has had a difficult time deterring revenge attacks or the emigration of tens of thousands of Kosovo Serbs. As in Bosnia, it is hard to imagine reconciliation between the major ethnic groups anytime soon. To make matters worse, Kosovo's political future is still uncertain. Will Kosovar Albanians be satisfied with anything short of independence? Will local autonomy satisfy the major parties? Until these questions are answered, Kosovo will likely remain a NATO protectorate. In the end, American troops are likely to remain in Bosnia and in Kosovo for a very long time. Strife in Kosovo also has the potential to destabilize its neighbors: for example, when the fighting has spilled

over into Macedonia. Regional destabilization could only enhance the likelihood of more humanitarian interventions in the future.

CONCLUSION

Following the Kosovo crisis, Clinton promulgated what has come to be known
as the Clinton Doctrine on Intervention: "I think there is an important principle here that I hope will be now upheld in the future. . . . And that is that
while there may well be a great deal of ethnic and religious conflict in the
world—some of it might break out into wars—that whether within or beyond
the borders of a country, if the world community has the power to stop it, we
ought to stop genocide and ethnic cleansing."[91] Soon after, the United States
supported a UN peacekeeping operation in East Timor (though U.S. troops
provided only logistical assistance). Are these recent interventions a harbin-
ger of things to come? Will the United States become more supportive of, and
active in, future international peace missions? Of course, only time will tell,
but the preceding analysis suggests that the answer depends first and foremost
on the person that occupies the White House. Clearly the president has the
greatest influence over how the U.S. government responds to humanitarian
crises. As commander-in-chief of the armed forces, only the president has the
power to send troops abroad. And because few humanitarian crises threaten
vital national interests, there will rarely be widespread consensus on the appropriate response. Thus, a president has much leeway in responding to humanitarian crises around the world. He or she can adopt a minimalist
approach with little fear of serious political or security repercussions, or go so
far as to intervene militarily. Or a president could choose any number of options in between.

In any case, the initiative lies within the executive branch. As we have
seen, Presidents Bush and Clinton often hesitated to act; however, once they
decided to intervene they were able to do so. In no instance did we see a president who was determined to intervene thwarted by congressional action, bureaucratic infighting, military abstinence, or public opinion (commonly
thought to restrict the president's ability to act). The reasons intervention occurred or did not occur differed from case to case, though we can categorize
them as either soft security concerns, humanitarian concerns, or domestic political concerns. Clearly, the Bush intervention in Somalia in 1992–93 was a
highly personal decision based on his humanitarian impulse to help, as well as
his desire to go out on a high note. For Clinton, domestic political concerns
were central considerations in his administration's policies toward Rwanda,
Bosnia, Haiti, and to a lesser degree, Kosovo. Whoever controls the Oval Office in the future will continue to enjoy a tremendous amount of discretion in
responding to humanitarian crises. What he or she decides to do with this
ability will likely depend more on his or her priorities and leadership skills
than other factors such as the opinions of Congress, the military, the foreign

policy bureaucracies, public opinion, or the media—each of which (if recent experience is any guide to the near future) will likely remain surmountable. Application of these considerations to the administration of George W. Bush can be found in the conclusion of this book.

ANNEX 1

Clinton Administration Policy on Reforming Multilateral Peace Operations (PDD25)

Released by the Bureau of International Organizational Affairs, U.S. Department of State, February 22, 1996

Executive Summary

Last year, President Clinton ordered an inter-agency review of our nation's peacekeeping policies and programs in order to develop a comprehensive policy framework suited to the realities of the post-Cold War period. This policy review has resulted in a Presidential Decision Directive (PDD 25)...

i. Voting for Peace Operations . . .

The Administration will consider the factors below when deciding whether to vote for a proposed new UN peace operation (Chapter VI or Chapter VII) or to support a regionally-sponsored peace operation:

- UN involvement advances U.S. interests, and there is an international community of interest for dealing with the problem on a multilateral basis.
- There is a threat to or breach of international peace and security, often of a regional character, defined as one or a combination of the following:

  International aggression, or;

  Urgent humanitarian disaster coupled with violence;

  Sudden interruption of established democracy or gross violation of human rights coupled with violence, or threat of violence.

- There are clear objectives and an understanding of where the mission fits on the spectrum between traditional peacekeeping and peace enforcement.
- For traditional (Chapter VI) peacekeeping operations, a ceasefire should be in place and the consent of the parties obtained before the force is deployed.

- For peace enforcement (Chapter VII) operations, the threat to international peace and security is considered significant.
- The means to accomplish the mission are available, including the forces, financing and mandate appropriate to the mission.
- The political, economic and humanitarian consequences of inaction by the international community have been weighed and are considered unacceptable.
- The operation's anticipated duration is tied to clear objectives and realistic criteria for ending the operation.

ii. Participating in UN and Other Peace Operations

The Administration will continue to apply even stricter standards when it assesses whether to recommend to the President that U.S. personnel participate in a given peace operation. In addition to the factors listed above, we will consider the following factors:

- Participation advances U.S. interests and both the unique and general risks to American personnel have been weighed and are considered acceptable.
- Personnel, funds and other resources are available;
- U.S. participation is necessary for operation's success;
- The role of U.S. forces is tied to clear objectives and an endpoint for U.S. participation can be identified;
- Domestic and Congressional support exists or can be marshaled;
- Command and control arrangements are acceptable.

Additional, even more rigorous factors will be applied when there is the possibility of significant U.S. participation in Chapter VII operations that are likely to involve combat:

- There exists a determination to commit sufficient forces to achieve clearly defined objectives;
- There exists a plan to achieve those objectives decisively;
- There exists a commitment to reassess and adjust, as necessary, the size, composition, and disposition of our forces to achieve our objectives.

Any recommendation to the President will be based on the cumulative weight of the above factors, with no single factor necessarily being an absolute determinant. . . .

Chapter 6

U.S. POLICY ON TERRORISM BEFORE AND AFTER SEPTEMBER 11

Mark J. Miller

The late F. H. Hinsley held that all wars could be explained in terms of distant and proximate causes.[1] Following the attacks on the World Trade Center and the Pentagon on September 11, 2001, President George W. Bush declared war against terrorism around the world. The first phase of the campaign was to be waged in Afghanistan against the Taliban regime allied to the presumed perpetrators of the September 11 attacks, the shadowy Al-Qaida movement, and its allies led by Osama bin Laden. The war against terrorism, however, was viewed as global and indeterminate in nature. The president vowed to extirpate terrorism around the world and to oppose and punish states harboring or supporting terrorism.

This declaration of war marked the culmination of a decades-long progression of counterterrorism to the top of the U.S. national security agenda. George W. Bush's predecessors, including his father, had previously declared counterterrorism to be a top priority in U.S. foreign policy. Indeed, President Bill Clinton had declared combating terrorism to be a top priority of his administration and had put counterterrorism on the agenda of G-7 meetings. Thus, the initial military and diplomatic campaign in Afghanistan reflected the culmination of a historical process that witnessed the violence called terrorism as it steadily became a preoccupation of U.S. foreign policy. In addition, it constituted an uncertain departure in the conduct of U.S. foreign policy, as terrorism appears endemic in global politics and there is no incontrovertible way to claim victory in the war against terrorism.

President Bush's declaration of war against terrorism committed the United States to the use of military and diplomatic means to combat an amorphous, complex phenomenon that will be impossible to eradicate through the use of force alone. The indeterminacy of the war declared against terrorism was re-flected in public statements made by President Bush and cabinet members that the U.S. public should be prepared for a protracted and difficult war unlike past U.S. conventional wars. Nevertheless, the president predicted that the United States would triumph in the end and portrayed the war against terror-ism in images familiar to U.S. foreign policy, namely as a struggle between forces of good and evil. When viewed as such, how could the forces of good not prevail?

The problem with President Bush's declaration of war reflected the broader and long-term problem of U.S. foreign policy coming to grips with terrorism and devising a credible strategy to counter it. Terrorism can be de-fined as the use of violence against civilian populations to achieve political goals outside of a conventional warfare context. Such violence has been an important concern in the conduct of U.S. foreign policy since the late 1960s. Yet more than thirty years after the U.S. government identified terrorism as an important concern, the United States has yet to evolve a credible strategy for attenuating it. Enormous resources, both human and budgetary, and a great deal of admirable expertise have been devoted to the elaboration of a credi-ble U.S. foreign policy response to terrorism.[2] And, in certain respects, great progress had been made prior to September 11. Terrorism had been declared a top concern. Key agencies such as the State Department, the CIA, and the FBI had developed expertise on terrorism and had begun to coordinate a more comprehensive policy in response to the threats posed by terrorism. Yet the shortcomings in U.S. counterterrorism were all too obvious and fully ex-posed by the attacks of September 11.

In the wake of those attacks, U.S. foreign policy entered a new era, one characterized by a great deal of uncertainty. The new era was defined by the centrality of the war against terrorism. The United States pledged to use all military and diplomatic means to oppose it. The commitment was open-ended and unambiguous. The phenomenon it was directed against, however, was not. One manifest problem is the lack of an international consensus on what constitutes terrorism. A second problem arises from the complex causes of terrorism. Political violence viewed as terrorism often arises in areas char-acterized by adverse socioeconomic and political circumstances, the so-called root causes of terrorism.

The central problem with U.S. counterterrorism strategy over the past thirty-plus years has been a propensity to avoid addressing complex socioeco-nomic and political background factors that foster terrorism. President Bush's declaration of war ushers in a new era in U.S. foreign policy because no cred-ible U.S. counterterrorism strategy can avoid addressing root causes. The use of force alone will not suffice. Hence, the declaration of war made during the highly emotionally charged atmosphere in the wake of the September 11 at-tacks would appear to entail a major recasting of U.S. foreign policy.

Ideologically, the George W. Bush administration appeared resistant to the types of engagements required for a credible global war against terrorism. Nevertheless, by the end of the first phase of the declared war against terrorism, a U.S. foreign policy characterized by pragmatism and a renewed commitment to multilateral cooperation had emerged. In key respects, post–September 11 U.S. foreign policy appeared discontinuous with the conduct of the second Bush administration's foreign policy prior to September 11, 2001.

It remains within the realm of possibility that the Bush administration (or its successors) will fashion a more credible counterterrorism strategy than preceding administrations. The shock of the losses and insecurity of September 11 should not be underestimated. Nevertheless, the challenges to fashioning a credible and comprehensive counterterrorism strategy are many and considerable. U.S. foreign policy will need to be systematically rethought and reassessed. The U.S. will need to fully engage the world and its many, many problems. It will need to work more closely with international and regional organizations and strive for enhanced bilateral cooperation with virtually all states around the world.

One early test of whether U.S. foreign policy would change fundamentally due to the war against terrorism came in January 2002. UN Secretary General Kofi Anan correctly interpreted the violence of September 11 as signaling an urgent need for the international community to address global poverty and the huge disparities in life chances between rich and poor lands. Several European states, the UN, and the World Bank launched a campaign to increase foreign aid to poor countries. But the United States refused to accept the UN goal of a transfer of 0.7 percent of total economic output to poor countries or even a compromise proffered that would have had the United States double its foreign assistance over an interim period. Instead, U.S. foreign assistance would remain at $10 billion per annum, a level at which it had been frozen for a decade and, by 2002, represented the lowest percentage of the total economy being given in foreign aid since 1945.[3]

Regardless of how successful the war against terrorism becomes, total victory is unlikely to be achieved. The problems and issues fostering recourse to terrorism defy short-term eradication, and the United States will remain vulnerable to violence committed at home and abroad. Indeed, progress in counterterrorism will be difficult to measure and, therefore, public debate over counterterrorism will endure. In the wake of September 11, it seems odd to recall that only three or four decades earlier terrorism was not on the U.S. foreign policy or national security agenda at all. There was virtually no scholarship devoted to understanding terrorism. Terrorism was dimly understood as something terrible that happened elsewhere—against the French in Algeria, against the British in Palestine, or against the Israelis. Few students or practitioners of U.S. foreign policy paid much attention at all to the phenomenon.

DISTANT CAUSES

Terrorism first became a U.S. foreign policy concern during the turbulence of the 1960s. Victorious insurgencies against the French in Indochina in 1954 and in Algeria in 1962 fostered a guerrilla mystique and belief in the righteousness of wars of national liberation. The fledgling Palestinian nationalist movement Al-Fatah, for instance, embraced the armed struggle model of the Algerian National Liberation Front. Communication and cooperation between nationalist and leftist anti-imperialist revolutionary movements increased and was fostered by certain states such as newly independent Algeria or Cuba. At this juncture, which roughly coincides with the advent of scholarly study of terrorism, the phenomenon was largely identified with the anti-imperialist movement. A long history of terrorism, however, preceded the moment that it became a concern in the conduct of U.S. foreign policy and, it should be obvious, that various nationalist and leftist revolutionaries of the 1960s held no monopoly over the method of terrorism.

An ideology of anti-imperialist struggle developed and was adhered to by many movements and groups around the world, including violence-prone elements of the New Left and student movements in many of the Organization for Economic Cooperation and Development (OECD) countries. Indeed, groups such as the Red Army Faction in the Federal Republic of Germany also emulated the Algerian model and began to cooperate closely with Third World revolutionary movements, especially the leftist Popular Front for the Liberation of Palestine. The outcome of the June 1967 Arab–Israeli war discredited Arab leaders such as Nasser and further radicalized many Palestinians and other Arabs as additional hundreds of thousands of Palestinian refugees were displaced.[4] Beirut, Lebanon, became a focal point of a shadowy network of movements with a common agenda of anti-imperialist struggle. The war in Vietnam, growing U.S. economic and military support for Israel, and U.S. preeminence in the Western bloc made the United States a principal target of anti-imperialist movements. Thus began the targeting of U.S. embassies and military installations, as well as U.S. citizens abroad, that catalyzed the new-found interest in the phenomenon of terrorism. In the early 1970s, George Bush played a key role in identifying terrorism as an important security concern during his tenure as CIA director.

The initial preoccupations of embryonic U.S. counterterrorism were with groups such as the Japanese Red Army, the Red Brigades in Italy, the Irish Republican Army in the United Kingdom, and a multitude of Palestinian-dominated movements. Such organizations frequently struck at U.S. targets and were viewed as threatening to U.S. interests and to those of close allies. Cooperation between anti-imperialist movements was considerable, and some early analysts of terrorism discerned an international terrorist network akin to the Second, Third, and Fourth Internationals of Socialist, orthodox (pro-Moscow) communist, and Trotskyist parties, respectively. The revolutionary government led by

Colonel Kaddafi that had overthrown a pro-Western Libyan monarch was viewed with growing alarm, as were states such as North Korea, for aiding the Japanese Red Army, or Cuba, viewed as supporting revolutionary movements in Africa and Latin America.

Later in the 1970s, Claire Sterling would view international terrorism as a network fostered and supported by the USSR.[5] A number of USSR-allied states, principally the German Democratic Republic and Bulgaria, did aid and abet terrorists, especially members of the German Red Army Faction. The USSR offered training and military assistance to certain Palestinian nationalist organizations, such as Al-Fatah or the Popular Democratic Front for the Liberation of Palestine (now the Democratic Front for the Liberation of Palestine). The Soviets viewed these groups as being engaged in legitimate national liberation struggles to create a Palestinian state in the territories occupied by Israel in 1967. Sterling greatly exaggerated the role played by the USSR in terrorism of the 1970s. Nevertheless, her views were quite influential and contributed to a narrative that elucidated and largely misconstrued terrorism in Cold War terms. Cold War and strongly pro-Israeli thinking marked much early scholarship on international terrorism and influenced emergent U.S. counterterrorism policy. This had several important consequences that still weigh heavily upon the post–September 11 environment.

By discrediting Egyptian President Gamal Abdul Nasser, as well as his modernist pan-Arab philosophy, the June 1967 war created a void that enabled a proliferation of competing, largely Palestinian guerrilla movements.[6] The emergence of the fedayeen (the Arabic term for "those who sacrifice themselves") threatened the Hachemite monarchy in Jordan and Maronite domination of Lebanese government. This was of more than passing concern to the United States, particularly because U.S.-supported diplomatic efforts to secure Arab–Israeli peace on the basis of UN Security Council Resolution 242 (1967) were repeatedly disrupted by fedayeen attacks and Israeli reprisals. Settlement of the Arab–Israeli conflict constituted an important foreign policy goal for the United States and its NATO allies since 1967.

Following the Black September crisis of 1970–71 in Jordan, which witnessed the crushing of the fedayeen by the U.S.-supplied Jordanian army, violence perpetrated by Palestinians, sometimes in tandem with groups such as the Japanese Red Army or the Red Army Faction, became of enormous concern to the United States. The attack by Palestinian guerrillas upon the Israeli team at the Munich Olympics in 1972 introduced many Americans to the growing and already global phenomenon of terrorism.

The UN and other international organizations began to study and debate international terrorism. The UN became the principal forum for debate. Many governments that sympathized with the plight of Palestinian refugees and favored the creation of a Palestinian state viewed the history surrounding the Arab–Israeli conflict as a root cause of political violence in the Middle East and its spillover elsewhere. The United States generally opposed such analysis as biased against Israel. U.S.-UN relations reached a nadir with the UN General Assembly's resolution that claimed Zionism constituted a form of racism. A principal casualty was U.S. support for any serious global discussion of the root causes of terrorism.

The United States largely ignored important signs of moderation of Al-Fatah (the principal Palestinian movement led by Yasir Arafat) goals in the early 1970s as did most, but not all, Israelis. The electoral victory of the right-wing Likud coalition in Israel in 1977 essentially precluded any negotiated settlement of Palestinian–Israeli issues for a decade or more, although the Camp David Accords, leading to the Egyptian–Israeli peace treaty, envisaged a five-year period of negotiations concerning the autonomy of Gaza and the West Bank. Meanwhile, the Likud government promoted Jewish settlement of the Occupied Territories and became more deeply involved in conflict in Lebanon, which culminated in the Israeli invasions of 1978 and 1982.

During the Nixon presidency, Henry Kissinger affixed three conditions to the start of any U.S.-Palestine Liberation Organization dialogue. The Palestine Liberation Organization (PLO) must eschew terrorism, recognize the legitimacy of Israel, and accept Security Council Resolution 242 as the basis for settlement of the Arab–Israeli conflict. Despite evidence of moderation of Palestinian goals in the 1970s, the PLO was unable to meet the three conditions set down by Kissinger until the late 1980s. In the absence of U.S.-PLO dialogue, given the importance of the Arab–Israeli conflict in global politics, probably no serious discussion of root causes of terrorism could have been expected. Instead, under President Reagan, U.S. foreign policy sharply veered away from an approach conducive to redress of socioeconomic and political issues viewed as fostering terrorism; indeed, such an approach became an anathema. A key means to influence environments conducive to terrorism, namely the provision of socioeconomic assistance, was scaled back. Most foreign assistance by the United States went to Israel and Egypt, and most of that was comprised of military assistance.

Fatefully, as the United States began to suffer direct effects of terrorism, which became a concern for U.S. foreign policy, the U.S. response was quite circumscribed and frequently limited to just military responses. The apogee was reached in the Reagan presidency with retaliatory attacks against Libya and against targets in Lebanon. U.S. foreign policy explicitly opposed North-South dialogue, thereby dooming global prospects for negotiations bearing on global socioeconomic disparities. Instead, the Reagan administration touted free market principles and extolled the virtues of unrestrained capitalism, which helped bring about the heightened globalization of the 1980s and 1990s with resultant growing disparities within and between states.[7]

The Reagan administration's decision to dispatch U.S. Marines to Beirut in August 1982 facilitated the departure of fedayeen from West Beirut who had been besieged there by the Israeli army and allied Lebanese forces since June. PLO Chairman Arafat had sought the creation of a multinational force to protect Palestinian and Lebanese civilians in West Beirut and surrounding areas in the wake of their evacuation. The U.S. Marines were deployed during the evacuation of the fedayeen and then redeployed to ships offshore. A bomb that killed Lebanese President-elect Bashir Gemayel, who was the leader of the Lebanese forces, and many of his adjoints, served as a pretext for occupation of West Beirut by the Israeli army. Killings of hundreds, probably thousands, of Palestinians and Lebanese Shi'a in the refugee camps of Sabra and Chatilla ensued. After several days of massacres, the U.S. Marines and other elements of the multinational force were redeployed to West Beirut.

Gradually the U.S. servicemen became enmeshed in Lebanese strife. U.S. support for rebuilding a Lebanese government led by Amir Gemayel was not viewed indifferently by local forces hostile to the government. When the Lebanese government initialed a peace agreement with Israel that was opposed by a large segment of the Lebanese population and by regional powers such as Syria and Iran, Lebanon's civil war resumed. West Beirut quickly fell to guerrillas opposed to the Lebanese forces and clashes with the encircled marines began. The violence culminated in the 1983 bombing of the U.S. embassy in Beirut and of a U.S. Marine barracks that took hundreds of American lives. Within several months of President Reagan declaring Lebanon to be a vital national security interest of the United States, the marines cut their losses and were withdrawn from Beirut in 1984.

U.S. involvement in Lebanese strife testified to the growing centrality of terrorism to U.S. foreign policy, but also to the limits of U.S. counterterrorism strategy. The use of U.S. force went badly awry. Israeli forces in Lebanon were forced to withdraw to the Israeli-created security zone along the Lebanese-Israeli border until that zone also was evacuated in 2001. Very significantly, the United States frequently criticized attacks on Israeli troops in Lebanon as terrorism, whereas most Arabs and much of the rest of the world did not regard the attacks as terrorism but rather as legitimate resistance to foreign occupation.[8]

The quarter century of strife in Lebanon after 1975 reflected many, if not all, of the principal long-term causes of terrorism with which the United States now must reckon at the global level. The legitimacy of the Lebanese state and its institutions was problematic.[9] The central government itself was weak. Enormous socioeconomic disparities exacerbated tensions over Lebanese identity and the place of the Lebanese state in regional and global politics. Mass displacement of Palestinian refugees to Lebanon and perpetuation of their plight eventually helped precipitate civil war by 1975. Several decades of conflict left the economy in ruins and large parts of Lebanese society in dire straits. Disparate rates of population growth and migration tended to undercut the stability of Lebanese institutions governed by the unwritten National Pact of 1943. Reform of Lebanese institutions under Syrian tutelage in the 1990s did not resolve the legitimacy questions surrounding the Lebanese state.

At the global level, socioeconomic disparities, illegitimate governance, and unresolved historical and ethnic disputes loom large among the root causes of terrorism. Prior to September 11, little was done to address these questions in U.S. policy against terrorism. Indeed, many aspects of U.S. foreign policy appeared to exacerbate rather than attenuate perceived root causes of terrorism, particularly in the Middle East.

PROXIMATE CAUSES

So-called Islamic terrorism was not on the radar screen of U.S. foreign policy until the 1980s. In retrospect, it is understood now that the 1967 war had also opened a political space for Islamic fundamentalism with the discrediting of Nasserism.

Islamic fundamentalism did not begin in 1967.[10] Many variants of it can be traced far back into the history of the Islamic world. Moreover, not all Islamic fundamentalists embrace political content. The magnitude of the Arab defeat in 1967 gave some credence to the notion that secular-minded regimes, or political parties such as Nasser's Arab Socialist Union, had deviated from Islamic governance and that political renewal was contingent upon a return to authentic Islamic rule.

The 1979 overthrow of the Shah of Iran, a major regional ally of the United States, led to the creation of a revolutionary Islamic Republic. Steadfast U.S. support for the Shah had helped to sustain a regime that was widely decried as autocratic, illegitimate, and repressive. Indeed, the United States had helped to oust a democratically elected Iranian government and then placed the Shah in power back in 1953.[11] Strong and consistent U.S. support for the Shah fostered the emergence of a radical Islamic opposition that was very hostile to U.S. interests. The new revolutionary government in Tehran viewed the United States after 1979 as the Great Satan, and militants soon seized the U.S. embassy.

In the early phases of the Islamic Republic, a goal of Iranian foreign policy was the export of Islamic forms of governance to the rest of the Islamic world. Iranian Revolutionary Guards arrived in Lebanon's Bekaa Valley and began to create Hezbollah, or "the Party of God." Hezbollah would thereafter figure centrally in political violence in Lebanon.[12] Secular regimes, such as the Iraqi government controlled by the Ba'ath party since 1968, viewed events in Iran with alarm. Iraq judged the time propitious and launched a war against Iran in 1980. The Iraqi offensive into Iran eventually bogged down, and a nearly decade-long military stalemate ensued, which caused hundreds of thousands of casualties. Many Arab states supported Iraq in its war with Iran. When an end to the fighting was finally achieved, disagreements over the financing of the "Arab" war against Iran would figure among the disputes that led to the Iraqi invasion of Kuwait and the subsequent Gulf War in 1990–91.[13]

The Soviet decision to intervene in Afghanistan in 1979 also was linked to repercussions of Iran's Islamic Revolution. Afghanistan had been politically unstable throughout the 1970s. The Soviet invasion of Afghanistan at the behest of a pro-Moscow Afghani Communist party eventually met with widespread, but politically disunited, resistance. Numerous Islamic fundamentalist organizations figured centrally in the resistance to the Soviet-backed government. Thousands of Arab volunteers flocked to Pakistan and Afghanistan in the 1980s to fight the Soviets. Among the volunteers was a wealthy Saudi of Yemeni background—Osama bin Laden. The Saudi monarchy supported Islamic resistance in Afghanistan, as did the U.S. government. Covert U.S. aid to Afghanistan's mujahadin was funneled mainly through a Pakistani intelligence service. The provision of quite sophisticated U.S. arms to these anti-Soviet guerrillas enabled a protracted military stalemate that ended with the evacuation of Soviet forces in 1989. The hard core of Al-Qaida (a term that means "the base" in Arabic) membership consisted of Arab volunteers who had fought against the Soviets in Afghanistan.

Bin Laden criticized the Saudi government for allowing American troops into Saudi Arabia after the Iraqi invasion of Kuwait in August 1990. He termed the U.S. military presence there a desecration. In the aftermath of the Gulf War, he began to campaign against the United States and its regional allies, especially from Sudanese soil. During this period, he appears to have nurtured ties between Al-Qaida and other Islamic fundamentalist organizations, including the Egyptian Islamic Jihad, whose members had assassinated the Egyptian president, Anwar el-Sadat, as punishment for his signing of the Camp David treaty. Members of the Egyptian Islamic Jihad were also involved in the bombing of the World Trade Center in 1993.

By 1998, bin Laden announced the creation of a coalition to fight the United States and its allies in the Middle East in what amounted to a declaration of war by the coalition against the United States.[14] The structure of the coalition was amorphous by design. A commonality of many of those involved in the network was service against the Soviets in Afghanistan in the 1980s or subsequent training at Al-Qaida bases in Afghanistan in the 1990s.

By the mid-1990s, a new force emerged in the continuing strife in Afghanistan, which raged on long after the departure of Soviet troops. The Taliban movement enjoyed the support of elements within the Pakistani military and intelligence community and espoused an austere form of Islam similar to the Wahabism practiced in Saudi Arabia. The Taliban seized control of most of Afghanistan but continued to meet resistance, particularly in non-Pashtun areas of northeast Afghanistan where the Northern Alliance continued to hold out against the Taliban with Iranian assistance. Iran was sharply critical of the Taliban government established in Kabul, especially after the killing of a delegation of Iranian officials by the Taliban.

The expansion of Taliban rule over much of Afghanistan was aided by Al-Qaida and its allies. Many Al-Qaida members appear to have fought for the Taliban against the Northern Alliance. This cooperation enabled Al-Qaida to maintain bases in Afghanistan for military training and indoctrination.

After Al-Qaida-organized attacks against U.S. embassies in East Africa in 1998 and on the USS *Cole* in Yemen in 2000, the Clinton administration retaliated against Al-Qaida bases in Afghanistan with cruise missiles. In the 1990s, however, Al-Qaida and confederate organizations had created a global network of cells and operatives, often operating among immigrant-background communities in Western societies. A number of mosques in cities such as London and Milan became centers for recruitment of immigrant Muslims, converts, and European Muslims into the Al-Qaida network, many of whom then flew to Afghanistan for training. Radical fundamentalist organizations such as the Algerian Armed Islamic Group (AIG) created cells in places such as Canada through asylum seeking and other migration processes. Shortly before the celebration of the new millennium, an alert U.S. customs agent stopped the Algerian Ahmed Ressam in a vehicle packed with explosives as he crossed the U.S.-Canada border near Seattle. He would later cooperate with U.S. authorities and explain how he and AIG confederates in Canada intended to bomb the Los Angeles airport.[15]

The attacks of September 11 prompted the U.S. declaration of war. Despite all of the warning signs, U.S. counterterrorism failed to detect and prevent a punishing attack. The transnational network that perpetrated the coordinated attacks appears to have trained and prepared for the attack over many months, if not years. All nineteen of the attackers were aliens who had been in the United States from a week to several years. Some of the militants involved were Egyptian and Saudi expatriates living in Hamburg, Germany. Sixteen entered the United States on student or tourist visas.[16] One French citizen of Moroccan background suspected of participating in planning for the attack but detained prior to it entered the United States without a visa because the visa waiver policy instituted in 1986 exempted French citizens from a visa obligation for a short-term visit. Of the 32 million aliens (excluding Canadians and Mexicans) who temporarily enter the United States each year, most are not required to obtain visas.[17]

U.S. FOREIGN POLICY AFTER THE NEW DAY OF INFAMY

Many observers have compared the events of September 11 to the Japanese attack on Pearl Harbor in 1941. The analogy drawn, however, is imperfect. The Japanese surprise attack struck at U.S. military forces. The attack on September 11 targeted civilians, thereby constituting terrorism. The United States responded in both 1941 and 2001 with declarations of war, but the war launched in 1941 was conventional and targeted enemy states. The war declared in 2001 was of a different nature and was principally directed against a nonstate, transnational movement—Al-Qaida and its allies, including the Taliban movement in Afghanistan. The differences between the two events reflected the fundamental changes that have occurred in global politics since 1941.

In the post–Cold War period, most conflicts do not involve conventional interstate warfare but, rather, rage within states. The role and nature of national states has also evolved. Many theorists interpret the profound changes wrought by globalization as a challenge to the primacy of nation-states.[18] Many view nation-states as weakened in a global order undergoing transformation. Nevertheless, as dramatically underscored on September 11, nation-states continue to provide security and are expected to do so. Provision of national security in 2001, however, constituted a very different challenge than it did in 1941. The quest for security that shaped U.S. foreign policy after September 11 differed profoundly from the quest for security pursued in 1941: military force alone cannot achieve victory.

The analogy drawn between these two Days of Infamy could not obscure the obvious: changes wrought by globalization and the evolution of world politics since 1941 had profoundly altered the national security environment of the United States. The war waged against terrorism could not be fought with the strategy and means used in World War II. Indeed, part of the explanation for the vulnerability exposed by the attack on September 11 arose from an inability to reconceptualize national security needs in light of global changes. The prosecution of the war against terrorism necessarily entails reconceptualization of the national security needs of the United States, and this could fundamentally reshape U.S. foreign policy in the wake of September 11.

Shortly after the attack, President Bush ordered the creation of an Office of Homeland Security to coordinate counterterrorism in the United States. His appointee to head the council, former Pennsylvania governor Tom Ridge, received a broad mandate to improve and foster interagency and intergovernmental measures to protect Americans from terrorism. His appointment quickly resumed debate over the adequacy of federal agency coordination on counterterrorism. Some proposed restructuring of the U.S. government to bring all agencies principally involved in the provision of homeland security, such as U.S. Customs, the Federal Aviation Administration, the border patrol of the Immigration and Naturalization Service (INS), the FBI, and consular services of the State Department into a new agency headed by the Coordinator for Homeland Security. In all, the Office of Homeland Security was mandated to coordinate the work of forty-six federal agencies.[19]

Overall coordination of federal agencies involved in counterterrorism improved after the 1993 bombing of the World Trade Center. That attack and the bombing of the Federal Courthouse in Oklahoma City spurred enactment of new federal laws concerning terrorism and immigration in the mid-1990s. In fact, the 1996 immigration law authorized the creation of a system to monitor foreign students in the United States and a system to verify the arrival and departures of aliens accorded temporary visas. About forty percent of the estimated 8.5 million aliens illegally living in the United States overstayed their visas.[20] Neither measure had been successfully implemented by 2001. American universities had vociferously criticized the mandated system to monitor foreign students and, before September 11, it remained stillborn. The entry-exit system to monitor temporary visa holders was to become effective in 1998, but it still functions inadequately. Some airlines do not comply with the requirement to return I-94 forms to the INS. Compliance with I-94 requirements at land border crossings has been incomplete. Some 130 million persons crossed the U.S.-Canada border in 2000.[21]

The adequacy of State Department screening of visa applicants came under intense scrutiny. Recent U.S. Congresses have funded the State Department at lower levels than requested. This slowed the State Department's ability to respond to recommendations made to improve security at U.S. embassies. Consular services are chronically understaffed, limiting the ability of Foreign Service officers to evaluate applicants. Moreover, the National Automated Immigration Lookout System used by the State Department, Customs, and the INS to prevent entry by known or suspected terrorists can be circumvented through adoption of a false identity supported by fraudulent identity documents.[22] Theft of passports from states whose citizens are exempted from visa requirements poses an additional dilemma.

In 2000, the National Commission on Terrorism concluded that the U.S. was a de facto land of open borders.[23] Not surprisingly, much of the immediate response to the events of September 11 centered on aliens in the United States. Hundreds of aliens of Middle Eastern and Islamic background were detained, many for violations of U.S. immigration law. Moreover, the attorney general ordered the interrogation of additional thousands of recent legal immigrants, mainly of Middle Eastern background.[24]

Western European allies similarly cracked down on immigrants of Middle Eastern background. Scores of suspected militants were detained across Western Europe, as the September 11 attack was interpreted as an attack against all member states of the North Atlantic Treaty Organization (NATO), thereby activating the common defense clause of the treaty. In December 2001, for the first time, immigration figured on the agenda of a seminar of the NATO Parliamentary Assembly, a meeting of the Mediterranean Special Group convened on Malta in midmonth.

Western European states and the EU took immediate steps to enhance counterterrorism. All of this augured well for the U.S.-declared war against terrorism, particularly because several Western European states have more experience in counterterrorism and more intelligence on organizations such as the Algerian AIG recently involved in plotting attacks in the United States. Better sharing of intelligence information and cooperation in prosecuting suspects loomed vital to the success of the war effort.

Concomitantly, significant divergences in the conceptualization of the war against terrorism emerged. European leaders suggested that the war effort should be limited to Afghanistan. They viewed with alarm public statements by U.S. Department of Defense officials that threatened extension of the war effort to Iraq and Iran because a certain outcome would be further mass migrations, which are viewed as threatening security and political stability throughout Europe.[25] Similarly, the U.S. viewpoint, which regards Hezbollah as a terrorist organization, is unlikely to be endorsed by European governments.

The initial phase of the war effort that was waged principally in Afghanistan with Afghani allies such as the Northern Alliance testified to the awesome skill and firepower of the U.S. military. The Taliban forces and many of their Al-Qaida allies were destroyed. But this did not appear to constitute a definitive victory in the declared war against terrorism. An ongoing, relentless counterterrorism effort would be required, and long-term success seemed to hinge greatly on bilateral and regional cooperation in suppression of terrorism. Ultimately, credible counterterrorism policies would need to address underlying socioeconomic issues and grievances fostering recourse to terrorism, and this would require much more of U.S. foreign policy than evidenced from the late 1960s until September 11. The attack testified to an enormous vulnerability and insecurity that Americans wanted to reduce. This new awareness born of disaster may significantly affect the conduct of U.S. foreign policy and enhance its stewardship of this planet.

U.S. rejection of the UN bid to secure pledges of increased foreign assistance for poor lands suggested the continuity of a narrow U.S. approach to counterterrorism in the wake of September 11. Secretary of State Colin Powell's address at the University of Louisville in late 2001, in which he proclaimed U.S. support for the creation of a Palestinian state, suggested a broadening of U.S. strategic vision and, at long last, a more credible approach to counterterrorism. However, after detection of a ship loaded with armaments destined for Palestinian forces in 2002, the Bush administration angrily admonished Palestinian leaders, particularly President Arafat, and the all-too-familiar contours of circumscribed thinking about terrorism and U.S. foreign policy reemerged.

Any lingering doubts about the centrality of the war against terrorism in U.S. foreign policy vanished after George W. Bush's first State of the Union address on January 29, 2002. Nearly half of the speech dealt with terrorism, and the president bluntly warned that the next phase would be directed against an "axis of evil" comprised of states such as Iraq, Iran, and North Korea and their terrorist allies. The choice of the term "axis" evoked images of U.S. enemies from World War II. The president also specifically referred to Hamas, the Palestinian Islamic fundamentalist movement opposing Israel, and Hezbollah as comprising, along with other groups, a "terrorist underworld."[26]

The president's address was certain to revive European and Arab fears of U.S. unilateralism in the war against terrorism. The possibility of the war against terrorism greatly straining long-established relations with key allies further testified to the fundamental reshaping of U.S. foreign policy underway since September 11. No evidence of a more comprehensive approach to counterterrorism emerged in Bush's 2002 address, suggesting that military action continued to constitute the core of U.S. counterterrorism strategy.

PART II
MARKETS

INTRODUCTION TO PART II

As the strategic Cold War against the USSR was ending, an economic cold war was emerging between the United States and its allies in Europe and Japan. In the 1990s there were hopes that the end of the Cold War would lead to a "peace dividend" (i.e., money saved from reduced military expenditures) that could be invested in rapid global economic development. There were also expectations that the end of the Cold War would lead to a more peaceful and less tense global order. None of these hopes and expectations have been realized. Military budgets fell slightly before September 11, but there was no peace dividend to invest in global development. Military conflict increased in the immediate post–Cold War period as ethnic violence erupted in Europe and Africa. International tensions over nuclear war have been replaced by constant international anxiety over trade wars. Ironically, the end of the Cold War led to a situation within the Western economic zone that shares many characteristics with the East–West enmity of the prior Cold War.

There are at least three key similarities between the old Cold War and the new economic cold war: (1) a never-ending situation of competition exists between nations that makes international tensions inescapable, (2) this competition (military or economic) is a central feature of international relations and a primary focal point for foreign policy among the major powers, and (3) although there are no direct military confrontations between the great powers, in both ages global politics exhibit what Rousseau called "a state of war." In other words, American foreign policy is now obsessed with concerns about economic competition (on a day-to-day basis) just as it was once obsessed with daily concerns about the Soviet military threat. Foreign economic policies now assume a role that is similar in some respects to the role once played by Cold War nuclear policies. Economic conditions in the post–Cold War era are typified by Rousseau's state of war.

Rousseau's concept of a state of war describes "a condition that we today would call a 'cold war.'"[1] Rousseau was one of the first philosophers to make a distinction between war itself and the state of war. When two or more states remain "on guard" against one another for any reason but take no punitive "actions against each other. . .the relationship has not changed as far as their intentions are concerned. Thus they are in a 'state of war.'"[2] This is an apt description of the economic conflict that typifies relations between the United States, the European Union (EU), and Japan. For Rousseau, "military conflict was only one [possible] aspect of the state of war. He saw greed as another major source of trouble, quite capable of causing states to want to weaken one another—an intention that is the essence of the state of war."[3] Trade is "an inevitable source of discord" between nations, and trade protectionism is a form of "overt hostility" that displays "aggressive intent."[4] Regulation of foreign trade becomes a "diplomatic weapon," and "peaceful international politics . . . [are] but the continuation of war by other means."[5] Commerce between nations does not "breed peace" as Kant and others believed, but rather "commerce only exacerbates greed and the competition among nations."[6] Hence the characterization of trade relations among the three economic superpowers (United States, EU, Japan) as an economic cold war, or as a "Cold Peace."[7]

Of course, there are also obvious differences between the old Cold War and the new economic cold war. The old Cold War was based on an implicit threat of direct military confrontation. The United States and the USSR threatened the physical survival of each other. Use of the military option against one another is not a viable alternative within the "security community" that has been established for the United States, Western Europe, and Japan. Now the implicit threats are economic in nature (e.g., trade sanctions, closing markets, imposing trade barriers, seeking alternative trading partners). It is the economic welfare of citizens that is threatened, not the physical survival of the state. But these economic threats are also felt at the individual level in a way that the threat of nuclear annihilation was not. Trade wars "hit home" for the average American in a more direct and consistent manner than did the less imaginable scenarios of global nuclear war. The costs of trade wars during the economic cold war can hit at the pockets of almost any and all American workers.

As the world moved from the old Cold War into the new economic cold war, theories of American foreign policy were forced to adjust. Realist theory was developed to guide national defense policy and was rarely relevant to foreign economic policy (FEP). The realist approach assumes that nation-states are the dominant actor in global politics[8] and that states are unitary actors. Realism is also based on the assumption that there is an identifiable hierarchy of foreign policy priorities, and national security is always at the top of this listing. Realists such as Kissinger have never had much interest in economic affairs. Their concerns are almost exclusively devoted to national security. Neorealism has been slightly more useful (than classical realism) regarding FEP, especially Gilpin's analysis of the connections between economic development and war.

The schools of liberalism and neoliberal institutionalism evolved to correct the weaknesses of realism when it comes to economic matters. One of the first major contributions came from Keohane and Nye's theory of "complex interdependence." Complex interdependence stresses three aspects of international politics that are often overlooked by realism: (a) the importance of nonstate actors (such as transnational corporations) (b) the fact that states are not unitary actors (they interact with one another through multiple channels), and (c) the realization that some national interests are separate and distinct from military security. Nations have economic interests that can often supersede concerns of national defense (depending on the context).[9]

Once again (as was the case with defense policy) the debate between realism and liberalism has defined the mainstream regarding theories of America's FEP. These broad schools of thought have also spawned a series of more specific approaches to international political economy. The end of the Cold War and the publication of Paul Kennedy's book on *The Rise and Fall of Great Powers* stimulated much interest in hegemonic stability theory (HST).[10] HST studies the extent to which global politics and American foreign policy have been structured by the rise and fall of hegemonic states. Is the United States today a former global hegemon that must develop policies to cope with its inevitable decline? Opinions differ; Kennedy is pointed to as the theorist who best defends the declinist view, whereas Nye and Nau argue against the validity of charges that America is a great power in decline.[11] Closely related to this debate are theories of economic and political cycles of power. These "long cycle" theories posit a view of history in which hegemons rise to global prominence, hold power for a time, and then eventually fall to challengers that become the new hegemon after a global trauma (such as a world war).[12] Those who subscribe to long cycle theory predict America's decline and a global war between 2030 and 2050 that will bring to power a new hegemon.

Theories of international political economy have also turned to the relatively new topics of international regimes and globalization. Regime theory focuses on international institutions that loosely govern interactions between states within a given issue area (such as trade or monetary relations).[13] Theories of globalization and global governance foresee a time in the future when the sovereignty of nation-states has eroded to such an extent that international organizations, transnational corporations, and global civil societies perform functions that have been dominated by state governments in the past (e.g., providing security, promoting welfare, protecting human rights and the environment).[14]

Finally, beyond the mainstream there are those critical theories of FEP and international political economy that tend to approach these issues from the perspective of underdeveloped nations. Theories of economic dependency and Wallerstein's world systems theory both emerge from a premise that all nations can be divided into "the haves" and "the have-nots:" into a rich core of industrialized nations versus an underdeveloped periphery of poor Third World nations.[15] According to these views, global capitalism and America's FEP exist to further the interests of the rich and powerful nations, while progressively impoverishing and disenfranchising the nations of the Third World. Neo-Marxist theories of political economy go even farther in terms of their critiques, arguing that a radical redistribution of wealth and political power (through revolution if necessary) are the only ways that justice and economic equity can be achieved at the global level, given the disparities created by 300 years of capitalist exploitation.[16]

Once again, as with theories of security policy, this text will not try to convince students that one of these theories is right and the others are wrong. Rather, we urge our readers to come to their own conclusions about the empirical and normative merits of these many theories. To facilitate that process, we once again offer a series of websites (cutting across the ideological spectrum) for gaining further information.

Internet Resources for Part II

Fifty Years Is Enough
www.50years.org

International Forum on Globalization
www.ifg.org

International Monetary Fund
www.imf.org

Jubilee 2000
www.j2000usa.org

Organization for Economic Cooperation and Development (OECD)
www.oecd.org

U.S. Agency for International Development
www.usaid.gov

U.S. Commerce Department
www.commerce.gov

U.S. International Trade Commission
www.usitc.gov

U.S. Trade Representative
www.ustr.gov

World Bank
www.worldbank.org

World Trade Organization
www.wto.org

WTO Action (anti-WTO)
www.wtoaction.org

UN Conference on Trade and Development (UNCTAD)
www.unctad.org

UN Development Program
www.undp.org

Chapter 7

A HISTORY OF AMERICA'S FOREIGN ECONOMIC POLICIES

HIGH POLITICS AND LOW POLITICS

The first six chapters of this book analyze areas of U.S. foreign policy that are traditionally given the most attention: defense, nuclear weapons, arms control, war and peace in the Middle East, U.S. military interventions, and terrorism. Such topics are sometimes lumped together under the heading of "high politics." High politics refer to policies regarding national defense, warfare, and all policy directly related to international security (when security is defined in terms of realpolitik). This chapter, the second subsection of this book, and indeed all topics in this text beyond chapter 6 are sometimes referred to collectively as "low politics." Low politics include all areas of policy that are not intimately tied to national defense and international war. Economic policy is perhaps the most important area of low politics in the post–Cold War era; hence, it is a logical point of departure when any discussion moves beyond defense policy into other areas. The end of the Cold War has increased interest in and attention to low politics in general and foreign economic policy (FEP) in particular.

One must be careful not to draw too sharp of a distinction between high and low politics, or between national defense and economic policy. Indeed, in many ways the two areas are ultimately inseparable. Defense policies often have economic purposes as their raison d'être. When the United States moved to create the North Atlantic Treaty Organization (NATO) after World War II, it was done in large part due to U.S. economic interests. In order for the United States to grow and prosper, it needed trade with Western Europe. If Western Europe had been allowed to fall under Soviet control, Stalin would have severed trade across the Atlantic, just as he had severed trade between Western Europe and his satellites in Eastern Europe after 1945. Therefore, due to economic imperatives, the United States had to keep Western Europe free from Soviet domination.

Conversely, economic means are often used to pursue military ends. For example, when the United States went to war against Iraq in 1990–91, special aid programs were extended to the "frontline states" that bordered the conflict (Israel, Jordan, Syria, and Turkey). Economic aid to frontline states was extended primarily to solidify the alliance against Iraq. Similar polices were used to rush new aid to Albania and Macedonia during U.S. intervention into Kosovo. Once again, aid to frontline states (this time in the Balkans) was used to buy support for American military policies.

TRADE WARS AND MILITARY AGGRESSION

Perhaps the best example of a connection between high politics and low politics is to be found in the perceptions of victorious Western powers after World War II. A consensus was shared among the victors (and even with some of the vanquished) that economic disputes had been a primary catalyst leading to the military aggression of World War II.[1] So common was this view that, even before the war was over, Allied leaders took steps to reform the structural dynamics of international trade and finance. These institutional reforms created an international system of economic interaction that is still largely with us to this day. By creating new organizations such as the International Monetary Fund (IMF) and the World Bank, and by creating new rules for international trade under the General Agreements on Tarriffs and Trade (GATT) system (which later evolved into the World Trade Organization [WTO]), post–World War II leaders believed that they could eliminate the international economic structures that helped to turn trade wars of the 1930s into world war during the 1940s.

In order to understand America's foreign economic policies or to explain the emergence of the IMF, World Bank, GATT, and the WTO, one must first understand the connection between economic relations and military aggression that existed in the minds of those who shaped the postwar international political economy. To understand the possible ties between trade wars and military aggression, one must understand the nature of international trade prior to the two World Wars.

From the seventeenth to the nineteenth centuries, international trade became based more and more on a system of imperial trade zones. Within each colonial empire, a system of preferential and exclusionary trade relations developed. Each major power (Great Britain, France, the Netherlands, the United States, etc.) had a string of colonies around the globe. The imperial powers, or "mother countries," traded with their own colonies and sought to expand trade as much as possible within their imperial zone. There was less trade between the major powers than there is today, and there was little or no trade between the colonies themselves. British colonies had little direct trade with other British colonies, despite the fact that many of them shared borders (the same was true of French colonies). The entire system worked primarily for the benefit of the colonizers. For example, economic interactions between Kenya and Uganda were funneled through middlemen in England, who gladly profited from such arrangements.[2] Furthermore, economic specialization accelerated growth within the imperial powers, whereas the economies of the colonies fell farther and farther behind.

Colonies provided raw materials to the mother countries. These raw materials were sent to Europe and North America where they were consumed or processed into manufactured goods. Many of the finished products were then exported back to the colonies, which served as guaranteed markets for the imperial powers. Colonies served both as sources of raw materials and as markets for manufactured goods. Only British businesses had access to British colonies, only the French were allowed to exploit the economic resources of French colonies, and so forth. Colonies were legally prohibited from manufacturing products that would compete with similar goods from the mother country. For example, British colonial rulers in India closed down textile plants on the Asian subcontinent. The Indian people were then forced to buy their cloth from the mills in Lancashire, Leeds, and Manchester.

This system of imperial trade preferences brought the economically less-developed parts of the world (Africa, Asia, and Latin America) into the global marketplace. The underdeveloped parts of the world were dominated politically and economically by those states that were among the first to industrialize and establish colonies (once again the British, French, Dutch, etc.). The United States was not a founding member of the imperial club, given its own early history as a set of colonies and its early industrialization based on growth via *domestic* expansionism. After the Spanish-American War, however, the United States gained its own colonies such as the Philippines and Cuba.[3] By the late nineteenth century, the United States had become an imperial power.

Also in the late nineteenth century, another set of actors came onto the global scene. Often referred to as "late developers," nations such as Germany and Japan industrialized after the Americans and British had already gained an economic and imperial head start. These late developers wanted "a piece of the action" in the game of colonial trading preferences. However, most of the world had already been carved up by the established imperial powers. Germany and Japan reached major powers status, both economically and militarily, later than did the United States the United Kingdom or France. There was almost no area for them to expand into without coming into direct confrontation with the established imperial powers.[4]

Despite their positions as incipient threats to the established imperial nations, Germany and Japan were especially strident in their pursuit of colonies and areas to place under their economic control. By the 1930s, both of these rising powers were demanding more "living space." Hitler claimed that the dynamic nature of the Germanic peoples gave them a moral right to more lebensraum. At about the same time, Japanese fascists were moving quickly to establish their "East Asia Co-Prosperity Sphere" (their term for a new Japanese empire). Germany expanded primarily on the European continent, taking its living space from Czechoslovakia, Poland, the Low Countries, France, Denmark, Scandinavia, and ultimately the USSR. Japan mounted its own blitzkrieg into the Pacific Rim. It took colonies away from the British, the Dutch, the French, and the United States. In the view of the late developers, such military aggression to establish economic zones was essentially the same action that established imperial powers had taken decades (or perhaps centuries) before.

Whether this scenario about trade wars leading to military aggression is empirically accurate or not is largely beside the point. The fact is that this is how leaders in the West perceived economic factors contributing to the outbreak of world war.[5] This view was especially common within the United States. The United States took the lead during the postwar era to see that this scenario would not be repeated.

POST-WORLD WAR II TRADE AND MONETARY REGIMES

After Germany and Japan had been defeated, there was general agreement among the Allied powers that economic factors (trade wars, exclusive economic zones) had contributed to the outbreak of military aggression.[6] To avoid a repeat of these prewar problems, international economic relations had to be reformed. In order to do away with the imperial system of trade preferences, the GATT system was created. To facilitate the liberal trading system of GATT, a new monetary system was established under the IMF and the World Bank. GATT, the IMF, and the World Bank were designed to promote international free trade and the currency stability necessary for free trade.

GATT was created in 1947. It was originally set up to promote free trade in manufactured goods. GATT was founded on the basis of three main principals: "most favored nation" (MFN) status, reciprocity, and multilateral trade negotiations (MTNs). MFN status discourages discriminatory trade practices. Each member of GATT was expected to extend MFN status to all other members of GATT. Under MFN, any favorable trade relationship established for one member of GATT was to be extended to all other members trading in the same commodity. For example, if the United States granted a six percent tariff to Belgium for steel products imported into the United States, then the United States was expected to grant the same low tariff to all other members of GATT who exported the same steel products. The expectation was that GATT members would not "play favorites" among their trading partners. GATT members were not supposed to discriminate against some members of the organization while providing more favorable trade arrangements for others. In the 1990s, the preferred term for this principle became "normal trade relations" (NTR).

Under GATT's second principle—reciprocity—tariff reductions are supposed to be mutual. To go back to the previous example, if the United States lowered tariffs on Belgian steel from six percent to four percent, then Belgium was expected to reciprocate. Belgium would be expected to return the favor by lowering its tariffs on U.S. steel to no less than four percent. Furthermore, due to MFN, such tariff reductions would then cascade down to all other members of GATT over time as the United States and Belgium extended the same deal to other states. Reciprocity would promote bilateral and mutual tariff reductions, and MFN would then diffuse such liberalization of trade to all members of GATT.

The third principle of GATT was MTNs. MTNs have been held about once every decade to promote widespread reductions of tariffs and to eliminate other barriers to trade (nontariff barriers or NTBs). Referred to as "rounds," the negotiations for one full round of MTNs can span many years. The Uruguay round of MTNs from 1986–94 spawned the new WTO, as well as many other major changes to GATT's ways of doing business (see following discussion).

By means of MFN, reciprocity, and MTNs, GATT's members hoped to drive trade barriers progressively lower. When exceptions were granted to the general principles of GATT (and the exceptions were many), it was done largely because these exceptions were consistent with U.S. national interests. For example, Japan was allowed to discriminate against American goods, whereas the United States provided relatively unrestricted access for Japan's goods into American markets. Japan was allowed to deviate from strict adherence to the principle of reciprocity because the United States wanted it that way. The United States used its power and influence to grant Japan preferential trade status in return for American military bases, the United States established bilateral and multilateral trade preferences for Japan in order to gain base rights on Japanese territory. Other nations, such as less-developed countries (LDCs), also asked for similar exceptions to GATT's trade rules, but they were consistently denied. For example, LDCs wanted to protect their infant industries (e.g., steel plants in Brazil) from international competition during the difficult start-up phases. The United States and the GATT agreements rarely allowed for such protectionism by LDCs, largely because it was not in America's interests (see chapter 11).

The United States also took the lead in the area of international monetary relations. Prior to the end of World War II, the United States and its allies met in Bretton Woods, New Hampshire. The Bretton Woods meetings created a new regime for international currency rates and international lending based on the IMF and the World Bank. International trade in goods is easier to conduct when the values of national currencies are stable and predictable. International trade is also facilitated by international lending. The IMF was set up to oversee currency exchange rates and to provide short-term loans (shorter than one year) to member governments. The World Bank, also known as the International Bank for Reconstruction and Development (IBRD), was designed to grant long-term loans (longer than one year) to member governments. In the immediate postwar period, the World Bank focused on reconstruction loans to help rebuild Europe and Japan after the devastation of World War II. More recently, the World Bank has made its loans primarily to LDCs in order to promote development. America's key position within the Bretton Woods institutions is just one aspect of the unique nature of U.S. FEP.

THE UNIQUE NATURE OF U.S. FOREIGN ECONOMIC POLICY: QUANTITATIVE AND QUALITATIVE REASONS FOR THE IMPORTANCE OF U.S. POLICY

U.S. international economic policies play a singularly important role in international relations. The importance of U.S. policies can be summarized according to quantitative and qualitative factors. The quantitative dimensions of American policies are perhaps the most striking. First and foremost, the United States has the largest single national economy in the world. Total gross domestic product for the United States at the opening of the new millennium was more than $8 trillion annually. The second-ranked national economy, that of Japan, was a distant second at just less than $4 trillion.[7] The *combined* output of the nations of the European Union (EU) exceeds that of the United States, but no other single national economy can match that of the United States. U.S. gross domestic product (GDP) is equal to about twenty-three percent of total world GDP.[8] Total U.S. trade (imports plus exports) accounts for roughly thirty percent of world trade.[9] At least twenty-five percent of all non-U.S. exports come to the United States, making America the most important foreign market for all other nations. The United States is every other nation's "market of first resort."[10] The U.S. market is especially important to developing nations, because roughly fifty percent of all Third World exports are sent to the United States.

The quantitative importance of U.S. FEP is also evident from measures of trade as a percentage of America's GDP. Imports plus exports are a rapidly growing segment of the overall economy. In 1955, exports and imports combined to make up about eight percent of U.S. GDP. By 1990, this had doubled to sixteen percent of GDP.[11] By 1995, trade had grown to twenty-five percent of GDP and is expected to account for a full one-third of U.S. GDP by the year 2010. International trade now directly or indirectly affects the incomes of all Americans.

There are also nonquantitative factors that highlight the importance of America's FEP for international relations. Qualitative dimensions of global politics show that the United States plays a special role in the international system. The U.S. dollar has a special status in international markets due to its importance as the primary currency for transnational business, and also due to its role as a reserve currency (see following discussion). Many commodities on the international market, such as crude oil, have their prices set in dollars even when these goods are not produced inside the United States. This means that fluctuations in the value of the dollar affect the values of such commodities. Interest rates inside the United States, which are also linked to the value of the dollar, affect the international debts of most foreign governments, especially Third World nations.

The burdens of leadership have been another factor that complicates U.S. FEP. The United States has more things to contend with when setting its FEPs than any other nation. American decision makers have more to consider, more goals to pursue, and more trade-offs to make.[12] Many of these complications are due to America's leadership role in the world. Other nations can concentrate their FEPs on promoting basic domestic economic factors. Most countries use their FEPs to increase exports, decrease unemployment, expand domestic growth, and attract foreign investment. They do so via a combination of protectionist measures used to guard their domestic enterprises and workers, plus export enhancement policies (e.g., subsidies) used to promote domestic goods in global markets. The United States must balance these same domestic economic concerns with plans to maintain international peace and security and with the additional need to promote expansion of the global system of free trade.

A liberal system of free trade requires open markets. Creating and expanding open markets requires leadership. The primary responsibility of leadership in a system of free trade is to maintain open domestic markets. Free trade agreements require that some nation or nations pay the "system maintenance costs." System maintenance costs are the costs entailed when markets remain open. Promoting free trade requires the leadership of nations that are willing to open their markets first, as a means to persuade other countries to reciprocate.[13] Leadership also requires *keeping* those markets open, even in the face of protectionist measures on the part of trading partners. The United States was willing to pay most of these system maintenance costs during the Cold War, keeping its markets open to Japanese and European goods as a way to solidify the alliance for containment (while at the same tolerating protectionism on the part many of its trading partners). As we shall see, now that the Cold War is over and now that the global strategic threat has dissipated, the United States is much less willing to shoulder the burdens of system maintenance costs alone. In the post–Cold War era of the new millennium, the United States wants more "burden sharing" on the part of the other major economic powers in the world. In order to understand this recent transition from unilateral economic leadership during the Cold War to a need for multilateral burden sharing in the new millennium, one must review a history of U.S. FEP.

ISOLATIONISM (1776–1941)

The history of U.S. FEP can be divided into three broad periods: isolationism (from the Revolutionary War to Pearl Harbor); unilateralism (from Bretton Woods in 1944 to the dollar crisis of 1971); and interdependence (from 1973 to the present). The longest period was that of economic nationalism and isolationism.

As we saw in chapter 1, isolationism was the hallmark of U.S. security policy prior to the two world wars. The central feature of strategic isolationism was the refusal to form any permanent military alliances. At the same time that the United States pursued a defense policy of isolationism, nationalism was the hallmark of America's international economic policies. Before the 1930s, the United States paid little attention to international economic problems. American leaders acted unilaterally when making foreign economic policy and had little regard for the consequences of their policies on other nations. Nineteenth-century U.S. economic strategies concentrated on the nation's "manifest destiny," building a continental state from the Atlantic to the Pacific.

During economic isolationism, the United States played a relatively minor role in the affairs of Europe. The United States rejected military ties to European powers as a way to stay out of European wars. The United States had comparatively little interest in foreign markets as well. Because America was largely self-sufficient in economic terms, it didn't need foreign trade or foreign economic resources. The country concentrated on internal economic growth and rapid industrialization on this continent. Almost everything that was produced could be consumed within the quickly growing nation. Domestic natural resources and raw materials were sufficiently abundant to keep factories operating at full capacity. Wave after wave of immigration provided more than enough cheap labor.

The international economic system of this age stood in stark contrast to that which came after the world wars. American FEP during isolationism reflected these prior structural realities. Most of the world was still made up of colonies controlled by European powers. The poorest areas of the world (which are now Third World nations) had almost no importance to the United States. There was no such thing as U.S. foreign aid. The dollar was no more important than other currencies; in fact it had much less international importance than the British pound. London was the financial center of the world. U.S. banks were not very important outside of the United States. International banking revolved around London. A few international businesses existed in the United States, but there were no multinational corporations (MNCs) as we know them today.

The international economic system of this prior era had been largely created and managed by Great Britain. International trade was based on the system of imperial economic zones described previously. Some aspects of that global system of trade were less than acceptable to the United States, but American leaders made no efforts to change the system. Americans were content to tend their own garden and leave matters of international economic management to the Europeans. FEP for the United States during this long age of isolationism was a combination of economic isolation and economic nationalism. First and foremost, the United States used protectionist measures regarding trade. The primary tool of international economic policy was the imposition of high tariffs. Protectionism insulated the U.S. economy from the rest of the world. Congress has direct authority over trade under Article I of the Constitution. Congress used this power during isolationism to build a wall of protectionist barriers. Tariffs were high and relatively inflexible. The age of economic isolationism and trade protectionism culminated with the Smoot-Hawley Act of 1930.

Smoot-Hawley was a congressional initiative in response to the Great Depression. It erected a wall of tariffs designed to keep out foreign goods. Smoot-Hawley raised tariffs to an average of forty percent.[14] Congress taxed imports at an average rate of forty percent in a misguided attempt to ameliorate the pernicious impacts of the Depression. Of course, other nations were doing the same thing at the same time in their own attempts to weather the Depression of the 1930s. This rapid spread of protectionist tariffs only made the global economic depression worse. To be successful, the United States had to develop new approaches.

Movement away from economic isolationism began slowly with the Reciprocal Trade Agreements Act (RTAA) of 1934. The RTAA was part of President Franklin D. Roosevelt's New Deal policies. The New Deal was FDR's design for getting the United States out of the depths of the Depression. Prior to 1934, Congress set tariffs. Congress, due to its sensitivity to special interest groups, almost always put those tariffs at very high levels. Presidents had little or no power to adjust these protectionist measures. President Roosevelt found a way around such congressionally mandated protectionism. FDR wanted to expand foreign trade to assist in America's economic recovery. FDR was very popular, and he usually got what he wanted. Under pressure from the president, Congress gave the executive branch the authority to negotiate new lower tariffs for foreign goods. President Roosevelt would offer better access to U.S. markets as a way to entice other governments to lower their barriers to American goods. The RTAA sought trade agreements that would include *reciprocal* reductions in trade barriers (a precursor to the principle of reciprocity later integrated into GATT). Reciprocal reductions, it was hoped, could be used to expand international trade and jump-start the moribund industrialized economies.

Roosevelt's RTAA was an enormous success in reaching its goals. During the first six years after the RTAA went into effect, twenty-eight new trade agreements were signed between the United States and its major trading partners.[15] The RTAA provided a temporary lifting of the isolationist policies that had been preferred by American FEP during this age. A permanent break from isolationism did not come until after World War II.

UNILATERALISM IN U.S. FEP (1944–1971)

Isolationism gave way to internationalism in American foreign policy after World War II. The United States abandoned isolationism not only in its economic policies but in political and military relations as well. In its military posture, the United States tied itself to the permanent defense of Western Europe through the NATO alliance. Politically, the United States took the lead in establishing a series of new international organizations such as the Organization of American States (OAS) and the UN, once again a departure from pre–World War II foreign policy. Internationalism also tied the United States into a web of economic relations around the globe. At Bretton Woods, the United States led in the creation of a new system for international monetary relations. The IMF and the World Bank were created to rebuild the world after the war and to create stable currencies that would facilitate movement of goods across national borders. American leadership was also a key to the creation of the GATT system for free trade. GATT was created to discourage the economic nationalism of the prewar age (which the United States had employed just as all other nations had). GATT would "outlaw" the extreme protectionist measures that had contributed to the hostilities leading up to World War II. In the grand design set by U.S. policy makers after the war, containment and military alliances would maintain international peace and security, the UN would be a great power forum that would advance a global political agenda (decolonization, etc.), and the Bretton Woods institutions and GATT would manage international economic relations.

All of these efforts were integrated, and they were consistent with perceived national interests. The number one goal of FEP in the immediate postwar era was to enhance national security. Unlike today, the United States felt little or no threat from foreign economic competition. Japan and most of Western Europe lay in shambles. The USSR withdrew economically from the world and established its own international economic regimes by dominating and exploiting Eastern Europe. The U.S. economy was so powerful and so much larger than any other nation that it could not suffer much from any form of economic rivalry. In 1950, U.S. GDP was equal to roughly half of total world economic production.[16] As the lead economy, America's output was double that of the USSR (then ranked second in total economic production), and three times larger than the British (number three in economic rankings of that time).[17] The United States also had a growing trade surplus for decades after the war's end.

Because of its overwhelming economic dominance, the United States felt secure enough to allow the Japanese and many European nations to discriminate against American goods, while at the same time opening American markets to their goods. Because of U.S. economic hegemony, closed markets in Europe and Japan seemed like a small price to pay for frontline allies against communism. The United States used its wealth and power; exchanging trade incentives for base rights and support of containment. FEP was used to enhance American security. This was the age of unilateral U.S. economic leadership. Perhaps the clearest example of America's unilateral leadership was its management of the Bretton Woods system during that system's first twenty-five years.

The Dollar Standard

Bretton Woods never functioned as it was originally designed. When America met with its allies in 1944 to shape postwar monetary relations, there were certain expectations about how the system would operate and how it would be managed. These expectations were never met, and the United States stepped in to exercise unilateral control over Bretton Woods. Spero and Hart have provided a very useful summary of Bretton Woods as it was designed to work in theory, versus Bretton Woods as it worked in practice for its first twenty-five years. The following discussion of Bretton Woods in theory versus Bretton Woods in practice is taken largely from Spero.[18]

Bretton Woods was based in theory on three key assumptions. First, all currencies would be of equal importance. Second, the system would operate under multilateral management. Third, all currencies would be tied to the value of gold. Bretton Woods exchange rates would "peg" (or link) each currency to a gold standard. If each currency was valued in gold, then any one currency should be almost as useful for international trade as any other. Each national currency would be stabilized via this gold standard. Permission to revalue currencies would require the approval of the IMF's Board of Governors, which would be managed cooperatively by all the major powers that joined the IMF. IMF authority over revaluing currency would eliminate the prewar problem of competitive currency devaluations. In the interwar era, states had used unilateral "beggar-thy-neighbor" currency devaluations to drive down the prices of their goods in foreign markets. Such practices would not be allowed under the IMF. Finally, each nation in the IMF pledged to maintain "convertibility." Each national treasury had to promise to cash in its own currency (exchange the paper money for gold) when asked to do so by another member of the IMF. Such was the original design of the Bretton Woods system in theory.

In practice, Bretton Woods operated on a much different system for its first twenty-five years. First, the U.S. dollar became much more important than any other currency. Second, through management of the dollar, the United States was able to impose its own unilateral control over the system. Third, only the dollar was tied to gold, in practice all other currencies were linked to the dollar (and hence only indirectly tied to gold). This was a system that came to be known as the "dollar standard."

The dollar standard was unique in many ways. The dollar became the most important international currency for a wide variety of reasons. Dollars, rather than gold, became the preferred reserve asset for nearly all nations. Governments hoarded dollars. Dollars were better than gold for national treasuries. Dollars deposited into a bank account earn interest, gold normally does not. Dollars were used for government-to-government economic transactions (or "balance of payment" transactions). Nations paid their debts to other nations with American dollars, not with gold. Because there were so many dollars in circulation, the dollar also provided international "liquidity."

After World War II, the United States flooded the world market with dollars. The Marshall Plan, payments for foreign military bases, NATO and other alliance commitments, and foreign aid of all types entailed massive outflows of dollars from the United States. With abundant supplies of a desirable currency in circulation, or with "high liquidity," trading became easier for all major economies. The dollar was the grease that allowed the machine of international trade to operate at full-bore.

One disadvantage for the United States during the days of the dollar standard was its own inability to "repeg." Other nations could repeg, or revalue their currencies (upon approval from the IMF), as one way to cope with trade imbalances. Nations with a deficit in their trade balance often devalue their currency as a way to reduce that trade deficit. After devaluation, foreign goods in domestic markets usually go up in price, whereas domestically produced goods sold in foreign markets go down in price. Under normal economic circumstances, the result is usually a partial correction of the trade deficit: exports increase and imports decrease. However, repegging the value of the dollar was not an option for the United States during the days of the dollar standard. The United States could not effectively revalue its own currency. The United States could change the value of the dollar in relation to gold, but because the value of other currencies was tied to the dollar (and not to gold), the dollar's value vis-à-vis other currencies remained the same both before and after repegging. Hence, the United States could not address trade deficits in the same way as other nations. This inability to effectively revalue the dollar did not become a problem until the U.S. trade surplus started to decline in the late 1960s.

The Dollar Crisis

Because of the unique nature of the dollar standard, the United States was able to exercise unilateral control over monetary relations in the 1950s and 1960s. The dollar standard, however, eventually led to the "dollar crisis" of 1971. The dollar crisis marked the end of U.S. unilateral economic control. The dollar crisis was a crisis in many respects. It was a crisis of confidence, as international confidence in the value of the dollar waned. It was also a crisis for the IMF, in terms both of reserve assets and in relation to currency exchange management. Finally, the dollar crisis was a crisis for American foreign policy. Each dimension of the dollar crisis requires a detailed assessment.

The dollar crisis emerged in 1971 due, in part, to the fact that there were so many dollars in circulation. In theory, the dollar had to be convertible into gold. In practice, the United States promised foreign governments that it would cash in dollars for gold on demand. By 1960–61, however, dollars circulating *outside* the United States were greater than the value of America's gold reserves.[19] This led to questions about the reliability of the dollar. If the dollar was not fully backed by gold, how could governments be sure of its value? If the dollar's convertibility could not be maintained, what would foreign governments want to use for reserve assets and balance of payment transactions? How would international trade be affected?

To address the monetary aspects of the dollar crisis, the IMF adopted a series of new policies. To make reserve assets more readily available, the IMF created a new financial instrument called special drawing rights, or SDRs. SDRs were once known as "paper gold" because they exist only on paper. SDRs exist only in the financial ledgers of the IMF (because this system has been computerized, perhaps they should now be called "electronic gold"). The IMF can create and issue SDRs at will. They are backed by deposits in IMF accounts from the major economies. The value of one SDR is based on an average of several major international currencies. They are used only for balance of payments transactions. SDRs are allocated according to national economic output and trade volume. In other words, the bulk of all new SDR allocations go to the wealthiest nations. Creation and issue of the first SDRs helped to solve the problem of reserve assets during the dollar crisis. SDRs were an alternative to the dollar for national savings and government spending.

Another problem revealed by the dollar crisis was the fact that currency exchange rates had become too rigid. The Bretton Woods system established "fixed" exchange rates. Governments were allowed to revalue their currency only with IMF approval, and then only within very narrow limits. The Bretton Woods system was based on an assumption that, without fixed exchange rates, international trade would be discouraged. It was thought that currencies had to be unchanging from day to day, and even from year to year, in order to increase the movement of goods across international borders. As it turned out, the original design made rates too rigid, and governments with trade deficits or with high inflation had trouble managing their economies within the confines of fixed exchange rates. The solution to this problem was to move to a system of flexible exchange rates, a transition that took many years to complete. By 1976, the Jamaica Agreement institutionalized floating exchange rates as part of the rules of the IMF.

Another dimension of the 1971 dollar crisis, perhaps the most important one, was the crisis it created for American foreign policy. This was the era of Nixon's détente policies and the turbulent days of American involvement in Vietnam. The dollar crisis (in that respect) was just one more problem on a long list of national crises, and not the most salient one at that. Although he was primarily concerned with other areas of foreign policy at the time, President Nixon did announce new programs to deal with the dollar crisis, programs that were part of his New Economic Policy (NEP). In many ways, the NEP of August 1971 was a last gasp for U.S. economic unilateralism. The NEP was announced without consulting, or giving prior notice to, our allies (the Japanese government was particularly shocked). The United States enacted the NEP with little assistance from its major trading partners.

To solve the problem of convertibility, Nixon announced that the dollar would no longer be exchangeable for gold. It is often said that Nixon took the United States off of the gold standard, or that he "closed the gold window" at the U.S. Treasury. Foreign governments could no longer cash in dollars for gold. By 1971, it was also obvious that the dollar needed to be devalued. But devaluing in relation to gold was not sufficient. The United States needed to establish new values for the dollar vis-à-vis other major currencies, especially in regard to the German mark and the Japanese yen. The NEP allowed the dollar to float temporarily on international currency markets. This effectively established new exchange rates in regard to foreign currencies.

Other economic problems brought about other aspects of the NEP. For the United States, 1971 was a time of high inflation and high unemployment. The United States also suffered its first post–World War II balance of trade deficit in that year. To deal with the trade deficit, Nixon's NEP imposed a ten percent surtax across the board on imports into the United States. To cool inflation, the NEP called for voluntary wage and price controls within the United States. By 1973, it was obvious that the dollar once again needed to be devalued, and once again a "temporary" float of the dollar was announced. For all practical purposes, 1973 marked the beginning of floating exchange rates among the major currencies. Floating exchange rates were made permanent by the IMF, after the fact, in the 1976 Jamaica Agreement. The end of fixed exchange rates, the closing of the gold window, and America's first postwar trade deficit were symbolic indicators that U.S. economic hegemony was coming to an end. With the relative decline in U.S. economic power came a concomitant end to unilateralism in America's FEP. The end of unilateralism further coincided with the emergence of international interdependence.

INTERDEPENDENCE AND U.S. FEP (1973–PRESENT)

Defining "Interdependence"

It is commonplace and largely uncontroversial to say that we now live in an interdependent world. However, the term *interdependence* means different things to different people. It is similar in that respect to terms such as *modernization* or *globalization*. Such terms become politicized, and therefore they can lose their empirical utility. Interdependence remains a useful term to describe the world around us only if we keep in mind some specific empirical denotations of this word. The concept of interdependence is especially useful for highlighting certain sea changes in world politics that emerged in the late twentieth century. Many of these changes became undeniable during the years 1971 through 1973. Four dimensions of international interdependence require special attention.

First, interdependence means that it is no longer possible for the United States, or any other nation, to be economically self-sufficient. During the age of isolationism, the United States could grow and prosper by means of its internal resource base. Now, in order to ensure its own peace and prosperity, the United States must rely to some extent on foreign markets, foreign raw materials, and foreign allies. All nations are dependent on things outside their borders. Thus all nations exist in a state of *mutual* dependence with other countries. However, dependence is a relative term, and not all states are dependent to the same degree. Therefore interdependence is *mutual, but not symmetrical.* Each state is dependent to a different degree. The United States is probably less dependent than most other nations, but interdependence has been an undeniable constraint on FEP since the early 1970s.

Second, theories of international interdependence are useful for stressing the differences between international relations today and international relations thirty years ago.[20] These differences are many. Military force is now less salient, and military options have decreased utility for U.S. foreign policy. The world's top economic powers are no longer the top military powers as well (or vice versa), as was largely the case in prior historical epochs. National power is no longer fungible. In other words, a state's military power is now less useful for attaining economic goals. Theories of interdependence also stress the importance of relatively new nonstate actors for world politics. These "new" actors include MNCs, transnational social movements, nongovernmental organizations (NGOs, such as Amnesty International), and former LDCs that are now referred to as the newly industrialized countries (NICs, such as Brazil, China, and India).

Third, although the seeds of interdependence have been growing for many decades (and even centuries), the unavoidable restrictions on U.S. foreign policy that interdependence represents did not become obvious until 1971 through 1973. There were several events during this time period that are symbolic of the "arrival" of interdependence for U.S. FEP. In 1971, the United States experienced its first trade deficit since World War II. During the same year, the dollar crisis came to a head and forced Nixon to adopt the NEP of August 1971. Part of the NEP was the first postwar "float" of the dollar on international currency markets. A second "float" for the dollar came in 1973. This was also the year that most scholars of the IMF point to as the time for the switch from fixed to floating rates.[21] Finally, 1973 was the year of the Organization of Petroleum Exporting Countries (OPEC) oil embargo. In 1973, Arab nations in OPEC used their "oil weapon" for the first time. During the 1973 Arab–Israeli war, OPEC cut supplies of oil to supporters of Israel. This led to the first "oil crisis" of the Cold War era and forced many nations to make significant changes in their foreign policies toward the Middle East. OPEC's 1973 oil embargo showed that, in an age of interdependence, international relations are not necessarily controlled by the nations with the greatest military power. Even a superpower such as the United States was vulnerable to a cutoff of Middle Eastern oil.

Finally, the most significant aspect of interdependence for America's international economic policies is the fact that unilateralism is no longer a viable option. The rise of interdependence coincided with the end of unilateralism in FEP. An end to unilateralism meant an end to unilateral U.S. leadership. The United States is no longer willing to pay the system maintenance costs for free trade. The United States also has had to fight many trade disputes in the age of interdependence. The remainder of this chapter will review FEP since 1973 in regard to these two key areas: interdependence and leadership, and trade disputes in the age of interdependence.

The Problem of Leadership

In many ways, the age of interdependence is a "time of troubles" for U.S. foreign economic policies. One of the persistent problems of this age has been the problem of leadership. During the unilateral period of FEP, the United States took the lead in setting up GATT, the IMF, and the World Bank. It managed the Bretton Woods system via management of the dollar. The United States paid the bulk of the system maintenance costs for free trade by keeping its markets open and tolerating protectionist policies by Europe and Japan. Such leadership was not purely altruistic. Unilateral leadership during the peak of the Cold War facilitated the economic growth and national security of the United States.

The United States is now retreating, even retrenching, from its prior position of unilateral leadership. It is not willing to pay as large of a percentage of the system maintenance costs. The United States wants increased burden sharing. Most of the political pressures on U.S. decision makers in this regard come from domestic interests. Organized labor, textile manufacturers, agricultural producers, and the steel and auto industries are just a few of the many special interests that have felt the sting of interdependence. Lost jobs and declining market shares due to foreign competition have raised cries of "America first." In response, a wave of neoprotectionist legislation swept through Washington in the 1980s and 1990s (see following discussion). The United States has threatened on numerous occasions to close its markets unless trading partners move to liberalize economic sectors that historically have remained protected.

At the same time, Japan and the EU have been unwilling to step in and replace the loss of U.S. leadership. Japan has the second-largest national economy in the world, but it has not shouldered a position of leadership and responsibility commensurate with its economic power. The members of the EU have a *combined* GDP that is greater than that of the United States. However, the EU nations have been unwilling and unable to achieve enough internal consensus and cohesion to become a unified world leader.

What is necessary in an age of interdependence is some degree of multilateral cooperation and shared leadership by the three biggest economic powers (the EU, Japan, and the United States). Instead, the world is moving toward three regional economic blocs that compete more than they cooperate. Therefore, a sharing of the burdens of leadership by these three economic superpowers is unlikely in the near future. Furthermore, given the economic power of NICs such as China, Brazil, and India, these nations also deserve a place at the table of international economic leaders. However the advanced industrialized powers of Asia, Europe, and North America are unwilling to democratize international economic institutions, or to share leadership power with Third World nations (see chapter 11 for more detail).

Trade Conflicts in an Age of Interdependence

The age of interdependence for U.S. FEP is perhaps best understood by looking at key trade disputes from recent decades. Along with these trade conflicts, certain new economic strategies have also emerged for the United States. The trade disputes are best summarized by reviewing the political maneuvering at the GATT round of MTNs known as the Uruguay round (1986–1994). Uruguay round debates tended to focus on three key areas of trade: agriculture, service industries, and intellectual property rights. While these issues were being hammered out, the United States also devised a new set of FEPs that strengthened its hand during the MTNs. These policies included new trade sanctions under Section 301 of the 1988 Trade Act (or "Super 301") and the creation of the North American Free Trade Area (NAFTA). A review of the Uruguay round, Super 301, and NAFTA informs our understanding of FEP in the age of interdependence.

Prior to the Uruguay round, GATT principles of low tariffs and free trade never applied directly to agriculture. In the beginning, this was how the United States wanted it. Protectionism was allowed for agriculture as a way to shield American farmers from foreign competition and as a way to keep prices and profits high for agribusinesses (often by means of direct government subsidies). The EU and Japan also have long histories of government subsidies combined with restrictions on foreign agricultural goods. By the 1980s, the United States strongly objected to these policies. The United States opened the Uruguay round by taking the position that GATT had to be expanded to cover trade in agriculture.

By the 1990s, agricultural subsidies in the EU ran at more than $80 billion per year. U.S. subsidies during the same period were roughly $35 billion per year. The United States used to export grain to Western Europe in the 1960s—now the EU is its biggest competitor. The United States currently exports approximately forty percent of all agricultural production. One-third of its corn and two-thirds of its wheat crops go to foreign consumers every year. Believing that government subsidies by all producers were, on balance, reducing American exports, the United States demanded an immediate end to all subsidies during the Uruguay round. Argentina, Australia, and Canada sided with the United States. The EU, however, refused. The United States insisted on an immediate end to subsidies and employed heavy diplomatic pressure on the Europeans to push its position. The Europeans accused the United States of being heavy-handed and arrogant in its negotiating tactics and walked out of the debates. Fortunately, a collapse of Uruguay round talks (due to disputes over ag subsidies) was avoided. The final results of this dispute will be summarized in the following discussion.

A second area of contention during the Uruguay round was service industries. This is another area of international commerce that did not fall under the original mandate of GATT. Prior to the Uruguay round, GATT principles of free trade did not apply to services. However, these are some of the fastest-growing sectors of advanced, postindustrial economies. Services such as banking, insurance, transportation, shipping, tourism, education, health care, advertising, telecommunications, and data processing are some of the most competitive and leading-edge sectors of the U.S. economy. Two-thirds of GDP and sixty percent of all jobs in the United States are now tied to service industries.[22] The U.S. battle over free trade in agriculture was fought primarily against the Europeans. The battle over free trade in services has been primarily against the NICs. The EU tends to be pro–free trade in services, due to its desire to gain better access to U.S. markets in these areas. NICs such as India and Brazil, however, favor protectionism as a means to develop their own service industries. Computer-based sectors, media, and other such infant industries in the NICs are not well-developed enough to face up to unrestricted international competition. However, the NICs feel that if they do not rapidly develop their own service industries, then they will fall even farther behind the more advanced economies. Especially important are telecommunications and data processing. The United States battled the NICs during the Uruguay round to open up trade in services to GATT principles of free trade. The United States was also in a battle with the NICs over intellectual property rights.

Intellectual property refers to copyrights, patents, trademarks, Internet addresses, and other trade-related intellectual products. This is yet another area of trade not covered by GATT agreements prior to the Uruguay round. According to the U.S. position, some NICs have developed their economies via "piracy" of foreign intellectual property. The United States also claimed during the Uruguay round that American companies were losing $60 billion per year in unpaid royalties for patents and copyrights (on computer software, movies, publishing, pharmaceuticals, etc.).[23] India, Taiwan, and Thailand were cited as some of the worst offenders. The United States insisted, once again, that new GATT-style agreements be adopted to protect trade-related intellectual properties (or TRIPs). The United States scored partial victories during the Uruguay round in the areas of agriculture, service industries, and TRIPs. Before we review the results of the Uruguay round, however, it would be instructive to look at the new U.S. FEPs that were devised during this same time period.

SUPER 301 AND NAFTA:
THE "HAMMERS" OF U.S. FEP

While the United States was battling with the EU and the NICs at the Uruguay round, it was also developing several "big sticks" for its FEPs. The biggest hammer which the United States has to beat its trading partners into submission comes from the 1988 Omnibus Trade and Competitiveness Act. Section 301 of the 1988 Trade Act, commonly known as Super 301, promises to impose unilateral trade sanctions against nations that the United States deems to be unfair traders. These sanctions are said to be "mandatory" in cases where foreign governments use unfair trade practices or for nations with large trade surpluses vis-à-vis the U.S. Super 301 sets up an annual policy process to identify and punish unfair traders.

First, Super 301 requires an annual review by the White House of all trading partners. The result of this annual review is supposed to be a "hit list" containing the names of unfair trading nations. The hit list for Super 301 usually comes from the office of the United States Trade Representative (USTR). The USTR is a cabinet-level office that works directly under the president. Created by an act of Congress in 1962, the USTR is responsible for representing the United States at international trade talks. The 1988 Trade Act gave the USTR the additional responsibility of putting together the annual hit list under Super 301. To give just two examples, in recent years Brazil has been put on the hit list for restrictions against U.S. imports, and India has been targeted for barriers to American direct investment. Once the Super 301 hit list is published, unilateral trade sanctions against the targeted nation(s) are supposed to "mandatory." Little or no discretion is allowed to the president. However, there is a national security loophole to Super 301. A president can wave sanctions against a nation targeted by the 301 hit list if he or she argues that America's security would be compromised. The original time frame for Super 301 was five years. In 1994, however, President Clinton renewed the provisions of Super 301 by executive order, and it remains a key coercive element of America's FEP to this day.

Another key innovation in FEP during the days of the Uruguay round was the creation of NAFTA. The roots of NAFTA go back to a 1989 free trade agreement between the United States and Canada. This agreement removed almost all remaining barriers to trade between America and Canada (the United States' largest trading partner). In 1992, Mexico accepted an invitation to join the U.S.-Canada free trade zone under NAFTA.[24] Approved by Congress in 1993, the NAFTA treaty went into effect in January 1994. The terms of NAFTA were negotiated by the Reagan and Bush administrations and supported by Clinton.

President Clinton made important additions to NAFTA before presenting it to Congress for approval. Clinton added side agreements on labor rights and environmental protection. The primary purpose of these side agreements was to get each nation (especially Mexico) to more vigorously enforce its preexisting laws on labor rights and environmental protection. NAFTA created no new laws in these areas. The NAFTA process also includes dispute panels containing representatives from all three nations. Some panels hear complaints regarding alleged violations of free trade. For example, the United States has brought complaints before the dispute panels regarding Canadian tariffs on milk, eggs, and chickens. Other NAFTA panels have the power to review charges of unfair labor practices (union-busting, etc.) and complaints regarding environmental destruction (illegal dumping of toxic wastes, etc.).[25] During his second term, Clinton proposed expansion of NAFTA into a Free Trade Area for the Americas (FTAA). In theory, the FTAA would be open to all nations in the Americas.

Debates in the United States over the wisdom of NAFTA and the FTAA tend to focus on the impact that such agreements have on jobs at home. Numerous studies have been released by NAFTA's critics and by its supporters. Studies from groups that support NAFTA claim to show a net increase in jobs due to NAFTA, whereas anti-NAFTA organizations have presented data claiming to show an overall loss of jobs in the United States due to NAFTA.[26] Although this debate may never be settled conclusively, it is also largely beside the point. The central fact is that the forces of interdependence and globalization of production are pushing all major traders toward regional free trade blocs. NAFTA, and the future expansion of NAFTA, are in that sense inevitable; just as the future expansion of the EU is inevitable. The irresistible tide of interdependence and the concomitant currents of economic globalization guarantee that global-level production and marketing by MNCs will continue to grow. As MNCs expand their global reach, all major trading states look to free trade zones to enhance their competitiveness.

Creation of NAFTA was, therefore, a good strategy for U.S. FEP at the global level. Because increased globalization of production and interdependence are inevitable, U.S. policy and American corporations need to get on the right side of these international changes. Creation and expansion of NAFTA strengthens the U.S. position vis-à-vis the other major trading blocs (e.g., the EU and Japan's web of Pacific Rim production). Like Super 301, NAFTA increased the pressure on America's opponents in the Uruguay round debates. Perhaps this is one reason that the United States was able to achieve some notable breakthroughs in the final agreements from the Uruguay round.

RESULTS OF THE URUGUAY ROUND: PARTIAL U.S. VICTORIES AND THE CREATION OF THE WTO

The United States scored a series of partial victories during the Uruguay round regarding agriculture, services, and intellectual property. An agreement was signed by the United States, the EU, and others to reduce agricultural export subsidies by thirty-six percent over a six-year period, with additional reductions to be phased in over ten to twenty years.[27] Past performance, however, raises doubts that the EU will follow through on their promises and fully implement the proposed reductions in ag subsidies. The EU is not the only habitual offender in this regard. At the beginning of the twenty-first century, the United States was still spending $9 billion per year on its own agricultural subsidies.[28] This issue will therefore remain a key area of contention in subsequent rounds of MTNs.

Partial victories and unsettled issues typify the results of the Uruguay round for services and intellectual property as well. The United States was able to achieve agreement in principle that GATT rules for free trade will be extended to include service industries and intellectual property rights. However, the quandary is in the many details yet to be worked out for both areas.

Post–Uruguay round negotiations have been ongoing for years in the areas of telecommunications, shipping, and other service sectors. The Uruguay round produced a new treaty under which free trade in services will be enhanced. This is the General Agreement on Trade in Services (GATS). As of now, the GATS treaty allows each government to decide for itself which services will be subject to free trade, and they do not necessarily have to treat all other GATT/WTO members the same when it comes to trade in services. In other words, although there is an agreement in principle to expand free trade to services, MFN requirements do not yet apply, and the specific services themselves are still subject to negotiations.

The same agreement in principle, although leaving the specific details subject to future negotiations, applies to trade-related intellectual property. The TRIPs agreement from the Uruguay round established a TRIPs council within the WTO to monitor international copyrights, trademarks, patents, and printed circuit designs. The TRIPs council can take cases of intellectual property infringement to the WTO dispute panels (see chapter 9 for more on GATS and TRIPs).

The most controversial result of the Uruguay round was the creation of the WTO. The WTO replaced GATT on January 1, 1995. The primary difference between the WTO and GATT is the WTO's power to impose trade sanctions via dispute panels. More detail on the WTO dispute process will be provided in chapter 9. For now, a brief description should suffice. WTO members can bring charges of unfair trade practices before the WTO. Panels made up of member nations then hear from both parties to the dispute. Each government in the WTO has one vote, and there are no weighted votes or veto powers. Dispute panels have the power to decide if any GATT/WTO regulations have been violated. When violations do occur, the WTO has the power to order the offending nation to end the unfair practice(s). If the offender does not comply, the WTO has the power to impose fines and/or trade sanctions that must be observed by all WTO members.

President Clinton called a special session of Congress after the 1994 national elections to secure ratification of the WTO treaty. The lame-duck Congress approved but attached the Dole Amendment. The Dole Amendment is an "escape clause" giving the United States the right to withdraw from the WTO if American decision makers decide that membership in the new organization is contrary to the national interest. Critics of the WTO on the right charge that this organization reduces national sovereignty. Critics on the left see the WTO as a club for the rich that is controlled by corporate interests. Anti-WTO demonstrations tend to focus on the alleged harm done by the organization to workers and environmental conditions (see following discussion).

Threats to national sovereignty from the WTO are probably overstated. There is no reason to believe that the WTO can impose its will on the United States (or the EU or Japan or any other major economic power) if the United States refuses to accept decisions handed down by the WTO dispute panels. The Dole Amendment is largely redundant because *every* nation has the right to withdraw from WTO membership at almost any time. Furthermore, to date the United States has been consistently successful in winning cases before the dispute panels.

WTO dispute panels dealt with more than 150 complaints during the 1990s.[29] One study shows that the United States won twenty-three out of the first twenty-five cases it brought before the WTO (1995–2000).[30] In its most notable loss to date, the WTO ruled that the U.S. government had to eliminate its Foreign Sales Corporation. The Foreign Sales Corporation was created in 1984 to give tax breaks to U.S. corporations by allowing them to set up subsidiaries in tax havens such as Barbados and the Virgin Islands.[31] If the United States simply refuses to abide by the WTO ruling (and indications are that this will continue to be the U.S. response), it will have to weather the sanctions imposed by other WTO members. But no coercive power of the WTO can force the United States to eliminate programs that it believes are, on balance, in the national interest.

U.S. FOREIGN ECONOMIC POLICY IN THE NEW MILLENNIUM

Unresolved issues from the Uruguay Round and debates over the value of membership in the WTO will set the tone for FEP in the early twenty-first century. The biggest dispute yet before the WTO puts the United States toe-to-toe with the EU, once again regarding trade in agriculture. The infamous "banana war" dispute is likely to be a make-or-break struggle regarding the WTO's power to effectively impose its decisions on the economic superpowers. Details of the banana wars will be discussed in depth in chapter 9. The final ruling in the banana war case must go against what one side or the other views as its vital national interests. Can the WTO impose its will against an economic superpower if that actor refuses to submit? See chapter 9 for a partial answer to this question.

Another key dimension for FEP in the future will be the interests expressed by the public and by NGOs. The WTO, once a relatively obscure part of international politics, became front-page news during protests in Seattle during 1999. An interesting coalition of labor groups, environmental organizations, consumer advocates, and Third World lobbies banded together to expose what they see as the pernicious impact of the WTO. Critics deride the WTO as an antidemocratic club for corporate interests that allegedly endangers the environment, undermines public health and safety, threatens accountable policy making, and endangers the economic interests of the developing nations.

Many groups came to Seattle in 1999 to pressure the WTO to open its proceedings to labor unions, environmental groups, and Third World NGOs. Global Exchange, Global Trade Watch, and Third World Network were among the most outspoken NGOs. Global Exchange criticized the WTO's preference for making decisions behind closed doors. Global Trade Watch fears that critics of the WTO will be either co-opted or excluded from the decision-making process. Third World Network cautioned that more liberalization of trade by the WTO would lead to political instability and economic hardships in developing nations. Although these criticisms are important, and especially relevant to the WTO's track record to date, there was also much more common ground between the protestors and the position of the U.S. government than either side seemed to realize.

Even before protesters took to the streets in Seattle, the U.S. position on necessary reforms in the WTO spoke to some of their concerns. President Clinton claimed that he wanted to "put a human face" on the global economy. He proposed a new round of global trade talks (the Millennium round). The 1999 ministerial meeting in Seattle was to be the first step in launching the Millennium round. As part of the new Millennium round, the United States wants to create a working group on trade and labor standards. Working groups lay the groundwork and draft resolutions for the plenary sessions of the WTO to consider. The goal of the working group on labor standards would be to expand WTO authority to include worldwide enforcement of basic labor rights (unionization; collective bargaining; standards for minimum wages, maximum hours, and job safety; etc.).

Similar reforms would be made to bring environmental concerns into the ambit of WTO authority. The United States has already conducted its own review of the likely environmental consequences from a new round of trade talks. The WTO has an Environment and Trade Committee that could function much like the new working group on labor, drafting new regulations that would enforce and improve existing environmental protections within member governments (similar to NAFTA's environmental dispute panel). The United States will push to eliminate all tariffs on environmental technologies (e.g., greener industrial equipment) as a way to facilitate trade in these goods, especially exports to the developing world. The United States also demands that member governments be given the right to retain environmental standards that are higher than those required by existing international agreements.

U.S. policy also favors increased "transparency" within the WTO. As stated by U.S. Trade Representative Charlene Barshefsky (during the Clinton administration), transparency would include rapid release of documents; enhancing the input of NGOs, allowing NGOs and other interested parties to file amicus curiae briefs at WTO dispute panels, and opening dispute settlement proceedings to public observers.[32] Dispute panels are the targets of the WTO's critics' primary concerns. In response to the unrest in Seattle, Clinton restated and emphasized his administration's prior offer to open up the dispute panels to NGO participation. Labor and environmental groups would be given a seat at the hearings and allowed to voice their concerns. Only WTO member governments, however, have a vote in the final decisions on whether or not to impose sanctions.

U.S. foreign policy has taken the position that new trade agreements should contain enforceable standards for labor rights and environmental protection. The United States is generally supported in this position by the countries in the EU and by its partners in NAFTA. The strongest political opposition to new WTO authority over labor and environmental standards comes from Third World governments. In many cases, these are the same Third World countries in which MNCs set up sweatshops. They are also the same countries favored by MNCs because of their lax (or nonexistent) enforcement of environmental protections. We can expect to see a long and bitter struggle in the early twenty-first century as rich and poor nations seek compromises and common ground on these issues. To better understand the politics of current U.S. economic policy, the next two chapters will present more in-depth looks at the IMF, the World Bank, and the WTO.

Chapter 8

DEBT CRISES,
THE ASIAN MELTDOWN,
AND U.S. POLICY TOWARD
THE IMF AND WORLD BANK

Daniel M. Green

The streets of Prague were teeming with life one blustery week in late September 2000, but not with tourists enjoying the city's beautiful historic architecture. Instead, Prague was host to thousands of protesters trying to disrupt the annual meetings of the World Bank and the International Monetary Fund (IMF) being held there. Many wore black masks and held inner tubes in front of their chests—to bounce off police shields and deflect blows—and indeed there were a few dozen injuries in clashes with police brigades during the three-day meeting. The protesters were chanting "London! Seattle! Continue the Battle!" in Wenceslas Square, site of the "Velvet Revolution" that shook Czechoslovakia a decade earlier during the fall of communism. Their demands? An international economic order that was more equitable and an end to abject poverty and unemployment due to free trade competition. The protestors had an impact, even on those against whom they were protesting. World Bank president James Wolfensohn seemed to agree with much of the spirit of the protests, saying, "[W]e live in a world scarred by inequality. . . . Something is wrong when the richest 20 percent of the global population receive more than 80 percent of the global income . . . and when 2.8 billion people still live on less than $2 a day. Our challenge is to make globalization an instrument of opportunity and inclusion—not fear."[1] The protesters succeeded in trapping the gathered dignitaries in their conference center for six hours at one point but did not seriously disrupt the proceedings. Nonetheless, at the closing ceremonies, IMF managing director Horst Kohler felt compelled to apologize to the people of Prague for the trouble that had been caused.

Amazingly enough, just a few months earlier Kohler himself had been at the eye of a diplomatic storm, a less public fight over the IMF, but with high stakes just the same. On November 9, 1999, Michel Camdessus suddenly announced that he would be stepping down from his post as managing director of the IMF, after thirteen years of service. The battle over who would succeed him became far more heated than anyone would have expected, as angry phone calls were exchanged between President Clinton and European leaders such as Chancellor Gerhard Schroeder of Germany. The head of the IMF is traditionally a European, but the United States did not like Schroeder's candidate, Caio Koch-Weser, although he was supported by nearly all of the European heads of state. No matter; U.S. Treasury Secretary Larry Summers had plans to reform the IMF, and he doubted that Koch-Weser had the stature and respect to get them pushed through. After repeatedly hinting that he was unsuitable, the United States finally had to go public and wage a campaign, brief but effective, to remove Koch-Weser and push the Germans to put someone else forward. The Europeans finally relented, and Horst Kohler (a compromise candidate) was quickly approved. Clinton had exercised America's traditional veto power over who would take up the IMF post, but this had not been taken well in European capitals. All sides were irritated and embarrassed. From the beginning of his term, Kohler was anxious to demonstrate independence from Washington's powerful influence.

What was at stake in these two public power struggles? In many ways, the very future of the world economic system. The current economic order that most dominates the principles of trade, international business, and economic development has been in place since about 1980 or so. This order is often referred to as the "Washington Consensus." The very existence of the Washington Consensus appears to be a sign of the supreme dominance of American interests and ideology in the international system. But these episodes illustrate some of the important themes we have seen in other chapters of this text: about the persistence of American power undoubtedly, but also about challenges to it from other major powers (including an EU on the rise, speaking increasingly with one voice) and so-called nonstate actors, in this case a newly important global civil society of individuals and organizations coalescing in a global social movement against free trade and excessive neoliberalism. This chapter is about the origins of this economic order, America's role in its evolution, and the likely directions of a world economic policy paradigm in the new millennium to come.

AMERICA AND THE POWER OF THE BRETTON WOODS INSTITUTIONS

The World Bank and the IMF, together known as the Bretton Woods Institutions (BWIs), were established at the end of World War II to promote global economic order and prosperity and thereby help prevent another world war. They were largely designed by the United States and Britain, strongly reflecting the interests of the former in particular, in a process that included a pivotal meeting of Allied country representatives at the Bretton Woods resort hotel in New Hampshire in the summer of 1944. To begin to understand the ways in which the U.S. government influences and controls the activities of these two organizations, we must review some details of their institutional missions and operations.

The World Bank's basic institutional mission has evolved considerably since it was first established in 1945. It began as a bank to provide funds for the reconstruction of Europe after World War II, but since the 1950s it has become a development bank, lending money to eligible countries (member countries not exceeding a certain level of development and per capita income). By the end of the 1990s, the bank was making loans totaling roughly $30 billion per year for various projects and programs throughout the world.

Governance at the World Bank covers issues such as bank lending policy, specific loans to individual countries, reforms to bank operations, and the approval of new initiatives. The World Bank's 180-plus member countries have representation on a board of governors that meets annually. Daily activities are managed by a twenty-four-member board of executive directors based at headquarters in Washington, D.C., which has effective power between annual meetings. The World Bank is led by a president with considerable influence and visibility, who has to date always been named by the U.S. government and has always been an American.

One can also get a sense of power relationships over bank policy by looking at its finances. To begin, the World Bank charges interest on most of its loans and earns a profit each year, just as commercial banks. The Bank gets a small portion of its funding from countries when they join, but most of its money is raised in international capital markets, through the floating of bonds or through borrowing, and from periodic replenishment drives (as in the case of funds for the International Development Association, the Bank's special facility for the very poorest countries).

The IMF differs from the World Bank in several important ways. The IMF's Articles of Agreement state that its purpose is to encourage the balanced growth of international trade and to facilitate international monetary cooperation. To do this, it is specifically tasked to monitor currency exchange rates and balance-of-payments problems, with an eye to promote exchange

TABLE 8.1: Recent World Bank Presidents

1968–81	Robert McNamara
1981–86	William Clausen
1986–91	Barber Conable
1991–96	William Preston
1996–present	James Wolfensohn

rate stability. Thus, the IMF is not a "banker" providing loans for economic development projects to its member countries, but it is rather a "police officer" seeking to maintain proper currency values and balanced trade and to promote global trade flows and economic expansion. It acts as a monitoring agency and credit union, keeping track of country performance and loaning governments money when their currency values and current account balances are in trouble.

The IMF enforces a code of conduct that must be agreed to by all member countries when joining. This gives the IMF power to give advice and make pronouncements about the economies of all its members. It routinely rebukes even wealthy and powerful countries such as the United States and the major European economies for high inflation rates or trade imbalances. Enforcement of IMF standards happens because all countries face policy "conditionalities" when they borrow from the IMF. These economic conditions impose financial stringency, currency devaluations, and government budget cuts upon countries in crisis, especially less-developed countries (LDCs), forcing them to set their economic houses in order. Because wealthy countries are rarely in dire need of IMF financial assistance, they are seldom forced by conditionalities to heed its advice. Third World nations, by contrast, have little choice but to submit to conditionalities if they want to borrow from the IMF. Originally, the IMF used mostly short-term "stand-by" loans and policy "shock treatment" programs of no more than one year's duration. But since the oil price shocks and economic crises of the 1970s, its loan/reform packages have stretched to three-year or five-year terms (and sometimes longer) to assist countries in making deeper structural changes to their economies.

The issues that face the IMF on a regular basis relate to its lending policies and supervisory powers over member countries; new initiatives such as those for debt management or debt relief; and bigger concerns about how the world economy should be run (or what has been recently dubbed the "international financial architecture"). These issues are dealt with through its institutional decision-making procedures, which are similar to those in the World Bank. The head of the IMF has the title of managing director and serves for a five-year term. It is a very important position in terms of policy making and public visibility and one by tradition held by a European. The deputy director of the IMF is traditionally an American.

The IMF is governed by an executive board of directors, usually made up of the finance ministers of member countries. They meet to approve all loan programs of the IMF and also to formulate "guidance statements," setting policy that the rest of the IMF's employees must follow. The executive board meets at big meetings, but most of its work is handled by an interim committee. Most recently, there has been a change in this schema as well. Since 1999, the interim committee has been replaced by a permanent International Finance and Monetary Committee (IFMC), currently chaired by Gordon Brown, the British finance minister.

TABLE 8.2: Recent Presidents of the IMF

Jacques DeLarosiere	1979–87
Michel Camdessus	1987–2000
Horst Kohler	2000 to present

The IMF's executive board rarely proceeds to a full, formal vote—mainly because the voting weights of each country are complicated, and voting is laborious. Instead, most decisions are taken by the "sense of the meeting." But voting power is still very important. America's voting strength in the IMF has dropped steadily, but it retains 17.8 percent of the vote in the IMF and, given the "eighty-five percent" rule, we can expect that it will not drop much further. (Or the veto threshold will need to be changed again.) The total voting power of the "Group of Seven," or G-7, countries is about forty-five percent, which means that the IMF is definitely under the control of the world's wealthiest countries and propounds an economic model, which reflects their interests.

The IMF provides credits to countries experiencing currency and balance-of-payments difficulties in funds that come from three sources. First, the IMF is like a credit union: each country has to pay the equivalent of a subscription fee based on the size and wealth of their economy, and they may withdraw a percentage of this "quota" in times of balance-of-payments problems (up to 300 percent of a given quota, and sometimes more). The IMF was founded in 1945 with pledged quotas totaling $7.4 billion, but by 1995 it had a working capital stock of $217 billion. It obtains much of its money through its quotas, but in recent years this source of funds is not as flexible and fluid as is sometimes desired—many country governments must obtain legislative approval to increase their quota contribution. Instead, it is easier for the IMF to resort to its second principal source of funds, its "general arrangements to borrow," to increase its lending capacity. These are standing lines of credit from several industrialized countries (and Saudi Arabia) or their central banks, allowing the IMF to borrow up to $28 billion at market interest rates. The United States wields considerable power in the IMF, much of it from its financial weight. The American quota contribution is the largest, at 17.8 percent, in monetary terms, $35 billion. (Overall, from combined sources, the United States provides about thirty percent of IMF funds.) The third source of lending capital is from special drawing rights (SDRs), a kind of international artificial currency based on an accounting innovation, a currency the IMF has the power to create if its directors approve. These financing mechanisms are central to understanding the politics of the IMF, as they are the constant subject of disputes between countries, especially the G-7 countries.

A commonly held perception, especially outside America, is that the IMF and the World Bank are in effect "handmaidens" of America and American foreign policy interests. There is a great deal of truth to this conclusion, but the true picture is much more complicated. As we will see, the precise makeup of American interests is not simple and monolithic. These interests change with the changes in administration and appointments to key positions in the U.S. government. Similarly, the United States is not purely self-serving; American interests are often more accurately described as the interests of advanced industrialized countries, or perhaps even global capitalism. And the American political system and the larger policy networks by which a Washington Consensus is made are both very open ones with dozens of access points, such that many voices and interests are heard in public battles over BWI policy. That said, the Washington Consensus does represent a consensus of a particular kind, closely linked to American interests as the U.S. government has perceived them; there are many policy paths *not* taken in the management of the world economy.

Before discussing the policy process in America by which the U.S. government influences the BWIs and the rules of the international economy, we should examine the origins and character of the Washington Consensus from the 1980s.

THE WASHINGTON CONSENSUS AFTER 1980

The United States has arguably the greatest influence in the BWIs, but what has it done with its power in these two institutions? The Washington Consensus, as it became famously (or infamously) known in the 1980s and 1990s, is a detailed, dominating ideology of economics and politics, of basically "neoliberal" economics since 1980 and of liberal democracy since 1990. The term *neoliberal* refers to the new return to free market principles, away from the regulated, "embedded" liberalism of the post-1945 period. In brief, the Washington Consensus' neoliberalism has meant a strict doctrine of free markets, free trade, and free currencies imposed, in many cases, on almost every country in the world.

The Washington Consensus policy prescriptions have their origins in the unusual global economic crises of the 1970s in general, and the 1979–80 period in particular. Oil price increases and global inflation meant that many countries were hard-hit by sudden increases in import costs. The situation through most of the 1970s was not initially believed to be serious. But World Bank president Robert McNamara signaled in his 1980 presidential address that the outlook for world growth was grim and that fundamentals had changed. Developing countries would have to "adjust" to the new economic conditions.[2]

These crises thus became unfortunate opportunities for a forced transfer of policy prescriptions from the BWIs. The World Bank and the IMF's consensus policies became the stranglehold prescription enforced throughout the world as countries fell victim to debt crises. Of course, both of these BWIs were always neoliberal in spirit, but they became more powerful and doctrinaire in the atmosphere of crisis. The changes were considerable. The World Bank abandoned its development strategy of the time, which focused on providing for the basic human needs of the poor through expenditures on health, housing, and education. The IMF suddenly shifted from short-term loans to alleviate payments problems to deep and intensive interventions in subject economies. What motivated such changes was the sense that the lessons to be learned from the unhappy conjuncture of 1979–80 were a) economic development was not going to come easily and naturally to poor developing countries, and b) what was required was more intensive supervision of structural reforms in crisis countries—dozens of profound policy changes bought with conditional lending, from both the World Bank and the IMF.

The World Bank chose the "structural adjustment loan" (SAL) as its main vehicle for enforcing neoliberal reforms. Between 1980 and 1986, thirty-seven SALs were negotiated with stricken countries by the World Bank.[3] The IMF chimed in with various longer-term lending programs of its own, usually done in conjunction with bank SALs. Both BWIs wanted fiscal balance (getting government budgets back in the black) and the promotion of exports (to improve trade balances and obtain hard currency for needed imports—and to pay back the BWI loans!). Basic fiscal preliminaries would include painful measures such as tax increases, cuts in government expenditures and subsidies, and increased interest rates to reduce inflation. The rest of the package of "structural" reforms was designed to promote free markets through deregulation of prices, privatization of state-owned enterprises, reform of banking sectors, creation of stock markets, and much more.

How was all this done? There are important differences in the ways in which the IMF and the World Bank bring their policy desires to bear on a given country. The IMF has only about 1,100 staff members in its Washington headquarters and very little staff presence in any member country, but it sends frequent missions to the countries in which it has programs. Its conditions tend to be highly quantitative and precise, and any deviation from targets usually brings quick punishment, via suspension of loan disbursements. The World Bank has a much bigger Washington staff and large resident missions in its member countries. Its omnipresent staff (plus a constant flow of consultant teams flying in from Washington) enables the bank to be intimately involved in the details of program design and all phases of implementation. Its conditionalities are more qualitative and easily fudged, such that its policy reform schedules appear again and again across different loans. Though they have problems coordinating their activities at times, and there is the problem of "cross-conditionality" (contradictory stipulations in agreements), the IMF and the World Bank pack a "one-two punch" to developing countries, combining very nicely to enforce neoliberalism in almost every country in Africa and Latin America during the 1980s.

From the perspective of the dozens of developing countries that undertook these programs in the 1980s, the programs had a strong taste of *austerity*.

Privatizations and the firing of redundant government workers meant rising unemployment. "Cost recovery" initiatives meant new fees for health care and education at all levels. The cuts were typically so difficult and controversial that riots were common, especially when the IMF was in town imposing the latest cutbacks in government spending or raising prices on essentials. Furthermore, the performance record of these BWI efforts, in terms of growth and development, was very poor. For Latin America, the 1980s were the "Lost Decade." In Africa, weak growth levels finally returned to the continent as a whole only after 1992. Though the BWIs imposed quick shock treatments, the benefits of this therapy were far from obvious.

Early Modifications to the Washington Consensus after 1987

In light of its poor record, by 1988 and 1989 some small but important modifications were being made to the Washington Consensus. The first of these was a new willingness to relent in the austere hardships of adjustment and provide for "adjustment with a human face." In 1987, the World Bank launched a Social Dimensions of Adjustment (SDA) program to focus targeted spending on "vulnerable groups" such as children, expectant mothers, and the newly unemployed. This involved many small changes, including new spending programs to ease the transition for fired government workers, promoting small and medium businesses, and targeted welfare spending. A bank-wide task force on poverty alleviation was created in 1988. The IMF, using funds from other loan programs, developed the new Structural Adjustment Facility (SAF) and Enhanced Structural Adjustment Facility (ESAF) in 1986 and 1987 to provide adjustment lending at concessional rates.

At about the same time, the bank began to take a greater interest in the environmental impact of its project lending and launched a series of operational reforms that were the opening steps in the so-called greening of the bank. President Barber Conable announced the creation of an environmental department in 1987. Since late 1989, all investment projects under consideration for bank funding must be screened for their environmental impacts. Then the bank became the chief implementing agency of a new multilateral global environmental facility, established in late 1990 and later endorsed by the UN Conference on Environment and Development (UNCED) in Rio, to deal with global warming, biodiversity, water pollution, and ozone depletion. Indeed, the UNCED conference pushed the World Bank into further environmental commitments, including the greening of the bank's entire loan portfolio by 1996.[4] In 1992, the Bank began assisting its countries with National Environmental Action Plans and new legislation on environmental protection, forestry, and coastal zone management.

Finally, world events such as the end of the Cold War, the breakup of the Soviet bloc, and a wave of democratization led to the appearance of "political conditionality" to accompany economic conditionality. Political conditionalities focused on "transparency" in government operations and a proper "enabling environment." Expectations increased regarding freedom of the press, ending corruption, and legal-judicial reforms.

The new political conditionality was part of a trend in the BWIs to push an ever-deepening adjustment agenda and to find more policy sectors for reform. As structural adjustment programs advanced into their second decade with little sign of success, the BWIs tried to explain their own failures in terms of host country mistakes rather than in terms of the SAL and ESAF loans themselves. Other parts of the deepening conditionality included addressing the financial sector and a general look at the role of the state. The World Bank added Sectoral Adjustment Loans (SECALs) as a means of financing reforms on a sector-by-sector basis. Closer scrutiny of reform activities was allowed by SECALs and Policy Framework Papers (PFPs), which were to coordinate all government and BWI activities in a given country.

THE MACHINERY OF POLICY CHANGE IN WASHINGTON

How does the policy process work through which the Washington Consensus is constructed, reconstructed, and reformed? How should we think about the means by which this consensus could break down and perhaps be replaced by an improved alternative? We have already seen that the United States holds a privileged position in the governance of both BWIs and their policy areas. The process of policy change thus takes place in Washington, D.C., or at least must pass through there.

Several branches of the American federal government are involved in the governance of these policy areas and of the BWIs themselves. One of the most important of these is the U.S. Department of Treasury, that branch of the American government that has the official liaison relationship with the BWIs. The secretary of the treasury is the U.S. government's lead person on the BWIs, but the Treasury Department's many assistant secretaries and subdivisions all have their roles to play in diplomacy with the BWIs. The high officials of the Treasury Department can place tremendous pressure on the BWIs to obtain a desired result. Indeed, at times they commit BWI resources or speak for the BWIs without consulting them, informing the World Bank and the IMF of their roles—in resolving a crisis, securing loans for a favored country—after the deal has been struck. In addition, U.S. government officials rotate in and out of the BWIs as staff, so they often have personal experience with their operations.[5]

The U.S. government, as we have seen, has veto power over the major decisions of both organizations, so the Treasury Department's dominance should not be surprising. But to understand the influence that the United

States wields, we must also look at the role of the U.S. Congress. The U.S. Congress is tremendously influential. It has so many means of influencing the World Bank and the IMF through its powers of the purse, publicity, and its oversight roles. Congress frequently holds hearings on the IMF and the World Bank. Many different congressional committees display no hesitancy in delving into even small operational details of the BWIs. Hearings tend to be held when the BWIs need money, and such meetings offer opportunities for members of Congress to address all kinds of issues. Hearings typically call on Treasury Department officials, U.S. representatives at the BWIs, and members of nongovernmental organizations (NGOs) to testify.

Political struggles in Congress over BWI policy reflect the basic political and ideological cleavages in America at large. The fate of BWI policy therefore depends a great deal on which American political party is in power in Washington. For example, President Clinton's arrival changed America's stance toward the BWIs in important ways. Under Clinton, the United States pushed consistently for increased sensitivity to environmental issues, and the BWIs have radically overhauled their approach to the environment since 1992. The Clinton administration also expended great effort to expand BWI lending capacities, though not always successfully.

Throughout most of the world, it is the political left that attacks the BWIs. Critics from the left in the U.S. government attack the World Bank for promoting a harsh, capitalistic style of development that exposes developing countries to ruthless global competitive forces but fails to produce a development payoff. They dislike the IMF for imposing its draconian austerity policies, sometimes referred to as "sado-monetarism," upon poor countries. These programs appear to be the worst kind of trickle-down economics, in which the bulk of a country's poor population suffers severely and immediately, in hopes of some improved level of economic growth and investment in the future.

Ironically, in America the political right *also* attacks the BWIs. Republican members of Congress are quite critical of the BWIs on philosophical-ideological grounds, essentially for the extent to which they interfere with market forces. Critics charge the World Bank with crowding out private investment and opportunities for private companies. They attack the IMF for encouraging the problem of a "moral hazard," the situation arising if a country is perceived as being "too big to fail," causing investors to be imprudent. The IMF and its rescue programs are thus characterized by the right as a kind of "international socialism," shielding bad decision makers and government from the discipline of the market. Poor, aid-dependent countries are deserving in some eyes and lazy "welfare cheats" in others' eyes.

Right and left in Washington exercise their power especially via funding issues and the power of the purse. Throughout much of 1997 and 1998, for example, certain members of Congress held the IMF hostage over the Clinton administration's request for $17.9 billion in appropriations to replenish IMF coffers.[6] Similar opportunities for interference arise in hearings on appropriations bills replenishing the World Bank's concessional lending arm, the International Development Association (IDA). The crucial point is that attacks from left and right coincide frequently enough that they threaten the BWIs and usually prod them into policy change.

Finally, another key mechanism—this time outside Washington—by which America exerts its influence on the BWIs is through the G-7 process. The G-7 includes annual meetings of the heads of state of the largest economies in the world, plus the more frequent meetings of their staffs and cabinet officials. American agenda setting and leadership are common at these meetings. G-7 countries hold roughly forty-five percent of the voting power in the IMF, so their approval of an initiative virtually guarantees that it will become policy. But it should also be noted that the BWIs and their thousands of trained, skilled personnel are sometimes far ahead of the leaders of the industrialized countries.

In all these ways, the Washington Consensus on national development and international economic order reveals itself to be a living creature, evolving as its environmental conditions change, though never truly changing its spots. This establishes the context for understanding BWI actions and the policy reform pressures that surrounded them in the 1990s. The other key ingredient to understanding international development and financial policy today—and America's role in these issues—is the experience of two major crises that shook the world in the second half of the 1990s, the Russian and East Asian crises of 1997 and 1998.

THE WASHINGTON CONSENSUS UNDER PRESSURE: PIECEMEAL CHANGE, 1992-95

The BWIs did not emerge unscathed from the 1980s. In development policy, by 1989 the backlash against the Washington Consensus' antistate policies was having an effect. Combined with the fall of the Soviet bloc and the end of the Cold War, the BWIs reinterpreted their stance on politics and the role of the state. They developed an entirely new focus on "good governance" that was part of the new "political conditionality." Democratic reforms became a precondition for aid. Indeed, the World Bank came to admit a role for the state, in Africa of all places. The mild embarrassment of these vacillations were compounded with new evidence of the general ineffectiveness of World Bank development projects. The World Bank's own internal survey, the Wapenhans Report of 1992, showed that bank lending policies and projects were largely ineffective in achieving their stated goals.

The World Bank also got hit at decade's end with environmental scandals and infamous controversies over dam and road projects in India, Brazil, and

China.[7] To its credit, the bank responded with some vigor to the environmental critique and began a process of greening bank policies and programs, which continues to this day. In 1993, the office of vice president for environmentally sustainable development was created at the bank.

If nothing else, by 1995 the bank had undergone a significant image makeover. The lingering problem to many critics, however, was the fact that the bank still promoted neoliberal policies and capitalist development above all. These changes also paradoxically garnered the bank new enemies among developing countries who did not, for example, want to obey First World environmental standards as they tried to promote economic growth.

The revolt against the BWIs accelerated appreciably with the "50 Years Is Enough" campaign in 1993–94, which hit at their poor record in promoting growth and ending poverty and publicized their environmental disasters. The other key event of the early 1990s was the election of a Democratic White House. Although President Clinton did not do as much as some hoped to push reforms and challenge the neoliberalism of the Washington Consensus, the Clinton administration began to use its position to launch a new review of the BWI's activities. For example, President Clinton began using the G-7 process and at the 1994 meeting in Naples began a debate about a new "International Financial Architecture."

THE WASHINGTON CONSENSUS UNDER ATTACK: THREE "NEW AGE" FINANCIAL CRISES

Sovereign debt crises and structural adjustment solutions were the context of the Washington Consensus in the 1980s, but the 1990s proved to be a different world. The world quickly became a global marketplace of instant transactions. New and unfamiliar problems aggravated the strong backlash against the BWIs that had originated in poor developing countries in the 1980s. In the 1990s, the BWIs became deeply involved in bigger and more complex economies—Russia, Mexico, South Korea—that vigorously protested and resisted their simple remedies. They came under much greater criticism in European and American policy circles and in the new global civil society emerging after the Cold War.

Three crisis episodes—in Mexico, East Asia, and Russia consecutively—proved to be tremendously important for redefining the BWIs' mission. These were not at all like the debt crises of the 1980s, nor were they typical imbalances in trade flows that the BWIs could handle. The BWIs have been undergoing organizational upheavals and soul-searching without break since 1995, and these three crises are much of the reason why—they bear closer examination. Each crisis was different, but each was a serious test of the wisdom and influence of the BWIs and American authority. World opinion and debate focused on the fundamental principles and practices by which the global economy should be managed.

Episode 1: Mexico

Lawrence Summers, then the undersecretary of the U.S. Treasury, called the Mexican crisis of December 1994 "the first crisis of the 21st century."[8] Mexico made the world newly aware that there was something called an "emerging market" and that, although they offered unique opportunities, such countries had special needs. Liberalization of the Mexican stock market and money markets had opened up the economy to huge inflows of highly liquid capital in the early 1990s. This caused a boom in the Mexican financial sector. A speculative investor "bubble" was fueled by the difference in interest rates between America (five to six percent) and Mexico (twelve to fourteen percent), which allowed investors to "arbitrage," or reap the difference. The Mexican peso was inflated by this situation and was valued at an unsustainably high level. This precarious situation, relying on investor enthusiasm for easy gains in the Mexican economy, was made more fragile by the U.S. Federal Reserve's policy of raising American interest rates throughout 1994. The Mexican government also tried to keep up the value of the peso by raising interest rates and expending its own hard currency to cover short-term debt. President Salinas delayed the more drastic solution of a devaluation of the peso until after the elections of August 1994 to secure the victory of his successor Ernesto Zedillo. It was an artificial bubble that burst in December 1994, when the Zedillo government botched the devaluation, and an international crisis unfolded.

The other side of the Mexican crisis was the so-called Tequila effect on other emerging markets. The ability of a crisis to spread and bring down other economies, as investors fear a meltdown, makes such crises lightning rods for international anxiety. What was required in response was a lot of money, and quickly, to restore confidence in the soundness of the Mexican economy and the peso's value. The U.S. government stepped in with an emergency bailout package that included $20 billion in its own credit guarantees. The IMF poured $17.8 billion into a rescue fund to help the Mexican government stabilize its financial system. This was ten times more than the Mexicans were due, based on their quota allowances, but the IMF had been asked (some say coerced) by the Clinton administration and the U.S. Treasury to step in.

The ultimate effect of the crisis on the Mexican economy was horrific in the short-and medium-term. Average industrial wages dropped forty-four percent in real terms in a few months, as economic activity contracted by seven percent, the worst results since the depression of the 1930s. Millions of middle-class families were made bankrupt by sudden rises in their mortgage rates and credit card interest rates. Fortunately, the Mexican crisis did not cause a global meltdown. The huge devaluation of the peso also ended up helping fuel a healthy export-led recovery in subsequent years, as trade with America exploded after NAFTA went into effect (in 1994).

Policy Responses to Mexico

By mid-1995, the IMF had learned two lessons from the Mexican crisis: 1) it needed more money to handle such emergency rescues, and 2) it needed to promote much better accountability and transparency in its member countries. This amounted to an expansion and tightening of the neoliberal Washington Consensus, with expanded supervisory and enforcement mechanisms.

The IMF and managing director Michel Camdessus had been asking for an expansion in funds available for troubled countries since early 1994 and pressed very hard for more funds in 1995 and 1996. The Clinton administration was in favor of these, but a new U.S. Congress, now dominated by Republicans, took this as an opportunity to examine and challenge the missions of the IMF and World Bank. American contributions were delayed for years. Conservative forces elsewhere in the G-7 also reined in IMF inclinations to grow, as Germany (with only 5.5 percent of votes on the IMF board) rallied forces to prevent gold sales from IMF reserves.

More profound responses appeared to be needed as well, and the new International Financial Architecture was again on the agenda at the G-7 meeting in Halifax in 1995. Key elements were an international program to strengthen disclosure and develop principles for supervision of emerging market financial systems. Indeed, the policy lessons from Mexico included an expansion of the Washington Consensus policies to include banking system reform and measures to promote healthy financial sectors in its troubled member countries. The G-7 agreed and called for more monitoring and transparency in the national accounts and banking systems of emerging markets.

Changes at the World Bank at this time reflected a different world order after Mexico but also an important change in leadership. The Clinton administration was able to appoint a new president of the World Bank. James Wolfensohn's 1995 appointment as president marked a turning point for the bank's operating style and substance. The bank proceeded more deeply into nontraditional policy areas (corruption, the internet, poverty alleviation) and deepened its efforts to present a gentler face to the world.

In early 1996, the World Bank and the IMF finally launched a concerted program to help the world's poorest nations escape from their "debt traps." At the time, dozens of Third World nations were spending up to sixty percent of their annual earnings merely to make the interest payments on their national debts, much of which was decades old and seemingly impossible to retire. It was a bizarre situation and one rather embarrassing to the BWIs and the G-7.[9] A new set of special measures for so-called highly indebted poor countries (HIPCs) began in September 1996, for which Wolfensohn was a chief proponent. The plan was to finally give real debt relief to the poorest. Unfortunately, the HIPC initiative, seemingly a generous break in the tough policies of the Washington Consensus, had unusually stringent conditions attached to it. To be eligible, countries had to have successfully completed *six years* of IMF supervision. After two years of the program only one country, Uganda, had actually qualified and benefited with a modest reduction in its debt, and only seven other of the poorest forty-one countries were ready to begin receiving assistance. Many of the HIPCs had debt service payments that were four times their export earnings. The effort was going so badly that it became an embarrassment, such that the time to qualify was extended from October 1998 until the end of 2000.

As noted earlier, Mexico was the beginning of the intensification of a political storm over the BWIs. Debates about their roles have not died since the Mexican crisis.

Episode 2: The East Asian Crisis

The enhanced supervision put into place by the IMF after Mexico was not sufficient to prevent a very similar crisis from occurring in East Asia two years later. The east Asian crisis began on July 2, 1997, with a devaluation of the Thai baht, which caused a run on banks in Thailand. The spread of this to other east Asian economies burst a "bubble" of international investor confidence in the region that had built up throughout the 1990s. The bursting of the bubble caused massive outflows of capital very quickly. Currencies began to drop, and soon there was a cycle of competitive devaluations. Other countries in the region immediately came under pressure as investors panicked.

The contagion hit South Korea in October 1997. Indonesia was the third country to be consumed by the problem. Malaysia, the Philippines, China, and Taiwan all suffered to a lesser extent. Hard currency inflows reversed to become dramatic outflows as international investors sought more reliable currencies and assets to spend their dollars and deutschmarks on.

Once again, the IMF was immediately involved, given its role as an international currency watchdog and its traditional task of enforcing macroeconomic stability. The World Bank was again more on the sidelines in an assisting role that would still involve it in controversy. This seemed to confirm a new role for the IMF, of an international "fire fighter" working frantically alongside the U.S. Treasury to put out international financial fires before they spread to the entire world.

The IMF-U.S. Treasury diagnosis fit within the realm of Washington Consensus experience and was not particularly insightful. Their explanations again relied on domestic faults rather than international problems of excessive liberalization or bad BWI policy advice. Their diagnosis was based on an out-of-control, corrupt "crony" capitalism of improper government-business relations, combined with excessive government involvement in the finance and banking sector. Critics argued that the BWI diagnosis of the problem was completely wrong and that the entire situation was the result of previous forced liberalizations of capital markets. These liberalizations had been forced by pressures from the BWIs and the U.S. Treasury in the early 1990s.

The policy remedies applied were also very much in line with the Washington Consensus: immediate neoliberal austerity and reform packages.

There would be a massive bailout and extensive liberalizing reforms, although the U.S. government contribution was less than in the Mexico case. The IMF began pushing higher interest rates so that more capital wouldn't flee. Unfortunately these produced a severe credit crunch that caused a wave of bankruptcies and bad bank loans to continue to pile up into late 1998. These moves also seemed to be prolonging the recession and adding to unemployment, though the IMF did exempt health and education expenditures from required government spending cuts in Indonesia and Thailand. The crisis was also an opportunity to insist upon full liberalization and the adoption of Western accounting practices in the South Korean and Thai financial sectors. Indeed, east Asian banks were so hurt that many of them were simply bought up by European and American competitors in fire sales.

The IMF and the U.S. Treasury responded with the defense that if South Korea's banks had collapsed into insolvency, they might very well have taken Japan's major banks with them. A meltdown of bankruptcies would have quickly spread across the Pacific and around the world. The situation was still serious a year later in the fall of 1998, causing some countries to flout the Washington Consensus. At this time, the Malaysian government stepped in to introduce its own national capital controls and lower interest rates. Hong Kong intervened to shore up its stock market. The role of the World Bank in east Asia was primarily a supporting one. It was coaxed into supplying $16 billion in emergency support funds in fiscal year 1998, a sum sizeable enough to put them in dicey financial straits as their reserves shrank.

The role of the IMF in the east Asian crisis was so roundly attacked that the experience marks a turning point in the organization's history. The first critical voice came from the World Bank itself, in the person of Joseph Stiglitz. In January 1998, Stiglitz warned that the IMF's harsh measures would only make things worse. Other major international economists began to line up with their positions on the crisis. Many critics pointed out that the IMF and U.S. Treasury seemed to simply copy their responses from their experiences with Latin American debt crises in the 1980s, when high inflation was usually a problem and had to be controlled with interest rates. In their own defense, the IMF argued that only the foolhardy would *lower* interest rates in a country hemorrhaging capital and that things would have been much worse if they hadn't gotten involved. Nonetheless, at the semi-annual World Bank/IMF meetings in September 1998, delegations from Indonesia, Thailand, and elsewhere arrived angry and belligerent, tired of being blamed for their countries' plights and pointing fingers at the IMF.

The full impact of the east Asia crisis was significant on several fronts. The five countries hit hardest—Indonesia, Malaysia, South Korea, Thailand, and the Philippines—saw their economies *contract* by an average of eight percent in 1998. In Indonesia, the Suharto government was toppled, and the country edged toward anarchy. The global economy saw growth cut in half, to two percent, in 1998. By 2000, some Asian economies had recovered considerably, though not to their pre-crisis levels, especially not in terms of employment. In addition, many of their flagship corporations and banks went out of business or were bought by foreign investors at artificially low prices.

Episode 3: Russia

In the middle of the Asian debacle, a somewhat different crisis broke out in Russia. The Russian situation, true to the country's problems at the time, was a mix of crisis and scandal. In the late spring of 1998, the Russian government was having horrible liquidity problems, but the IMF insisted the situation was not serious. However, the American and German governments were convinced otherwise and pushed very hard to get the IMF to concoct a rescue package. In June 1998, the Russian government happily announced that it had secured a sizeable $17 billion loan from the IMF to help it meet its external debt burden and support the value of the ruble. The scandal portion of the Russian crisis came next. Amazingly, most of the first disbursement of the loan ($4.8 billion) appears to have disappeared almost as quickly as it entered Russia in the form of capital flight, as privileged Russian "oligarchs" converted their rubles to dollars for export. The banking system subsequently seized up, Russia hemorrhaged capital, and there was a free fall in the ruble as President Yeltsin reneged on his promise and simply let it devalue.[10] In August 1998, Russia conducted a unilateral debt restructuring and defaulted on domestic debt, the result of which was a total collapse of all IMF monitoring and programs, totally undermining international confidence in the Russian economy.

The situation was particularly embarrassing because of the pressure applied to the IMF by the U.S. government to bail out Russia, even though this act was not in compliance with any sensible rules of economic management. That the IMF did make the loan anyway was widely viewed as a sign of America's improper dominance of the IMF, and it besmirched the IMF's already weakened reputation.

U.S. policy in this case was based on purely political considerations. America wanted to prop up the Russian economy and Russia's fledgling democracy at a time when Yeltsin was on the verge of being voted out of office and replaced by a revived Communist Party. When the loan unraveled and the economic scandal emerged, the U.S. government and the IMF engaged in behind-the-scenes recriminations, which heightened the sense of fiasco.

The IMF and others were at pains to point out that Russia's situation did not signal bankruptcy for all emerging markets or countries in transition. Russia had financed an "unduly large" budget deficit for an "unduly long" period of time, leading to a short-term exposure that proved unmanageable.[11] Nonetheless, a Russian contagion effect fueled further problems and worsened the grave situation of the global economy. Indeed, in a sense, at first the Asian crisis was tolerable because money had flowed out and went elsewhere, even if it was to other risky markets. Then the unthinkable happened—Russia defaulted in September 1998—and the situation suddenly went from "too big to fail" to "too big to save."[12] This contagion spread in September and October 1998 to Argentina and Brazil. Brazil was forced to raise interest rates to fifty percent

The World Bank/IMF meetings in October 1998 marked the beginning of a way out of these crises. The G-7 countries agreed to be engines of world growth, and several cut their interest rates. U.S. efforts were crucial. Federal Reserve chairman Alan Greenspan cut interest rates at the end of September 1998 and then conducted a further unscheduled "emergency" cut just two weeks later on October 13, which sent the American stock market soaring. The beginning of a global turnaround was underway, pulled along by the American economic locomotive. At the same time, the U.S. Congress finally freed up money for an expansion of the IMF credit pool (a new "general arrangements to borrow" package), which bolstered the IMF's financial position and capabilities.

CRISIS, REFLECTION, AND RANCOR

A common feeling in the international system and in American policy circles was that the IMF had not only mismanaged the crises of 1997–99 but had been found to be more fundamentally flawed in its very procedures and philosophy as well: unusually closed-minded and unable to learn from its mistakes. Oddly enough, the U.S. Treasury was also very much to blame but had somehow managed to escape punishment. There was real dissent and argument in the policy circles that maintain the Washington Consensus, leading to serious proposals for major changes. These have yet to produce major policy reforms, but there have been important smaller changes that may portend for the future.

Dissension within the Ranks

As we have seen, the crises greatly heightened tensions between the BWIs, causing some at the World Bank to break what had long been seen as a cardinal rule of the BWIs: one institution must not publicly criticize the other. Part of the reason for this is related to the individuals occupying key positions in the Washington Consensus policy network. The World Bank made statements highly critical of the IMF, but the chief protagonist was actually the World Bank's top economist, Joseph Stiglitz. Stiglitz was a Clinton appointee, having joined the Bank in December 1996 after a stint as chairman of President Clinton's council of economic advisers. He caused such a fuss in his critiques of IMF handling of the east Asia crisis—going public with his own articles in the popular press—that he had to be disciplined by James Wolfensohn. He also antagonized the U.S. Treasury Department.[13] Oddly enough, the World Bank had supported most of these same policies for decades, though newcomers Wolfensohn and Stiglitz had not, thus signaling the importance of these individuals in such positions.

In September 1998, Treasury Secretary Rubin felt compelled to publicly ask the two institutions to stop sniping at each other, and a patching up was arranged. But in November 1998 the World Bank's Global Economic Prospects report came out and criticized the IMF response in Asia once again. Wolfensohn was forced to defend and explain the report, in what became a major public relations fiasco for both organizations. He also ended up effectively promising to keep Stiglitz quiet. Stiglitz, who ultimately resigned his World Bank position in November 1999, may have been a rogue element in disobeying his own bosses, but his criticisms had tremendous impact, coming as they did from within the BWI fortress. Efforts to clearly define and harmonize the roles and relationships of the two are ongoing.

"Architectural" Changes?
The Global Policy Apparatus Starts Rolling

Because world attention was suddenly focused on the BWIs as never before, it should not be surprising that new proposals for reform came in from all over. The British, for example, proposed the merger of the IMF, the World Bank, and the Basel-based Bank for International Settlements (BIS) into one superorganization. Many argued for a retreat of the IMF. Shouldn't the IMF shift away from emergency lending, as its presence seemed to have a catalytic effect in signaling looming insolvency?

The G-7 meetings and coordination process became especially crucial in discussing what to do in a more permanent way to prevent the east Asian crisis from ever happening again. The June 1999 Cologne G-7 meeting was unusually critical on this score, bringing forth some plans for a new financial architecture and a debt initiative. One key decision was to make the IMF Interim Committee into the permanent IFMC, in which the head of the World Bank would have privileged status. This move went a long way toward realizing France's desire to transform the interim committee into a more formal, policy-making "super-council," as was actually envisioned in many years previously in the IMF original Articles of Agreement. The Cologne meeting also gave impetus to the creation of a new umbrella organization for international financial reform and coordination, a Financial Stability Forum, especially designed for liaisoning with large banks and money managers to promote financial stability in the West.

An attention-grabbing move in U.S. policy circles that paralleled international discussions was the creation of the International Financial Institutions Advisory Council (IFIAC) by the U.S. Congress in mid-1998. The IFIAC very nicely illustrates how politicized the position of the BWIs had become in a polarized Washington of the 1990s. The IFIAC was established at the behest of conservative American Congressmen and was headed by economist Allan Meltzer. Its very mission represented a profound critique of the IMF in particular along extreme free market lines. Professor Meltzer had called for the abolition of the IMF many times over the years, and his commission attacked the IMF as an interloper rather than a preserver or expander of market forces in world financial markets.

From this perspective, the main problem in international finance is "moral hazard"—the possibility that IMF rescue packages will allow investors to make overly risky decisions. In essence, the argument is that there would never have been a Thailand if there hadn't been a Mexico, because Mexico sent the signal that emerging market countries would not be allowed to collapse.[14]

Though they may seem threatening, such appearances are deceiving. These debates and proposals have not shaken the Washington Consensus in a profound way. Indeed, it is extremely unlikely that the World Bank, the IMF, or the U.S. Treasury will ever deviate substantially from the Washington Consensus. And America's official positions increasingly lean toward a deepening of the rigors of the Washington Consensus, rather than abandoning them. All that was conceded to critics was that, on these issues, the IMF had more to learn. In other words, the more drastic hypothesis suggested by the east Asian experience—that globalization, capital market liberalization, and full marketization were somehow fundamentally flawed and dangerous—was rejected out of hand by the Consensus makers. Globalization and financial liberalization would yield huge benefits as long as sound fiscal policies were maintained. In other words, the global market *required* discipline; exactly the same point that critics of globalization have increasingly focused on, beginning in Seattle in 1999.

Policy Details: Modifying (and Deepening) the Consensus

Modifications to specific policies within the enduring framework of the Washington Consensus can be seen in three areas. In development policy, slight changes have meant more of an emphasis on attacking poverty and doing more to directly achieve growth. In exchange rate policies there has been some shake-up of accepted orthodoxy. And the issues of debt and extreme poverty have been advanced, promising improved treatment for the highly indebted poor countries (HIPCs). On the HIPC initiative there has been considerable noise, and some action, since 1998. The HIPC initiative is regularly trotted out as an example of how the BWIs are responding to demands of global civil society, with renewed attention allegedly paid to the quality of growth and the alleviation of poverty. It is a central element of Wolfensohn's limited reforms within the Washington Consensus. What is most telling, however, is the way the HIPC relief has been used, and the severe restrictions placed upon access to it, forcing the poorest countries to submit to intense scrutiny and heavy policy commitments. Subsequent to the huge crises of 1997–99, there have been limited efforts to finally loosen these strictures. The Clinton White House, for example, made a major push for the easing of HIPC restrictions. At the 1999 World Bank and IMF meetings, the HIPC initiative was expanded.

At the same time, global civil society was proposing far more radical solutions such as Jubilee 2000: a full cancellation of all debt to poor developing countries in honor of the millennium. Oxfam proposed that, at a minimum, debt service payments should be limited to ten percent of annual government revenue. These more generous steps have never been seriously considered by the BWIs, the G-7, or the United States. Relaxed HIPC eligibility requirements did allow eleven very poor countries to qualify for BWI debt relief, with relief packages reducing the debt service for these nations by one-third in the year 2000. The other big change in HIPC policy is a new emphasis on protecting social programs through increased funding as part of the agreements with the BWIs. In other words, debt relief should be spent on health and education programs (and nothing else).

This is important recognition of the special status of some countries, especially their needs for profound assistance. In effect, this is an admission by the BWIs that not all countries are in a position to benefit from globalization and open market policies; an important example of "fine tuning" the Washington Consensus.[15] It is also almost certainly part of the new BWI perception that poverty alleviation for the poorest countries will garner increased support for the BWI mission across a broader political spectrum.

Exchange rate policy has been another area of controversy and movement within the Washington Consensus. The east Asian crisis marked the end of an era of currency pegging to the U.S. dollar. The period after 1997 has registered "the sound of dollar pegs tumbling" throughout Asia. Following the Asian crisis, it was Brazil that fell next, and then Argentina's peg to the dollar was severely shaken. By the end of 1999, the only major economies to employ currency targeting were China, Argentina, and Malaysia. The transition from pegged to floating rates is a difficult one for the country that undertakes it, usually producing large devaluations that shake investor confidence. But stronger economies—such as South Korea and Singapore—have so far had a favorable experience with free-floating currencies once they've made the transition. It does appear that the IMF needs to be more active in helping countries adjust their exchange rates. Many argue that it is the G3 (United States, EU, Japan) that need to be much better at coordinating their exchange rates, because misalignments in their relative values and especially in the dollar-yen rate have been so destabilizing to the world economy.[16]

Another alternative to floating is "dollarization," or the full adoption of the U.S. dollar by other countries as their official currency. Uruguay was the first to follow this option. Dollarization removes much national political discretion over economic policy. There is no further need for a central bank, for example, and no mechanism for monetary policy or exchange rate policy to adjust an economy to changing conditions. Instead a country creates a currency board to handle money issues.

Have these policy developments diminished the role and power of the United States and the Washington Consensus? Not exactly. The HIPC initiative, as we have seen, actually does an excellent job of spreading a tough form of the Washington Consensus' openness and austerity. Similarly, both of the newly favored paths in currency exchange policy (floating exchange or adopting the dollar) further cement countries into Consensus policies. Floating exposes countries fully to the rigors of the international economy. And dollarization means further integration into the international system and with the U.S. economy. As it has become a hot topic for Latin American countries, it paves the way to further trade openness and American influence. Thus, crises appear to fuel more floating and dollarization, in both cases exposing a given country even more fully to the rigors of the international system.

REFORM AGENDAS IN THE NEW MILLENNIUM

Talk of reform continues in earnest today, especially as the international financial institutions (IFIs) have emerged bloodied and tarnished from their Russian and east Asian experiences. This process has been marked by the startling protests at the Seattle World Trade Organization (WTO) meetings in December 1999 and the large protest events at the semi-annual IMF/World Bank meetings in Washington in April 2000 and Prague in September 2000.

IMF Leadership and the New Financial Architecture

The Meltzer Commission released its final report to Congress in March 2000 and, though it didn't seek to dissolve the IMF, it did propose restricting it rather severely, in favor of the international private sector and private finance. This included a recommendation that no concessional aid or loans be provided to developing countries, except for the very poorest. Instead, viable development and other projects would be financed by the private sector because they were expected to be profitable. Furthermore, the IMF should have nothing to do with longer-term lending for development. The IMF's role in currency/finance crises such as those in Mexico and South Korea would be similarly restricted, as the IMF would intervene only selectively in countries that were already very compliant with its standards. These proposals did not receive much support at their launching. The report was panned as misguided by many in the Clinton administration. However, the Meltzer report does represent the current position of an important element within the Washington Consensus' policy network, one that may find itself in power one day depending on changes in Washington leadership or the outcome of the next world financial crisis.

Changes in leadership in the IMF may also have an impact on the Washington Consensus. New IMF managing director Horst Kohler has spoken favorably of regional surveillance mechanisms, in effect decentralizing some of the IMF's role. Such a move could create new and important centers of power outside Washington. Amazingly, Kohler has also suggested on occasion that the IMF need not rigidly enforce trade liberalization upon developing countries if the advanced industrial countries continued to practice protectionism. This "fair free trade" idea is an interesting one, though one that would, again, paradoxically deepen the hold of neoliberalism on policy makers throughout the world.

The World Bank Gets Warm and Fuzzy?

The World Bank is also moderating its position, no doubt in part due to protest and publicity in Seattle and Prague. As we saw at the beginning of this chapter, Wolfensohn is increasingly capable of "talking a good talk" about global poverty and inequality. Indeed both the World Bank and the IMF are ever more vocal in their concerns for the massive poverty still present in too much of the developing world.[17]

In the World Bank, this is evidence of attention to the HIPC issue and to new bank initiatives on "quality growth," an effort to purposely fine-tune growth strategies to directly improve the lives of the poor.[18] This means programs to reduce inequities in access to health and education, including a huge education initiative for countries that present plans to eliminate illiteracy and educate girls. It also means going after the old bugaboo of inflation, which is increasingly cast as a political rights issue, as a kind of official repression. A stated goal of such moves is to improve country ownership of neoliberal reforms: if reforms show better results, they will garner greater public support, and the BWIs will look less like global bad guys.

The World Bank also chimes in on the notion of free trade for all, in effect calling upon rich countries to grant poor countries full market access. And it has given great attention to the HIV/AIDs crisis since early 2000.

CONCLUSIONS

What can we conclude about the Washington Consensus, its evolution, and future direction? First, when we think back to the first tough years of neoliberal shock treatment in the early 1980s, it is apparent that the Washington Consensus today has been modified and softened. But this does not mean it has retreated. Indeed, as we have seen, its program has deepened and penetrated several new economic areas as well as politics. And the BWIs' capacity to monitor and enforce compliance with the Washington Consensus has also expanded. There have been important developments in debt relief for HIPCs, improving the quality of growth and pushing the developed world to truly adopt the free trade dogma it espouses; but we have also seen such efforts fail in the past. In short, it is still not easy to be a poor country in the world of the

Washington Consensus. Many countries still feel that the world and the Washington Consensus are stacked against them.

Another issue is whether it is still fair to label our subject the "Washington" Consensus. It appears that the transition of the Consensus from an America-based ideology to a global ideology—propagated by the BWIs but also by a variety of other actors—is nearing completion. American common sense on economic thinking is becoming a G-7 or North Atlantic Consensus, and from there it spreads to the rest of the world. These steps are signs of movement toward a world of slightly greater institutional pluralism and lessened American dominance.

The United States undoubtedly remains extremely powerful in the Consensus' policy circles, and the United States still has an implicit veto over any significant changes in the BWIs. The U.S. Congress can delay funding for currency crises or for aid to poor countries for years at a time (if it so chooses). But, as we have seen, the policy network "brain" that directs the Consensus is expanding, it is becoming more complex, and it is globalizing at a rapid pace.

Chapter 9

AMERICAN POLICY AND THE WTO

Candace C. Archer

INTRODUCTION

In the fall of 1999, thousands of angry protestors stormed the streets of Seattle during the Ministerial Conference of the World Trade Organization (WTO). These protestors had various goals. Some were concerned about the environment, others about labor practices. But the sheer number of protestors and their sometimes violent acts brought increased attention to American membership in the WTO. The United States was an active participant in the Uruguay round of trade negotiations when the WTO was created and has been a member of the WTO since its founding in 1995. Yet prior to the demonstrations in Seattle, most Americans probably had never heard of the organization, nor thought much about American membership being controversial; now all that has changed. During the "battle in Seattle," prominent political figures and environmental advocates debated the merits of the WTO. Advocates presented the WTO as a necessary organization that would promote global welfare. Critics argued that the WTO promoted poverty, endangered the environment, and abused labor; therefore the United States should terminate its membership in the WTO. Why all the brouhaha over the WTO? What is this organization, and why is the United States a member? Should the United States remain within the WTO, or should American foreign policy seriously consider leaving the WTO?

To shed light on some of these policy questions, one needs to look carefully at the history, structure, and major components of the WTO. This chapter will examine the legally binding decisions of the WTO Dispute Settlement Body (DSB), highlight specific DSB decisions, chronicle a few interesting cases, and discuss the manner in which countries have reacted to DSB decisions. Knowledge of the structure and legal power of the WTO will provide a better understanding of the concerns that both policy makers and the public have regarding this organization.

POST-WORLD WAR II FOUNDATIONS

Prior to World War II, protectionism caused great tensions in the global economy. In the 1930s, global trade all but stopped as states erected barriers to imports. These trade barriers, exacerbated by the absence of a world leader to promote free trade, were key contributing factors to the outbreak of global war.[1] Before the war was over, the United States took the lead in laying the foundations of the post-war global economic order. As we have seen in previous chapters, American leadership was instrumental in creating the International Monetary Fund (IMF) and the World Bank at the Bretton Woods conference. To complement the Bretton Woods Institutions, a third organization was proposed after World War II: the International Trade Organization (ITO). Its purpose would be to facilitate free trade and to reduce the domestic barriers that had restricted the free flow of goods prior to the war.

The United States was actively involved in promoting these economic institutions. The World Bank and IMF met with little resistance from the U.S. Congress, but the proposal for the ITO presented problems from the outset. In 1948, a multilateral meeting was scheduled in Cuba, where the Havana Charter establishing the ITO was to be signed. Prior to the Havana meeting, the participating governments created a separate agreement to lower tariffs until the Havana Charter could be completed.[2] This document was the General Agreement on Tariffs and Trade, or the GATT. It was assumed that after the ITO was established, the GATT rules would be included as part of the larger trade organization. However, the ill-fated ITO never came into existence. Even though the United States had proposed the creation of an international organization to establish trade rules, the ITO would have faced considerable congressional opposition. Therefore, President Truman decided not to put the doomed Havana Charter before the Congress, and no vote was ever taken to ratify the ITO treaty.

Congress was leery of the ITO due to concerns that the organization would not be in the best interests of the United States. Critics were especially opposed to the proposed legal power of the ITO. According to the Havana Charter, countries that violated trading rules could be prosecuted by means of a judicial system within the ITO. The highest level of this system would have been the International Court of Justice, which would have had the power under the ITO charter to issue binding opinions.[3] Congress feared that the United States would have to sacrifice some of its sovereignty over trade policy if it ratified the ITO. It soon became apparent that without United States support, the ITO could never be an effective organization. Lack of an American presence in the ITO would seriously compromise the organization's ability to regulate world trade. The ITO was never established, but a stopgap measure had already been approved. The GATT agreement would now have to serve some of the functions that had been proposed for the ITO. Though only an agreement and not designed as an organization, the GATT was forced to fill the institutional gap left by the failure of the ITO. GATT managed global trade for nearly fifty years.

A SECOND-BEST SOLUTION: THE GATT

In 1947, the GATT began to reduce tariff rates for states that adopted the agreement (called contracting parties). Over the next four decades, it became the primary international forum for trade negotiations. The GATT functioned primarily as an ad hoc organization, even though it lacked those characteristics that typified more formal international bodies such as the IMF or World Bank. Most notably, contracting parties to the GATT could choose for themselves which sections of the agreement they wanted to implement. The GATT also had problems settling disputes between contracting parties. Trade disputes were common. Contracting parties regularly accused one another of not abiding by the rules of the GATT. Over time, a rudimentary dispute settlement system became established. But it was problematic at best, because the proceedings could be stopped if one contracting party disagreed with the charges —including the member who was being accused of breaking the agreement! Because its dispute settlement system was so weak, the GATT had little power to make sure that its rules were adhered to or enforced.

One result of this weak dispute settlement system was that many contracting parties avoided the system altogether. Economically powerful countries would rarely change their policies, even when a dispute was decided against them. Often, the more powerful contracting parties chose to settle disputes on a bilateral basis, rather than through the GATT system. Less developed countries avoided the system as well, because there was little hope that their grievances would be addressed or rectified, especially if the accused party was a powerful country. All contracting parties had the right to stop the proceedings.[4]

Because the GATT was merely an agreement instead of an international organization, it was more appealing to the U.S. Congress. Having an agreement such as the GATT provided a set of rules that helped facilitate trade relations between contracting members, thus the worst of the pre–World War II trade problems would be avoided. Yet, because the GATT system was essentially weak, the United States was still free to settle trade disputes on its own terms and to negotiate individually with countries that it felt had broken the rules. In addition, when charges were brought against the United States for breaking the GATT agreement, it could unilaterally stop the proceedings. It would seem that, for the United States, the GATT created an ideal situation—but there were problems. If the United States could easily ignore the rules, so could other powerful countries. This may not have been an issue when the United States was the unrivaled global economic leader, but as other countries began to challenge American economic dominance in the 1980s, organizational problems in the GATT system became more troublesome. Eventually, U.S.

decision makers were driven to push for a system that would place more binding commitments on all contracting parties.

Eight rounds of multilateral trade negotiations (MTNs) occurred from the GATT's inception in 1947 through 1993. During each of these rounds, significant steps were taken to expand GATT's free trade regime. Liberalization became more widespread, tariffs were lowered, and reciprocity expanded. In addition, through the successive rounds of MTNs the scope of the GATT grew; more products were covered and more countries participated. However, with each improvement in the rules, the problems inherent in GATT's structure became more evident.

By the mid-1980s, new trade relationships put considerable pressure on the GATT system. Japan and the newly industrialized countries (NICs) of Southeast Asia became powerful actors in international trade, producing highly desirable commodities such as automobiles and electronics. Both Japan and the Asian NICs achieved this status in part by employing protectionist policies that circumvented the GATT system of free and open trade.[5] By the 1980s the United States was facing stiff new competition. In response, the United States began pursuing neoprotectionist policies of its own in the form of nontariff barriers (NTBs), including quotas and export restraint policies.

The resurgence of protectionism in the European Union (EU), the United States, and Japan during the 1980s raised serious questions about GATT's ability to manage international trade and ensure open markets. American policy needed to respond to these pressures. At first, the United States pursued a multilateral approach to these problems. In the early 1980s, the United States strongly supported a new round of GATT negotiations. The Uruguay round of MTNs was launched in 1986 in Punta del Este, Uruguay. U.S. negotiators came to the table in Uruguay promoting the most ambitious agenda ever seen in GATT negotiations. They proposed bringing new economic sectors under GATT rules (e.g., services and intellectual property), and they wanted to strengthen the process by which disputes were settled. But the negotiations were difficult. By 1988, it appeared as though the Uruguay round talks would collapse. Frustrated by the slow pace and lack of success at the Uruguay round, the U.S. Congress chose to take matters into its own hands. As was discussed in chapter 7, the 1988 Trade Act promised to impose unilateral U.S. trade sanctions under the provisions of Section 301, otherwise known as "Super 301." The United States therefore pursued both unilateral and multilateral policies simultaneously. It continued to negotiate in the Uruguay Round but threatened unilateral Super 301 action. Many countries were critical of Super 301 and argued that unilateral trade sanctions were contrary to the antiprotectionist position that the United States had taken throughout the Uruguay round of negotiations.[6]

Pursuit of both multilateral and unilateral strategies in response to protectionism by other countries exemplifies the complexity of American trade policy. These actions would seem to contradict one another. In fact, American trade policy must constantly deal with such conflicting pressures. Understanding these pressures is crucial to assessing the U.S. role within the WTO. Prior to the founding of the WTO, Congress faced domestic demands to punish countries that discriminated against American products; therefore they strengthened Super 301 legislation. However, the United States must also shoulder the responsibilities that come with global economic leadership. Thus the United States is necessarily involved in pursuing liberal and multilateral solutions to trade problems. The United States was the primary advocate for strengthening the GATT system, and it was a founding member of the WTO in 1995. As will be discussed later, these conflicting pressures on American trade policy have not disappeared. They continue to shape the United States' relationship with the WTO to this day.

STRUCTURAL DIFFERENCES BETWEEN THE GATT AND THE WTO

The Uruguay round of GATT negotiations produced results that went far beyond what most observers had anticipated. A new organization to facilitate world trade was established. The rules and products subject to the jurisdiction of this new organization expanded considerably. The new rules were so extensive that the final documents from the Uruguay Round were 26,000 pages long and weighed nearly 75 pounds! In many ways, the WTO is significantly different from the former GATT system. By joining the WTO, member-states promise to follow all of the rules established by the organization. Institutionally, the WTO is an international organization that administers the agreements facilitating world trade. Substantively, the agreements on world trade were expanded during the Uruguay round; thus, the WTO administers rules covering more products and trade issues than did the GATT. All sections of the GATT's agreements were updated and several important new sectors were added, the most important of which are services, intellectual property, and agriculture. The following sections will outline the major institutional changes made from the GATT system to the WTO and discuss how the WTO works.

INSTITUTIONAL CHANGES

It is important to emphasize that the WTO, as an international organization, has one primary function: it administers the trade agreements that have been endorsed by member-states. It performs this function in two ways. First, it provides the bureaucratic structure necessary to administer the agreements. Over time the GATT developed limited administrative capabilities that were needed to manage world trade, but the powers of the WTO were designed to include much more than simple administrative capability. Unlike the GATT, the WTO has strict rules and procedures that it must follow. It is required to hold regularly scheduled meetings. It has the ability to create committees and working groups that can determine which trade rules need to be changed or added, and it provides reports that monitor the trade policies of all member-states. Second, the WTO administers trade agreements by providing a forum within which members can file grievances against states that violate WTO rules. The WTO DSB then interprets the rules, determines which rules have been broken, and orders compensation.

Bureaucratic Structure

The WTO is considered an umbrella organization because it provides one unified administrative structure for all agreements negotiated through the time of the Uruguay round. The most important of these agreements is the 1994 update to the General Agreement on Tariffs and Trade, called *GATT 1994*, which updated the earlier rules on tariffs and trade. There are also several other agreements that are separate and distinct from *GATT 1994*. These other agreements were negotiated during the Uruguay round and include the agreement on trade-related aspects of intellectual properties (TRIPs), the agreement on trade-related investment measures (TRIMs), and the General Agreement on Trade in Services (GATS). Upon joining the WTO, member-states agree to abide by the rules established in all of these agreements. To further tie the rules together, the WTO has an integrated dispute settlement system. This means that all grievances regarding any of the agreements must be brought before the same Dispute Settlement Mechanism (DSM).

The WTO is similar to most other international organizations in that it is has a hierarchical structure to facilitate administration and decision making. However, it is also relatively unique for an international economic organization because each member-state has an equal vote, regardless of the member-state's size. The highest level of decision making in the WTO is the Ministerial Conference. Each member has a representative at the Ministerial Conference, and this organ is responsible for the major policy decisions of the organization. The Ministerial Conference meets at least once every two years. Representatives to the Ministerial Conference are usually high-ranking trade officials from member-states. The Ministerial Conference's first three meetings were held in Singapore (1996), Geneva (1998), and Seattle (1999). The Ministerial Conference has the power to create committees and working groups for the purpose of determining if new rules should be developed by the WTO. For example, although no WTO agreement is yet specifically committed to environmental issues, a committee has already been established to investigate linkages between trade and the environment. The Ministerial Conference can also establish working groups to determine if member-states are in favor of the WTO expanding trade rules in new sectors. For example, in 1999 President Clinton proposed that the Ministerial Conference establish a new working group on trade and labor standards.

Much of the day-to-day work of the WTO is done by the second-highest body, the General Council. Like the Ministerial Conference, the General

Council has a representative from every member-state. Unlike the Ministerial Conference, the General Council meets every six to eight weeks and is staffed by permanent diplomats. The General Council has three main duties. First, it acts as the Dispute Settlement Body (DSB), addressing trade disputes that arise among members. Second, it administers the Trade Policy Review Mechanism, which is a periodic review of all members' trade policies. Finally, it supervises the lower tier of councils and committees that oversee the proper functioning of the agreements covered under the WTO. Although the Ministerial Conference is the highest body of the WTO, the General Council has a considerable amount of power to interpret the agreements and to establish policies that guide the WTO on a daily basis.

Beneath the General Council are three important subcouncils that report directly to the General Council: the Council for Trade in Goods, which administers *GATT 1994*; the Council for Trade in Services, which administers the GATS agreement; and the Trade Related Intellectual Property Council (or TRIPs Council), which administers the TRIPs agreement. Below these subcouncils are approximately twenty committees that deal with specific issues covered by each of the agreements and work to make sure that all agreements are being implemented correctly. The main job of the respective committees is to collect information from member-states and determine if the rules on specific issues are being followed. Each member-state is entitled to have a representative on every committee, working party, and council of the WTO.

The last important organ of the WTO is the Secretariat. Unlike many other international secretariats, the WTO Secretariat has no independent decision-making powers. It acts as the main administrative body of the WTO, handling daily organizational duties such as scheduling meeting times, taking minutes at meetings, managing translation concerns, and supervising external relations with other organizations and the media. The director general, who is chosen by consensus and appointed to serve a four-year term, heads the Secretariat. Four deputy director generals also help carry out administrative tasks. All of these offices are considered administrative and apolitical, meaning that these appointed officials serve the WTO, not their home countries.

When one member-state accuses another member-state of violating the rules of a WTO agreement, the General Council acts as the DSB. Although the DSB is simply the General Council acting in a different role, because of the significance of dispute settlement in the WTO, it is important to give special attention to this particular dimension of the organization.

DISPUTE SETTLEMENT

The most important institutional change from the GATT to the WTO was the creation of an integrated dispute settlement system. After expanding trade rules during the Uruguay round, it was also important to expand dispute settlement to ensure that the new multilateral agreements would be followed. The dispute settlement system plays a central role in the organizational structure of the WTO. In many ways, it is the institutional glue that binds together all WTO agreements. The same dispute settlement rules and procedures apply to all agreements under the WTO's jurisdiction and to all member-states.

If a trade dispute cannot be resolved through bilateral means, then member-states are required to go through formal WTO proceedings. Only the WTO can authorize trade sanctions. The DSB creates panels to investigate violations of WTO rules. Each panel is made up of three to five people who are chosen from a list of experts maintained by the WTO. Parties to each dispute have the right to oppose the selection of specific panel members. The panel must make an objective assessment of the facts and determine whether or not WTO agreements have been violated. Each state presents its case to the panel. After considering the facts, the panel compiles a report describing whether or not trade laws have been broken. The panel also makes recommendations for settling the dispute. Member-states can appeal panel decisions to the Appellate Body, which reexamines the facts of the case and reviews the decision of the panel. After all reviews are completed, recommendations on how to resolve the dispute are submitted to the DSB and General Council by the panel (or by the Appellate Body), and the offending party is ordered to implement the panel's recommendations.

Usually the recommendations are designed to force one member-state to compensate another member-state for the trade distortions caused by the offending policy. If the recommendations are not implemented, the winning member(s) can ask for further action from the DSB. Such action would likely entail some form of suspension of concessions, which means that the targeted state would lose some of the free trade benefits that it had gained from joining the WTO. For example, imagine that Japan and the United States had a dispute over unfair tariffs being place on cars exported from Japan to the United States. If the United States was found to have broken WTO rules and did not change its policies, the WTO could allow Japan to retaliate in order to regain what it had lost due to the U.S. tariff. The WTO would allow U.S. goods to be penalized by Japan. Most likely, the WTO would advocate that a tariff be placed on U.S. goods until Japan was compensated for the monetary losses resulting from the unfair American policy.

Dispute settlement cases are important because they are the key indicator of whether or not major economic powers will submit to the supranational authority of the WTO. By examining the cases, one can determine how well the system is working. Are states abiding by the rules? When the DSB discovers violations of WTO rules, will member-states be willing to change their policies even if those changes hurt their economies? Answers to these questions will reveal much about the ability of the WTO to compel members to honor their trade agreements. Examining dispute settlements can also help us understand the U.S. relationship with the WTO. Whether the United States chooses to comply with DSB rulings or not is an indication of how committed the United States is to the WTO.

DSB Cases: Wars over Bananas and Beef

Since its inception in 1995, the DSB has received more than 200 requests for consultations on more than 150 separate matters.[7] There were more requests in the first five years of the WTO than were made in the forty years of the GATT dispute settlement system. The new system remedies some of the problems that existed with the previous system; therefore it appeals to members and is used more frequently. Developed countries are far more active in filing grievances than developing countries, but developing countries have filed more than one-fourth of all complaints.[8] Several cases before the DSB have received special attention due to their outcomes and because they provide evidence of how well the WTO's dispute settlement mechanism is working. Important early disputes before the DSB have involved common products such as bananas and beef.

It may seem strange that bananas and beef would receive so much attention in international trade given the fact that these products account for a very small percentage of total world trade. However, these products have put the WTO dispute settlement system to the test. The United States and the EU have been central players in both of these cases. In many ways these cases are about far more than fruit and meat; they are an example of whether the WTO can be effective when the two biggest economic powers in the world disagree. In both cases, the WTO found in favor of the United States and against the EU. In both cases the EU was extremely reluctant to adopt the DSB decision and change its policy. Given the EU's position, the United States requested the right to retaliate against EU products in order to make up for the losses it incurred.

In the case of the "Banana Wars," the United States charged that the EU's preference for bananas from French and British colonies over those from Central and South American producers constituted a barrier to free trade. Central and South American producers are tied to American multinational corporations such as Dole and Chiquita, whereas former European colonial producers (mostly in Africa and the Pacific) are not. Europeans claim to favor their former colonial producers because they are concerned with the economic development of these regions. The United States, Mexico, Ecuador, Honduras, and Guatemala filed a complaint charging that the EU was unfairly excluding American bananas. The WTO found in favor of the United States et al. and ordered the EU to change its banana buying policies. The EU appealed the decision, lost the appeal, and then made minor changes to their banana buying policies. After three more appeals, the DSB found that EU banana policies were still in violation of WTO rules. The United States asked for the right to retaliate and place $500 million in tariffs on EU products. The DSB authorized retaliation for the amount of $191.4 million. The United States then created a list of products imported from the EU to be subject to a 100 percent tariff. These tariffs are supposed to remain in place until the EU changes its policies on bananas.[9] As of this writing, the United States and EU are still meeting to resolve this matter.

The beef case dealt with what the Europeans consider a health issue. In the United States and Canada, beef cattle are given hormones to promote growth. According to international food-safety experts, there is no decisive scientific evidence that these hormones constitute health hazards.[10] Europeans, however, are suspicious of hormone-treated beef and have banned U.S. and Canadian beef. The United States and Canada charged that the EU was unfairly discriminating against their beef. The DSB panel found in favor of the United States and Canada, arguing that the European ban was not based on scientific facts. The EU appealed the decision, lost the appeal, but refused to allow the hormone-treated beef within their borders. The United States again asked for the right to retaliate, and the WTO sanctioned $116.8 million in retaliation. The United States placed 100 percent tariffs on a wide range of products including Roquefort cheese and French chocolate.[11] As with the banana case, these tariffs will remain until the EU changes their policies.

What these cases have in common is the situation in which a major trading entity refuses to abide by the DSB's ruling and therefore faces a penalty. On both issues, the EU is convinced that their policies are consistent with the agreements they signed regulating trade, but in both instances the DSB has ruled that these policies are in violation of WTO rules. On the one hand, EU refusals to abide by WTO rulings make the DSB look weak. Further, the United States has looked like a sanctimonious bully by insisting on retaliation against EU products. On the other hand, the EU is facing penalties for breaking WTO rules, and the DSM is working as designed. It is encouraging that the United States did not retaliate unilaterally. It accepted WTO limits to its retaliation, which were far lower than the amounts the United States requested. Actions by the United States and the EU are having a major impact on the effectiveness of the DSM; whether that effect is, on balance, positive or negative is yet to be determined.

SHRIMP, SEA TURTLES, AND GASOLINE

The DSB has ruled against the United States in two notable cases: the importation of shrimp and trade in gasoline. In these disputes, the United States was accused of breaking WTO agreements by banning foreign shrimp and gasoline from the American market. The DSB panel eventually ruled that both American policies were inconsistent with WTO rules. The United States had to decide whether to change its policies or ignore the ruling. Regarding gasoline, the dispute centered on Environmental Protection Agency (EPA) regulations that require all gasoline to meet standards for purity (in order to reduce air pollution). The DSB case was triggered because the United States had different standards for foreign gasoline than it did for domestically produced gasoline. Foreign gasoline was required to have a higher level of purity than domestic gas. Venezuela and Brazil opposed this difference and brought the matter before the WTO. A panel was formed and EPA regulations were found to be in violation of WTO rules. Faced with the possibility of $150 million in trade sanctions, the United States modified its policy regarding foreign gasoline. The foreign refinery standard for purity was made equal to the American refinery standard and both standards will increase over time. The WTO decision and the American decision to change EPA policy had domestic political consequences; it outraged environmentalists in the United States. They argued that such changes to EPA policy would hurt the environment.

Environmentalists were also angered by the shrimp decision. In 1989, to protect endangered sea turtles, the EPA passed the "shrimp-turtle statute." This policy banned imported shrimp that were caught in nets not equipped with a device to exclude sea turtles. India, Pakistan, Malaysia, and Thailand, large shrimp-exporting countries, protested this policy and brought their case to the DSB. A panel ruled that American import restrictions were inconsistent with WTO rules and that the United States had to change its "shrimp-turtle statute." The United States appealed the decision and the Appellate Body overturned some of the panel's ruling. In the end, the WTO stated that the United States had a right to adopt a law that protected sea turtles, but the law had to be implemented more carefully and consistently. The law had to provide the same treatment and technical assistance to both eastern and western hemisphere producers, and countries facing a possible ban had to be allowed to participate in hearings before their shrimp were banned.[12]

In both of these cases, the United States changed its policies to abide by the final decisions of the DSB. If the United States had not made changes, it probably would have faced trade sanctions similar to the ones Europe faced in the beef and banana cases. Also in both cases, the environmental lobby in the United States was quick to point out how the WTO was affecting American sovereignty. Environmentalists have argued that the United States has the right to set its own environmental policy. When that policy must change to comply with WTO rules, they contend, the United States is losing sovereignty to an organization that is not concerned with the environment. The U.S. Trade Representative's Office sees the situation quite differently. It argued in both cases that the United States did not give up any sovereignty and that the WTO rulings have actually led to better U.S. policies.[13] The U.S. Trade Representative further argued that the United States should comply with WTO decisions because that is the behavior we expect from our trading partners.[14] Future cases and domestic opposition to WTO rulings will certainly play a big role in how committed the United States remains to DSB rulings. To date, it appears that the United States has respected WTO decisions.

WHAT DO THESE CASES MEAN?

Mixed lessons can be drawn from DSB rulings to date. Members are using the DSM to resolve trade disputes much more frequently than they did under the GATT system. In some cases, even the biggest trading states are conceding to WTO rules. In other cases, when issues are perceived to be of utmost importance (such as bananas and beef in the EU) member-states are far less likely to comply with DSB decisions. Although the United States may appear to be more committed to WTO rules than the EU, clearly the strength of America's commitment has not been tested because the United States has not lost a case that seriously challenges its sovereignty. In both the shrimp and the gasoline cases, the United States did not have to significantly change its policy to abide by WTO rulings.

There is another potential problem with the DSB. What if countries refuse to take their complaints to the DSB? What if they choose to retaliate unilaterally against trading partners without approval from the WTO? Countries may choose to bypass the DSB for several reasons. Some may decide that the DSB is not protecting their interests. If the biggest states bypass the DSB, or if they choose not to abide by its decisions, the DSM loses its legitimacy. If this happens, the system, and perhaps the WTO itself, becomes useless. An article in the *Economist* about the banana case sums up the problem nicely: "America and Europe, the leading proponents of world trade rules, must show they are willing to stick by them, their behaviour over bananas sets a bad precedent that invites others to play fast and loose with the law. America's bully-boy tactics will stiffen European resolve in disputes over beef and much else. And Europe's refusal to scrap its regime will only encourage growing feelings of hostility towards the WTO in the American Congress."[15] At issue, therefore, is much more than who gets their way with bananas, beef, and shrimp. Will the major players give legitimacy to the WTO system and abide by its rules?

THE U.S. RELATIONSHIP WITH THE WTO

Since the end of World War II, U.S. foreign economic policy has supported open markets. This policy goal has been achieved through multilateral cooperation via the GATT/WTO system. In the 1980s, the United States was a major proponent of strengthening GATT rules and pushed for the creation of a dispute settlement system to make sure all WTO members would follow the strengthened rules. U.S. negotiators worked hard throughout the Uruguay round to get these concessions. The United States was largely successful in getting what it wanted with the creation of the WTO, so one might expect that the United States would strongly support the WTO, but this is not always the case. Even though U.S. negotiators worked hard to construct a regime to facilitate and monitor free trade, Congress has not embraced the WTO. Sectors

of the public, such as environmentalists and union members, have been highly critical of the WTO. This has meant that although the United States continues to pursue an agenda that widens the scope of the WTO and gives it more
power, there is also constant pressure from special interest groups in favor of
the United States leaving the organization.

The strongest proponents of the WTO have been presidents of the United States. Presidents Reagan, George Bush, and Clinton were all committed
to the creation of the WTO. Each of these presidents did their utmost to see
that the new trade organization would have binding legal authority far
beyond that of the GATT system. Despite the public backlash since 1995,
leaders of both major political parties favor remaining in the WTO. Clinton's
Trade Policy Agenda 2000 made a strong argument for continued membership in the WTO:

> A strong and healthy trading system, exemplified by the World Trade Or-
> ganization, is critical to America's economic and security interests, and
> thus central to our trade policy. America, as the world's largest exporter
> and importer benefits perhaps most of all: the efficiency of our industries
> and the high living standards of our families reflect both the gains we re-
> ceive from open markets abroad and our own open-market policies at
> home, as well as from a framework of rules designed to ensure that Amer-
> ican products receive fair and predictable treatment around the world.[16]

Corporate interests have been another driving force behind American
trade policy. American corporations often call on the government to help
increase their access to foreign markets. But whereas corporations are simply
interested in profit, the executive branch must be responsive to public demands. It therefore must be aware of the rising opposition to the WTO and
balance the politics of public opinion with the economic agenda of American
corporations.

An unusual alliance of interests that range from right-wing conservatives
to left-wing liberals are opposed to U.S. membership in the WTO. Some conservatives fear runaway globalization and favor a United States that is more
isolationist and less engaged in the global system. Liberal interests are more
varied. The liberal groups that oppose the WTO tend to represent labor
unions, environmentalists, and human rights activists.

Many labor unions oppose the WTO because they feel that American jobs
are disappearing and that the WTO is to blame. Wages are lower in many
foreign countries, and this has caused numerous American corporations to
relocate their manufacturing operations to other countries. With no international labor standards to control wages, there is nothing to stop companies
from locating in the countries that have the cheapest wages. Nor is there anything to stop companies from employing children in countries where it is
legal to hire child labor. Labor unions share concerns about child labor with
human rights activists who largely oppose the WTO due to its indifference to
human rights issues. Human rights activists believe the WTO values economic

profits more than human rights. Child labor issues and economic exploitation in the Third World top the list of concerns that lead human rights activists to oppose the WTO.

Environmentalists object to the WTO because they feel the organization puts corporate profits ahead of environmental concerns and fosters a "lowest common denominator" mentality. It would seem that countries that have stronger environmental laws are punished. If tough environmental laws are struck down by the WTO, then environmental protections will be lowered to the weakest standard that all countries can agree on. In the United States, environmentalists are particularly concerned that laws created to protect endangered species and clean air have been weakened because they are seen as barriers to free trade.

Environmental concerns have been expressed through well-known groups such as the Humane Society, the Green Party, Public Citizen (Ralph Nader's organization), and the Sierra Club, just to name a few. Dozens of local small groups such as churches and student organizations have also expressed anti-WTO sentiments. Whereas conservative critics have been most active in voicing their opposition to the WTO through spokespeople such as Pat Buchanan, liberal critics have found their voice in the streets. The Seattle protests brought together a potpourri of left-wing groups, including environmentalists, labor unions, human rights organizations, student groups, French Roquefort cheese manufacturers, animal rights activists, and the Free Tibet movement. Even anarchists, who are difficult to place on the right/left political spectrum, made a violent but strong appearance in Seattle opposing the WTO.

THE PROBLEM IS SOVEREIGNTY

What ties these disparate interests together? What do environmentalists, right-wing conservatives and labor unions have in common? The opposition seems to be tied to the fear that the WTO is a threat to U.S. sovereignty. Critics of the WTO argue that the United States is handing over too much of its decision-making power to an international organization. This is by far the most important issue for Congress regarding the WTO.

Concerns about losing U.S. sovereignty to an international trade organization are nothing new. In the 1940s, the fear of diminished sovereignty is what drove congressional opposition to the ITO. Similarly, in March 2000, several members of the House of Representatives introduced a resolution demanding that the United States withdraw from the WTO.[17] Those supporting a U.S. exit from the WTO presented arguments full of references to American sovereignty. They often cited the alleged constitutional illegality of giving an international organization the power to make decisions that are binding on the United States. Representative Jack Metcalf from Washington stated: "I firmly believe that any participation in multilateral organizations that in any way affects the independence and sovereignty of these United States is wrong and should be discontinued. Unfortunately, it has become obvious that the WTO will be able to remove jurisdiction over virtually any economic activity from the federal, state and local governments."[18]

The resolution sponsored by Metcalf and others that would have forced the United States to withdraw from the WTO was soundly defeated by a vote of 56 in favor and 363 opposed. Remarks by Representative Thomas Reynolds of New York summed up the thinking of the majority in Congress who supported the WTO: "Continued U.S. participation in the global trading system is vital to America's long-term economic and strategic interests, continued prosperity and strengthening the rule of law around the world. This is not a time for the U.S. to move away from the global economy by sending the wrong message to its trading partners."[19] Thus isolating the United States from the WTO would damage its leadership in the international economy and undermine U.S. national interests.

Although the WTO can demand that the United States change its trade policy or face penalties, no WTO decision is self-executing in U.S. law. Congress has to pass new or revised legislation before any DSB decision can have an impact inside the United States. The United States also always has the right not to implement any WTO decision, just as the EU has chosen to do in the cases of beef and bananas. The United States may face fines and economic penalties if it chooses to ignore a WTO decision, but in the final analysis, American sovereignty remains largely unchanged. For the moment, those supporting the WTO have won the battle regarding U.S. membership, but the war is far from over. In the meantime, strong contradictory pressures continue to exist, and the American relationship with the WTO will remain ambivalent at best.

THE FUTURE

What is the United States' relationship with the WTO going to look like in the future? Will the United States remain committed to the WTO, or will it abandon its membership in this organization? Although it is difficult to predict what the future will bring, there are specific issues that have the potential to change both the WTO itself, as well as the U.S. relationship within that organization.

The Seattle Issues

Although the interests of the protestors in Seattle seemed diverse, there were several issues that gained enough public attention to have a potential impact on the future of the WTO. Protestors argued that the WTO needs to do more to enhance environmental protection, to promote labor standards, and to increase its institutional transparency and accountability. The link between trade and the environment is something that the WTO has been sensitive to since the Uruguay round. To better understand this connection, the WTO has established the Committee on Trade and the Environment, which is overseen by the General Council. The WTO was not created to be an environmental protection organization. Its goal is to ensure a free and open trading system, but at times it is clear that trade issues and environmental issues overlap. The Committee on Trade and the Environment studies how free trade can affect the environment and makes recommendations for new WTO policies.

Trade and the environment are linked in several ways. Often in their quest to be stronger economic actors, less-developed states damage their environment while developing their industries. States without laws to protect the environment can also attract companies that are looking for a cheaper place to do business. When there is no need to comply with environmental laws, many products can be produced at lower costs. When economic growth and trade are given higher priority than environmental issues, many times the environment will suffer. Environmentalists would like to see countries pursue sustainable economic development policies that are based on sound ecological strategies. Environmentalists argue that member-states with high environmental standards should be able to refuse products from member-states that do not meet those higher standards. This way all members will be forced to adopt industrial policies that are environmentally friendly or they will lose their best markets.

Labor standards are another issue that mobilized protestors in Seattle. Labor standards include a wide range of issues such as child labor, forced labor, unionization, collective bargaining, and minimum wages. Protestors objected to the fact that the WTO promotes free trade in goods with no attention to working conditions or labor practices. Labor activists would like to see the WTO allow members to cite unfair or unsafe working conditions as a legitimate reason for discriminating against foreign goods. For example, some countries would like to keep products made by child labor from entering their markets. America's 1992 Child Labor Deterrence Act is a case in point. Labor activists hope that such laws will force countries to stop using child labor. However, the WTO has tried to avoid promoting labor rights and has rejected the inclusion of labor standards as part of trade agreements to date. Instead, the WTO has deferred the issue of labor standards to another international organization, the International Labor Organization (ILO). American foreign policy took the position at Seattle that, in the future, WTO rules should be expanded to include basic labor rights. Eventually, the WTO will be forced to deal with this issue.

All developed country member-states have policies to protect workers, but many developing country member-states do not. As in the case with weak environmental laws, low wages permit developing countries to attract manufacturing businesses because they can offer cheaper workers. Establishing uniform international labor standards may cause some countries to lose economically, therefore, many developing countries tend to be opposed to such standards.

Transparency and accountability were other issues that prompted protests in Seattle. Protestors argued that decisions made by the WTO are undemocratic because they are made by a small number of nonelected bureaucrats in the organization. If decision makers are not elected, then they are largely unaccountable. In addition, these decisions are not transparent; the general public has not been allowed to attend WTO meetings. Of particular concern to the protestors was the DSM that allows a panel of three to five experts to make trade decisions on the basis of their expertise, without considering public opinion.

The WTO responded to these allegations by arguing that member-states decide all issues by consensus. Each member-state is allowed to have representation on all committees and councils. DSB panel reports are approved by the general membership before being adopted. In addition, new WTO policies will open up the decision-making process in the future by providing documents to the public about DSB proceedings. Once again, American policy has led the way. Clinton's Trade Representative Charlene Barshefsky called on the WTO to allow nongovernmental organizations (NGOs) to participate in all proceedings and to publish a full account of all WTO meetings.

The protests in Seattle brought many new issues into the public eye: the environment, labor standards, transparency, and accountability are among the most important. Although the WTO has been working to address some of these concerns, both prior to and certainly after the Seattle protests, how it responds to these issues could seriously affect the American relationship with the WTO. Therefore, environmental issues, labor standards, transparency, and accountability are vital issues for the future of the WTO.

CONCLUSION

This chapter has provided an introduction to the WTO by explaining its history, structure, and legal authority. It has further sought to understand the nature of the United States' relationship with the WTO. The United States has a complex relationship with the WTO. On the one hand, the United States has been a driving force behind creating a multilateral organization to regulate global trade. Evidence of this dates back to the end of World War II and throughout the Uruguay round. The American negotiating agenda strongly supported developing institutional methods to enforce the new trade agreements. However, the United States is ambivalent about the WTO because it must sacrifice some sovereignty to this organization. American discomfort with ceding any sovereignty to an international trade organization has a long history dating back to the late 1940s.

The United States is the global leader for both imports and exports. It benefits greatly from an open global trading system, far more so than most other countries. Therefore, the benefits of participating in the WTO far outweigh the costs. But the U.S. Congress continues to be skeptical, and popular social movements (e.g., labor activists and environmentalists) are also leery of the organization's power. The central issue is the extent to which the United States is willing to sacrifice some amount of its national independence to remain in this international organization. Critics of the WTO believe that the loss of U.S. sovereignty has already been too great. As the WTO expands its legal power and the scope of its authority, domestic opposition to U.S. membership will escalate. How the WTO deals with issues such as the environment, labor, and accountability will help transform the organization and the U.S. relationship with the WTO.

PART III

VALUES

INTRODUCTION TO PART III

To what extent do standards of morality shape American foreign policy? Should morality be the basis for international policy? These questions are more controversial than they might appear. Parts I and II of this text reviewed defense and economic policies, but readers may have noticed by now that neither discussion raised the issue of ethics and foreign policy. Of course, there are ethical dimensions to military policy or trade policy. But most histories and assessments of American foreign policy do not use ethical standards as criteria for evaluation. Defense policy is usually judged according to how well it protects America's "national interests." A "good" defense policy is one that protects national interests, whereas a "bad" policy is one that threatens perceived national interests. Similarly, economic policy is usually evaluated according to the standard of "competitiveness." A "good" economic policy enhances America's competitiveness, whereas a "bad" economic policy reduces competitiveness.

In the final section of this book, we will discuss areas of U.S. foreign policy that seem most directly relevant to standards of morality. We will not go back through defense and economic polices while using our new moral lens. Rather we will discuss ethics and foreign policy indirectly by moving on to policies regarding human rights, Third World development, and the international environment. Each of these areas raises certain moral questions that U.S. policy is forced to address to some extent.

(A) Is the way a government treats its own people purely an internal political matter? Does the international community of nations, following America's leadership, have a need or a right to set limits to how any government treats its own citizens? What areas of human rights are the most important? How can American foreign policy be used to improve human rights standards around the world? Should the United States impose economic or military sanctions on foreign governments that commit egregious violations of human rights?

(B) Do rich nations, including the United States, have any direct or indirect responsibility for the poverty of Third World nations?[1] How can U.S. aid and U.S. foreign policy promote better living conditions in the Third World? Should economic relations between rich and poor nations (e.g., the United States versus the Third World) be restructured in such a way as to promote international distributive justice? Is a redistribution of international wealth and global economic power now required?

(C) What moral obligations do we owe to future generations to protect and repair the environment? Who is responsible for international environmental degradation? What nations should shoulder the burdens and pay the costs for cleaning up the environment? How can the world undo the environmental damage from prior industrial development without forcing impoverished nations to forgo rapid economic development in the future?

Although foreign policy makers in the United States may not spend time every day wrestling with the weighty moral questions in the previous list, American foreign policy is faced with a series of salient political issues that have these questions as their subtext. Should the United States continue its normal trade relations with the People's Republic of China despite the massive and consistent violations of rights there? Should the United States support massive debt relief for Third World countries? A U.S. secretary of the treasury recently stressed the ethical dimensions of debt relief when he referred to forgiving some Third World debt as a "moral imperative."[2] In light of renewed concerns about the poor health of the American economy, should the United States now abandon the promises it made in a 1997 treaty to reduce its emissions of greenhouse gases? These ethical issues are relevant to the international policies reviewed in the next three chapters.

Theories of international ethics have recently turned to how international norms (or values) arise, spread, and become widely accepted. There are two major schools of thought that focus on international norms: the economic approach and the constructivist view.[3] Economic approaches have shown how broad international ethical standards can evolve over time through the interactions of successive generations.[4] Social constructivist theory is more interested in showing how specific norms arise and change at particular times in history. Normative theory has postulated a life cycle for ethical standards: (a) starting with the emergence of a norm, (b) moving on to a period of "cascading" norms when the values spread to at least two-thirds of all states, and (c) culminating in the institutionalization of normative standards.[5]

When ethical theorists turn to matters of policy, they tend to focus on issues of rights, obligations to promote development, and environmental responsibility. These are the very areas of American foreign policy to which we now turn our attention. Chapter 10 begins by drawing connections between realist theory, idealist theory, and morality. Before beginning that discussion, however, our readers are invited to explore the following web resources and make their own ethical evaluations of U.S. foreign policy.

Internet Resources for Part III

Amnesty International
www.amnesty.org

Derechos–Human Rights
www.derechos.org

Environmental Protection Agency
www.epa.gov

Freedom House
www.freedomhouse.org

Friends of the Earth
www.foe.org

Global Exchange
www.globalexchange.org

Greenpeace
www.greenpeace.org

Green Parties of North America
www.greens.org

Human Rights Internet
www.hri.ca

The Human Rights Page
www.hrweb.org

Human Rights Watch
www.hrw.org

International Human Rights Law Group
www.hrlawgroup.org

Lawyers Committee for Human Rights
www.lchr.org

UN Environment Program
www.unep.org

UN Framework Convention on Climate Change
www.unfccc.de

UN High Commissioner on Human Rights
www.unhchr.ch

U.S. Department of State (annual reports on international human rights)
     www.state.gov

World Organization Against Torture
     www.omct.org

Chapter 10

FOREIGN POLICY
AND HUMAN RIGHTS

Moral principles have always played a prominent role in American foreign policies. This chapter addresses the morality of U.S. policy by focusing on post–World War II policies regarding international human rights. Before proceeding to a history of human rights policy, however, a review of two key theories on the proper relationship between ethics and foreign policy is in order.

ETHICS AND FOREIGN POLICY

Opinions on the proper role that should be played by ethics in U.S. foreign policy cover a wide spectrum. Some analysts and practitioners argue that private standards of morality cannot be the basis for international policy. Others take an opposing view, positing private ethical standards as the ultimate foundation for any workable foreign policy. This wide range of opinions can best be understood by explaining two ideal types. At the extremes are the theoretical stances of realism and utopianism (the latter is also known as "idealism," or "liberalism"). These are ideal types in the sense that they represent alternative conceptual frameworks for linking ethics to foreign policy. The view of any particular individual will tend to lean more toward one side or the other (realism vs. utopianism), and most authorities on foreign policy use language that partakes of both positions. Discussing realism and utopianism in their purest forms will facilitate the following detailed explanation of actual policies on human rights.

Early twentieth-century views on ethics and foreign policy were akin to the ideal type of utopianism. Popular among politicians and intellectuals in the 1920s and 1930s, utopianism became almost synonymous with Wilsonianism because of its congruence with the foreign policies of President Wilson. Utopianism is characterized by four basic elements:

1. Utopianism was the dominant view during the interwar period (between World Wars I and II).
2. Utopianism is optimistic. It emphasizes how national leaders *ought* to behave. Utopianism argues that behavior can be morally improved. Utopianism also

tends to view human nature as something that can be molded and guided through ethical instruction and education.

3. Utopianism stresses the importance of international law and international organizations. Utopians seek to create new laws that will limit and regulate the behavior of nations. They also favor the creation of international organizations as a way to manage and prevent interstate conflict.

4. Utopianism seeks to establish a widely shared set of international norms. These moral rules and ethical principles are to serve as the proper basis for international laws, international relations, and foreign policies.[1]

The utopian nature of this view is most evident in its desire to make the world a better place. Utopians look to private ethical standards as a way to create a morally defensible world order. Interwar utopians were optimistic enough to believe that they could effectively outlaw war. The Kellogg-Briand Pact of 1928 claimed to do just that. This was a moralistic declaration that purported to prohibit war between nations.

Utopianism in the United States found its impetus in U.S. reactions against the horrors of World War I. A war that was different in kind from all prior conflicts, the Great War of 1914–18 exhibited a barbarity and wrought destruction on a scale the world had never seen. New techniques of mass destruction (aerial bombardment, gas warfare, the machine gun) were introduced. Trench warfare and tactical maneuvers designed with *expected* casualty rates of fifty percent or more led to the decimation of entire armies for little or no military gain. Led by President Wilson, many Americans expressed desires after the war for a more moral and peaceful world order. They argued that European power politics had been the cause of World War I. Wilson's design for the League of Nations after the war was an attempt to transcend power politics. Wilson's hopes for a new world order based on the League of Nations were a concrete manifestation of utopianism in post–World War I U.S. foreign policy.

Utopians such as Wilson tend to disdain the use of military force. They will try to avoid the turn to military options in foreign policy if at all possible. Utopians prefer the use of other means: diplomacy, treaty obligations, and economic sanctions. Utopians will also tend to resort to force only when that military pressure is applied in a collective fashion and by a multilateral alliance that has been sanctioned under an international organization (e.g., the League of Nations, or more recently, the UN Security Council).

The most common criticism of utopianism is that it lacks any effective enforcement mechanisms. Collective security as demonstrated by the League of Nations failed to stop fascist aggression in the 1930s. The Kellogg-Briand Pact had no way to enforce its moralistic prohibition against war. A more recent example can be found in the foreign policy of President Carter. Carter sounded very much like a utopian in 1979 when he announced that the United States would not employ force or the threat of force to rescue U.S. hostages in Iran.[2] One of Carter's first actions during the Iranian hostage crisis was to declare publicly that he would not resort to military force as a way to free the hostages. His subsequent efforts to end the crisis through diplomacy and economic sanctions largely failed. Carter therefore seemed powerless to do anything that would effectively end the crisis.

The failure of the League of Nations to prevent aggression in the 1930s subsequently resulted in the commencement of World War II. After the war, the Cold War came to dominate U.S. foreign policy. The Cold War led to the demise of utopianism. Cold War politics were guided by realism and the tenets of realpolitik. As we shall see, realism is the dominant view in U.S. policy to this day. Although the intellectual history of realism dates back to ancient Greece, the four basic elements of realism were established from the following post–World War II characteristics:

1. Realism is the dominant view after World War II (during both the Cold War and post–Cold War periods).
2. Realism is a pessimistic view of politics and human nature. It is suspicious of political idealism and emphasizes how leaders and nations do behave (rather than how they ought to behave). It emphasizes the evil elements of basic human nature.
3. Realism focuses on power and the balance of power. Power, not law or organizations, is used as the means to regulate behavior.
4. Realism makes a distinction between private morality and public morality. Realism argues that private moral standards are not directly applicable to the actions of nations.

Textbook treatments of realism trace its origins back to the Greek philosopher Thucydides and to the early modern works of Machiavelli and Hobbes.[3] The intellectual staying power of realist arguments has helped political realism remain the mainstream view throughout the Cold War and post–Cold War eras. Perhaps the best defense of these arguments is still to be found in the writings of Machiavelli. Of all classical realists, Machiavelli has been the most influential among modern day followers of this view.

Realists believe that utopian goals and crusades to make the world a better place can only lead to ruin. Utopianism tends to distort national policy, according to this view, and inhibits effective leadership. Although often misinterpreted as an amoral or even an immoral position, realism is better understood as that view which holds utopian idealism to be simply counterproductive. In the words of Machiavelli:

> To go to the real truth of the matter . . . how we live is so far removed from how we ought to live, that he who abandons what is done for what ought to be done, will rather learn to bring about his own ruin than his preservation. A man who wishes to make a profession of goodness in everything must necessarily come to grief among so many who are not good. Therefore it is necessary for a prince, who wishes to maintain himself, to learn

how not to be good, and to use this knowledge or not use it, according to the necessity of the case.[4]

Machiavelli's book *The Prince* was the first realist handbook. This realist text contains extensive reflections on the nature of power. Realists study power rather than law or international organization as their preferred means for protecting national interests and managing conflict. Acquisition of power, maintenance and expansion of power, displays of power, the use of force and diplomacy backed by the threats of force—these are the tools of realist foreign policy. Realists argue that only the study of power politics and history can instruct us on the ways to prevent war. Only power and balances of power can guide or alter the behavior of nations. Law and political institutions cannot effectively restrain the actions of nations, but force and diplomacy backed by military force can. Machiavelli's handbook on power has often been referred to as the first political science textbook.

Machiavelli also gives us the most succinct and definitive statement on the differences between public and private morality: "It must be understood that a prince. . .cannot observe all those things which are considered good in men, being often obliged, in order to maintain the state, to act against faith, against charity, against humanity, and against religion. . .in the actions of men, and especially of princes. . .the end justifies the means. Let a prince therefore aim at conquering and maintaining the state, and the means will always be judged honourable and praised by every one."[5]

Realists believe that the moral standards applicable to the public actions of national leaders are not necessarily the same as those that we apply to our private activities. Again, often misinterpreted as a view that argues for amoral or even immoral behavior, realism instead seeks to present a distinct moral calculus for public actions. The supreme moral obligation for any leader, according to realism, is the preservation of the state. Beyond that, leaders are also obligated to do their best to protect the interests of their people. These moral requirements of leadership may oblige a president or a prime minister to take public actions that are contrary to private or religious moral standards. Nevertheless, realists since Machiavelli have argued that a national leader must do what is necessary to protect national interests, even if that means learning "how not to be good." History shows that leaders often behave badly, and one must learn how not to be good or risk losing power and security altogether.

Realists criticize utopians for being misled by their preoccupation with private standards of morality. Pre–World War II utopians in the League of Nations were condemned for their unwillingness and inability to use force to stop aggression by Germany, Italy, and Japan.[6] To avoid war, realists argue that U.S. foreign policy must concentrate on a stable international balance of power. This was the basic logic behind Cold War policies of containment against the Soviet bloc. Realists such as George Kennan and Henry Kissinger constructed policies in which force was met with military force, and the power of enemies was balanced by countervailing U.S. power. Realists fear that a preoccupation with morality for morality's sake will lead to distraction, muddle one's thinking, and result in campaigns to change the world that must necessarily fail. The end product, according to this logic, would be the failure to protect the United States, Americans, and U .S. national interests.

On the other hand, realism is not devoid of morality. Every leader has the supreme moral duty to provide for national security and the physical safety of the citizenry. According to Kissinger, "Peace is the fundamental moral imperative."[7] Realists concentrate on balance of power politics because they believe that, without a balance of power, without international order, without stability and security, no moral behavior of any kind is possible in the international arena. When once asked to compare the relative importance of order versus justice, Kissinger quoted Goethe: "If I had to choose between justice and disorder, on the one hand, and injustice and order on the other, I would always choose the latter."[8] Without order, the result is often the kind of all against all state-of-nature war of witnessed in Lebanon during the 1970s or in the Balkans during the 1990s. In a world of anarchy and rampant disorder, no one is safe and anything goes. Events in Liberia, Rwanda, and Somalia in the 1990s are additional cases in point.

Realism heavily influenced U.S. foreign policy during the Cold War. As we shall see, even after the end of the Cold War realpolitik remains the dominant view. However, one cannot push the distinction between realism and utopianism too far. Utopians such as Wilson and Carter were not ignorant when it came to power politics, nor were they averse to the use of force when they deemed it absolutely necessary. Wilson took the United States into World War I in order to make the world safe for democracy. He also deployed more than 10,000 troops into Russia after the war as part of an unsuccessful attempt by the Allies to overthrow Lenin.[9] Carter attempted an unsuccessful military rescue of the hostages in Iran, after having sworn publicly against just such an action (a sequence of events as Machiavellian as anything undertaken by any realist). Utopians can and do use force, only perhaps not as often or as quickly as would a realist. Realists—at least the more sophisticated realists—also understand the importance of international law and international morality when it comes to national security. A sophisticated realist acknowledges that protection of national interests can depend at least in part on ethical considerations and the ethical consequences of foreign policy. In the view of some, the so-called late Kissinger moved to such a position when he argued during the Ford administration that the United States must take international human rights more seriously.

It is in the area of human rights policy that the tension between utopianism and realism becomes most readily apparent. It is also in regard to international human rights that the need for a synthesis of these two views becomes most necessary. Tonelson has argued that ignoring human rights abuses by pro-U.S. dictatorships often backfires on the United States and leads in the long run to endangering U.S. national interests.[10] Donnelly reminds us that, despite the realists' definitions of national interests in terms of power and security, human rights and "other moral concerns" might well constitute necessary additional elements of the national interest.[11] In the long term, utopian concerns such as human rights and realist concern for national security may ultimately converge. Before this can become apparent, however, a review is needed of the particulars of U.S. foreign policies on human rights. Although they have their limitations as ideal types, the conceptual categories of realism and utopianism will inform a historical review of human rights policies. Human rights, as such, have been a factor relevant to the study of foreign policy only since World War II. However, there are certain important precedents that date back to the United States' earliest days as a sovereign nation.

FROM INDEPENDENCE TO THE FOUR FREEDOMS

Since the birth of the United States, ideas about rights and public policies on rights have been inextricably intertwined with the United States' evolution as an international actor. When Jefferson wrote the Declaration of Independence, he spoke of the "inalienable rights" to "life, liberty and the pursuit of happiness." Violations of these rights by the British government constituted the moral and philosophical grounds on which Jefferson argued in favor of a right to independence (self-determination) for the thirteen colonies. Following Jefferson and throughout the nineteenth century, U.S. leaders based their foreign policies on notions of morality and self-images that were widely shared across the country.

Separated from the Old World by the Atlantic and lacking the overseas colonies that were prized by European powers, Americans saw themselves as politically and morally unique. They eschewed standing armies as a symbol of European autocracy. U.S. leaders extolled the virtues of democracy, written constitutions containing a bill of rights, and free enterprise. However, U.S. foreign policies during this period were also decidedly isolationist. The United States made no efforts to remake the world in its own image during the 1800s. Its role in the world was to stand as a moral example that other nations could emulate, if they so wished. The United States was the shining city on the hill that other nations could and should try to copy. U.S. exceptionalism, especially in terms of active foreign policies, meant that its leaders would be content to tend their own garden. The rest of the world would have to find its own way, largely without the direct help or intervention of the United States.

The first halting steps away from U.S. isolationism were taken by Wilson after World War I. Wilson's foreign policies might appear to be a clear break from the isolationist past. However, they were also essentially consistent with nineteenth-century policies in that, at their core, these new policies were likewise based on a vision of the moral role that the United States should play in the world. Wilson's Fourteen Points (1918) were to become the basis of a new world order, a global order that would make the world safe for democracy and that would for the first time declare certain inalienable rights at the international level. Among the rights expressed in the Fourteen Points was the right of self-determination for nations that were under a "colonial claim."

The "sovereignty" and "interests" of the colonized peoples were to be given "equal weight" as compared to the claims and demands of the colonizers (Point V). "[M]utual guarantees" of "political independence and territorial integrity" were to be given by all states to all other "great and small states alike" (Point XIV).[12]

The aggression that led to World War II, along with the coincident failure of the League of Nations to prevent such aggression, meant that Wilson's new order was not to be achieved. However, this did not prevent a subsequent U.S. president from offering his own vision of the proper moral basis for a just world order. In his State of the Union Address of 1941, President Franklin Roosevelt declared the "Four Freedoms." These freedoms were to be universal. Roosevelt argued that they should be enjoyed by all peoples everywhere. They are freedom of speech, freedom of religion, freedom from want, and freedom from fear.[13] Roosevelt declared the Four Freedoms prior to U.S. entry into World War II. However, the wars that were already raging in Asia and Europe were clearly on the president's mind when he declared these freedoms to be the ethical minimum that all people had a right to expect from their own governments. The implication was that fascist governments, by definition, did not ensure such liberties.

FROM THE UNIVERSAL DECLARATION THROUGH THE EARLY COLD WAR

The historical connection between World War II and the international human rights movement is definitive. The horrors of the Holocaust and the various war crimes committed by fascist governments led to two immediate results at the war's end. First, war crimes tribunals were established to punish the guilty. Second, in the newly formed United Nations, the Commission on Human Rights was established. The first chair of this commission was Eleanor Roosevelt. The commission was charged with drafting an international bill of human rights (IBHR). The first element of the IBHR became the Universal Declaration of Human Rights (UDHR), adopted by the UN General Assembly on December 10, 1948. The tenth of December has been commemorated ever since as International Human Rights Day.

During this early post–World War II period, the United States was at the forefront of the international human rights campaign. U.S. leadership, most notably the work of Eleanor Roosevelt, helped to push the UDHR through the United Nations. Written primarily by Roosevelt and one of her top aides, the UDHR is a nonbinding standard of achievement. U.S. leadership regarding international human rights quickly dissipated, however, with the advent of the Cold War. Foreign policy in the 1950s was dominated by desires to contain communism and to prevent Soviet expansion.

Presidents Truman and Eisenhower showed little interest in promoting human rights as such. Their top concerns were to establish a string of military alliances, anchored by the North Atlantic Treaty Organization (NATO), and to enforce the Truman Doctrine, which promised U.S. aid to any nation fighting against communist aggression. U.S. foreign policy in the 1950s exhibited a narrow focus on realism. The only rhetoric used during this period on human rights was in regard to the need to protect the "free world" (America's allies) from the Soviet bloc. Eisenhower gave in to congressional critics of the United Nations, led by Senator John Bricker of Ohio, who opposed all treaties on human rights. The United Nations drafted binding covenants on rights as a follow-up to the UDHR. These binding treaties were largely completed by 1954.[14] However, the opposition led by Bricker forced Eisenhower's administration to announce that the United States would not be a party to any human rights treaties produced by the United Nation. To this day, congressional opposition to human rights documents is still referred to as Brickerism.[15]

Bricker made three kinds of arguments against ratification of human rights treaties.[16] First, he argued that rights and protections of rights are domestic political issues and therefore not proper subjects for international treaties. Because, in his view, the U.S. Constitution always takes precedence over any treaty and because international law does not apply directly to U.S. citizens (in Bricker's opinion), rights are not subject to foreign treaties. In this instance, Bricker was simply restating the position that had been the dominant view on rights prior to World War II. A second set of arguments from Bricker involved Cold War politics. Bricker characterized the UN General Assembly as a forum dominated by America's enemies, specifically the Soviet Union and its allies in Third World socialist nations. Because most human rights treaties are a product of General Assembly resolutions, Bricker saw them as threats to U.S. national interests. Finally, Bricker expressed the opinion that human rights documents represent "socialism by treaty," a charge that one still hears to the present day from such members of Congress as Jesse Helms of North Carolina. Treaties on second generation rights—specifically the Covenant on Economic, Social and Cultural Rights—posit jobs, housing, and medical care (among others) as areas that are to be promoted through the provision of rights. Because such things are not recognized as rights under the U.S. Constitution, becoming a party to this treaty would allegedly bring socialism into the U.S. political system through the back door.

Bricker's ultimate goal was a constitutional amendment prohibiting the United States from joining any international treaties on rights. Bricker failed in his attempt to amend the U.S. Constitution. He succeeded, however, in preventing U.S. foreign policy from supporting any international human rights obligations throughout the early Cold War era.

POSITIVE AND NEGATIVE DEVELOPMENTS IN THE 1960S

When President Kennedy redesigned U.S. foreign policy in the 1960s, he gave increased attention to international issues other than the Soviet threat. Development in the Third World, especially within Latin America, was elevated in importance to become a primary objective of U.S. policy. There was a markedly more generous approach to foreign aid. New assistance programs were set up under the Peace Corps and the Alliance for Progress (AFP). President Johnson followed up on these policies and expanded the Food for Peace program that had been established in 1954. This was also the age of the domestic civil rights movement capped by the Civil Rights Act (1964), signed by Johnson. All of these policies were designed to promote equality at home and abroad and to help people everywhere better meet their basic human needs. The United Nations finished the two international covenants on human rights in 1966: the Covenant on Civil and Political Rights and the Covenant on Economic, Social and Cultural Rights. The covenants are binding treaties for those nations that ratify them. The two covenants and the UDHR make up the three parts of the IBHR. Falk describes the Kennedy-Johnson years as a period of "expansive international liberalism" and paints a rosy picture of Kennedy in particular as "an idealistic force in international society."[17] A more balanced history of the period, however, such as the one given by Schoultz, reveals a darker side to U.S. foreign policy.[18]

The AFP was economic aid directed toward Latin America. The hope was that economic development would reduce the likelihood of more Castroite revolutions. The AFP would enhance growth and defuse some of the economic tensions that might result in political unrest. The other side of this coin was the Office of Public Safety (OPS), also created by the Kennedy administration. Whereas the AFP brought economic growth to Latin America, the OPS was designed to keep the lid on communist insurgencies. The latter program provided arms, training, and technical know-how for fighting guerilla wars waged by national liberation fronts. The OPS created an International Police Academy (IPA) that trained forces from fifty-two nations.[19] Most of this training was for internal security. The targets of OPS-IPA programs were leftists of various sorts. Critics charged that the IPA was teaching torture and other forms of repression. Similar charges have been made recently in regard to the International Military Education and Training program and the School of the Americas, both successors to the IPA.[20] Schoultz cites a congressional report from 1971 that detailed the kinds of training provided to Latin American security forces through these programs:

> Courses were offered in riot control, intelligence, psychological warfare, counter-guerilla operations . . . censorship . . . defoliation, electronic intelligence, the use of informants, insurgency intelligence, counterintelligence, subversion, counter-subversion, espionage, counterespionage, interrogation of prisoners and suspects, handling mass rallies and meetings, intelligence photography, polygraphs, populace and resources control, psychological operations, raids and searches, riots, special warfare, surveillance, terror, and undercover operations.[21]

The OPS was also implicated in violations of rights in South Vietnam during the same period. The OPS itself was part of the larger Agency for International Development (AID). The OPS was intimately linked to the South

Vietnamese police forces, and AID provided the funding for the notorious "tiger cages" on Con Sol Island, cages used by the South Vietnamese security forces for interrogation and torture of suspected Viet Cong rebels. A congressional aide named Tom Harkin photographed the tiger cages and published the photos in *Life* magazine in 1970. Prisoners were bolted to the floor of the cages in such a way that they could not stand, sit, or recline for weeks, even months, at a time. Congressional testimony about the effects of this form of torture showed "severe nutritional deficiency coupled with prolonged immobilization. Each man had spent months or years without interruption in leg shackles while subsisting on a diet of three handfuls of milled white rice and three swallows of water per day. This combination of prolonged immobilization and starvation has . . . never occurred before on such a scale."[22] The Air Force doctor who gave this testimony concluded by noting that "their paralysis together with the causative conditions are unique in the history of modern warfare, and the U.S. bears a heavy burden of complicity."[23]

The legacy of the Kennedy-Johnson years and the programs initiated by these presidents thus leaves a checkered balance sheet regarding U.S. foreign policy and human rights. The admirable goals and the good works of the Peace Corps and the AFP were offset by the repression enhanced by the OPS and the IPA. When these Democratic administrations were succeeded by Republican presidents, the stage was set for a battle between the White House and Congress for control of foreign policy, especially policy in regard to human rights.

KISSINGER VERSUS THE CONGRESS

Kissinger was the principal architect of U.S. foreign policy in the Nixon and Ford administrations. Well known for his scholarship and practice of political realism, Kissinger aided Nixon in the creation of détente during the 1970s. Détente was an effort to promote peaceful coexistence while containing communism through new means. Kissinger pursued nuclear arms control, trade with the Soviets, and policy in Vietnam. The Nixon administration escalated the war in Vietnam before negotiating a withdrawal of U.S. forces. Kissinger was awarded the Nobel Peace Prize in 1973 for his achievement at the Paris peace talks with North Vietnam. Although famous for détente, Kissinger also has received considerable attention from those who study the history of U.S. policy on human rights.

Falk claims that Kissinger was "openly scornful of introducing human rights concerns into serious diplomacy."[24] As a realist, Kissinger argued that introducing human rights matters into policy would interfere with more important issues, such as maintaining a stable balance of power and limiting nuclear weapons. Stressing human rights violations, even those in the Soviet Union, was set aside by Kissinger to pursue détente. Kissinger would not broach the subject of human rights in his dealings with the Soviets. He wanted to avoid embarrassing the Soviet Union in any way that might increase tensions between the superpowers and thereby endanger détente.

Schoultz describes Kissinger as a man who had a change of heart on the issue of human rights. Schoultz details what he calls the "early" as opposed to the "late" Kissinger. The early Kissinger was a dyed-in-the-wool realist. The early Kissinger saw only two options for U.S. policy when it came to human rights violations: "In our bilateral dealings we will follow a pragmatic policy of degree. If the infringement on human rights is not so offensive that we cannot live with it, we will seek to work out what we can with the country involved in order to increase our influence. If the infringement is so offensive that we cannot live with it, we will avoid dealing with the offending country."[25]

For the early Kissinger there were only two choices. Either the United States could turn a blind eye toward human rights violations, ignoring abuses and conducting business as usual in its foreign policy, or it could cut all ties with the repressive regime when rights violations became too egregious. Reducing the policy options to these two extremes, in effect stacks the deck in favor of turning a blind eye toward rights violations. Kissinger, in both his early and his late periods, never advocated cutting ties to any regime because of its human rights violations. Kissinger also opposed using aid as leverage. Leverage is the reduction or suspension of foreign aid to a government as punishment for human rights abuses. Kissinger argued that linking foreign aid to human rights was too utopian, that it was part of a misguided "temptation to crusade," and he said cuts in aid would damage national security.[26] Instead of leverage, Kissinger preferred quiet diplomacy as his means to improve human rights.

The late Kissinger described by Schoultz experienced a change of heart regarding the issue of human rights, a change allegedly reflected in his 1976 speech before the Organization of American States (OAS). Present at this speech were representatives from the government of Chile. Headed by General Pinochet, Chile's military junta had become notorious by 1976 for its human rights atrocities. Speaking before the OAS, Kissinger said: "One of the most compelling issues of our time, and one which calls for the concerted action of all responsible peoples and nations, is the necessity to protect and extend the fundamental rights of humanity."[27] In the same speech, Kissinger referred to human rights as "the very essence of a meaningful life."[28]

There are at least three ways to interpret Kissinger's 1976 conversion on human rights. One interpretation would be simply that he was sincere in his change of heart. Perhaps this great statesman decided during his last year in the State Department that his prior realism had to be tempered with a greater concern for international morality and human rights. Schoultz seems to lean toward this view of Kissinger.[29] A second interpretation is that Kissinger lied when speaking before the OAS. His speech may have been a cynical use of rhetoric to fool the U.S. public into believing that he had experienced a change of heart. Forsythe seems to lean toward this view when he says of the 1976 speech that "Kissinger was nothing if not duplicitous."[30]

A third interpretation of Kissinger's talk before the OAS would view the speech as something designed primarily for domestic consumption in the

United States. After all, 1976 was an election year. A Democrat running for president, Jimmy Carter of Georgia, was using the rhetoric of human rights to garner national attention for his campaign. Kissinger had also been under pressure from Congress for years to make human rights leverage a part of official government policy (something Kissinger consistently resisted). Kissinger may have recognized the political value of human rights rhetoric; he may simply have been trying to steal Carter's thunder while defusing the human rights movement within Congress.

While Kissinger was orchestrating White House policy, congressional leaders initiated a countertrend that sought to reduce or remove U.S. support for right-wing governments that abused human rights. Congress was bothered by the moral complicity of the United States in regard to the Vietnamese tiger cages and training by the OPS at the IPA.[31] Concerns of Congress led to a series of legislation that required the White House to integrate new human rights policies into its agenda. Human rights strings were attached by Congress to economic aid and military aid.

In 1974, Congress amended Section 502B of the 1961 Foreign Assistance Act to apply human rights leverage to foreign military aid. As amended, this law states that "no security assistance may be provided to any country the government of which engages in a consistent pattern of gross violations of internationally recognized human rights . . . unless the President certifies in writing . . . that extraordinary circumstances exist warranting provision of such assistance."[32] Hence under Section 502B military aid cannot be extended to governments that consistently violate human rights standards. However, the "extraordinary circumstances" clause is a national security loophole that allows repressive regimes to receive military aid if a president argues that such aid is necessary for U.S. national interests. At different times in the past, this loophole has been invoked to ensure continued military aid to nations such as Iran, the Philippines, and South Korea.

In 1975 Congress moved to attach the same conditions to economic aid. The OPS was also shut down by a separate act of Congress in 1975. Economic aid was made subject to human rights leverage under the provisions of an amendment to Section 116 of the Foreign Assistance Act. Also referred to as the Harkin Amendment in honor of its author, Tom Harkin of Iowa (onetime congressional aide who photographed the tiger cages, later a member of Congress), this law is a "cornerstone of human rights legislation."[33] As amended, Section 116 denies economic aid "to the government of any country which engages in a consistent pattern of gross violations of internationally recognized human rights, including torture or cruel, inhuman, or degrading treatment or punishment, prolonged detention without charges, or other flagrant denial of the right to life, liberty, and the security of the person, unless such assistance will directly benefit the needy people in such country."[34]

The Harkin Amendment goes on to require of the White House "annual presentation materials" certifying that nations that receive U.S. economic assistance do indeed uphold international standards of human rights. The "needy people" loophole of the Harkin Amendment allows economic aid to be granted to a nation that displays gross human rights violations if that aid goes to the direct benefit of the most needy. Haiti is an example of a country for which the needy people loophole has been invoked as a way to ensure continued aid. On such occasions, however, Congress will further require that the aid be channeled through nongovernmental organizations (NGOs), such as the Red Cross. Use of NGOs under these circumstances is a way to see that needy people are not penalized for crimes committed by their government. At the same time, corrupt officials in a repressive regime have no direct access to the aid themselves.

The Harkin Amendment also has had a lasting impact on U.S. foreign policy because it has institutionalized the processes of human rights reporting by the State Department and certification of human rights compliance by the Congress. This act led to annual publications from the State Department on human rights conditions around the world. Released in February of each year, the country reports on human rights from the State Department have become an increasingly important source of information for Congress and the public alike.[35] Once subject to politicization, the reports have become progressively more objective over time.

Section 502B and the Harkin Amendment stand as the key pieces of human rights legislation governing military and economic aid, respectively. Both acts were vigorously opposed by Kissinger and the White House when originally drafted. Presidents Nixon and Ford resisted the human rights leverage on foreign policy that these acts represented. President Carter, on the other hand, came into the White House very much in favor of such legislation and of increasing the role that human rights would play in his administration.

THREE CHARACTERISTICS OF THE CARTER POLICY

President Carter came into office promising a change from the old way of doing things under Nixon and Kissinger. He promised a change from the immorality of the Watergate scandal and the dirty tricks of the Nixon White House.[36] Carter ran for the presidency as an outsider. A former governor of Georgia, Carter was unconnected to the old boy network of Washington. He ran against the idea of politics as usual. His campaign stressed Carter as an idealist, and he spoke of himself as a former Sunday school teacher. A man who focused on his moral beliefs, Carter even confessed in a published interview to the weakness of having "lusted in his heart" after women other than his wife, but he quickly added that he would never act on such feelings. He wore his heart on his sleeve and displayed morality as his badge of courage.

Carter's early foreign policies were consciously constructed on utopian grounds. He said he wanted to make the U.S. government as good as the American people. He believed that morality had to be the basis of international policy. This meant no more turning a blind eye toward human rights violations by allied governments. Carter sought to distance the United States from right-wing dictatorships, especially those in Latin America. He came into office very much in favor of using aid leverage to exert pressure on rights abusers.

Carter promised to make human rights the moral focus of his foreign policy. He said that his administration's commitment to rights would be absolute. Upon taking office, Carter moved quickly to display his devotion to the cause of human rights. He signed the American Convention on Human Rights, which is a regional rights treaty from the OAS. He signed the two UN covenants on human rights, both the civil-political covenant and the covenant on socioeconomic rights.[37] Within the State Department, Carter created the Bureau of Human Rights and Humanitarian Affairs, headed by an assistant secretary of state for human rights. The president elevated the preexisting office of human rights within the State Department to the assistant-secretary level. The first assistant secretary for human rights was Patricia Derian, a diplomat who became famous for scolding Chile's General Pinochet and others for their use of torture. Carter took all of these actions within his first year in office as a way to show the high priority he placed on human rights as a key element of foreign policy.

Carter's approach to human rights is best summarized according to three principal features:

1. A single standard. Carter vowed to have a single standard of human rights for all nations, friend and foe alike.
2. Publicity. Carter chose to use public criticism of human rights abusers. He wanted to publicly denounce the worst abusers of rights.
3. Leverage. Carter promised to cut off aid to violators of human rights.

The single standard employed by Carter promised to bring an evenhanded approach to human rights policy. Tonelson criticized Carter for adopting the "pipe dream" of evenhandedness and then failing to live up to his own goals.[38] Forsythe also makes much of the differences between the rhetoric of Carter's declared policy on rights and the reality of Carter's actual policies.[39] In theory, the single standard was going to apply the same rights criteria to the behavior of both pro-U.S. and anti-U.S. regimes. Communist dictatorships and right-wing juntas that violated rights were to be treated equally, regardless of their strategic relationship to the United States.

The single standard was based on three areas of human rights, ranked in order of importance to the Carter administration. Secretary of State Cyrus Vance articulated the elements of the single standard in a speech to the University of Georgia's law school in 1977. First and foremost were rights involving the security of the person (e.g., the right to be free from torture). Second in importance were social and economic rights to the things that help fill basic human needs. These include the rights to food, health care, and shelter. Carter's was the first U.S. administration to formally recognize the existence of some second-generation socioeconomic rights. Finally, civil and political liberties such as free speech and freedom of religion were ranked third in order of importance by Carter and Vance.[40]

Carter's use of publicity and criticism of rights abusers in the mass media replaced the Nixon-Kissinger preference for quiet diplomacy. Publicity and the media spotlight were used to denounce major violations of rights. Carter was vocal in his condemnation of the pro-U.S. Somoza dictatorship in Nicaragua. Carter also led international criticism of the Republic of South Africa (RSA) when anti-apartheid activist Stephen Biko was beaten to death by security officers in 1977. In practice, the White House seemed to direct its harshest attacks against governments that sided with the United States in the Cold War, bringing into question the evenhanded principles that Carter had espoused.

The consistency of Carter's human rights policies was also brought into question by his use of aid leverage. Carter came into office in favor of the Harkin Amendment, Section 502B, and additional legislation that applied human rights leverage to other assistance programs. The Carter administration ended aid to Paraguay, Uruguay, and the Somoza regime in Nicaragua. Aid was reduced to the Shah of Iran and Pinochet's Chile. Aid was redesigned to go directly to the most needy in Guatemala and Haiti.[41] However, Carter did not cut aid to the right-wing Marcos dictatorship in the Philippines, nor did he use aid as leverage against South Korea, even though both governments were widely known for their repression. Furthermore, Carter reduced aid to Chile during a time when private investment into Chile's economy and private lending to Chile's government were booming.[42] Increases in private funds flowing into Chile offset and vastly surpassed the cuts in public assistance imposed by Carter.

Carter's public criticism and use of leverage tended to focus primarily on America's allies. Right-wing, anticommunist regimes were much more likely than leftist regimes to feel the sting of Carter's rhetorical barbs. Thus, his administration seemed to undermine in practice the evenhanded single standard that it proclaimed in principle. There is a logical reason for this. As Tonelson points out in his critique of the Carter approach:

> America can withhold aid only from aid recipients, deny weapons only to arms clients, embargo trade only to trading partners. Thus any peaceful human rights policy involving deeds must fall most heavily on countries linked most closely to the United States. Every concession to this reality, no matter how well explained, sabotages the claim of evenhandedness and compromises the credibility of U.S. policy the way each leak compromises the credibility of a dam.[43]

Despite the lack of rigid consistency in the Carter approach, U.S. policy did experience some notable successes in the late 1970s in terms of improving human rights around the world. Thousands of political prisoners were released in Asia and Latin America during Carter's tenure.[44] No doubt at least some of the credit for the release of these prisoners of conscience goes to Carter's use of aid leverage and public criticism. Some of those released even thanked Carter for their freedom.[45] Leverage imposed by Carter undermined the political strength of military dictators who relied heavily on U.S. security assistance to stay in power. The Carter staff would claim credit for starting a trend toward replacing dictatorships with democracies in Latin America, a trend that came to fruition only after Carter had left office.

Carter's use of public pressure also helped to bring almost to a halt deaths of prisoners in confinement in South Africa. In the two years before Carter made the murder of black leaders held in South African prisons a major issue in bilateral relations, twenty-seven suspicious deaths were recorded (during 1976 and 1977). This number includes Stephen Biko's death by torture on September 12, 1977. After Carter helped to publicize the brutal death of Biko, the killing of black leaders dropped to approximately one per year for the remainder of Carter's term in office. Deaths of blacks in RSA jails escalated dramatically once again after Carter left office and when the Reagan administration replaced Carter's use of public pressure with its preference for quiet diplomacy.[46]

Carter also used the power and prestige of the U.S. presidency to bring the issue of human rights to center stage in world politics. He did what perhaps only a U.S. president can do. He took an international issue that had received only token attention and moved it higher up on the agenda of global political priorities. Evidence of this fact is most readily observable in the area of presidential politics. Although no president before Carter articulated a policy on human rights qua human rights, every president since Carter has felt obliged to develop a specific set of policies that addresses human rights as such. No president since Carter has ascribed to all three of Carter's principles on rights (single standard, publicity, and leverage), but each president has taken the time and effort to work out a detailed set of policies on human rights. This is perhaps the most important legacy of the Carter administration regarding human rights.

Carter also had his notable failures in the area of foreign policy. Although his failures were not in the area of human rights policy itself, Carter's critics were quick to point out that, in their opinion, his preoccupation with international rights led him into foreign policy blunders in other areas.

His most notable foreign policy failures were the hostage crisis in Iran and the Soviet invasion of Afghanistan. Carter often gave the appearance of being too soft on the Soviets and other enemies of U.S. interests. Revolutionary governments came to power in both Iran and Nicaragua during Carter's administration and then developed anti-U.S. ideologies. During his last eighteen months in office, Carter wavered in his support for human rights as the guiding principle of U.S. foreign policy. Tensions developed between his human rights ideals and the geopolitical necessities determined by an international balance of power. Vance resigned as Carter's secretary of state to protest the unsuccessful use of force to try to free the hostages. Vance (a utopian) was replaced as Carter's top foreign policy advisor by Zbigniew Brzezinski. The latter was clearly a political realist. Carter then proceeded on more of a case-by-case basis in his bilateral dealings, in essence giving up on the single standard.

Ronald Reagan defeated Carter in the 1980 election in part because of Carter's weaknesses in foreign policy. Reagan charged many times during the campaign that Carter's preoccupation with human rights had allowed the United States' enemies to take advantage of its interests. Reagan believed that Carter's approach to human rights had punished America's allies and abetted its enemies. Because he was too much of a utopian purist, Carter's single-minded devotion to human rights had been counterproductive to U.S. strategic interests, according to the Reagan critique.[47]

Carter succeeded in bringing the issue of human rights to center stage in international relations. This was perhaps his broadest and most lasting contribution as president.[48] However, in so doing, Carter "raised the stakes" involved in supporting human rights as a key element of foreign policy. Falk has argued that Carter raised the stakes by investing so much energy, so much of his own prestige, and so much political capital in the area of human rights.[49] Then, when Carter seemed to fail in his foreign policies in other areas, the results did indirect harm to the international human rights campaign. Carter's failures (the hostages, Afghanistan) became associated with the failure of a human rights agenda as the guiding light for U.S. foreign policy. Carter's floundering led to a realist-oriented backlash in U.S. politics, a backlash against the failures ascribed to Carter's utopian views.

Reagan capitalized on this pro-realist backlash in the 1980 campaign. Upon taking office, Reagan made good on his promises to redirect U.S. foreign policy and to once again stress power politics (a realist approach). Reagan also redirected policy on human rights in such a way as to make it a tool in the resurgent Cold War of the 1980s.

The swing toward realpolitik in foreign policy helped Reagan unseat Carter. This is a trend that is still very much with us after the end of the Cold War. The trend away from utopianism and toward realism also translates into a greatly diminished probability that the U.S. public will support human rights policies in the future that are akin to those of the early Carter years.[50]

THREE ELEMENTS OF THE REAGAN POLICY

The focus of President Reagan's foreign policies was on power, especially military power. Reagan was primarily concerned with the international balance of power between the West and the Soviet Union. Reagan oversaw a huge buildup in U.S. military forces. Total military expenditures under Presidents Reagan and Bush exceeded $3 trillion (FY 1982–93). There was much less attention paid by the White House to human rights as such, both in comparison to the previous administration and in comparison to the Reagan administration's affinity for power politics. As had been the case in the early 1970s, major human rights policies during the Reagan years were pushed by Congress, often with stiff opposition from the White House. The most important piece of human rights legislation of the 1980s, the Comprehensive Anti-Apartheid Act (CAAA) of 1987, had to be passed over Reagan's veto. Human rights issues did play a part in Reagan's foreign policy, but in most cases, primarily as a strategy for pursuing Cold War campaigns against the Soviets.

The Reagan administration's early rights emphasis was to concentrate on violations of rights in communist nations: the Soviet Union, the People's Republic of China (PRC), Cambodia, and the anti-U.S. Sandinista regime in Nicaragua. They also tended to downplay violations in allied states: the Republic of South Africa, El Salvador, the Philippines, and South Korea. Reagan was very much a realist, but unlike Kissinger before him who refused to criticize the Soviets for fear of endangering détente, Reagan was willing and eager to denounce Soviet transgressions.

The particular rights that Reagan focused on were first generation civil and political rights. Especially important were freedom of the press and regularly scheduled, honest elections. Emphasizing these rights brought international pressure to bear on the Soviets and the Sandinistas. The first annual human rights report out of the Reagan State Department in 1982 included a special introduction declaring that there are no such things as economic and social rights. The Reagan administration also defined international terrorism as a human rights violation. In fact, terrorist acts were identified as entailing the most egregious forms of rights violations. Of course this tactic also had its residual Cold War utility. Because Reagan believed that almost all terrorism was traceable to Soviet instigation or to Soviet proxies, focusing the human rights debate on terrorism would help the White House in its diplomatic battles against the Soviet Union.

A sharp contrast between Reagan's human rights policies and Carter's policy emerges from comparing three principles of the Reagan approach to the prior Carter matrix:

1. A double standard. The Reagan administration had two distinct sets of criteria for evaluating a nation's record on rights. One standard was applied to authoritarian regimes and a separate standard was applied to totalitarian regimes.
2. No public criticism of allies. Reagan preferred to deal with violations of rights in friendly states by means of quiet diplomacy.
3. No leverage against allies. Reagan opposed denying aid to pro-U.S. regimes because of violations of rights.

The rationale for the double standard was laid out by Reagan's ambassador to the United Nations, Jeane Kirkpatrick. In an article entitled "Dictators and Double Standards," Kirkpatrick argued that major violators of human rights come in two types: authoritarian versus totalitarian regimes.[51] The Kirkpatrick Doctrine holds that Carter's single standard was hopelessly flawed because it did not take into account the differences in kind between left-wing regimes and right-wing regimes. Public criticism of allies and denials of aid based on Carter's utopian approach only served to undermine allies and endanger U.S. security interests.[52] Instead, the Reagan policy would be based on a more "realistic" understanding of rights and politics. According to this view, both authoritarian and totalitarian regimes violate rights. However, authoritarian regimes tend to be rightist and pro-United States, whereas totalitarians are almost always leftist and anti-United States. Furthermore, according to Kirkpatrick, authoritarians are usually content to control the political system, imposing dictatorships and one-party rule, but allowing considerable latitude and relative freedom in nonpolitical areas. Authoritarians are more likely than totalitarians to permit a capitalist economy, private property, and at least some religious and cultural liberties. There is allegedly a "far greater likelihood of progressive liberalization and democratization" in authoritarian regimes, as compared to totalitarian ones, because there are more freedoms in nonpolitical spheres on which to base a campaign for political liberalization.[53]

According to the Kirkpatrick Doctrine, totalitarians will never transform themselves into a more liberal polity. Precisely because they seek to control the totality of human existence, left-wing communist totalitarian states "claim jurisdiction over the whole life of society."[54] Hence there is no economic, cultural, or religious space within a totalitarian state where the roots of liberal reforms can take hold and spread.[55] Policy implications follow from Kirkpatrick's distinction between the two types of human rights violators. The United States should maintain its ties to the authoritarian regimes, including provision of official assistance. Because authoritarian regimes are uniformly anticommunist, aid from the United States serves not only as a force for change from within but also to bolster strategic interests. Conversely, the policy best suited to totalitarian regimes is one that "tightens all screws" by putting as much formal and informal pressure on them as possible.

The other two elements of the Reagan approach follow logically from the first premise of the double standard. There was to be no public criticism of allied states for their lapses in human rights protection. Rather, this administration preferred to work behind the scenes, applying pressure informally and off the record. The Reagan White House returned to the quiet diplomacy toward allies option used previously by Kissinger. A notable difference between Kissinger's and Reagan's realism, however, was the latter's public criticism of the Soviet Union. Kissinger had eschewed human rights agendas vis-à-vis the Soviets in deference to his détente initiatives. Reagan, by contrast, took advantage of every opportunity to denounce violations of rights in Russia during both his first and his second terms.

The Reagan administration did agree with Kissinger when it came to opposing the use of aid as leverage against friendly governments. Reagan worked very hard to get legislation through Congress in 1985 that eliminated special human rights restrictions on aid to El Salvador.[56] Reagan also tried to prevent passage of the economic sanctions against the RSA contained in the CAAA. The Reagan administration did impose economic leverage in one case. It was directed against totalitarians in Poland for their crackdown on the Solidarity labor movement in December 1981. A prior policy of preferential terms for trade and loans to Poland was suspended by Reagan.[57]

The lack of public criticism and the refusal to use leverage against pro-U.S. regimes was exemplified by the policy of constructive engagement toward South Africa. Constructive engagement (CE) was the term coined to describe policies developed by Chester Crocker, Reagan's assistant secretary of state for African affairs. CE was a set of incentives, rather than sanctions, that were aimed at promoting reform in South Africa. CE offered increased aid, increased trade, and other incentives to the RSA as a way to lessen the pressure felt by the white minority regime. The hope was that if the whites felt less pressure they would be more likely to allow increased political and economic freedom to the nonwhite majority. Liberal reforms might then lead to the dismantling of apartheid. However, during the period of CE as official U.S. policy, repression in South Africa increased. A state of emergency was imposed by the white minority regime,[58] and deaths of black anti-apartheid leaders in confinement skyrocketed. By 1985, the Reagan administration had to admit that CE had failed.

Meanwhile, a countermovement in Congress had grown, demanding the imposition of tough economic sanctions against the RSA as a way to help bring down apartheid. Reagan tried to defuse the congressional movement toward sanctions by imposing token economic pressure through presidential decree. In 1985, Reagan suspended importation of gold Kruggerands (coins minted by the RSA government), ended sales of high-tech equipment (such as computers) to the RSA security forces, and allowed public loans to the RSA government only if those funds were to be used for the benefit of the nonwhite majority (e.g., new housing).[59] These were token sanctions in the sense that they seemed designed to have little or no impact on the economic position of the whites.

Rather than placating Congress, the weak nature of the 1985 presidential sanctions stimulated even greater desires on Capitol Hill for a general trade embargo against South Africa. This took the form of the CAAA of 1987. The CAAA was first vetoed by Reagan and then became law by a vote of Congress overriding that veto. The CAAA prohibited importation into the United States of most RSA exports, outlawed exportation of petroleum products to the RSA, and denied all public loans to the RSA government (regardless of purpose). Perhaps the harshest economic blow to the RSA, however, was the CAAA ban on all new investment into South Africa's economy. Direct foreign investment from the United States to the RSA had run at a level of about $2 billion per year prior to 1987. All such new investment was halted by the CAAA.

A notable loophole in the CAAA was the provision allowing continued importation of strategic minerals from South Africa. Strategic minerals, such as manganese and vadium, are necessary to U.S. defense industries. They are key components for making alloys with high tensile strength used in the production of armored vehicles and fighter aircraft. Given existing technologies, many of these strategic minerals could be exported in quantity only by South Africa and the Soviet Union. Hence the Congress deemed it in the national interest to allow trade in strategic minerals to continue throughout the period of economic sanctions against South Africa.

Although the presidential sanctions of 1985 had little or no economic impact within South Africa, the CAAA combined with sanctions imposed by the European Union (EU) had a major effect. A report released within the RSA two years after the CAAA went into effect summarized the impact of foreign economic sanctions.[60] According to Bankorp, sanctions against the RSA cost that nation $40 billion in economic output, reduced the economic growth rate by ten percent, and cost South Africa 500,000 jobs. Such economic pressure, combined with the internal resistance to apartheid led by the African National Congress (ANC), was too much for the white regime to bear. In 1990 Nelson Mandela, the leader of the ANC, was released after twenty-six years in prison. The ANC was also legalized at that time, ending a political ban dating back to 1963. Mandela's release and the legalization of the ANC quickly led to new political talks that established a democratic constitution and the first fully free elections in South Africa's history. By 1991, most of the laws of apartheid had been stricken from the books. In 1994, Mandela was elected president of South Africa.

The success associated with the use of economic pressure against the RSA, however, came in the face of White House opposition to these congressionally mandated sanctions. Reagan, like Carter, had both notable failures and important successes in the area of human rights and foreign policy. The most notable failure of the Reagan years was the complete inefficacy of constructive engagement toward South Africa.[61] By contrast, policies of quiet diplomacy did help to further the cause of rights in South Korea and the Philippines. When Corazon Aquino led a popular uprising against the Marcos dictatorship in the Philippines in 1986, the Reagan administration did not try to prop up Marcos but instead used behind-the-scenes pressure to convince Marcos to abdicate power.[62] A quiet diplomacy approach also seemed to have an effect on the military-backed government in South Korea in 1988. Demonstrations and riots preceded the scheduled opening of the Seoul Summer Olympics of 1988. The Reagan White House once again pursued a strategy of quiet diplomacy and convinced the South Korean leaders to hold competitive elections prior to the games (something the government had sworn in early 1988 that they would not do). A wave of democratization in Latin America also came to a head from 1982 to 1989.[63] As noted earlier, the Carter administration believed its policies of public criticism and aid leverage were behind the eventual fall of military dictatorships in South America. However, because these juntas were voted out in most cases during the Reagan years, Carter's successor also claimed credit for that international trend.

Finally, a review of the Reagan years would not be complete without mentioning the end of the Cold War and the fall of communism in Eastern Europe. The heady days of the communist collapse began with the fall of the Berlin Wall and the election of the first noncommunist governments in the former Soviet bloc, both of which came in 1989. Although these events took place after Reagan left office, officials in the Bush administration and the Republican Party accorded most of the credit for this breakthrough to Reagan himself. The most common explanation for the fall of communism and the end of the Cold War (although not necessarily the most valid explanation) is that the military buildup of the 1980s under Reagan bankrupted the Soviet system. This account views Soviet efforts to keep up militarily as the single most important factor leading to communism's demise in Europe.[64]

The end of the Cold War, and the spread of democracy throughout Europe and the Americas have many possible explanations. It would be overestimating the power of U.S. foreign policy to assume that either trend was due largely to the actions of one or more U.S. presidents. The internal politics of communist regimes and Latin American dictatorships may be affected to some extent by U.S. policy. However, it would be a gross oversimplification to give the credit for these trends to U.S. leaders. There is also some question as to whether any president has ever adopted a set of human rights principles and then consistently stuck to those principles. The changes in Carter's policy on rights during his last year in office have already been discussed. At least one author has argued that Reagan's foreign policy on rights also experienced fundamental changes. Forsythe believes that Reagan's policies during his second term were actually more akin to those of Carter than they were to Reagan's own policies during his first term.[65] He cites as an example the increased willingness by the Reagan administration in its second term to criticize authoritarians as well as totalitarians. Forsythe also argues that "the Soviet Union and its allies were no longer special targets of U.S. public criticism" during Reagan's second term.[66] This slant on the Reagan years tends to overlook what the president himself said.

During his last year in office, President Reagan gave a speech in Chicago honoring the fortieth anniversary of the UDHR.[67] During his last major presidential address on rights, Reagan took a position that was essentially the same one he had espoused when he first took office nearly eight years earlier. Reagan counseled Americans concerned about human rights in 1988 to focus their attention primarily on the Soviet Union. Reagan argued that if one wants to criticize human rights violations or promote respect for human rights internationally, then one should start with the human rights problems within the Soviet Union. Furthermore, according to Reagan, one should keep one's attention and human rights pressure fixed mainly on the Soviets. In this crucial respect, Reagan's approach to human rights stood in stark contrast to that of Carter or even Kissinger. Regarding his emphasis on rights in the Soviet Union, Reagan was consistent throughout his years in the White House.

TEST CASES DURING THE BUSH YEARS (1988–92)

President George H. Bush's administration expressed a view on human rights that, at least on the surface, appeared to be a synthesis of the Carter and Reagan policies. In theory, Bush claimed to be willing to use public criticism of violations wherever they might occur. These claims reflected the themes of publicity and evenhandedness expressed by Carter. In practice, however, Bush's policy was much closer to that of Reagan, as one would expect. Bush's policy was a continuation of the Reagan approach in several important respects. They shared the same general definition of human rights. Bush, like Reagan, restricted the denotation of rights to only civil and political rights. According to the Bush administration, what some call economic and social rights require active promotion and affirmative steps by governments, they are not therefore rights as such. Rather, economic and social welfare (jobs, medical care, shelter) should be left to the work of private enterprise and market forces; they should not be the subjects of guarantees or promotion by the public sector.[68] The first annual human rights report out of the Bush administration in 1990 tried to sort out some of the alleged confusion that lead others to speak mistakenly of socioeconomic rights. The same report also detailed the Bush policies for addressing international rights.

The 1990 report by the State Department set two ends and two means for Bush's policies on rights.[69] The ends were to oppose specific human rights violations "wherever they occur" and to work to strengthen democracy around the world. The first goal was stated in such a way as to recall Carter's single standard. The second goal, bolstering democracy, was to become especially important because Bush was the first U.S. president required to develop post–Cold War foreign policies. The means for pursuit of these goals were to be "traditional" (quiet) diplomacy as a first option and "public statements" as a fallback position if the first option was unsuccessful.[70] The first means, quiet diplomacy, was to become the almost exclusive tool for Bush, whereas the second means, public pressure, once again harkened back to the Carter days but was almost never utilized by Bush. A series of test cases served to take the Bush approach to task.

Lithuania

The first test case for the Bush approach to human rights, and a key case also in regard to the end of the Cold War, was Lithuania. Lithuania was one of the fifteen republics that made up the Soviet Union. Like its Baltic neighbors,

Latvia and Estonia, Lithuania had experienced political independence between the World Wars, only to be forceably annexed into the Soviet Union by Stalin in 1940. During the Cold War, the United States did not officially recognize the Baltic states as part of the Soviet Union. However, at least since 1975, U.S. policy had been not to recognize the Baltics as fully independent either.[71]

In March 1990 Lithuania unilaterally declared its independence. Gorbachev, despite his rhetoric in favor of glasnost (openness), responded to Lithuania's declaration of independence with force. The Red Army conducted new military maneuvers inside Lithuania. Printing presses were seized. Radio and television broadcasting in Lithuania, claimed by both the local government and the regime in Moscow, were taken over at Gorbachev's orders. Control of government buildings was seized by Soviet "black berets" (special forces). Gorbachev also imposed an economic embargo against Lithuania, cutting off badly needed goods, especially oil.[72]

The Bush response to Gorbachev's repression in Lithuania was limited. The president refused to support demands by the Baltics for independence. Bush also refused requests from Congress to deny most favored nation (MFN) trading status to the Soviets as a way to punish Moscow for its crackdown on Lithuania. Temporary MFN status was first granted to the Soviet Union in 1990, a status that was made permanent in 1991. Trade with the Soviets took precedence in the Bush White House over the right of self-determination for the Baltic republics. There was little or no pressure by Bush on the Soviets to grant non-Russian republics their freedom. He even made public statements to the contrary.[73]

With the thaw in the Cold War stimulated by the fall of the Berlin Wall in 1989, Bush was keen to promote a new era of détente between the superpowers. Like Kissinger before him, Bush did not want tensions over human rights to stand in the way of increased trade with the Soviets (e.g., MFN status). Kissinger and Bush were both more concerned with trade and arms control than with human rights violations inside the Soviet system.

The dissolution of the Soviet Union in December 1991 brought the demands for independence by Lithuania and the other non-Russian republics to a successful conclusion. The fact remains, however, that their demands found no support within the Bush administration. The president put a realist's emphasis on the necessities of international stability and stability within the Soviet Union ahead of the requests of the Lithuanian people.

China

MFN status for a communist dictatorship became a key test of the Bush policies on human rights in a second case as well: that of the PRC. Repression inside the PRC peaked during the massacre in Tiananmen Square in June 1989, forcing the Bush administration to deal with violence committed by another communist regime. The events leading up to the 1989 massacre found their origins in a 1987 movement for student democracy.

Students in the PRC demonstrated in 1987, asking for political rights. Specifically, student leaders wanted the right to form their own political parties independent of the Chinese Communist Party and to run candidates for office in student governmental organizations. Hu Youbang, a top party official, refused to use force against the student protests and was ousted from the party's inner circle by Deng Xiaoping, the unquestioned ruler of the party.[74] Hu was succeeded as China's second in command by Zhao Ziyang; Hu later died in 1989.

Students marched in early 1989 to honor Hu Youbang on his death. Their activities quickly coalesced into a renewed democracy movement. Students gathered in Tiananmen Square in the heart of Beijing to demand freedom of speech and the right to assemble. By all indications, Deng Xiaoping and Zhao Ziyang disagreed on how to respond to the student's demands. Zhao, like Hu before him, did not want to use force against the students.[75] Deng subsequently ousted Zhao from the ruling elite in favor of Li Peng. Deng and Premier Li Peng then declared martial law and ordered army units to clear the square on June 4, 1989. The subsequent massacre of unarmed protesters produced hundreds, perhaps thousands, of casualties.[76]

The Bush response to the egregious violations of the Tiananmen massacre was mild. Human rights activists called for economic sanctions against the PRC, including suspension of MFN status. Bush defended China's MFN status. Bush announced that all high-level diplomatic contacts would be suspended as a result of the massacre, but he also consistently supported continued MFN trading arrangements. Furthermore, in December 1989, Bush's national security advisor, Brent Scowcroft, was seen in Beijing toasting Deng Xiaoping at a state dinner.[77]

Bush's arguments in favor of MFN status for China held that economic sanctions against the PRC would be counterproductive. Bush stated many times that he thought it would be a mistake to isolate China in response to the violence at Tiananmen. He argued that U.S. businesses in China could serve as a force for economic liberalization from within. In a variation on the Kirkpatrick Doctrine, Bush believed that political reform in the totalitarian PRC would be more likely if U.S. economic ties were expanded rather than restricted. Because Deng had already allowed limited capitalism in the PRC, despite the political repression, continued trade with the United States was the best hope for promoting reform, in Bush's view. MFN status was extended to the PRC throughout the remainder of the Bush administration. Bush did impose an annual review of human rights conditions in the PRC before agreeing to renewal of MFN status every year. Bush threatened to suspend MFN status unless there was consistent improvement in rights. However, despite his critics' wishes to the contrary, Bush never made good on those threats.

El Salvador

A third case that tested the first Bush administration's commitment to human rights was El Salvador. Politically motivated murders by so-called death squads in El Salvador became a contentious issue in bilateral relations with the United States during the 1980s. Death squads are right-wing private armies of the night that target leftist politicians, labor leaders, and church activists for assassination. Research has also shown that most of these death squads are made up of off-duty military personnel who receive support from the military-backed government of El Salvador.[78] The United States extended heavy military aid to El Salvador's right-wing government during the Reagan and Bush administrations ($40–$50 million per year). A civil war between the government and leftist guerillas resulted in more than 75,000 deaths between 1979 and 1992.

A key test for the Bush administration came with the killing of six priests by uniformed military personnel in 1989. Members of the Jesuit order and suspected by the government of being communists or communist sympathizers, the priests were killed along with two of their housekeepers. Bush publicly condemned the killings, and Secretary of State Baker called the killings a "turning point" in U.S.-Salvadoran relations. However, Bush also argued against ending military aid to El Salvador's government in response to the killings.[79] Congress voted to freeze $42 million in aid to El Salvador until the priests' killers were tried. The president wanted the aid released by Congress as soon as possible. A long trial eventually led to the conviction in 1992 of two military officers for ordering the killings (including the former head of the National Military Academy in El Salvador). This opened the way for a renewal of military aid, something Bush had long favored. In the case of El Salvador, Bush once again employed a realist approach when it came to human rights violations. He consistently opposed use of leverage against the Salvadoran regime despite death squad activities and the murder of priests by the military. A campaign against Marxist revolution was given priority over the human rights abuses of the allied government waging that campaign.

South Africa

U.S. policy toward the RSA was another controversial case during the years of President George Bush. As Reagan's vice president, Bush had opposed the economic sanctions against the RSA contained in the CAAA. In July 1991 President Bush announced that, in his opinion, enough progress had been made within South Africa to allow the suspension of CAAA sanctions.[80] By this time, Mandela had been freed, the ANC had been legalized as a political party, and most of the laws of apartheid had been stricken from the books. Talks were also underway in 1991 to establish a new democratic constitution and free elections in the RSA. All of these conditions had been stipulated within the CAAA as necessary preconditions to ending U.S. economic sanctions.

Based on this progress, Bush announced that he was ending economic sanctions by executive order. Some members of Congress protested, arguing that Bush's actions were premature. Bush's critics were supported in their position by Mandela himself, who thought that Bush should wait until all political prisoners had been released. Mandela also argued that international sanctions should remain in place until the new constitution was in place, guaranteeing political rights to the black majority.[81] Despite these sentiments to the contrary, CAAA sanctions ended under the Bush administration in 1991.

CLINTON: A SYNTHESIS OF REALISM AND UTOPIANISM?

As the United States moved into the twenty-first century, a possible synthesis of realist and utopian views on human rights and foreign policy seemed to be in the making. The outlines of such a policy were evident in the way that President Clinton addressed human rights crises during his administration.

The issue of human rights surfaced in the 1992 presidential campaign. During televised debates, candidate Clinton criticized President Bush for being soft on China. Clinton implied that, if elected, he would take a harder line in regard to violations of rights in the PRC.[82] Once in office, however, Clinton did no more than to continue the Bush approach of reviewing human rights in the PRC before agreeing to renew MFN status in 1993. Furthermore, in 1994, Clinton went so far as to drop the annual review of rights. Clinton dropped all connection between rights and trade with China during his second year in the White House. He argued that it was not fair to U.S. businesses to have to fear the annual rights review or possible suspension of special trade ties between the United States and the PRC.[83] During his last year in the White House, Clinton persuaded a reluctant Congress to support China's admission into the World Trade Organization (WTO). As part of that trade agreement, MFN (or normal trade relations, NTR, as it is now known) became permanent for the PRC.

The Clinton approach to human rights did inject one relatively new element. Clinton seemed to be more willing than his predecessors to employ military force and humanitarian intervention as a means to ensure protection and promotion of human rights. Clinton's justifications for intervention employed a Carter-like rhetoric of utopian motives. A closer look, however, reveals that military intervention by the Clinton administration was driven primarily by realism. Four cases in point show both the utopian nature of Clinton's declared policy as well as the realpolitik of the actual policy behind the rhetoric. Somalia and Rwanda are negative examples of the Clinton policy; these are cases in which humanitarian intervention was either not employed (Rwanda) or was terminated when it became too costly (Somalia). Haiti and Bosnia stand as positive examples of the Clinton approach; these are cases in which intervention was pursued for reasons that were justified in terms of utopianism but which were better understood as realist policy. Military actions in Bosnia and Haiti were primarily motivated by national interests and domestic political dynamics.

Somalian intervention was a policy Clinton inherited from Bush. Bush ordered the intervention in December 1992 with the objectives of feeding the starving victims of the Somali civil war and then turning the peacekeeping mission over to the United Nations once security had been established.[84] Humanitarian efforts to feed the Somali people were successful, but subsequent plans for disarming the warlords and for nation-building to produce a permanent peace failed miserably. Then, when eighteen U.S. servicemen were killed during a fight with the militia loyal to Mohamed Aidid on October 3, 1993, Clinton moved quickly to arrange a phased withdrawal of U.S. forces. Clinton canceled efforts to disarm the Somali factions and ended a search for General Aidid.[85]

The lesson of Somalia for U.S. foreign policy was that humanitarian intervention would not be pursued if it posed too great a risk to military personnel. Protection of American lives was given priority over the more idealistic goals of the original intervention mandate set down by Bush in 1992.

Having been burned during the Somalian incursion, Clinton adjusted his intervention policies accordingly in the cases that followed. In both Haiti and Bosnia, Clinton justified intervention in terms of utopian goals for protecting human rights. However, in these cases troops were dispatched because of a combination of domestic political considerations and perceptions of U.S. national interests. In those crucial respects (domestic politics, perceptions, national interests), U.S. actions in Haiti and Bosnia were not significantly different from Cold War campaigns such as Vietnam.

When Clinton dispatched troops to Haiti in 1994 and to Bosnia in 1995, he defended his decisions in terms akin to the utopian project of preventing further abuses of human rights. The Haitian intervention was needed, according to the president, because of the massive rights violations committed by General Cedras and his regime.[86] Likewise in Bosnia, U.S. troops were needed to put an end to the form of genocide known as ethnic cleansing. The president even compared ethnic cleansing in Bosnia to the genocide of the Holocaust.[87] In both Haiti and Bosnia, the stated policy was one that pointed to a utopian concern for humanitarian action compelled by abuses of rights. However, upon closer examination, the actual policy in both cases was one of realpolitik.[88]

In the case of Haiti, Clinton was forced to act by a wave of refugees spilling out of the island nation toward Florida. Domestic political interests opposed to absorbing these immigrants pressured the president to take action.[89] National interests defined as the inability (or unwillingness) to relocate the Haitian masses were more of a motivating factor than the concomitant desire to end the suffering of Haitians trapped inside that country. If desires to stop the bloodshed had been the primary reason for intervention, Clinton would have taken action much sooner in both Haiti and Bosnia. Instead, he delayed the military option as long as there was no perception of a threat to the national interest; this was a classic realist calculation.[90]

In the case of Bosnia, 250,000 people died and an estimated 20,000 rapes occurred before the United States became militarily involved. Once again, Clinton used the utopian rhetoric of protecting the innocent and preserving rights to justify sending in troops.[91] Once again, however, it was a realist desire to protect U.S. interests that compelled Clinton to act when he did. Utopian desires to protect human rights would have been relevant to any intervention following the first acts of ethnic cleansing in Bosnia beginning in 1992. The Clinton administration waited until 1995 to dispatch troops because of a realist calculus that disputed the existence of a threat to any vital U.S. interest before that time.[92] The UN Security Council, the World Court, and the UN Commission on Human Rights declared ethnic cleansing in Bosnia to be acts of genocide long before Clinton took military action.[93] Clinton was able to overlook these abuses and failed to invoke human rights violations as a justification for intervention until after U.S. global leadership and credibility were squarely on the line (leadership and credibility, once again, being considerations relevant to realist policy—such as in Vietnam—but not necessarily linked in any direct way to utopian concerns for protecting rights).

By the time the United States finally did intervene in Bosnia, the United States had been thrust into a leadership role for seeking a settlement because of the repeated diplomatic failures of the UN and the EU. There was also a widely shared realist perception that events in Bosnia, if left unchecked, could "disrupt irreparably" NATO and other U.S. security commitments.[94] The immediate task given to U.S. and other NATO forces was the enforcement of the 1995 Dayton agreements brokered by U.S. negotiators. Military intervention was structured so as to ensure disengagement of the warring factions behind the cease-fire lines established at Dayton. The forces were explicitly *not* given the charge of locating and arresting those individuals indicted for war crimes by the international tribunal established through the Security Council. U.S. troops were told to apprehend war criminals if they came across them in the course of their other duties, but the task of directly seeking them out was too utopian and too dangerous, especially in the context established by the debacle in Somalia.

The pattern thus established during the Clinton years was not to act when human rights atrocities occurred, unless those abuses were also related in a direct way to U.S. interests defined in terms of power, prestige, credibility, and domestic political concerns. Rwanda was the case that most clearly demonstrated the fact that massive violations alone would not be sufficient to move the United States to action. Genocide on the scale of 500,000–800,000 dead in Rwanda during 1994 did not result in humanitarian intervention by the United States.

By contrast, when intervention because of realist policies of protecting national interests has been used in the post–Cold War era, the consistent rhetoric has been one of idealism spurred on by violations of human rights. The 1990s rhetoric of humanitarian concerns and motivations is yet another example of the long-term legacy of the Carter administration when it comes to presidential politics. Carter, who has maintained an active role by negotiating the departure of a dictator in Haiti and by acting as an international observer of human rights conditions in Bosnia, still stands as the patron saint for rights as a part of U.S. foreign policy. Clinton's refusal to intervene unless realpolitik dictated the need to protect interests, however, shows that recent U.S. policy has remained essentially consistent with the kinds of calculations that drove foreign policy during the prior Cold War. In both ages, U.S. foreign policy has been one typified primarily by realism.

THE FUTURE OF U.S. HUMAN RIGHTS POLICIES: DOUBLE STANDARDS VERSUS THE KOSOVO PRECEDENT

Throughout most of the Cold War and post–Cold War eras, U.S. policy on human rights has operated according to double standards. The double standard of the Cold War was most clearly articulated by the Reagan administration. American policy favored right-wing, anticommunist regimes, showering these authoritarians with economic and military aid.[95] Left-wing communist regimes were targeted for economic and military sanctions, including (in some cases) military intervention and covert destabilization. Carter was the only president to make a notable break from this Cold War double standard, and he did so with only limited success. Carter's temporary break from the Cold War double standard was the exception that proves the rule: American foreign policy during the Cold War largely ignored human rights abuses in states that were considered strategically important to the United States. Now that the Cold War is over, America has adopted a new double standard: an economic double standard.

The new double standard was most evident in Clinton's policy, especially his handling of China.[96] According to Lewis, Clinton was willing to criticize human rights violators only if they had little or no commercial importance to the United States.[97] Nations that were singled out by the Clinton administration for sanctions due to their human rights abuses were countries that had little or no trade with the United States. This would include Burma (now known as Myanmar) and the Sudan. On the other hand, Clinton would not criticize or sanction nations that were notorious human rights abusers if those countries had an economic (or strategic) importance to the United States. The PRC is the most obvious case, but others would include Indonesia and Turkey. Once again, as during the Cold War, abuses of human rights are overlooked by the United States if it is in the perceived national interest to do so. The post–Cold War double standard punishes only those human rights violators that have no economic importance, whereas key trading partners who violate rights get off virtually scot-free.

To be fair to Clinton, however, his is also the administration to set what could be a new precedent for U.S. foreign policy and human rights, a policy that may one day lead to the end of these debilitating double standards. That was the case of military intervention into Kosovo. Most discussions of Kosovo start with the connections between intervention there and in Bosnia. After the Serbian dictator Milosevic encouraged ethnic cleansing in Bosnia and was eventually defeated in his efforts there by NATO intervention, Serbian forces turned to acts of genocide in their own province of Kosovo. Having already witnessed the threat to international peace and security represented by Serbian aggression in Bosnia, the United States and its NATO allies were much quicker to intervene in Kosovo, despite the fact that in this case they were invading a sovereign state. If NATO's actions were designed merely to put a leash on Milosevic, then U.S. policy was acting in a manner largely consistent with the same realpolitik considerations that led to intervention in Bosnia. An alternative interpretation of intervention into Kosovo would be that the United States acted there largely due to humanitarian considerations.

The small province of Kosovo has little strategic value to NATO. Unlike Bosnia, in Kosovo Milosevic's minions were engaged in atrocities within their own borders. American actions in Kosovo seemed to be provoked largely by the media coverage showing hundreds of thousands of ethnic Albanians fleeing in terror from Serbian ethnic cleansing. NATO moved with relative speed to stop these massacres. One could argue that Kosovo was the first case of U.S. intervention in which the pressures to take military action were almost entirely nonstrategic in nature. If that was the case, then Kosovo was indeed a new precedent. George W. Bush implied during his 2000 campaign that he might pull American forces out of Kosovo due to the lack of any U.S. national interest in that fight. But once in office, the second President Bush decided to continue the U.S. presence in Kosovo.

In conclusion, one could view Kosovo as the case that finally demonstrates the false dichotomy that was drawn during the Cold War, a false dichotomy pitting U.S. strategic interests against America's humanitarian concerns. In the long run, realist concerns for national interests and utopian concerns for human rights complement each other; they need not be cast as alternatives or as competing priorities for American foreign policy. The United States acted in Kosovo to stop genocide in a province that had no obvious strategic priority. This stands in stark contrast to America's failure to act in the case of Rwanda during 1994. But the United States also wanted to bring down Milosevic in Serbia, and his subsequent fall from power was an indirect result of his defeat in Kosovo at the hands of NATO. Thus in Kosovo, humanitarian intervention to stop ethnic cleansing (a utopian priority) also helped to topple an anti-American dictator who represented a military threat to U.S. national interests. The Kosovo precedent is one that deserves closer study from both decision makers and students of U.S. foreign policy.

Chapter 11

AMERICAN POLICY TOWARD THIRD WORLD NATIONS

FOREIGN POLICY
AND INTERNATIONAL REGIMES

During the Cold War, decolonization produced a significant number of newly independent states. In most cases, these new nation-states were former colonies of the European powers. As new nations in Africa and Asia became independent (primarily in the 1950s and 1960s), American foreign policy had to develop new approaches to deal with these "Third World" countries.[1] Seeking power through numbers, Third World nations formed a loose alliance at the United Nations (UN) known as the Group of 77. They have often acted as a bloc when dealing with the United States. Political maneuvering between the United States and the less-developed countries (LDCs) of the Third World is commonly fought out within the context of international regimes. To understand U.S.-Third World politics during and after the Cold War, one must attend to the politics of international regimes.

Defining International Regimes

The most often cited definition of an international regime is the one popularized by Stephen Krasner. Krasner defines a regime as: "Principles, norms, rules and decision-making procedures around which actor expectations converge in a given issue area."[2] Regimes are issue specific or area specific. For example, there is a regime for trade (the WTO) and a separate regime for monetary relations (the IMF and World Bank). The most highly developed regimes include (1) an institutional framework (e.g., an international organization), (2) a set of specific rules and more general norms, and (3) a set of shared expectations regarding acceptable behavior by member-states. Part II of this text was, in a sense, an extended discussion of American foreign policy regarding the trading regime under the GATT/WTO, and the monetary regime governed by the IMF/World Bank.

The international trading regime is an especially illustrative example. (1) The institutional framework of the trading regime used to be loosely organized under the GATT agreements. In 1995, the trading regime gained a much more authoritative structure under the new World Trade Organization (WTO). (2) The rules and norms of the trading regime have been expressed through concepts such as most favored nation (MFN) status and reciprocity. (3) Broad expectations regarding behavior were based on the assumptions of free trade and liberal economics.

The trading regime is also a good example of how regimes are created and controlled. When the International Trade Organization (ITO) was proposed after World War II, the United States (specifically the Congress) blocked its creation. At that time, the United States was opposed to a regime that gave binding power over trade disputes to an international body (the ITO). Due to the dictates of American foreign policy (AFP), the much weaker GATT system became the postwar trade regime by default. The United States first killed the ITO and then approved the weaker GATT. However, as AFP and perceptions of national interests changed over time, the United States reversed its position in the 1980s. At the Uruguay round, America successfully pushed for the creation of a powerful, binding organization to enforce trade rules—the WTO.

Regimes are created by the great powers of world politics. For example, the victors during World War II established a global monetary regime at Bretton Woods in 1944. Because they are created by the great powers, regimes operate in a manner that is consistent with the interests of the most powerful nations. Great powers establish regimes for a wide variety of reasons. Regimes make international relations more stable. Strong regimes make the behavior of other nations more predictable. Because the most powerful countries create and manage regimes, they can sometimes mold a "world order" that is consistent with their national interests. Regimes establish certain "rules of the game" for global politics. Regimes express values. Regimes promote the spread of certain values (those consistent with the interests of great powers) while inhibiting the diffusion of competing values (values contrary to the interests of the regime's founders).

This chapter will discuss AFP toward the Third World within the context of international regimes. The primary focus will be on economic and environmental regimes. This will provide a setting within which one can better understand what the Third World wants from the United States. Regime politics also helps to illustrate what the United States is willing to concede when faced with LDC demands. The discussion will focus on Third World attempts to work within existing regimes, as well as efforts by developing nations to establish new regimes. The relative success of these efforts will also be assessed. Before examining regime politics in particular, however, it helps to have an understanding of the general politico-economic cleavages that separate the United States from the Third World.

What Does the Third World Want?

The politics of rich nations versus poor nations is often fought out within international regimes. The poor nations of the Third World tend to have a list of priorities that carries over from one setting to another. The United States has tended to resist these Third World demands and has usually thwarted efforts by LDCs to turn international regimes toward a direct focus on Third World needs. Third World nations want, above all else, rapid economic development combined with what Krasner has called "metapower."

Because of their desperate economic situations, most Third World governments must concentrate their efforts on development. Third World leaders as a group tend to believe that successful economic development for LDCs requires nothing less than an international redistribution of wealth. Without a more *equitable* distribution of global wealth, LDCs fear that they will forever be relegated to nothing more than economic dependency, or "dependent development." They see the gap between rich and poor nations getting larger, not smaller, and wonder how they can ever hope to catch up. For example, Third World leaders have demanded more favorable terms for technology transfers from the rich industrialized nations of the North to the poor developing nations of the South. Ideally (from their point of view) these technology transfers would be made free of charge and without any strings attached as to how the developing world uses the technology.

In addition to rapid economic development (to be financed by aid from the United States and others), Third World nations also want more international political power and respect. They want to be treated as equals by the United States. They desire international power that is equivalent to that of the advanced industrialized nations. In terms of regime politics, they want metapower. Metapower is power over international regimes.[3] Metapower for LDCs would give them more authority over setting the agendas for international regimes. Metapower entails control over regimes, especially control over management. For example, rich nations have metapower within the International Monetary Fund (IMF) and the World Bank. The North dominates international financial institutions through a system of weighted voting on the managing boards of the IMF and the World Bank. Poor nations in the Third World, by contrast, have little or no metapower.

American foreign policy during and after the Cold War has denied Third World nations most of what they want. AFP tends to counsel restraint and self-reliance for LDCs. The U.S. view is that LDCs must rely on their own resources and their (limited) comparative advantage in order to achieve development. The United States is also adamantly opposed to sharing metapower over regimes with the Third World. Refusing to be stymied by American intransigence, LDCs have banded together and advanced their cause over and over again in numerous international settings. Third World nations have sought to alter existing regimes to make them more amenable to LDC interests. They have also made several attempts to establish new regimes over which they would have more control and more metapower. As we shall see, the Third World has not been very successful in these efforts. However, that has not stopped them from trying. By reviewing Third World efforts to reform old regimes and to create new regimes, along with U.S. responses to these efforts, one can get a better understanding of AFP toward the Third World.

REFORMING ECONOMIC REGIMES: THE GSP AND THE "LINK"

In 1971, the GATT system established the Generalized System of Preferences (GSP) to give Third World nations more favorable terms of trade. The GSP was created to enhance Third World development by promoting some of their export capabilities. GSP programs eliminated tariffs on selected Third World exports. GSP advantages reduced tariffs on LDC raw materials. However, GSP preferences do not usually apply to trade in textiles, electronics, or steel. During the 1990s, GSP products imported into the United States averaged $10 billion per year (equivalent to roughly four percent of total imports).[4] Nearly 150 LDCs qualified for GSP incentives, but many Third World nations were excluded. Oil exporters rarely qualified, and some former LDCs (such as South Korea) have "graduated" out of the GSP. Newly industrialized countries (NICs) in the Third World do not receive this kind of assistance. The NICs include Singapore, South Korea, and Taiwan (excluded from the GSP since 1989). Although important in some respects, the GSP has not been very successful from a Third World point of view. The advantages provided by the GSP are not what LDCs really wanted.

What the Third World wanted most under the GSP was a permanent system, one that would cover *all* Third World exports (including both manufactured goods and raw materials). Third World nations also hoped for duty-free access to all developed states. However, not all advanced industrial states created GSP programs (they have been limited to the United States and eighteen other states).[5] It is also, in essence, a temporary system. GSP preferences usually have a ten-year life span and are then subject to renewal. GSP policies never cover all Third World products. It is common for clothing and leather goods to be excluded. These are the very products for which many LDCs have a comparative trade advantage. Furthermore, products that do qualify for low GSP tariffs can be restricted by means of quotas (limits to the total quantity of imports). Although the United States has maintained its GSP policy in the post–Cold War era, renewal of GSP advantages are no longer guaranteed, and Congress frequently has threatened to eliminate the GSP program altogether.

A second Third World effort to work within existing regimes can be found in the campaign to link allocation of special drawing rights (SDRs) to economic need. The "Link" proposal would tie the distribution of IMF SDRs to economic development in the Third World.[6] Recall that SDRs are special financial instruments used within the IMF system as reserve assets and for balance of payment transactions (see chapter 7). SDRs can be created at will by the countries that control the IMF. SDRs were first created during the Cold War to alleviate some of the problems created by the Dollar Crisis of the late 1960s and early 1970s. IMF rules tie allocation of SDRs to the "quotas" that each member-state must keep on deposit with the IMF. Because quotas are calculated by means of GDP plus percentage of global trade, the richest nations have the highest quotas. A larger quota brings in more SDRs. Therefore, allocation rules within the IMF require that most SDRs go into the coffers of rich states.

For decades, LDCs have demanded that SDRs be tied to developmental needs, a process that would bring most of the SDRs to the Third World (during times of initial allocation). The Link might help jump-start some of their moribund economies. Unfortunately for the Third World, the board of governors that controls the IMF has consistently refused to accept the Link. SDRs have not been tied to development. Votes on the board of governors are weighted (and also tied to quotas).[7] Hence advanced industrialized nations control the IMF by means of weighted votes on the board. Because the United States in particular has opposed the Link, there is little reason to believe that the IMF will ever change its policies in this area. Third World nations have campaigned in favor of the Link for decades, but they have always been denied.

Reliance on GSP preferences and (failed) attempts to promote the Link have not been very helpful for LDCs. Therefore, the Third World bloc has turned to other attempts to change the rules of international economic relations. Coalitions of Third World governments have sought to force trade concessions from the United States (and the rest of the developed world). In a series of attempts to gain metapower over trading regimes, the Third World adopted a dual-track approach to creating new rules for trade and new economic regimes. Prior to the 1990s, the two tracks of this approach focused on producer cartels and on proposals for "new international orders."

METAPOWER VIA CARTELS OR THE NIEO?

The best example of a successful Third World cartel is, of course, the Organization of Petroleum Exporting Countries (OPEC). OPEC is controlled by Third World nations. OPEC has been a major force in global politics ever since the 1973 oil embargo. The embargo (imposed on the United States and others during an Arab-Israeli war) effectively quadrupled the price of a barrel of crude oil. The oil embargo was cited in chapter 7 as one of the events that brought international economic interdependence to the attention of U.S. decision makers. OPEC's embargo was a clear case of nonaligned nations banding together to force a change in North-South relations.

Cooperation within the Third World during the OPEC embargo forced changes in the pricing structure of North-South oil trade. OPEC's actions in 1973 are the clearest example of a Third World bloc acquiring greater metapower over the terms of international trade. Now OPEC would set the price of oil, taking this power away from the Western oil corporations. OPEC took control of the international agenda in oil trade, and it was largely successful in achieving the goals it had set for the embargo: many advanced industrialized nations were forced to rethink their Middle East policies and give more attention to the problems of Arab nations. For example, Japanese foreign policy largely overlooked Arab interests prior to 1973. After the embargo, Japan started to speak out on the importance of protecting the rights of Palestinian Arabs. OPEC was such a rousing success during the 1970s that it became a model for other parts of the Third World to emulate.

LDCs tried to capitalize on OPEC's 1973 success. Third World countries control significant production of many raw materials other than oil. If a cartel worked for oil, why not create Third World producer cartels for copper, bauxite, rubber, and even agricultural goods (e.g., coffee and bananas)? A wave of cartelization swept through the Third World on the heels of the OPEC oil embargo. However, these attempts to create cartels for resources other than petroleum largely failed.[8] Cartels have not been an effective means for most Third World states to gain metapower. Even the OPEC cartel does not enjoy the internal unity, international power, or economic influence that it once had. Cartels no longer look like a long-term solution to economic problems in the Third World. Cartels have rarely helped Third World nations to get, and *keep*, metapower. This led many in the Third World to seek an overhaul of international economic relations by establishing "new orders" for global politics.

The first and most important proposal for a new order came in 1974, just months after the shock of the OPEC embargo. At a special session of the UN General Assembly, Third World nations proposed the New International Economic Order (NIEO). The NIEO, if created, would have been nothing less than a new economic regime for trade. The NIEO fell through, but a brief review of the original proposal will help us understand the evolution of U.S.-Third World relations. It is also important to keep in mind the time frame for the NIEO proposal. The period immediately after the oil embargo was a time of great international uncertainty. American leaders did not know what to expect. To Third World leaders, almost anything seemed possible in regard to overhauling the international system of trade. Average Americans were so caught up in the price hikes and the "energy crisis" (e.g., long lines at the gas pumps) spawned by the OPEC embargo that they feared the worst.

The NIEO came out of the UN General Assembly as a series of recommendations. NIEO proposals of 1974 were expressed in a series of nonbinding General Assembly resolutions. Nothing required UN members to abide by these proposals, but the hubris created by the OPEC embargo gave Third World nations the impression that, through force of numbers and internal solidarity, they could use their combined economic power to make the NIEO a reality. They were badly mistaken.

The heart of the NIEO can be summarized under six key points.

1. LDCs were to be given absolute sovereignty over their own economic resources, including the right to nationalize foreign industries. Nationalization occurs when a Third World government takes possession of economic enterprises (within its borders) that were previously owned by foreign corporations.
2. The NIEO called for the creation of Third World cartels in all exports. OPEC was championed as a model for other parts of the Third World to follow.
3. The NIEO would have given preferential treatment to Third World goods in Western markets. This included across-the-board increases in prices paid for all Third World exports; guaranteed shares of Western markets for Third World enterprises; and indexing the costs LDC imports to the prices paid for LDC exports.[9]
4. Trade between Third World nations was to be increased and subsidized by the wealthy nations of the North. Trade between North and South would be reduced, along with the alleged economic dependency that North-South trade promotes.
5. Technology transfers from North to South would take the form of grants or outright gifts, without cost for LDCs, and with no strings attached as to the uses of that technology.
6. LDCs would be given new powers to regulate Western multinational corporations (MNCs) within their borders.

The United States was adamantly opposed to the NIEO. American leaders refused to fund all but the most inexpensive elements of the NIEO.[10] Without support from the United States (or any of the Western industrialized powers) the NIEO was going nowhere. One might wonder what would possess Third World nations to make such radical and costly proposals for reforming international trade? The impact of the OPEC embargo cannot be overstated. Third World nations assumed that, if OPEC could bring the rich and powerful nations to their knees in 1973, then LDCs as a bloc could force a new order in economics upon recalcitrant rich countries. American policy is opposed to anything that goes against the dictates of free market economics; hence there was no support from U.S. decision makers for the NIEO. To this day the NIEO is still invoked by Third World nations at annual meetings of the General Assembly, but to no avail.

Despite its lack of success, Third World nations did not abandon the NIEO. Instead they extended its principles to other areas of North-South relations. Not long after the NIEO proposal, Third World nations proclaimed the need for a new order in media and communication as well. In 1980, Third World countries at the United Nations Educational, Scientific and Cultural

Organization (UNESCO) proposed the New International Information Order (NIIO). The NIIO adopted the basic elements of the NIEO and then adapted them to the areas of information and communication:

1. Developing nations would have absolute sovereignty over all "informational resources" within their borders, including control of foreign media and foreign journalists. The NIIO proclaimed a right for Third World nations to censor news about their own countries and to keep out foreign media that they felt endangered their cultures.
2. The NIIO promoted what could be called "media cartels" by advocating Third World news pools and the creation of news services that would be under Third World control.
3. The NIIO supported preferential treatment for Third World news and information in Western media markets. News from LDC media would be given guaranteed percentages of the total media markets in the West. Western media would also be required to carry more of the "good news" out of the Third World, especially reports about the economic and political successes of developing countries.
4. Communication between Third World nations would be increased, whereas dependency of LDCs on Western media would be decreased.
5. Transfers of advanced communication and media technology (broadcasting equipment, computers, satellites, video links) from rich to poor countries would be made free of charge.
6. Third World nations would be given control over the Western MNCs that dominate international communication; particularly the major news wires (AP, AFP, Reuters, and UPI) that are all based in the West.[11]

As was the case with the NIEO, the United States was vehemently opposed to the Third World's proposal for an NIIO. President Reagan was so firmly opposed to the anti–free press elements that he saw in the NIIO that he withdrew U.S. membership from UNESCO in 1984. Implementing the NIIO, like the NIEO before it, would have required tremendous amounts of money. Without America's financial support, neither of the new order proposals stood a chance. Neither of these new orders ever came into being. UNESCO backed off its support for the NIIO in the 1990s in an attempt to entice the United States to rejoin.

CONFERENCE DIPLOMACY AND GLOBAL SUMMITS IN THE 1990S

Third World nations have not had success in promoting their interests by working within the regimes established by great powers. The GSP in GATT and proposals for the Link between SDRs and development at the IMF are cases in point. In the 1970s and 1980s, developing nations tried to establish new regimes for trade and communication under the NIEO and the NIIO. These efforts also failed. LDCs then turned to conference diplomacy in the 1990s, using their majority at the UN General Assembly to organize a series of "world summits" on topics that are of utmost importance to the Third World. The Third World hoped to use their force of numbers at global conferences to push through changes in international relations and American foreign policy. The overall objective of these global summits was, once again, to invest Third World nations with greater metapower in world affairs. Once again, most of their efforts failed. The remainder of this chapter will review these global summits with a special focus on environmental politics at the Rio Earth Summit (as well as the follow-up meetings after Rio).

The United Nations Conference on the Environment and Development (UNCED) was held in Rio de Janeiro, Brazil, during 1992. The Rio Earth Summit, as it was popularly known, was just one of several global summits in the 1990s. A Human Rights Summit was held in Vienna (1993), a Population Summit took place in Cairo (1994), and a Poverty Summit convened in Copenhagen (1995). At each summit, Third World nations tried to act as a bloc to exact certain concessions from the United States and from other rich countries.

Most global summits in the 1990s were massive failures from a Third World point of view. The Copenhagen poverty summit was the best example of failure.[12] The meager results of Copenhagen also stand in stark contrast to the important treaties that came out of Rio. Copenhagen was a good example of what the Third World should *not* do if they hope to influence American foreign policy.

LDCs demanded a plan at Copenhagen to eliminate all poverty in the Third World. They advanced a related demand that all Third World debts be cancelled.[13] LDCs wanted massive increases in foreign aid from the United States. They wanted this new aid to come with no strings attached and in addition to existing aid programs. They wanted to be able to spend the new aid as they saw fit.

The American position at Copenhagen was to oppose all requests for new aid moneys. The United States also opposed cancellation of Third World debts, and it would agree only to redirect *existing* aid dollars toward meeting basic human needs (e.g., food, shelter and medical care).

The politics of the Poverty Summit were indicative of a general trend that was played out at other global summits in the 1990s. Third World nations came to the meeting with a grandiose agenda. They advanced unrealistic demands and set unattainable goals. The goals were admirable (e.g., eliminating all poverty), but they were unrealistic nonetheless. The results of the Copenhagen summit were also typical of most global conferences in the 1990s. Third Word nations got little or nothing of what they requested. The Rio Earth Summit, however, was a different story.

THE RIO EARTH SUMMIT

Third World governments arrived in Rio in 1992 seeking to create a new regime for the international environment while conferring metapower upon themselves. They achieved some limited success at Rio and at the follow-up conferences after Rio, because they found an area of international relations that is now of utmost importance to the United States (and other wealthy nations). A review of Third World tactics at environmental conferences can highlight the necessary conditions for LDCs to get what they want (or at least part of what they want) from the United States.

In most of their attempts to reform international relations, LDCs have met with negative reactions from the United States. The United States opposed the NIEO and NIIO. The United States has opposed creation of producer cartels or massive increases in foreign aid. In most cases, the United States has been what regime theorists call a "blocking state."[14] That is, the United States has tried to block or veto proposals for radical changes in North-South relations. Success will be possible for the Third World only if they can find some bargaining leverage to use against the United States. First, they must find areas of global politics that are salient to the United States. The environment is a good example of such an area (drug trafficking and illegal immigration might be others). Second, after they have identified an area important to U.S. policy, LDCs must look for a "global bargain"—or a global tit-for-tat—a trade-off that can extract concessions from the United States in return for reforms in the Third World (reforms that the United States would like to see). Environmental politics is an area in which the issues are important enough to the United States that a global bargain or global trade-offs may be possible as a means to achieve some Third World goals.

The origins of the Rio Earth Summit can be traced back to 1972. UNCED (1992) was the second UN global conference on the environment. The first was held in Stockholm during 1972. It was known as the UN Conference on the Human Environment. One hundred and fourteen nations attended the Stockholm environmental conference. Northern views dominated, and Communist nations did not attend. No binding agreement came out of Stockholm. The meeting did produce a Declaration of Principles that contained 109 recommendations on the environment. The most significant result of Stockholm was the creation of the United Nations Environmental Program (UNEP) to coordinate UN environmental activities.

In 1989, the General Assembly called for a second global summit on the environment to be held on the twentieth anniversary of the Stockholm conference. Rio de Janeiro was selected as the site. From 1989 until 1992, there were annual meetings of UN members to prepare documents for Rio. At these preparatory meetings, there was much politicking and political maneuvering by both the United States and the Third World.

Prior to Rio, the Third World took the position that the Earth Summit must include both environmental and development issues. The United States preferred to keep the conference focused on environmental issues alone. The United States very much wanted an international conference on the environment to take place due to concerns about the rain forests, destruction of the ozone layer, and the possibility of global warming. Third World nations made it clear that they would not participate in an environmental summit unless development issues were also on the agenda. The United States and Third World nations struck a global bargain to address both environmental and developmental issues at Rio. Hence the official name of the summit became the UN Conference on the Environment *and* Development.

The Third World Versus the United States at Rio

UNCED was another attempt by LDCs to restructure international relations. Third World nations played the game of linkage politics at Rio. They tried to use environmental treaties to get what they wanted out of the United States in regard to economic development and political influence. Bargaining over environmental agreements was used to pursue many of the same economic goals that LDCs had failed to secure through the NIEO. At Rio, the Third World requested new transfers of technology, especially the newest generation of environmentally safe industrial technology (or "green technology"). They wanted new aid—assistance that would be *in addition to* existing aid programs (the so-called principle of additionality). Third World nations also demanded that the new aid go through multilateral, rather than bilateral, channels. Third World nations proposed that a new international organization be created to distribute this aid. They did not want aid to be distributed by the old economic institutions that are controlled by the great powers (e.g., the World Bank). The new institutions would be jointly managed by all nations, large and small, on a democratic basis, in the process conferring instant metapower on the Third World.

Third World countries tend to blame international environmental problems on wealthy nations such as the United States.[15] They blame overconsumption in the North for degradation of the global environment. Because the North allegedly made this mess, the North should pay to clean it up. LDCs also blame developmental policies promoted by the IMF and the World Bank. For decades, these institutions imposed economic strategies on LDCs that required them to rely on cash crops for export. Due to this approach, overtilling has destroyed much of the Third World's topsoil. Low-tech industrial plants exported from the North to the South also get part of the blame. Such technology leads to high-pollution methods of production.

On the other hand, LDCs (particularly the NICs) refuse to forego future development, industrialization, or harvesting of their rain forests, Northern concerns for the global environment notwithstanding. Brazil and India, homes to the most important rain forests, reserve their sovereign rights to exploit natural resources within their borders as they see fit, even if this means "mining" the rain forests.[16] If the United States tries to tell Third World nations how to develop or how to protect their own environment, Americans can be branded with the label of "environmental imperialism" or "green imperialism."

Third World environmental priorities tend to differ from those of the United States. LDCs are most concerned about the "old" or "first generation" environmental problems: air pollution, water pollution, soil erosion, toxic dumping. At Rio, Third World nations demanded better compensation and profit sharing for new biotechnology developed from rain forest resources. This would include payments to the Third World for new plant and animal species developed from rain forest hybrids. Western pharmaceutical corporations would have to share profits for drugs derived from rare elements found only in the rain forests.

America's position at Rio, as presented by the first Bush administration, could not have been farther removed from LDC opinions. On almost all major points, Bush and Third World governments were in fundamental disagreement. The United States cited overpopulation (a Third World problem), not overconsumption, as the root cause for most environmental problems. President Bush responded to charges that overconsumption in the United States was a major cause of environmental destruction by saying: "America's lifestyle is not negotiable."[17] The Bush administration opposed all proposals for new environmental aid based on additionality. The farthest Bush would go was to promise to redirect existing aid toward environmental priorities. The United States preferred bilateral aid (over which it has more control) instead of multilateral aid. If any aid was to be distributed through multilateral institutions, the United States insisted that preexisting organizations be used, specifically the World Bank (which is dominated by the Northern powers).

America's environmental priorities are significantly different from those of the Third World. Top concerns include the hole in the ozone layer, fears of global warming, preserving the rain forests, and protecting biodiversity (endangered species).[18] These tend to be the "new" issues or "second generation" environmental issues. Answers to these problems require reducing greenhouse gasses,[19] ending production of CFCs,[20] and setting aside most of the rain forests for nondevelopment. These are hardly the policy prescriptions favored by the Third World. China feels that it must burn coal (a major source of greenhouse gasses) to catch up with the West. India was among the world's largest producers of CFCs, and ending CFC production would hinder India's development.[21] Brazil and India both oppose foreign interests that want to put limits on their uses of the rain forests.

Results of the Rio Earth Summit

The Rio Earth Summit became a major media event. It was the largest gathering of heads of state up to that time, with 116 in attendance. Each leader was given a few minutes to address the gathering. Fidel Castro was applauded and cheered by Third World delegates, George Bush was booed. More important than the personalities in attendance, however, were the results of Rio. The Earth Summit produced two nonbinding declarations, two new international treaties, a plan of action, and one attempt by the Third World to create a new regime for environmental politics.

The Rio Declaration included twenty-seven principles to promote environmental protection, but this declaration created no specific legal obligations for governments. The Rio meetings also produced a Declaration on Forest Principles to promote preservation of the rain forests, but this was another nonbinding agreement. The binding treaties finalized at Rio promise to have greater long-term impact than either declaration.

The Biological Diversity Convention from Rio outlines certain steps toward international protection of endangered species. A Convention on Climate Change established the first treaty to reduce the dangers of global warming. The Climate Change treaty, along with a series of follow-up agreements (see following discussion) seeks the reduction of greenhouse gasses emissions, especially reductions in carbon dioxide. Twenty-four states committed to reductions in their carbon dioxide emissions; all were advanced industrialized nations of the North. Third World governments were not required to reduce their emissions under the Rio treaty.

Agenda 21 was the name given to Rio's program of action. It was touted as a "blueprint" for implementing the combined environmental reforms found in the Earth Summit's various declarations and treaties.[22] Agenda 21 called for new environmental programs and technologies. It also advocated diffusion of green technologies to the Third World, primarily via transfers from the North to the South under concessional terms (e.g., grants or low-interest financing). Agenda 21 received a great deal of attention because it was the most important document at Rio in terms of the estimated costs for cleaning up the environment. Maurice Strong, chair of the Earth Summit, placed the price tag for Agenda 21 at around $125 billion per year. The assumption was that the North would have to foot the bill, because only more developed nations have the necessary financial resources.

Also very much in the spotlight at Rio was the new Sustainable Development Commission (SDC). The SDC was established to monitor national compliance with the many Rio agreements. The SDC was, in essence, yet another attempt by the Third World to create a new international regime and to give themselves metapower. The SDC is a fifty-three-member panel that operates on a basis of democratic management; each nation on the SDC has an equal voice.[23] LDCs had visions of the SDC as a powerful international organization that could channel their political pressures and impose new behaviors on the North. The SDC was given the job of gathering annual reports from governments and NGOs. The primary responsibility of the SDC is to monitor how well states carry out the terms of Agenda 21. However, the SDC also represents another failed effort by the Third World to create and control a powerful regime. The fundamental weakness of the SDC lies in its lack of enforcement powers. It has no power to impose economic sanctions or any other coercive measures. It cannot force a state to carry out its agreements from Rio. The SDC must rely on publicity and public opinion to shame recalcitrant governments into honoring their commitments.

Environmental activists and some policy makers in the United States shared the hopes of Third World governments that the SDC would have the power and authority to force compliance with international environmental standards.[24] However, the harsh realities of international relations quickly became apparent after Rio. It soon became obvious that the SDC did not have the funding, authority, or enforcement powers needed to make it an effective institutional arm for a new environmental regime. Once again, Third World efforts at regime building were thwarted.

U.S. ENVIRONMENTAL POLICY AT RIO AND BEYOND

The first Bush administration found itself diplomatically isolated due to the positions it took at Rio. Bush was in a very small minority that opposed almost all of the documents signed at Rio. One hundred and fifty-six nations signed the biodiversity treaty to save endangered species. Bush did not. Bush signed the Convention on Climate Change, but only after forcing UNCED to water down this treaty. The United States forced UNCED to take out all specific targets and all specific deadlines for reducing carbon dioxide emissions.[25] The United States leads the world in carbon dioxide output. 1992 was an election year, and Bush was running for a second term. In that context, he argued that specific targets and dates for reducing emissions would harm America's economic growth. Bush also refused requests for new aid to finance transfers of green technology to the South. The only new aid that the Bush administration would agree to was an additional $150 million to help save the rain forests. However, this aid would come with strings attached. The United States wanted the power to control how the rain forest aid was spent. India and Brazil balked. They refused to accept aid that required external oversight of how to manage their rain forests. Bush responded to harsh criticisms of his views by taking a hard line. In regard to Rio, he said, "We have nothing to apologize for."[26]

Bush lost the 1992 election, and in 1993 President Clinton reversed American environmental policy in several key respects. Clinton signed the Biological Diversity Convention. He also agreed to the targets for carbon dioxide reductions that Bush had removed from the Convention on Climate Change. The Rio target was to reduce carbon dioxide emissions to 1990 levels by the year 2000. Clinton pledged $2 billion in government funds toward meeting this target. He also called on private industry to spend $60 billion of their own money to help the United States reach the target of 1990 levels for carbon dioxide emissions by 2000.[27] Because Clinton's call for industry to switch to low-emissions technology relied on voluntary compliance, it was largely ignored. Of the twenty-four nation-states in the North that committed to the Rio target, only one (Germany) reached that target by the year 2000. Germany was able to do so only because it closed down inefficient and out-of-date industries from the former communist sections of eastern Germany. Those plants were scheduled to be closed anyway due to the fact that they could not compete at the global level with newer technologies.

Follow-up to Rio: Berlin, Kyoto, and Buenos Aires

The first follow-up conference to Rio was held in Berlin in 1995. The United States arrived in Berlin with a new proposal. The Clinton administration proposed the use of environmental "credits." Under this plan, rich nation in the North could earn credits by transferring green technologies to the South. Third World nations would get newer, better, and more efficient industrial technologies. In return, the United States would be allowed to exceed its carbon dioxide emission restrictions because it was helping to reduce emissions elsewhere (through the export of green technology). The United States would gain environmental credits and then "cash in" these credits as its own emissions exceeded the Rio targets.[28] Clinton was, in effect, proposing another global bargain. Third World nations would get something they wanted (technology transfers), and America would gain new advantages in return (credits to authorize greater pollution levels inside the United States). The Clinton proposal also would allow nations that earn credits to sell or otherwise exchange these credits between governments. Finally, the United States took the position in Berlin that the Rio target of reaching 1990 emission levels by the year 2000 should apply to *all* nations, including the Third World.

Third World nations, led by China and India, rejected the Clinton proposals at Berlin. They opposed the idea of environmental credits. They also refused to put their own emissions under the terms of the Rio agreement. They argued that their needs for rapid development meant that it was unfair for the North to expect the South to reduce its emissions. They need to pollute in order to catch up with the richer countries. Because (in the opinion of Third World governments) LDCs did not create the global mess of environmental degradation, it is also unfair to expect them to clean it up. If the North made this mess during centuries of economic development (dating back to the Industrial Revolution), then rich nations must bear the burden of the necessary corrective measures. The Third World bloc presented its own proposal at Berlin. They called on the North to reduce its emission levels to twenty percent *below* the Rio target. Northern states refused.[29]

No new agreements came out of the Berlin conference in 1995. A second follow-up to Rio was held in Kyoto, Japan, during 1997. The Kyoto conference did produce significant new agreements.

The Kyoto agreement on global warming calls on the North to make cuts in carbon dioxide emissions beyond the Rio target. The new reductions were hammered out during long, contentious, eleventh-hour negotiations. These further reductions vary according to country. Japan pledged to make a cut that is six percent below the Rio target. The United States promised to reduce emissions to seven percent below the Rio target of 1990 levels. The EU's target at Kyoto was an eight percent reduction below 1990 emission levels. Each region of the North is to reach their respective target levels by the year 2010.[30]

Like the Earth Summit, the Kyoto conference set up no binding mechanism by which to enforce its agreements. Once again, LDCs were not required to join the reduction regime. Any nation that is party to the Kyoto Protocol can opt out of the treaty by giving other member-states one year's notice (weakening these agreements even more).[31]

The Kyoto meetings were significant in that advanced industrialized nations were willing to make a public commitment to address global warming beyond what was required by their promises at Rio. Implementation of this agreement, however, is problematic at best. The U.S. Senate quickly expressed its view of the Kyoto Protocol by voting 95-0 against ratification of any treaty that did not include Third World participation in emission reductions. China, once again playing the role of champion for the Third World cause, refused to join into Kyoto reduction targets and denounced the idea that LDCs should cut back on industrial output in order to protect the environment.

A third environmental conference after Rio was held in Buenos Aries in 1998. Negotiators arrived in Buenos Aires in a general state of diplomatic "exhaustion" after their hard-fought battles at Rio, Berlin, and (especially) Kyoto. By 1998, the movement for creating an effective regime for international environmental politics was losing momentum.[32] Although no new treaties came out of Buenos Aires, there was one notable element of progress. The host government, Argentina, was the first Third World government to voluntarily commit itself to enter into the terms of the various global warming pacts. Argentina pledged to reduce its own carbon dioxide emissions in accordance with the Rio targets. Perhaps Argentina's move can help break the logjam separating North and South when it comes to international environmental politics.[33] If Third World nations hope to achieve any success in this regard, they are going to have to follow Argentina's lead. They must also find a global bargain that is attractive to the United States.

CONCLUSION: A NEW GLOBAL BARGAIN FOR ENVIRONMENTAL POLITICS?

Third World efforts to reform existing international regimes have been generally unsuccessful. Likewise, LDCs' attempts to garner metapower by establishing new regimes have failed. American foreign policy has consistently sought to veto or otherwise thwart Third World efforts in this regard. In the area of environmental politics, however, one can find elements of a strategy that might be more successful in achieving Third World goals.

The overall dynamics of U.S.-Third World relations are unlikely to change in the foreseeable future. LDCs will continue to demand extensive aid and trade advantages to speed up their own development. They will also continue to seek metapower within regimes. The United States will continue to resist increased aid and will counsel market-based development strategies. The United States will also oppose efforts to democratize international regimes. However, this impasse can be overcome if Third World nations adopt a win-win approach.

First, developing nations must identify areas of international relations that are important to America's interests. Then they must be willing to make concessions to reform in exchange for U.S. largess. These global bargains should begin in the area of environmental politics.

As a start, Third World nations need to follow Argentina's lead and be willing to enter into environmental regimes as full participants. They must be willing to accept some nominal reductions in output of greenhouse gasses. These negotiations could be structured in a manner similar to trade regulations. Third World nations have regularly been allowed some limited advantages in regard to trade liberalization. The accession of China into the WTO is the most recent example. Although expected to adhere to the general principles of the regime, developing nations such as China have been allowed to deviate from strict compliance with WTO norms. The United States pushed for China's membership in the WTO and was willing to negotiate terms of the agreement that gave China higher tariff structures on U.S. goods than the American tariffs on Chinese products. These trade advantages will be equalized slowly and over a long period of time.

A similar approach could serve the environmental interests of both the United States and LDCs. Instead of a flat refusal to enter into required reductions under the climate change regime, Third World nations could agree to higher targets for total emissions (perhaps stabilizing at 2000 emission levels, instead of reaching 1990 levels or less). They could also be given more time to meet these targets. Good faith efforts in this regard would then be rewarded with new aid based on additionality. Furthermore, the Third World should agree to some variation of the environmental credits proposal that would give the United States pollution "vouchers" if America exports advanced green technology to the South. This would increase prospects for the technology transfers that Third World nations seek.

Similar global bargains may be possible in the areas of drug trafficking, illegal immigration, and the war against terrorism. The United States would be called on to exchange increased aid and technology in return for LDC efforts to reduce the flows of illicit drugs and illegal immigrants or to help root out terrorist cells. The one thing Third World nations may never attain is metapower. By sacrificing their more lofty goals of controlling regimes, however, global bargains are the most likely means for them to achieve greater success in attaining their more limited ends.

Chapter 12

U.S. INTERNATIONAL ENVIRONMENTAL POLICY

Richard T. Sylves

Environmental problems have been recognized for many hundreds of years. Most of these problems were initially believed to be local and manageable. For many years these problems were poorly understood both in human and in natural terms. Few suspected that environmental damage could cumulate, cause damage elsewhere, or defy correction. Many believed that humans were such an insignificant part of nature that human behavior could never have a measurable impact on the natural environment. Experience and scientific knowledge gained over the second half of the last century; some gathered from satellite telemetry and space research, have proven how wrong these assumptions are. Glantz, among others, has documented the fact that human industrial and developmental practices have had measurable impacts on a global scale.[1] Some popular environmental writers (such as McKibben) allege that humans have so changed the environment and the natural world that there no longer exists a pure state of nature. When industrial and automotive pollution measurably changes global atmospheric chemistry, when polar bears show measurable levels of human-invented carcinogens such as dioxin in their bloodstreams, and when remote high-altitude forests evidence significant damage from industrial air pollutants, one might conclude that humans have managed to produce global environmental impacts. Some of these effects have perhaps permanently altered major ecosystems.

In the United States during the twentieth century, environmental protection and sustainable natural resource management rose from local to state to regional to national prominence. Problems in maintaining the purity of the Great Lakes compelled the United States and Canada to form a joint commission for the Great Lakes under an agreement predicated in part on curtailing pollution. This bilateral organization has assumed many important responsibilities, among them improved pollution control and the restriction of damaging industrial and municipal discharges into the Great Lakes. When the environmental behavior of one country has a negative effect on another country, cross-national and international controversy ensues. There are literally

289

hundreds of bilateral or multilateral treaties in effect, which owe their origin to an environmental dispute or controversy of some kind. Where common property resource exploitation has produced Hardin's "tragedy of the commons," as in ocean contamination and atmospheric pollution, new modes of governance have become necessary.[2]

SCIENCE AND ENVIRONMENTAL POLICY

A tremendously important force in U.S. domestic and foreign environmental policy has been the scientific community. Scientists across a broad range of disciplines, such as climatology, meteorology, natural biology, agronomy, marine sciences, toxicology, chemistry, and many others, have entered the world of policy making with trepidation. Their research findings document environmental damage, disclose disturbing trends, measure the success and failures of existing environmental policies, and help to model the world's environmental future. Their analysis is sometimes a barometer of both public and environmental health and welfare. However, moving from the world of research to the world of "science advocacy" is difficult and controversial for most scientists.

The forecasting and scientific modeling developed and studied by scientists has done much to warn humankind about damage to the stratospheric ozone layer, the buildup of carbon dioxide in the atmosphere, the threats of extinction that humans pose to many species of plants and animals, the broad implications of acid rain deposition, and, of course, the environmental damage that human behavior has imposed and continues to impose via water, air, and hazardous substance pollution. However, scientific research by its very nature also points to unresolved uncertainties. Many policy makers worldwide remember the doomsday scenarios projected by the respected Club of Rome scientific group in the 1970s. Nearly all of their prognostications proved to be wrong. The credibility gap created by past scientific and engineering predictions often elicits skepticism or indifference on the part of public policy makers.

However, the persuasiveness and influence of scientists on matters of environment is in ascendance as perhaps never before. Tremendous advances in high speed computing, the growth of the Internet, quantum leaps forward in genetic research, application of remote sensing technologies, the ability to monitor in real-time environmental changes across vast expanses of the Pacific (to detect El Niño and La Niña phenomena), and development of geographic information systems technology have increased the influence, status, and credibility of modern science and scientists.

Owing to the huge costs of research expertise and technologies used in science, governments themselves have established sizable and active research programs and institutions. The U.S. Environmental Protection Agency's (EPA) laboratories; the National Oceanic and Atmospheric Administration's centers for studying atmospheric research, climate change data, marine studies; and

NASA's research facilities are unlikely to confine their research to domestic environments. Government scientists in the United States and elsewhere are active players in policy making, particularly with respect to international policy. More than ever, American scientists, whether they are government employees or not, are likely to carry their work into the international arena. The point is, American foreign policy on environmental issues is likely to be influenced by scientists at both ends. In other words, American scientists (many actually employed by the federal government) use their influence to effect American foreign policy relating to environmental matters. Correspondingly, scientists outside the United States follow similar avenues in influencing their home governments and other national and international authorities, including U.S. government officials.

According to Susskind; "the importance of scientific considerations, the need to involve large numbers of non-governmental groups, and the overwhelming uncertainty surrounding the scope and dynamics of ecological change, require a unique approach to environmental diplomacy."[3]

THE EARTH SUMMIT

In 1989, the UN General Assembly Conference on Environment and Development set the agenda for the so-called Earth Summit to be held in 1992. The agenda proved to be both ambitious and unrealistic. Hopes were high in 1992 that treaties would be negotiated on climate change, transborder air pollution, deforestation, soil loss, desertification, drought, conserving biodiversity, protection of the oceans and seas, protection of freshwater resources, and development of the means to fund the implementation of these treaties.[4]

In 1992, the Earth Summit convened in Rio de Janeiro with some 4,000 officials and 30,000 unofficial negotiators in attendance.[5] The meeting lasted two weeks and drew worldwide media attention. This was one of those rare international conferences in which the United States did not play a leading role. The Earth Summit was extraordinary for many other reasons as well. The division between so-called North (developed) and South (developing) nations became more pronounced, this time over global environmental issues. Nongovernmental organizations (NGOs) had access and were consulted in panel meetings more than ever before. Fear of global environmental disasters stemming from such intractable problems as climate change, ozone layer depletion, loss of biodiversity, ocean pollution, and rising sea levels gave participants a sense of urgency.

President George Bush, confronting a stubborn economic recession and engaged in a heated presidential campaign during 1992, could ill afford to alienate his conservative base of support by approving environmental treaties calling for American economic sacrifice. The president also had to consider the likelihood that the U.S. Senate could muster the two-thirds majority vote required to ratify any environmental treaty he might sign. As it turned out,

Bush attended the Earth Summit, but his inaction and uncompromising behavior cost the United States international respect. He refused to sign either of the two main conventions proposed. The convention on climate change was weak by anyone's standards. It set no time tables and no targets. Yet the climate convention was signed by more than 150 nations, ultimately taking effect March 21, 1994; nevertheless, the president refused to sign it. Many American pharmaceutical companies opposed the Earth Summit's convention on biodiversity, owing to disputes over patent ownership and intellectual property rights.[6] President Bush used this as the main basis for his opposition to the convention. This was unfortunate for two reasons. First, 165 nations and the European community had agreed to sign the biodiversity convention. It took effect on December 29, 1993. The United States by refusing to sign, appeared both selfish and uncaring about this serious environmental problem. Second, by refusing to sign, the United States managed to alienate many developing countries whose representatives hoped that they could retain ownership of their species and genetic resources in some form before foreign drug companies could capitalize on them.

One of the Earth Summit's top priorities was a nonbinding action plan known as "Agenda 21." According to Hempel, "Agenda 21 was intended to stimulate cooperation on more than 120 separate initiatives for environmental and economic improvement, each of them commencing by the turn of the century."[7] The action plan was one of the most comprehensive frameworks ever developed by governments for global environmental policy making.[8] Yet the effort to win broad agreement yielded relatively weak measures and little support for their implementation. Agenda 21 represented an agreement among nations to act on environmental problems but without the force of binding deadlines or the fear of sanctions for failing to act.[9]

Clinton administration policy on climate change and biodiversity policy moved American foreign policy closer to world acceptability. However, President Clinton (having signed the biodiversity convention that the first President Bush would not) made no bold moves to address climate change. The U.S. produces one-third of the world's carbon dioxide emissions. Carbon dioxide emissions are thought to be the chief anthropogenic contribution to global warming. However, the vast number of politically and economically powerful domestic interests affected by the need to reduce American carbon dioxide emissions virtually ensures that the U.S. will follow a "go slow" approach to climate change policy. The Clinton administration, over the objections of Republican majorities in both houses of Congress, gingerly began a greenhouse gas emission inventory in the late 1990s, as called for in the Rio Summit's climate convention. However, the Clinton administration moved forward reluctantly.

The Clinton administration agreed after the Rio Summit to "reduce its greenhouse gas emissions to 1990 levels by the year 2000."[10] When the International Panel on Climate Change—a body composed of eminent scientists and experts—concluded that the United States and most other developed countries would not meet promised greenhouse gas reduction targets, another international conference was held in 1997 in Kyoto, Japan. The Kyoto conference met under fractious circumstances. Industrial and corporate interests lobbied cheek to cheek with international environmental organizations. The Kyoto meetings nearly ended in failure, but Vice President Al Gore, speaking for the Clinton administration and buoyed by American public opinion polls favoring stronger commitment to abating climate change, told delegates that the United States would commit to tough greenhouse gas emission controls. What the administration could not promise was Senate ratification of the Kyoto Protocol. A follow-up conference in Buenos Aires in 1998 was remarkable only because the host country went on record promising that it would commit to greenhouse gas reduction. The Clinton presidency ended without submission of the Kyoto Protocol to the Senate. With the inauguration of George W. Bush in January 2001, there is little expectation that the United States will ratify the Kyoto Protocol (see the conclusion of this text). When meetings on climate change issues occurred at The Hague in November 2000, America's representative advocated U.S. compliance through emissions trading. His stance earned him a pie in the face heaved by a young woman who was a German environmentalist.

THE WTO AND THE ENVIRONMENT

It is impossible to address matters of American foreign policy on environmental issues without considering the World Trade Organization (WTO). The WTO was created in December 1993 during the Uruguay round of General Agreement on Trade and Tariffs (GATT). The talks themselves were aimed at reducing tariffs by fifty percent. One hundred and seventeen nations participated in the talks. The WTO was assigned exclusive authority to adopt interpretations of GATT reforms. The GATT/WTO system affects more than ninety percent of the world's trade.

As environmental and natural resource problems become regional, multinational, and global in scale, they must invariably become part of multilateral trade and tariff negotiations. Introducing environmental and natural resource issues into trade negotiations is no simple task. This is because, as one researcher put it, "Environmental costs are seldom internalized in market prices, and environmental property rights are rarely defined, assigned and enforced."[11] American foreign policy has always had a mercantilist bias. The U.S. government was a major force in establishing both GATT and its successor, the WTO. What is notable with regard to environmental policy is that the same crosscurrents of trade versus environment in domestic U.S. policy making are evident in the ebb and flow of international trade negotiations. Despite the fact that the United States is the world's only superpower, America is just as likely to be influenced by other governments and foreign environmental interests as those very same governments and interests are likely to be influenced by the United States. For example, the European Union's (EU) strong promotion of relatively aggressive environmental policies has produced changes in both U.S. domestic environmental policy and U.S.-based multinational corporate behavior.

In 1999, environmental activists staged a highly publicized and controversial protest during WTO meetings in Seattle, Washington. Protestors railed against the WTO's decision-making secrecy and against its alleged disregard of environmental and social problems. Some insisted that environmental concerns should not take a backseat to matters of trade and commerce. Some maintained that elite representatives were ignoring environmental concerns and social justice in negotiating trading rules. These rules would have to be obeyed by every nation seeking to be part of the WTO's trading regime. Environmental activists accused the WTO of being undemocratic, a tool of powerful multinational corporations, and cavalier in its regard for the environment.

Others made counterclaims. Some dismissed environmental protests as radical, quixotic efforts to fight globalization of national economies; as sour grapes labor protests over job losses attributable to business internationalization; and as antidevelopment. Article XX of GATT "made formal exceptions for restrictions to protect human, animal or plant life," but these exceptions "have not faired well before Dispute Resolution Panels."[12] Yet Eisner adds that the Marrakesh Agreement setting forth the WTO called for promoting traditional economic goals "while allowing for the optimal use of the world's resources in accordance with the objectives of sustainable development."[13]

Some critics of trade rules aimed at advancing environmental causes call them a "green form of protectionism."[14] In other words, domestically imposed environmental restrictions are allegedly an excuse to continue protectionism and favoritism on behalf of domestic commerce.[15]

Disputes such as these have led some to ask whether nations are entitled to exercise "environmental sovereignty." In a 1991 GATT ruling, the United States squared off with Mexico in the dolphin-safe tuna controversy. That dispute resulted from the objections of Mexico's fishermen. They did not want to incur the expense of preventing the incidental catch of dolphins in the course of their tuna fishing, something the United States attempted to force them to do under provisions of the U.S. Marine Mammal Protection Act of 1972. In brief, the United States tightened regulatory standards and encouraged use of improved fishing technology to reduce dolphin mortality by U.S.-registered vessels. The act did not apply to foreign fishing fleets, and they continued to operate with higher dolphin kill rates than the law allowed. Under a 1990 federal court decision, the United States prohibited imports of tuna from Mexico, Venezuela, and other nations responsible for high dolphin kills in U.S. waters. "Mexico challenged the U.S. embargo on the grounds that GATT rules prohibit a nation from using trade policies to affect regulatory policies outside its jurisdiction."[16] The GATT ruling went in favor of Mexico and against the United States. It stipulated that "the United States cannot dictate to Mexico how it can harvest tuna; it cannot make access to its domestic market contingent on Mexico's adopting dolphin protection practices similar to its own."[17]

Controversies such as the dolphin-safe tuna case have impelled some to ask if advanced industrialized nations are trying to impose their environmental standards on developing countries. Can the WTO induce developing nations to better manage and conserve the natural resources needed for economic development? Or will the WTO undercut environmental concerns on behalf of developing nations whose leaders wish to disregard responsible resource management? Some critics have accused environmentalists of "two-level gaming." This means that if environmentalists lose political fights with various industrial or commercial interests on the domestic national government level, they attempt to overcome this setback by imposing environmental restrictions at the WTO international level.[18] For this to be possible, environmentalists would have to have significant influence in WTO negotiations, something few believe that they now have.

Environmentalists would like nations to retain their rights to impose export controls for the purpose of conserving important natural resources.[19] Protecting export of tropical hardwoods is an example.

The principle of subsidiarity means keeping the locus of decision making as close to the people and their direct representatives as possible. Some have questioned whether the WTO is preempting the principle of subsidiarity in its decision making on environmental issues. Relatedly, some have alleged that the old GATT and its new WTO are subsuming a nation-state-centered world under a global trade imperative. In other words, the WTO is forcing nations to surrender some of their national sovereignty as the price of joining an international trading regime. The WTO is an international organization whose leaders and major participants are unelected and therefore politically unaccountable.

Trade liberalization helps many multinational corporations and many national economies but may undercut environmental protection in some respects. Some assume that environmental conditions will first deteriorate due to trade liberalization but will later rebound to protect the environment in the long run (after higher levels of economic development have been reached).

The WTO might judge a nation's tough health and safety standards to be a trade barrier unless its authorities determine that those standards are scientifically justified. Judgments such as these are not easy to make. Many countries, including the United States, have tough health and safety standards based more on precautionary principles than on definitive scientific evidence.[20] The Clean Air Act of 1990 requires the application of strict government standards over nearly 200 air toxins. Many experts suspect that these air toxins pose meaningful risks to human health and to the environment. However, toxicological research has not presented definitive scientific causal evidence of the

harms posed by air toxins in every case. Does this mean that foreign manufacturers releasing air toxins in the United States have a grievance they can take to
the WTO?

There was a concession to environmental interests at the Uruguay round,
which came in the form of a committee dedicated to promoting sustainability.
Sustainability is at the heart of *Our Common Future*, a 1987 report of the World
Commission on Environment and Development.[21] The work is also referred
to as the Brundtland Report, named for Gro Harlem Brundtland, prime minister of Norway and chair of the World Commission. The report's goal was to
examine critical environment and developmental problems and to formulate
realistic proposals to solve them. Human progress was to advance through development that did not bankrupt the resources of future generations.[22] The
World Commission's sustainability study had a strong effect on the international community, so much so that the WTO established the Sustainability
Committee mentioned earlier.

CORPORATIONS AND THE ENVIRONMENT

For-profit corporations are embedded in American foreign policy and international environmental issues in a variety of ways. Their industrial and manufacturing behaviors produce workplace and natural environmental
consequences. Their trading, employment, investment, and natural resource
consumption activities often have important environmental effects. Their
willingness to comply with pollution control regulations, as well as their
stance on conforming to voluntary environmental protection norms advocated by trade associations and NGOs, is important. Private industry plays a crucial role in the research, development, and marketing of pollution control
equipment. As the globalization of commerce has progressed, many corporations have grown well beyond their original national home boundaries to become multinational.

In 1970, the UN identified some 7,000 multinational corporations
(MNCs). By 1996 the number had jumped to more than 35,000, with another
170,000 firms as foreign affiliates of MNCs. Half of the total foreign assets represented in cross-border trade and direct corporate investment comes from
the top 100 MNCs. In the United States, the top 1,000 corporations, most of
them MNCs, account for two-thirds of the U.S. Gross National Product.

Major MNCs can transfer environmental technology quickly and can draw
on research and development programs and information networks regarding
waste management and pollution control programs. They can compare notes
about environmental innovations in the countries in which they do business.
They can adapt to local environmental restrictions more easily than smaller
domestic firms. They often have integrated markets for goods and services enabling them to influence consumption and production of natural resources

even in undeveloped and remote parts of the world. Some observers fear that MNCs may act as "recolonizers," owing to their mobility, secrecy, and financial leverage. Because they are often able to circumvent local or national environmental laws, they can evade regulation and accountability for their actions.

Yet there are studies suggesting that economic performance of firms is not usually hurt by strict environmental regulation. Some corporations may in fact benefit from environmental regulation owing to their great economic competitiveness.[23] There are also "green" technology industries, which thrive on selling products that improve the environmental performance of other businesses. Some students of business believe that the "greening of capitalism is a reality."[24] The International Standards Organization's (ISO) 14000 series defines key elements of environmental management systems, and many corporations around the world are endeavoring to establish and maintain these systems for a variety of reasons. According to Eisner, many corporations have set forth environmental mission statements and environmental management systems, and a growing number have agreed to third party auditing of their environmental behavior. Passing audit review confers certification. By June 1999, some 10,439 firms had achieved certification. Japan, Germany, the United Kingdom, and Sweden reported the most certifications. Taiwan, South Korea, and the Netherlands each have about as many certifications as the United States.[25] Nonetheless, there are those who see such corporate behavior as deception and corporate "greenwash."[26]

Globalization has expanded the field of business competition; governments have begun to accede to colossal corporate mergers today that would have triggered titanic antitrust challenges in the past. We are now entering the era of supranational corporations (SNCs). SNCs are unfettered by loyalty to any nation-state, independent of local labor pools, able to respond to global capital flows, and likely to pounce on regional investment opportunities. Fair questions might be: How can SNCs be induced to obey WTO rules? Will these rules hold them accountable for their environmental actions? Will supranational corporations possess enough power to shape the rules of the WTO to their own advantage? Can SNCs be trusted to self-regulate and monitor their behavior?

Hempel maintains that there are no actual free markets, only "designed markets,"—that is, markets designed as products of governments, business entrepreneurs, and financiers. In his book *The Lexus and the Olive Tree*, Thomas Friedman lucidly demonstrates the immense power of organizations such as Moody's or Standard & Poor's.[27] Both firms, by grading financial security risks, affect economic exchange at both the national and the international levels. The World Bank and the International Monetary Fund are examples of other bodies capable of influencing so-called free markets in dramatic fashion. Most market designs to date, according to Hempel, encourage the systematic destruction of nature's ecological services in return for fleeting forms of profit and capital accumulation.[28]

CONCLUSIONS

American foreign policy has many aims and is conducted along a variety of tracks. The United States has many environmental interests. Most Americans would like to see the environmental policies they favor at home pursued on global terms. This is because ecological matters have become regional, continental, or even global in scope. Successes in domestic environmental policies may be undercut by the failure of other nations to act on the international or global stage. In some respects, Americans want their environmental examples emulated globally.

Conversely, the United States has many interests and policies that cannot be considered pro-environmental. The nation's extremely heavy dependence on oil and other fossils fuels makes it an easy target for climate change activists who seek to move the world away from prodigious fossil fuel use in order to reduce carbon dioxide emissions accountable for greenhouse gas buildup in the global atmosphere. Many Americans support abstract principles of environmentalism, but they resist or deny the need to change their lifestyles in order to advance environmental objectives. This ambivalence of Americans in regard to environmentalism is mirrored in the nation's foreign policy. For example, many Americans support government enactment and enforcement of tough pollution control measures imposed on industry. However, when stringent pollution control measures are alleged to drive industry out of the country at the expense of industrial employment, powerful interests can create a backlash against those environmental measures.

Americans have been at the forefront of the international campaign to protect endangered species. Despite many fits and starts, the U.S. government has pursued endangered species policies and programs. The same interest groups that promoted endangered species protection domestically have allied with groups outside the United States interested in pursuing the same goals. The Convention on International Trade in Endangered Species (CITES) has been a significant contributor to global action on species protection. Yet other American interests, such as wealthy sportsmen, have worked to undermine this treaty because it restricts various hunting pursuits and makes the importation of certain game trophies illegal.

American foreign policy in the environmental realm, such as American domestic environmental policy, is vulnerable to intervening counterpressures from other realms of policy. Economic recessions are poison for environmentalism because some of the greatest environmental advances are only feasible during prosperous times. During prosperity, companies are more likely to invest in cleaner, newer technologies; consumers have the money to make "greener" purchasing decisions; added leisure time allows more people to appreciate the great outdoors via tourism and recreation; and governments have the tax revenues to invest in cleaner and more efficient technologies.

Has there really been a fundamental shift in American attitudes about the environment? Is the "greening" of American business in firms such as McDonald's and General Motors a genuine transformation of those firms or merely a marketing ploy? Are American consumers themselves becoming "greener"? What is the state of American environmental literacy and environmental education in elementary and high schools? Clearly, answers to these questions will help to explain American foreign policy regarding the environment. There is reason to believe that Americans will endorse scientifically sound environmental measures, especially if most of the rest of the world follows suit. But there is less evidence to assume that they will make public and private sacrifices aimed at protecting the interests of future unborn generations. As the saying goes; "the future is no one's constituency." Most policy makers discount the value of future benefits and inflate the value of present benefits in their reasoning. The future cannot reward or punish those in the present. Nonetheless, American foreign policy is likely to be shaped domestically and internationally by the pressures imposed via environmental imperatives and by the force of young people who fear a future their ancestors have jeopardized.

CONCLUSION:
CONTINUITY AND CHANGE
IN A NEW MILLENNIUM

THE FIRST YEAR

At the time of this writing, President George W. Bush had spent slightly more than one year in the White House. His primary focus upon taking office was domestic politics: specifically his new tax cut and his proposed budget cuts. Prior to September 11 of his first year, foreign policy was a much less important area. However, by the end of his first year, and in large part due to September 11, the president was forced to focus most of his energy on foreign policy. Preliminary assessments of the extent to which we can expect continuity or changes in U.S. foreign policy under the George W. Bush's administration are now possible. This concluding chapter will summarize the consistencies and reforms in American foreign policy that are likely under the first administration of the new millennium. We will consider both general changes and specific reforms in the areas of defense, trade, the environment, and human rights.

During the 2000 presidential campaign, Governor George W. Bush ran against Vice President Al Gore. Gore laid out a foreign policy design that would have been a continuation of the Clinton approach. Gore spoke of his international policies with a mixture of realism and idealism. George W. Bush's campaign rhetoric was strictly realist in tone. The best example of their contrasting styles emerged during a debate over humanitarian intervention. Gore spoke of the need to use military force to stop genocide "wherever it occurs." Bush countered that America's armed forces should be used only to protect U.S. national interests (narrowly defined to exclude genocide in general). Bush spoke of the need to exhibit "restraint" and "humility" in foreign policy. He also said that U.S. troops ought to return home from places like Bosnia and Kosovo.

His critics accused Bush of proposing a neo-isolationist foreign policy that would lead to international disengagement. Once in office, Bush's secretary of state, Colin Powell, moved quickly to dispel these rumors. Powell declared during his confirmation hearings before the Senate that the new administration would not withdraw "into a fortress of protectionism or an island of isolationism."[1] In terms of specific foreign policies, Powell called for continued economic sanctions against Iraq, engagement with China, talks with North Korea, U.S. involvement in the Middle East peace process, greater attention to Africa, and the need for a national missile defense (NMD) system. In every one of these areas, Powell's comments reflected an essential consistency between the Clinton and Bush administrations. In terms of more detailed international policies, however, we can expect many changes to be instituted by President Bush and his advisors. To get a better idea of the changes and consistencies in Bush's foreign polices, this chapter will use the book's tripartite division of foreign policy into the areas of defense, economics, and morality.

CONTINUITY AND CHANGE IN DEFENSE POLICIES

During his first 100 days, George W. Bush proposed immediate changes in the defense budget to increase military pay and to improve the living quarters of America's service men and women. The Bush administration initially proposed increases in total defense spending in the range of $5–15 billion per year. Prior to September 11, defense expenditures were projected by the White House to run in the range of $325–365 billion annually.[2] After September 11 these projections increased to $390 billion for fiscal year 2003, representing the largest one-year increase in military spending since the Korean War.[3]

The Bush administration began its term by establishing a comprehensive, top-down strategic review of all security policy. Such comprehensive reviews of defense policy are common for a new administration, especially when the turnover in the White House includes a change of parties (in this case from the Democrats to the Republicans). A strategic review begins by postulating the most likely threats to America in the foreseeable future. The review then proceeds to the step of establishing the best military force posture to meet these threats.

One of the biggest reforms proposed by the Clinton administration, but yet to be carried out, was put on hold. This was based on a report from the Army's chief of staff, General Eric Shinseki. Shinseki wanted the United States to move out of a Cold War military posture based on heavily armored divisions. Instead, the Pentagon would create a "new calvalry" based on "medium-weight brigades."[4] Aging heavy armor, like the M-1 tank, would be gradually phased out in favor of more lightly armored defense vehicles. Shinseki argued that the United States should stop planning for Cold War–type military engagements (a la Korea and Vietnam); instead, future planning must emphasize medium-weight fighting units trained in quick response tactics.

Shinseki's proposals required the Army to give careful consideration to seemingly mundane issues such as whether the next generation of armored personnel carriers will be fitted with tracks (as on a tank) or equipped with tires (as on a car). Those who advocate tracks on armored personnel carriers envision future Army operations that are much like those of past wars: ground forces would be designed primarily to take and hold large areas of rough terrain within a hostile military environment (as in Korea, Vietnam, or the Gulf War). Those who advocate wheeled armored vehicles (such as Shinseki himself) predict that future military operations will be distinctly different from those of the past. The likely scenarios according to this view are ones in which the United States is involved in more urban types of warfare, possibly during civil wars between hostile ethnic factions within unstable states (as in Bosnia and Kosovo). If such predictions are accurate, future wars are likely to be ones in which the United States is forced to take sides in internal disputes, defending pro-American factions or U.S. proxies.

Members of the Bush administration were against Shinseki's preference for reordering the American army. Movement toward wheeled armored vehicles and training for urban warfare implies an increased likelihood for military operations involving peacekeeping, peace-enforcement, and nation-building within "failed" states. These are operations that President Bush expressed opposition to even before he attained the White House.

Prior to September 11, the aspect of defense policy that received the most attention was Bush's vigorous advocacy for a new generation of NMD. Bush's views on NMD are perhaps the most significant and controversial aspects of contemporary strategic policy. NMD is another area in which one can identify both continuities and changes as compared to the Clinton administration.

Clinton had proposed a "thin" NMD system to protect all fifty states from a limited intercontinental ballistic missile (ICBM) attack. Clinton's NMD would have been a strictly land-based system using interceptor missiles launched from Alaska. NMD policy under Bush is managed by Secretary of Defense Donald Rumsfeld. Before joining the Bush administration, Rumsfeld chaired two commissions that studied technology and defense. His 1998 report noted that North Korea and Iran were closer than previously believed to deploying missiles capable of reaching the United States. A 2001 report outlined likely threats to U.S. satellites—satellites that are necessary for military and civilian communications.

NMD and satellite defenses are necessarily linked in the minds of Bush and Rumsfeld. They want the United States to establish military control over outer space in order to "defend our own satellites and engage those of the enemy."[5] They also want a far more ambitious NMD than that proposed by Clinton. The Bush administration is considering the use of space-based weaponry. Powerful lasers would be mounted on satellites to destroy other satellites and enemy ICBMs. Such space-based weapons were prohibited under the terms of the 1972 ABM treaty (see chapter 3). Therefore, President Bush declared that the United States would abandon the ABM treaty.

The Impact of September 11 on Defense Policies

Defense policy under George W. Bush began with a preference for unilateral American actions, then shifted for a short time to multilateralism due to September 11, and more recently has returned to Bush's original bias in favor of unilateral means. Abrogation of the ABM treaty was just one example of the early unilateralism displayed by the Bush administration (Colin Powell's claims to the contrary notwithstanding). During his early months in office, George W. Bush also exhibited a preference for unilateralism when he suspended U.S. participation in the Kyoto Protocol on global warming, renounced American cooperation with the new International Criminal Court, stood alone among Western leaders in opposing a new mechanism for enforcing the 1972 Biological Weapons Convention, and insisted on watering down an international agreement to curb illegal trafficking in small arms.[6] Richard Haas, Bush's director of policy planning within the State Department, coined a new term for this approach to foreign policy. Haas called the Bush approach "a la carte multilateralism."[7] A la carte multilateralism, a clever new way to say "unilateralism," means that President Bush feels free to "pick and choose which treaties he wants to adhere to and which ones he scraps."[8]

September 11 highlighted the importance of "authentic" multilateralism for the Bush administration, if only for a short while. Many of the initial policy reactions to the terrorist bombings of September 11 relied on multilateral approaches. The United States went to the UN Security Council on September 28 to get a vote freezing the assets of all terrorist organizations. The United States also began working with the General Assembly on a new international convention against terrorism. Coalition-building with dozens of nations also became an instrumental part of pursuing the new war against terrorism (see chapters 4 and 6).

However, this use of multilateral means by Bush was short lived, and his innate preference for unilateralism had reemerged before the end of his first year in office. The Bush administration made it clear that America would stand alone, if necessary, to pursue the most important aspects of his foreign policy. Examples of this resurgent unilateralism were easy to find. In 2002, the Pentagon prepared plans for a unilateral invasion of Iraq, relying on 150,000 to 300,000 ground troops and five aircraft carriers, all drawn from U.S. forces if no other nation chose to stand with the United States.[9] The same plan assumed that the United States would go ahead with the invasion of Iraq even if Saudi Arabia denied America the use of its bases for staging the attack.[10] Members of the Bush administration spoke at length of the need to prepare U.S. public opinion for this war and pointed out that Americans would (in their opinion) accept as many as 30,000 U.S. wartime casualties under the right circumstances.[11]

Unilateralism was also evident in Bush's nuclear policies after September 11. Bush created a shift in strategic doctrine toward the use of offensive nuclear weapons, ones that could be employed against so-called rogue states such as Iraq. A defense policy memorandum drafted during the George Bush administration under Dick Cheney (then secretary of defense, later vice president under George W. Bush) was revived and updated. The Cheney report, both the 1992 and the 2002 versions, argued that the United States should not allow the rise of any global or regional challengers to American power.[12] Members of the Pentagon and the State Department began to discuss openly the "need to effect regime changes in six or seven countries."[13] At the top of this hit list of governments to be removed from power (by force if necessary) was Saddam Hussein, followed by the other countries identified by the State Department as sponsors of terrorism (Cuba, Iran, Libya, North Korea, Syria, and Sudan). Largely due to frustration over an inability to remove Saddam from power long after the 1991 Gulf War, George W. Bush ordered a crash program to develop new "bunker-busting mini-nukes" that could reach the Iraqi dictator, even if he was secluded in one of his many hardened underground command posts (see chapter 3 for more on this change in nuclear policy).[14]

CONTINUITY AND CHANGE IN NONDEFENSE POLICIES: TRADE, THE ENVIRONMENT, AND HUMAN RIGHTS

Economic Policy

In respect to trade policy, President Bush has expressed reservations regarding the Clinton preference for mixing labor and environmental issues into free trade pacts. Recall that Clinton added side agreements on labor rights and environmental protection to the NAFTA free trade agreement. The Clinton administration also negotiated a subsequent bilateral trade agreement with Jordan that was the first pact to include labor and environmental provisions within the main text. Bush's trade representative, Robert Zoellick, has criticized the Clinton approach of using trade sanctions to enforce international labor and environmental standards. President Bush and Zoellick both support continuation of NAFTA and expansion of the Free Trade Area for the Americas (FTAA), as did Clinton. However, both Bush and Zoellick want to renegotiate the labor and environmental elements of the Jordan trade agreement before they ask for Senate ratification of the pact. Bush's White House does not want to set a precedent for necessarily incorporating labor and environmental standards into future trade agreements.[15] This is a clear reversal of the policy followed by the Clinton administration in the wake of the 1999 "battle in Seattle" (protests at WTO conferences: see chapters 7 and 9).

During his second year in office, George W. Bush scored a key victory in his trade policy that had eluded Clinton. In 2002, the Congress voted to restore "fast-track authority," now known as trade promotion authority (TPA), to the president and his advisors. Fast-track authority, or TPA, denies Congress the ability to amend new trade agreements once they have been signed by a president. Once Congress agrees to grant TPA, it must vote a proposed trade agreement up or down in its entirety. Congress relinquishes (in advance) its ability to alter the terms of any trade agreement when it grants the president

TPA. Congress could still reject a trade agreement under TPA, but it cannot micromanage the details of any agreement once it has been signed by the president. TPA is supposed to give presidents more leverage in negotiating trade agreements because trading partners cannot hope to put indirect pressure on the White House by lobbying Congress to oppose specific elements of presidential trade policy. Hence with TPA in place, it is hoped that the United States will get better trade agreements than it might otherwise have if there was no TPA.

The economic cold war between the United States and the European Union (EU) also heated up under George W. Bush's administration. In early 2002, the president announced that he was imposing new tariffs that would run up to thirty percent on foreign steel. The three-year time frame for these steel tariffs was necessary to give America's domestic steel industry time to become more competitive, according to Bush. Almost immediately, the EU retaliated by threatening its own tariffs of up to twenty-six percent on U.S. steel. The EU also drew up a list of $355 million worth of U.S. exports ranging from citrus to textiles that could be hit with 100 percent tariffs if the Bush administration did not back off on its steel tariffs.[16] The products subject to possible 100 percent tariffs included "citrus from Florida; apples and pears from Washington and Oregon; textiles from North and South Carolina; and steel from Pennsylvania, Ohio and West Virginia."[17] Each of these states is either a key battleground for presidential races, or a state where key congressional races were being contested in 2002. Both the United States and the EU argued that its use of punitive steel tariffs was allowable under WTO regulations, whereas those of its opponent were not. At the time of this writing, both sides were also preparing cases to take before the WTO's dispute panels regarding the other's steel tariffs. The battle over steel tariffs has joined the "banana wars" discussed in chapter 9 as key test cases for the ability of the WTO to manage such high-profile trade disputes between the economic superpowers.

Environmental Policy

A series of environmental edicts during his first year brought criticism and controversy to the Bush White House. Within this period, Bush a) advocated drilling for oil in the Arctic National Wildlife Refuge in Alaska, b) rescinded a new environmental standard that would have lowered levels of arsenic in drinking water, c) suspended new cleanup requirements for mining operations, and d) challenged a ban on logging in nearly 60 million acres of national forest reserves. Furthermore, the most controversial decision by far, and the one most directly related to foreign policy, was Bush's policy reversal on global warming. Candidate Bush promised in 2000 to require reductions in carbon dioxide emissions from power plants once he became president. Reductions of carbon dioxide would have been accomplished by conversion from coal to natural gas. Once in office, President Bush reversed himself and abandoned these promises. President Bush said in 2001 that the costs to America's economy would be too great for forced conversion from coal to gas. Bush also declared an end to America's participation in the Kyoto Protocol. Kyoto would require the United States to cut carbon dioxide emissions to seven percent below 1990 levels by the year 2012. Bush proposed an "alternative" to the Kyoto Protocol based on economic incentives that he claimed would encourage businesses to voluntarily cut emissions, develop cleaner energy technologies, and promote conservation.[18] Environmental groups criticized the Bush alternative, pointing out that it would actually lead to the release of more (not less) greenhouse gases.[19] Bush's rejection of the Kyoto process to reduce global warming also brought angry reactions from Europe and Japan. The other major industrialized powers declared their intentions to go ahead with the Kyoto process without America's help. U.S. relations (particularly with the Europeans) are bound to suffer in the meantime. Global warming is one of the top issues on the EU's international political agenda.

Human Rights

During the presidential debates in 2000 against Gore, candidate George W. Bush had cautioned against military intervention for purely humanitarian purposes. He spoke of the need to maintain "humility" in American foreign policy. In his view, humility requires that we not impose our values or our policy preferences on other nations. Humility is good for U.S. policy if it is used as a way to avoid cultural imperialism. Humility would not be a good thing, however, if it is used merely as a smokescreen to hide American indifference to ethnic cleansing and other human rights violations in foreign lands.

The most significant human rights policies during the transition from the Clinton to the Bush administration concerned the International Criminal Court. At the last possible moment, the Clinton administration signed the international treaty to establish an International Criminal Court (ICC). The ICC was created by a 1998 treaty in Rome. The United States did not sign the ICC treaty during the Rome convention due to fears that the court could be used by America's enemies to persecute U.S. soldiers.

The ICC is the first permanent court ever created to try individuals from any country on charges of genocide, war crimes, and crimes against humanity. The ICC finds its precedents in the Nuremberg Tribunal for World War II and in the two ad hoc tribunals for the former Yugoslavia and Rwanda created by the Security Council during the 1990s. The tribunals for World War II, Yugoslavia, and Rwanda were temporary and only for crimes committed in those specific case. The ICC is a permanent court claiming universal jurisdiction.

The Senate must ratify the ICC treaty before the United States can become a member of the ICC. Opposition to the ICC has been very strong in Congress. When the treaty was signed, Clinton expressed his own concerns about the ICC's claims to universal jurisdiction. American foreign policy has always taken the position that treaties are legally binding only on nations that ratify the treaty. The official U.S. position is that the same restrictions must apply to the ICC. However, the Rome treaty claims that the powers of the ICC will extend to all states, including nonmembers of the treaty.

U.S. policy would also like to see the ICC treaty amended to give a veto over prosecutions to permanent members of the Security Council (like itself). In that way, the United States could protect its military from war crimes accusations that may arise during what America considers to be legitimate intervention campaigns (e.g., charges that bombing Belgrade during the Kosovo campaign constituted "war crimes"). Clinton qualified his support for the ICC treaty in the following way: "Given these concerns, I will not and do not recommend that my successor submit the treaty to the Senate [for ratification] until our fundamental concerns are satisfied."[20]

ICC membership was another key policy choice facing the first new presidential administration of the twenty-first century. George W. Bush responded by "unsigning" the ICC treaty during his second year in office. President Bush took the unprecedented step of "renouncing" the presidential signature placed on the ICC treaty by Clinton (it was never ratified by the Senate, and ratification was not even at issue). The universal jurisdiction claimed by the ICC (over parties to the treaty and nonparties alike) was "particularly troubling" to the Bush administration in the mdst of its war against terrorism.[21] The Bush administration declared that the United States would never recognize the right of an international organization to put Americans on trial without its consent or without a UN Security Council mandate to do so.[22]

Human rights and the ICC; trade and labor/environmental protections; military interventions, the war against terrorism, and the NMD system—these are the key issues and the enduring controversies for American foreign policy in the new millennium.

POSTSCRIPT ON IRAQ, 2003

As this book went to the printer, American forces were massing for a new war against Iraq in 2003. The stated goal of this new war was the overthrow of Saddam Hussein. With luck, U.S. casualties in the new war could be kept low, as was the case during the 1991 Gulf War. Even if the war to unseat Hussein turns out well, however, America may find it much harder to "win the peace" in Iraq after the war. Policy regarding the war and the subsequent occupation of Iraq, therefore, promises to be another enduring problem for America throughout the foreseeable future.

SELECTED BIBLIOGRAPHY FOR PART I

Allison, Graham. *Essence of Decision.* Boston: Little-Brown, 1971.

Amirahmadi, Hooshang, ed. *The United States and the Middle East: A Search for New Perspectives.* Albany: State University of New York Press, 1993.

Becker, William, and Samuel Wells Jr., eds. *Economics and World Power: An Assessment of American Diplomacy since 1789.* New York: Columbia University Press, 1984.

Beckman, Peter R., Paul Crumlish, Michael Dobkowski, and Steven Lee, eds. *The Nuclear Predicament: Nuclear Weapons in the Twenty-First Century.* Upper Saddle River, N.J.: Prentice Hall, 2000.

Bennett, A. Leroy. *International Organization.* Englewood Cliffs, N.J.: Prentice Hall, 1999.

Bert, Wayne. *Reluctant Superpower: United States' Policy in Bosnia, 1991–95.* New York: St. Martins Press, 1997.

Beschloss, Michael, and Strobe Talbott. *At the Highest Levels: The Inside Story of the End of the Cold War.* Boston: Little, Brown, & Co., 1993.

Bill, James. *The Eagle and the Lion: The Tragedy of American-Iranian Relations.* New Haven, Conn.: Yale University Press, 1988.

Blackwill, Robert, and Michael Sturmer, eds. *Allies Divided: Transatlantic Politics for the Greater Middle East.* Cambridge, Mass.: MIT Press, 1997.

Brinkley, David. "Democratic Enlargement: The Clinton Doctrine." *Foreign Policy* no. 106 (spring 1997).

Brune, Lester. *The United States and Post–Cold War Interventions: Bush and Clinton in Somalia, Haiti, and Bosnia, 1992–1998.* Claremont, Calif.: Regina Books, 1998.

Brzezinski, Zbigniew, Brent Scowcroft, and Richard Murphy. "Differentiated Containment." *Foreign Affairs* 76 (May/June 1997).

Burch, R. Kurt. "Illustrating Constructivism: George Kennan and the Social Construction of the Cold War." *Swords and Plowshares* 6, no. 1 (1996).

Calvocoressi, Peter. *World Politics since 1945.* New York: Longman, 1991.

Clarke, Walter, and Jeffrey Herbst. *Learning from Somalia: The Lessons of Armed Humanitarian Intervention.* Boulder, Colo.: Westview Press, 1997.

Council on Foreign Relations. *Future Visions for U.S. Defense Policy.* New York: Council on Foreign Relations Books, 2000.

Donaldson, Gary. *America at War since 1945.* Westport, Conn.: Praeger, 1996.

Draper, Theodore. "Nuclear Temptations." *New York Review of Books* 30, nos. 21 and 22 (1984).

Drew, Elizabeth. *On the Edge: The Clinton Presidency.* New York: Simon & Schuster, 1994.

Durch, William J., ed. *UN Peacekeeping, American Policy and the Uncivil Wars of the 1990s.* New York: St. Martin's Press, 1996.

Ellsberg, Daniel. *Papers on the War.* New York: Simon & Schuster, 1972.

Flournoy, Michael A. *Nuclear Weapons after the Cold War.* New York: Harper Collins, 1993.

Gaddis, John Lewis. *The United States and the End of the Cold War: Implications, Reconsiderations, Provocations.* New York: Oxford University Press, 1992.

―――. *The United States and the Origins of the Cold War, 1941–1947.* New York: Columbia University Press, 1972.

Gutman, Roy. *Witness to Genocide.* New York: Macmillan Publishing, 1993.

Haass, Richard. *Intervention: The Use of American Military Force in the Post–Cold War World.* Washington D.C.: Carnegie Endowment, 1994.

―――. *The Reluctant Sheriff: The United States after the Cold War.* New York: Council on Foreign Relations Press, 1997.

Hastedt, Glen P. *American Foreign Policy: Past, Present and Future.* Englewood Cliffs, N.J.: Prentice Hall, 2000.

Herring, George C. *America's Longest War.* New York: McGraw-Hill, 1996.

―――. *LBJ and Vietnam.* Austin: University of Texas Press, 1994.

Hirsch, John L., and Robert B. Oakley. *Somalia and Operation Restore Hope: Reflections on Peacemaking and Peacekeeping.* Washington D.C.: U.S. Institute of Peace Press, 1995.

Hoolbrooke, Richard. *To End a War.* New York: Random House, 1998.

Ikenberry, John G. *American Foreign Policy: Theoretical Essays.* New York: Longman, 1999.

Jentleson, Bruce W. *Perspectives on American Foreign Policy.* New York: Norton, 2000.

Kahin, George McT. *Intervention: How America Became Involved in Vietnam.* Garden City, N.Y.: Anchor, 1987.

Kennan, George (Mr. X). "The Sources of Soviet Conduct." *Foreign Affairs* 25 (July 1947).

Kinder, Hermmann, and Werner Hilgemann. *Anchor Atlas of World History.* New York: Anchor/Doubleday, 1978.

Kissinger, Henry. *Nuclear Weapons and Foreign Policy.* New York: Harper, 1957.

Klare, Michael, and Daniel Thomas. *World Security: Trends and Challenges at Century's End.* New York: St. Martin's, 1991.

LaFeber, Walter. *America, Russia and the Cold War.* New York: McGraw-Hill, 1997.

―――. *The American Age: United States Foreign Policy at Home and Abroad since 1750.* New York: W.W. Norton & Co., 1989.

Lamb, Christopher J. *How to Think about Arms Control, Disarmament and Defense.* Englewood Cliffs, N.J.: Prentice Hall, 1988.

Lesch, David, ed. *The Middle East and the United States: A Historical and Political Reassessment.* 2d ed. Boulder, Colo.: Westview Press, 1999.

MacKinnon, Michael G. *The Evolution of U.S. Peacekeeping Policy under Clinton: A Fairweather Friend?* London: Frank Cass Publishing, 2000.

Macridis, Roy. *Foreign Policy in World Politics.* Upper Saddle River, N.J.: Prentice Hall, 1992.

Melanson, Richard A. *Reconstructing Consensus: American Foreign Policy since the Vietnam War.* New York: St. Martin's, 1991.

Minear, Larry, and Philippe Guillot. *Soldiers to the Rescue: Humanitarian Lessons from Rwanda.* Paris: OECD, 1996.

Nathan, James, and James Oliver. *Foreign Policy Making and the American Political System.* 3d ed. Baltimore: Johns Hopkins University Press, 1994.

———. *United States Foreign Policy and World Order.* 3d ed. Boston: Little, Brown, & Co., 1985.

Natsios, Andrew S. *U.S. Foreign Policy and the Four Horsemen of the Apocalypse: Humanitarian Relief in Complex Emergencies.* Westport, Conn.: Praeger, 1997.

Oberdorfer, Don. *Tet!* Garden City, N.Y.: Doubleday.

O'Hanlon, Michael. "Star Wars Strikes Back." *Foreign Affairs* 78, no. 6 (1999).

Prendergast, John. *Frontline Diplomacy.* Boulder, Colo.: Lynne Rienner, 1996.

Quandt, William. *Peace Process: American Diplomacy and the Arab-Israeli Conflict since 1967.* Berkeley, Calif.: University of California Press, 1993.

Rhode, David. *Endgame: The Betrayal and Fall of Srebrenica, Europe's Worst Massacre since World War II.* New York: Farrar, Straus and Giroux, 1997.

Rose, Michael. *Fighting for Peace, Bosnia 1994.* London: Harvill Press, 1998.

Russett, Bruce M., and Bruce G. Blair. *Progress in Arms Control?* San Francisco: W. H. Freeman, 1979.

Sagan, Scott D., and Kenneth N. Waltz. *The Spread of Nuclear Weapons: A Debate.* New York: Norton, 1995.

Smoke, Richard. *National Security and the Nuclear Dilemma.* New York: Random House, 1987.

Snow, Donald M. *National Security: Defense Policy in a Changed International Order.* New York: St. Martin's, 1998.

Sobel, Richard. *The Impact of Public Opinion on U.S. Foreign Policy since Vietnam.* New York: Oxford University Press, 2001.

Strobel, Warren P. *Late Breaking Foreign Policy: The News Media's Influence on Peace Operations.* Washington D.C.: United States Institute for Peace, 1997.

Truman, Harry S. *1946–1952, Years of Trail and Hope.* New York: Norton, 1954.

Turner, Stansfield. *Caging the Genies: A Workable Solution for Nuclear, Chemical and Biological Weapons.* Boulder, Colo.: Westview, 1999.

Weston, Burns, Richard Falk, and Anthony D'Amato. *Basic Documents in International Law and World Order.* St. Paul, Minn.: West Publishing, 1980.

Woodhouse, Tom, Robert Bruce, and Malcolm Dando, eds. *Peacekeeping and Peacemaking: Towards Effective Intervention in Post-Cold War Conflicts.* New York: St. Martin's Press, 1998.

Woodward, Susan. *Balkan Tragedy: Chaos and Dissolution after the Cold War.* Washington D.C.: Brookings Institute, 1995.

Young, Marilyn B. *The Vietnam Wars, 1945–1990.* New York: Harper, 1991.

Zimmermann, Warren. *Origins of a Catastrophe.* New York: Times Books, 1996.

SELECTED BIBLIOGRAPHY
FOR PART II

Bello, Walden, and Stephanie Rosenfeld. *Dragons in Distress: Asia's Miracle Economies in Crisis*. New York: Penguin Press, 1992.

Bergsten, C. Fred. "Empire Strikes Back." *The International Economy* (May/June 2000): 10–13, 52–53.

Cohen, Stephen D. *The Making of U.S. International Economic Policy*. Westport, Conn.: Praeger, 2000.

Cohn, Theodore H. *Global Political Economy: Theory and Practice*. New York: Addison Wesley Longman, 2000.

Croome, John. *Reshaping the World Trading System*. Brussels, Belgium: World Trade Organization, 1995.

DeVries, Margaret Garristen. *The IMF in a Changing World*. Washington, D.C.: International Monetary Fund, 1986.

Engelen, Klaus. "A Good Start." *The International Economy* (September/October 2000): 48–51.

———. "Koch-Weser Gang Bang." *The International Economy* (March/April 2000): 26–31.

Executive Office of the President, U.S. Trade Representative. *USTR Announces Procedures for Modifying Measures in EC Beef and Bananas Cases*. May 26, 2000.

———. *1999 Annual Report of the President of the United States on the Trade Agreements Program*. Washington, D.C.: Government Printing Office, 2000.

———. *2000 Trade Policy Agenda*. Washington, D.C.: Government Printing Office, 2000.

"Fruitless but not Harmless (World Trade Organization Rules against European Union's Banana Import Rules)." *The Economist*, April 10, 1999, 18.

Gilpin, Robert. *War and Change in World Politics*. Cambridge, England: Cambridge University Press, 1983.

Greider, William. *One World, Ready or Not: The Manic Logic of Global Capitalism*. New York: Simon and Schuster, 1997.

Hancock, Graham. *Lords of Poverty: The Power, Prestige and Corruption of the International Aid Business*. New York: Atlantic Monthly Press, 1989.

Hoekman, Bernard M., and Michael M. Kostecki. *The Political Economy of the World Trading System: From GATT to WTO*. Oxford, England: Oxford University Press, 1995.

Isaak, Robert. *Managing World Economic Change*. Englewood Cliffs, N.J.: Prentice Hall, 1995.

Jackson, John H. *The World Trading System: Law and Policy of International Economic Relations*. 2d ed. Cambridge, Mass.: MIT Press, 1997.

Kennedy, Paul. *The Rise and Fall of Great Powers*. New York: Random House, 1987.

Keohane, Robert. *After Hegemony*. Princeton, N.J.: Princeton University Press, 1984.

Keohane, Robert, and Joseph Nye. *Power and Interdependence*. Boston: Little-Brown, 1977.

Kindleberger, Charles P. *The World in Depression, 1929–1939*. Berkeley: University of California Press, 1973.

Malmgren, Harald. "Dollar Politics," *The International Economy* (January/February 1999): 10–13.

Meyer, William H. *Human Rights and International Political Economy in Third World Nations: MNCs, Foreign Aid and Repression*. Westport, Conn.: Praeger, 1998.

———. *Transnational Media and Third World Development*. Westport, Conn.: Greenwood, 1988.

Mosley, Paul, Jane Harrigan, and John Toye. *Aid and Power: The World Bank and Policy-Based Lending*. Vol.1. London: Routledge, 1991.

Nau, Henry. *The Myth of America's Decline*. New York: Oxford University Press, 1990.

Noble, Gregory, and John Ravenhill, eds. *The Asian Financial Crisis and the Architecture of Global Finance*. Cambridge, England: Cambridge University Press, 2000.

Nye, Joseph. *Bound to Lead*. New York: Basic Books, 1990.

"Omnibus Trade and Competitiveness Act of 1998" (PL 100-418, August 25, 1988) 102. *U.S. Statutes at Large*, 1107. Available from Congressional Universe (online) *www.lexisnexis.com/academic/3cis/cismnu.htm*, Bethesda, Md.: Congressional Information Service.

Preeg, Earnest H. *Traders in a Brave New World: The Uruguay Round and the Future of the International Trading System*. Chicago: University of Chicago Press, 1995.

Qureshi, Asif H. *The World Trade Organization: Implementing International Trade Norms*. Manchester, England: Manchester University Press, 1996.

Raworth, Philip, and Linda C. Reif, eds. *The Law of the WTO: Final Text of the GATT Uruguay Round Agreements, Summary and Fully Searchable Diskette*. New York: Oceana Publications, 1995.

Ryan, Missy. "10 Sovereignty Issues Now before the WTO." *National Journal* 20 (November 1999): 3384–90.

Schott, Jeffrey J. *The Uruguay Round: An Assessment*. Washington, D.C.: Institute for International Economics, 1994.

————. *WTO 2000: Setting the Course for World Trade.* Washington, D.C.: Institute for International Economics, 1996.

Sek, Lenore. *The Uruguay Round: A Review of Major Issues.* Washington, D.C.: Congressional Research Service, 1994.

Spero, Joan E., and Jeffrey Hart. *The Politics of International Economic Relations.* New York: St. Martin's, 1997.

Srinivasan, T. N. *Developing Countries and the Multilateral Trading System: From the GATT to the Uruguay Round and the Future.* Boulder, Colo: Westview Press, 1997.

Stewart, Terence P., ed. *The GATT Uruguay Round: A Negotiating History 1986–1992.* Vols. 1–3. Boston: Klewer Law Publications, 1993.

Thurow, Lester. *Head to Head.* New York: William Morrow, 1992.

Ullmann, Owen. "Mad Dog." *The International Economy* (March/April 1999): 24–27.

U.S. Congress. House, "Any Participation in Multilateral Organizations that Affects the Independence and Sovereignty of the United States Is Wrong and Should be Discontinued." In *The Congressional Record.* 106th Congress, 2d sess., April 10, 2000, H1989 (*http://thomas.loc.gov*).

————"Withdrawing Approval of the United States from the Agreement Establishing the World Trade Organization." In *The Congressional Record.* 106th Congress, 2d sess., June 21, 2000, H4788 (*http://thomas.loc.gov*).

Walters, Robert S., and David A. Blake. *The Politics of Global Economic Relations.* Englewood Cliffs, N.J.: Prentice Hall, 1992.

World Trade Organization, "Overview of the State-of-Play of WTO Disputes." *http://www.wto.org/english/tratop_e/dispu_e/dispu_e.htmebsite* (August 1, 2000).

SELECTED BIBLIOGRAPHY
FOR PART III

Amnesty International. *Human Rights and US Security Assistance.* New York: Amnesty International USA Publications, 1995.

Benedi, Claudio F. *Human Rights: The Theme of Our Times.* St. Paul, Minn.: Paragon House, 1997.

Boyd, Andrew. *Atlas of World Affairs.* New York: Routledge, 1990.

Brown, Peter, and Douglas MacLean. *Human Rights and U.S. Foreign Policy.* Lexington, Mass.: D. C. Heath, 1979.

Brown, Seyom. *Human Rights in World Politics.* New York: Longman, 2000.

Carleton, David, and Michael Stohl. "The Role of Human Rights in US Foreign Assistance Policy." *American Journal of Political Science* 31, no. 4 (1987).

Carr, E. H. *The Twenty Years' Crisis.* New York: Harper, 1939.

Cingranelli, David Louis. *Ethics, American Foreign Policy, and the Third World.* New York: St. Martin's, 1993.

Club of Rome. *Reshaping the International Order.* New York: E. P. Dutton, 1976.

Donnelly, Jack. *International Human Rights.* Boulder, Colo: Westview, 1998.

Dougherty, James E., and Robert L. Pfaltzgraff. *Contending Theories of International Relations.* New York: Harper and Row, 1990.

Eisner, Marc Allen. "Green from Greed? Corporate Environmentalism and the Future of Regulation." Professional paper presented at the Annual Meetings of the American Political Science Association, August 2000.

Falk, Richard. *Human Rights and State Sovereignty.* New York: Holmes and Meier, 1981.

Friedman, Thomas L. *The Lexus and the Olive Tree.* New York: Farrar, Straus and Giroux, 1999.

Forsythe, David. *Human Rights and World Politics.* Lincoln: University of Nebraska Press, 1989.

———. *The Internationalization of Human Rights.* Lexington, Mass.: D. C. Heath, 1991.

Glantz, Michael H. "The Global Challenge." In *Annual Editions: Environment 2000-2001.* Ed. John L. Allen. Sluice Dock, Guilford, Conn.: Dushkin, 2000.

Hadar, Aron. *The US and El Salvador.* Berkeley, Calif: US-El Salvador Research Center, 1981.

Hall, Bob. *Gold and Green.* Durham, N.C.: Institute for Southern Studies, 1994.

Hardin, Garrett. *Exploring New Ethics for Survival.* New York: Penguin Books, 1976.

Hempel, Lamont. *Environmental Governance: The Global Challenge.* Washington, D.C.: Island Press, 1996.

Holsti, Ole R. "Public Opinion and Human Rights in American Foreign Policy." *American Diplomacy* (on-line) 1, no. 1, *www.unc.edu/depts/diplomat/Holsit* (1996).

Human Rights Watch. *El Salvador's Decade of Terror.* New Haven, Conn.: Yale University Press, 1991.

Jentleson, Bruce W. "Who, What, Why and How: Post-Cold War Military Intervention." In *Eagle Adrift.* Ed. Robert Leiber New York: Longman, 1997.

Kirkpatrick, Jeane. "Dictatorships and Double Standards." *Commentary* (November 1979).

———. "Establishing a Viable Human Rights Policy." *World Affairs* (spring 1981).

Krasner, Stephen. *International Regimes.* Ithaca, N.Y.: Cornell University Press, 1985.

Machiavelli, Niccolo. *The Prince.* New York: New American Library, 1952.

McKibben, William. *The End of Nature.* New York: Anchor Press, 1999.

Meyer, William H. *Human Rights and International Political Economy in Third World Nations.* Westport, Conn.: Praeger, 1998.

Porter, Gareth, and Janet Welsh Brown. *Global Environmental Politics.* Boulder, Colo.: Westview, 1991.

Robertson, A. H., and J. G. Merrills. *Human Rights in the World.* New York: Manchester University Press, 1992.

Rosenbaum. Walter A. *Environmental Politics and Policy.* Washington, D.C.: CQ Press, 1998.

Schoultz, Lars. *Human Rights and U.S. Policy toward Latin America.* Princeton, N.J.: Princeton University Press, 1981.

Steiner, Henry J., and Philip Alston. *International Human Rights in Context: Law, Politics, Morals.* New York: Oxford University Press, 2000.

Susskind, Lawrence. *Environmental Diplomacy: Negotiating More Effective Global Agreements.* New York: Oxford University Press, 1994.

Timerman, Jacobo. *Prisoner without a Name, Cell without a Number.* New York: Random House, 1981.

Tokar, Brian. *Earth for Sale: Reclaiming Ecology in the Age of Corporate Greenwash.* Boston: South End Press, 1997.

Tonelson, Alan. "Human Rights: The Bias We Need." *Foreign Policy* 78 (winter, 1982).

Unger, Sanford, and Peter Vale. "South Africa: Why Constructive Engagement Failed." *Foreign Affairs* 64, no. 2 (1985).

Vance, Cyrus. "Human Rights and Foreign Policy." *Georgia Journal of International and Comparative Law* 7, supplement (1977).

Van Dyke, Vernon. *Human Rights, the U.S. and World Community.* New York: Oxford University Press, 1970.

Vasquez, John A. *Classics of International Relations.* Englewood Cliffs, N.J.: Prentice Hall, 1987.

Woodward, Susan L. *Balkan Tragedy.* Washington, D.C.: Brookings Institute Press, 1995.

World Commission on Environment and Development. *Our Common Future.* New York: Oxford University Press, 1987.

Young, Oran R. *The Effectiveness of International Environmental Regimes.* Cambridge, Mass.: MIT Press, 1999.

———. *Global Governance: Drawing Insights from Environmental Experiences.* Cambridge, Mass.: MIT Press, 1997.

———. "International Regimes." *World Politics* 32, no. 3 (1980).

Zolberg, Aristide, and Robert Smith. *Migration Systems in Comparative Perspective.* New York: International Center for Migration, 1996.

CONTRIBUTORS

Candace C. Archer is an assistant professor in the Department of Political Science at Bowling Green State University. She received her Ph.D. from the University of Delaware in 2003. Her dissertation on "International Financial Crises: The Evolution of Multilateral Responses" studied the development of international reactions to financial crises over the past two hundred years. Archer wrote her master's thesis on the WTO dispute settlement mechanism (while at the University of Delaware). She has served as a program assistant for the U.S. Department of State's Fulbright Scholars program and for the International Studies Association.

Robert C. DiPrizio is an assistant professor at the Air Command and Staff College, part of the U.S. Air Force's Air University. He received his Ph.D. from the Department of Political Science and International Relations at the University of Delaware in 2000. His book on military intervention, *U.S. Humanitarian Interventions in the Post–Cold War Era,* is forthcoming from the Johns Hopkins University Press.

Daniel M. Green is an associate professor in the Department of Political Science and International Relations at the University of Delaware. His publications include *State Construction in the International System* (Lynne Rienner, 2001) and a series of articles on democratization, globalization, structural adjustment, and African politics in journals such as *Comparative Political Studies, Governance,* and *Review of African Political Economy.*

William H. Meyer is a professor of international relations at the University of Delaware. His prior research has focused on human rights and on international communication. His publications include *Human Rights and International Political Economy in Third World Nations* (Praeger, 1998), *Transnational Media and Third World Development* (Greenwood, 1988), and a series of articles in journals such as *Comparative Political Studies,* the *Cornell International Law Journal, Human Rights Quarterly, International Interactions,* and *Social Science Quarterly.*

Mark J. Miller is a professor of comparative politics at the University of Delaware. He is an internationally recognized expert in the areas of terrorism and migration studies. He is on the board of editors for the *International Migration Review,* has authored over a dozen books and monographs, and has published more than forty journal articles and government reports on immigration, terrorism, and U.S. security. Miller teaches courses at the University of Delaware on regional studies, international conflicts, and American foreign policy.

Bahram Rajaee is the director of international projects at the University of Delaware's Center for International Studies. He received his Ph.D. from the Department of Political Science and International Relations at the University of Delaware in 2000. His dissertation on "The U.S. and Southwest Asia Beyond 2000" employed international relations theory to critically examine American policy in the Middle East. He has published articles on Iranian refugee policy and on the geopolitics of oil diplomacy in the *Middle East Journal* and in *International Politics* (respectively).

Richard T. Sylves is a professor of public policy at the University of Delaware, where he also directs the Environmental and Energy program. He has published four books: *Declaring Disaster* (SUNY Press, forthcoming); *Disaster Management in the U.S. and Canada* (edited with William Waugh, Charles C. Thomas Publishers, 1996); *Cities and Disaster* (edited with Waugh, Charles C. Thomas, 1990); and *The Nuclear Oracles* (Iowa State University Press, 1987). His research and teaching encompasses environmental, energy, and disaster policies.

ENDNOTES

Preface

1. This line is from the song "What It's Like" by Everlast (from the album *Whitey Ford Sings the Blues*), house-of-everlast.8m.com/whitey2.html.
2. Bahram M. Rajaee, "The United States and Southwest Asia beyond 2000: A Regional Approach to U.S. Policy" (Ph. D diss., University of Delaware, 2000); "Regional Politics, the Legal Regime of the Caspian Sea, and U.S. Policy in Transcaspia," *International Politics* 37, no. 1 (2001).
3. Robert C. DiPrizio, *US Humanitarian Interventions in the Post–Cold War Era*, Johns Hopkins University Press (forthcoming); "Adverse Effects of Humanitarian Interventions into Complex Emergencies," *Small Wars and Insurgencies* 10, no. 1 (1999).
4. William Schultz, Executive Director for Amnesty International USA, "Report on Human Rights Abuses in the U.S.," public address on the CSPAN network, April 10, 2002.
5. Daniel M. Green, "The Way the World Works: The Burdens of Globalization," *Governance* 13, no. 3 (2000); "Ghana's Adjusted Democracy," *Review of African Political Economy* 22, no. 6 (1995); "Structural Adjustment and Politics in Ghana," *TransAfrica Forum* 8, no. 2 (1991).
6. Candace C. Archer, "International Economic Crises: The Evolution of Multilateral Responses" (Ph. D diss., University of Delaware, 2003); "Understanding the WTO: The Dispute Settlement Mechanism and International Relations Theory" (masters thesis, University of Delaware, 1999).
7. Environmental protection and sustainable development are key topics in the growing literature on "human security" (as opposed to "national security"). See, for example, Barry Buzon, Ole Waever, and Jaap de Wilde, *Security: A New Framework for Analysis* (Boulder, Colo.: Lynne Rienner, 1998).
8. Richard T. Sylves, "An Introduction to Trends in Extreme Weather and Climate Events," *Bulletin of the American Meteorological Society* (forthcoming); "Human Factors Explain the Increased Losses from Climate Extremes," *Bulletin of the American Meteorological Society* 81, no. 3 (2000); "US Disasters and Climate Research," *Aspen Global Change Institute Proceedings* (forthcoming); "How the Exxon Valdez Disaster Changed Oil Spill Management," *Journal of Mass Emergencies and Disasters* 16, no. 1 (1998). Sylves is also the director of the environmental and energy policy program at the University of Delaware.
9. See, for example, G. John Ikenberry, ed., *American Foreign Policy: Theoretical Essays* (New York: Longman, 1999); James Nathan and James Oliver, *United States Foreign Policy and World Order* (Boston: Scott Foresman, 1988); Robert Isaak, *Managing World Economic Change* (Englewood Cliffs, N.J.: Prentice Hall, 1995).
10. See, for example, Glenn Hastedt, *American Foreign Policy* (Englewood Cliffs, N.J.: Prentice Hall, 1997); Roger Hilsman, *The Politics of Policy Making in Defense and Foreign Affairs* (Englewood Cliffs, N.J.: Prentice Hall, 1990); James M. McCormick, *American Foreign Policy and Process* (Itasca, IL.: F. E. Peacock, 1992); John Spanier and Eric Uslaner, *American Foreign Policy Making and the Democratic Dilemma* (New York: Macmillan, 1994).
11. That which purports to be foreign policy theory is not even "theory" in its strictest sense (most other social science approaches are open to the same criticism). What foreign policy "theory" usually provides is empirical analysis, description, and prescription. Description and prescription are good things, but they do not provide us with analytic models that have predictive or explanatory power. Prediction and explanation are required of theory

in all disciplines outside of the social sciences (as in Newton's laws or Einstein's theory of relativity). It is the strength of good social science that we do description and prescription (not prediction—that's not possible). But we should not fool ourselves into thinking that, simply because social scientists often loosely apply the term *theory* to their typologies of foreign policy (e.g., bureaucratic politics, realism, neoliberal institutionalism, etc.), these typologies can be elevated to a level of theory that is similar to theories in the hard sciences (such as physics).

Introduction to Part 1

1. For more on the ethical aspects of realism and idealism, see chapter 10.
2. Thucydides, *History of the Peloponnesian War* (Harmondsworth, England: Penguin Books, 1972); Niccolo Machiavelli, *The Prince* (New York: New American Library, 1952); Thomas Hobbes, *Leviathan* (New York: Collier Books, 1962); Jean Jacques Rousseau, *The State of War and The Project for Perpetual Peace: Two Essays by Jean Jacques Rousseau* (New York: G. P. Putnam's, 1920).
3. E. H. Carr, *The Twenty Years' Crisis, 1919–1939* (London: Macmillan, 1939); Hans J. Morgenthau, *Politics among Nations* (New York: Knopf, 1948); George F. Kennan, *Realities of American Foreign Policy* (Princeton, N.J.: Princeton University Press, 1954); Henry A. Kissinger, *A World Restored—Europe after Napoleon* (New York: Grosset and Dunlap, 1964).
4. Kenneth N. Waltz, *Theory of International Politics* (Reading, Mass.: Addison-Wesley, 1979); Robert Gilpin, *War and Change in World Politics* (Cambridge, England: Cambridge University Press, 1981).
5. Waltz, *Theory of International Politics.*
6. Hugo Grotius, *The Rights of War and Peace* (Oxford: Clarendon Press, 1925); Baron de Montesquieu, *The Spirit of the Laws* (Berkeley: University of California Press, 1971); Immanuel Kant, *Perpetual Peace* (New York: Macmillan, 1957).
7. Woodrow Wilson, "The World Must Be Made Safe for Democracy," and "The Fourteen Points," in *Classics of International Relations,* ed. John A. Vasquez (Upper Saddle River, N.J.: Prentice Hall, 1996); Robert O. Keohane and Joseph Nye, *Power and Interdependence* (Boston: Little, Brown, 1977); Francis Fukuyama, "The End of History?" *The National Interest* 16 (summer 1989).
8. See chapter 11 for more on theories of international regimes and U.S. policy toward these regimes.
9. Ole R. Holsti, "Public Opinion and Foreign Policy," *International Studies Quarterly* 36, no. 3 (1992); Richard Sobel, *The Impact of Public Opinion on U.S. Foreign Policy since Vietnam* (New York: Oxford University Press, 2001); John Dietrich, "Interest Groups and Foreign Policy," *Presidential Studies Quarterly* 29, no. 2 (1999).
10. Graham Allison, *Essence of Decision: Explaining the Cuban Missile Crisis* (Boston: Little, Brown, 1971).
11. Irving L. Janis, *Groupthink: Psychological Studies of Policy Decisions and Fiascoes* (New York: Houghton Mifflin, 1982); Thomas C. Wiegele, Gordon Hilton, Kent Oots, and Susan Kiesell, *Leaders under Stress: A Psychophysiological Analysis of International Crisis* (Durham, N.C.: Duke University Press, 1985).
12. Noam Chomsky, *The Culture of Terrorism* (Boston: South End Press, 1988); James R. Kurth, "The Political Consequences of the Product Cycle," *International Organization* 33, no. 1 (1979).
13. Christine Sylvester, "Empathetic Cooperation: A Feminist Method," *Millennium* 23, no. 2 (1994); Cynthia Weber, *Simulating Sovereignty: Intervention, the State and Symbolic Interchange* (Cambridge, England: Cambridge University Press, 1994).
14. See Cynthia Enloe, *Bananas, Beaches and Bases* (Los Angeles: University of California Press, 1990), especially Enloe's chapters on diplomacy and banking; R. Kurt Burch, "Illustrating Constructivism: George Kennan and the Social Construction of the Cold War," *Swords and Plowshares* 6, no. 1 (1996).

Chapter 1

1. Roy Macridis, *Foreign Policy in World Politics,* chap. 13 (Upper Saddle River, N.J.: Prentice Hall, 1992).
2. Wilson's model of collective security within the League failed, at least in part, due to the fact that the U.S. Senate voted (against Wilson's wishes) not to join the League of Nations.
3. See chapter 2.
4. Bush used the term *new world order* frequently, especially during the 1991 Gulf War against Iraq.
5. Recall that, at this time, China still had a noncommunist government.
6. Chapter I of the UN Charter lists three purposes for creation of the organization. They are M.I.P.S., protection of human rights, and promotion of economic and social development. See A. Leroy Bennett, *International Organization,* Appendix 1 (Englewood Cliffs, N.J.: Prentice-Hall, 1999).
7. The Monroe Doctrine asserted the United States' position that non-American powers were prohibited from establishing a sphere of influence within the Americas. The Monroe Doctrine originated as a statement against European colonialism in the Americas. By the time of the Cold War, the Monroe Doctrine was interpreted to mean that the United States would not tolerate attempts to establish communist dictatorships in the Americas.
8. Before he died (near the end of World War II), President Roosevelt spoke of his desires for a system of regional dominance managed by what he called the "four policemen." See Walter LaFeber, *America, Russia, and the Cold War* (New York: McGraw-Hill, 1997). 12.
9. *http://www.uncg.edu/psc/yalta.htm*
10. Burch, "Illustrating Constructivism," 3–22.
11. LaFeber, *America, Russia, and the Cold War,* 3.
12. Key elements of the 1939 Soviet-German pact were kept secret. These provisions divided Poland between the two powers after Hitler's invasion of Poland in September 1939 started World War II.
13. The Azerbaijan province in Iran should not be confused with the former Soviet republic, also known as Azerbaijan, which became an independent state in 1991.
14. The 1936 International Straits Conference in Montreux recognized Turkish hegemony over the Dardanelles. See Hermann Kinder and Werner Hilgemann, *Anchor Atlas of World History, vol. 2* (New York: Anchor/Doubleday, 1978), 167, 229.
15. Peter Calvocoressi, *World Politics since 1945* (New York: Longman, 1991), 234.
16. After the Cold War, Czechoslovakia divided peacefully into the independent nations of the Czech Republic and Slovakia.
17. LaFeber, *America, Russia, and the Cold War,* 72.
18. The Cold War will be dated in this text from 1948 until 1991: 1948 is used as a beginning date because of the Berlin crisis; 1991 is used as an end date because that was the year of the final collapse of the USSR (see chapter 2).
19. For more on the foreign policy of isolationism, especially its economic aspects, see chapter 6.
20. Thomas Risse-Kappen, "From Mutual Containment to Common Security: Europe during and after the Cold War," in *World Security: Trends and Challenges at Century's End,* ed. Michael Klare and Daniel Thomas (New York: St. Martin's, 1991), 128.
21. Mr. X, "The Sources of Soviet Conduct," *Foreign Affairs* 25 (July 1947).
22. Risse-Kappen, "From Mutual Containment."
23. To fund an aid program today comparable to the Marshall Plan, more than $90 billion would be necessary.
24. LaFeber, *America, Russia, and the Cold War,* 59.
25. North Atlantic Treaty in Burns Weston, Richard Falk, and Anthony D'Amato, *Basic Documents in International Law and World Order* (St. Paul, Minn.: West Publishing, 1980), 97.
26. Madeleine K. Albright, "NATO: Collective Defense against the Threat of Aggression," in *World Politics,* ed. Helen Purkitt (Guilford, Conn.: Dushkin 1999), 77.
27. "Crisis in Asia—An Examination of U.S. Policy," *Department of State Bulletin* 22, no. 551 (January 23, 1950).

28. Gary A. Donaldson, *America at War since 1945* (Westport, Conn.: Praeger, 1996), 15.
29. "Appeasement" was a policy used in the 1930s by British Prime Minister Chamberlain to deal with Hitler's demands for territory. At the Munich conference of 1938, Chamberlain agreed to Hitler's takeover of part of Czechoslovakia. Chamberlain hoped that such negotiations could avoid war by satisfying the dictator's demands for territory. Of course, appeasement was a colossal failure, as it only whetted Hitler's appetite for more land and helped to lead to World War II.
30. Harry S. Truman, *1946–1952, Years of Trial and Hope* (New York: Norton 1955), 379.
31. Donaldson, *America at War*, 54.
32. "Treaty on the Non-Proliferation of Nuclear Weapons," in Weston *et al.*, *Basic Documents*, 126–27.
33. The CIA estimates that North Korea has already developed and now possesses at least a few nuclear devices.
34. Joseph Nye, "Conflicts after the Cold War," *Washington Quarterly* 19, (winter 1996).
35. Many NATO leaders in Europe during the Vietnamese War saw this issue in almost the exact opposite terms. They worried that U.S. involvement in Southeast Asia would reduce America's ability to support NATO, especially when some U.S. troops were pulled out of Europe to be sent to Vietnam.
36. Marilyn B. Young, *The Vietnam Wars, 1945–1990* (New York: Harper, 1991).
37. *Ibid.*
38. Donaldson, *America at War*, 87.
39. See Donaldson, *ibid.*, chapters 5–7 for an excellent discussion of how the French and the United States created a series of puppet regimes that had little or no popular support from the Vietnamese people.
40. George C. Herring, *America's Longest War* (New York: McGraw-Hill, 1996).
41. Donaldson, *America at War*, 94.
42. See Oliver Stone's movie *JFK* for one of the more fanciful, and exaggerated, conspiracy theories about the agents allegedly involved in Kennedy's death (including not only loose canons in the CIA but also the Pentagon, Vice President Johnson, and just about everyone else in the military-industrial complex).
43. George C. Herring, *LBJ and Vietnam* (Austin: University of Texas, 1994).
44. *Ibid.*
45. Johnson's duplicity was later unmasked when Daniel Ellsberg published secret government files as part of the "Pentagon Papers." See Daniel Ellsberg, *Papers on the War* (New York: Simon and Schuster, 1972).
46. Herring, *America's Longest War*.
47. LaFeber, *America, Russia, and the Cold War*, 247.
48. Air Force planes sprayed eleven million gallons of Agent Orange on Vietnam between 1962 and 1971. Subsequent studies have shown connections between exposure to Agent Orange and increased likelihood of heart disease or diabetes. Veterans' groups also claim that Agent Orange has caused cancer among troops that were exposed to it. See "Statistics Link Agent Orange to Diabetes," Wilmington, Del. *News Journal*, March 30, 2000.
49. George McT. Kahin, *Intervention: How America Became Involved in Vietnam* (Garden City, N.Y.: Anchor, 1987).
50. LaFeber, *America, Russia, and the Cold War*, 247.
51. Don Oberdorfer, *Tet!* (Garden City, N.Y.: Doubleday, 1971).
52. Kahin, *Intervention*.
53. CBS News and the *New York Times*, "The War in Vietnam," CD-ROM (New York: Simon & Schuster, 1995).
54. *Ibid.*
55. Richard A. Melanson, *Reconstructing Consensus: American Foreign Policy since the Vietnam War* (New York: St. Martin's, 1991).
56. Macridis, *Foreign Policy*.
57. Melanson, *Reconstructing Consensus*.

Chapter 2

1. See Donaldson, *America at War*, 120–21.
2. Richard Smoke, *National Security and the Nuclear Dilemma* (New York: Random House, 1987), 127.
3. Christopher J. Lamb, *How to Think about Arms Control, Disarmament, and Defense* (Englewood Cliffs, N.J.: Prentice Hall, 1988).
4. "Treaty between the USA and the USSR on the Limitation of ABM Systems," in *Basic Documents in International Law and World Order*, ed. Weston et al. (St. Paul, Minn.: West, 1980).
5. "Selections from the ABM Treaty, Interim Agreement, and Related Documents on SALT I," in *Progress in Arms Control?*, ed. Brice M. Russett and Bruce J. Blair (San Francisco: W. H. Freeman, 1979).
6. "Final Act of the Conference on Security and Co-operation in Europe," in Basic Documents in International Law and World Order, ed. Weston et al. (St. Paul, Minn.: West, 1980).
7. *Ibid.*
8. See Robert J. Art, "America's Foreign Policy," in *Foreign Policy in World Politics*, ed. Roy C. Macridis (Englewood Cliffs, N.J.: Prentice Hall, 1989), 149.
9. Calvocoressi, *World Politics since 1945.*
10. The draft, and even registration for the draft, had been suspended after the Vietnam War. The fact that young men have to register for the draft to this day is a legacy of the Soviet invasion of Afghanistan and Carter's reaction to that invasion.
11. An INF weapon is part of the intermediate-range nuclear forces (INF) that were deployed in Europe by both sides during the 1980s. INF weapons have a range of between 300 and 3,000 miles. See chapter 3 for more on INF weapons, especially the 1987 INF treaty that eliminated these weapons in Europe.
12. "Reagan Escalates Campaign Rhetoric," *New York Times,* June 13, 1980.
13. The cause for global instability (the USSR) identified by Reagan is now long gone. However, global instability has not diminished since the collapse of the Soviet Union.
14. The one notable exception to Reagan's tightening of all economic screws against the Soviets was grain sales. Candidate Reagan, while running against Carter in 1980, promised to reestablish the grain sales that Carter had embargoed after the invasion of Afghanistan. This was an obvious political ploy designed to gain votes for Reagan in the politically conservative farm belt. Once elected, President Reagan made good on his promise to American farmers.
15. Brian P. White, "British Foreign Policy," in *Foreign Policy in World Politics*, ed. Roy C. Macridis (Englewood Cliffs, N.J.: Prentice Hall, 1992).
16. Readiness expenditures are the costs that are required to have military forces prepared to go into battle on short notice (training, transportation, airlift, and sealift, etc.).
17. See the next chapter for a more detailed description of many of these weapons systems.
18. See the discussion of nuclear deterrence theory—especially the NUTs approach—in chapter 3.
19. Savimbi and UNITA have a decidedly socialist ideology of their own, making UNITA and the Reagan administration strange bedfellows indeed.
20. Early on, the Contras included such notable fighters as Eden Pastora, a.k.a. "Commandant Zero," who had once fought with the Sandinistas against the Somoza dictatorship that was unseated by the Sandinista revolution in 1979. Pastora had also been a member of the first post-Somoza ruling council, sharing power with the Sandinistas. As the Sandinistas' policies became more decidedly Marxist in the early 1980s, Pastora left their government and took up arms against them. However, when he began to feel that the United States particularly the CIA, had too much influence over the Contras, he also left the Contras and abandoned the Reagan-sponsored campaign against the Sandinistas.
21. Glenn P. Hastedt, *American Foreign Policy: Past Present and Future* (Englewood Cliffs, N.J.: Prentice Hall, 2000), 192–93.

22. Peter Stavrakis, "Soviet Foreign Policy" (public talk presented at the University of Delaware, September 1994).
23. Richard Nixon first rose to national political prominence by pursuing alleged communists in the U.S. government. As a young politician during the early Cold War years, Nixon made a name for himself through his attacks on Alger Hiss, a prominent member of the State Department.
24. Gorbachev broached this suggestion at a summit with Reagan in Iceland during 1986.
25. Hastedt, *American Foreign Policy*, 75.
26. This description of Clinton's foreign policy assumptions is taken from Robert Herman, "Democracy and Foreign Policy in the New Millennium" (public talk presented at the University of Delaware, January 2000). Herman was a member of the Clinton administration's policy planning staff in the State Department.
27. These priorities were first listed by Secretary of State Warren Christopher and later expanded into more detail by John Stremlau, Deputy Director of the State Department's policy planning staff. Stremlau spoke on "U.S. Policy in the New World Order" at the University of Delaware in January 1993.
28. APEC stands for the Asia-Pacific Economic Cooperation forum.
29. "Colin Powell Maps Out an Activist Foreign Policy," *Wilmington (Del.) News Journal*, January 18, 2001.
30. For more on the foreign policy of George W. Bush, see the conclusion of this text.

Chapter 3

1. Calvocoressi, *World Politics since 1945*, 4–5.
2. For more on the Baruch Plan, see Calvocoressi, *World Politics since 1945*, 11–12, Kinder and Higlemann, *Anchor Atlas*, vol. 2, 272, and LaFeber, *America, Russia and the Cold War*, 41–42. The U.S. proposal was popularly known as the Baruch Plan. LaFeber refers to it using the official title for the plan: the Acheson-Lelienthal Proposal.
3. Russia's quick acquisition of atomic weapons led to a witch-hunt in the United States to find spies that may have handed American atomic secrets to the USSR. Julius and Ethel Rosenberg were tried, convicted, and executed for atomic espionage on the basis of questionable evidence.
4. See Herbert F. York, "The Debate over the Hydrogen Bomb," in *Progress in Arms Control?*, ed. Bruce M. Russett and Bruce G. Blair (San Francisco: W. H. Freeman, 1979).
5. The atomic bomb dropped on Hiroshima was equal to 12 kilotons of TNT. The largest nuclear device ever tested was a 53-megaton bomb exploded by the USSR.
6. Henry Kissinger, *Nuclear Weapons and Foreign Policy* (New York: Harper, 1957), 175 ff.
7. *Ibid.*, 134.
8. The acronym NUTS has also been translated as "nuclear utilization target selection." What is more important than the specific translation of NUTS, however, is the idea that NUTS strategies are different in kind from MAD strategies. There is also some obvious tongue-in-cheek humor at play here by thinkers on both sides. If theorists of minimum deterrence are MAD, then theorists of flexible deterrence are NUTS. Such is the logic of plans for nuclear armageddon. See Spurgeon M. Keeny and Wolfgang K. H. Panofsky, "MAD versus NUTS: Can Doctrine or Weaponry Remedy the Mutual Hostage Relationship of the Superpowers?" *Foreign Affairs* 60 (Winter 1981/82).
9. See Fred M. Kaplan, "Enhanced-Radiation Weapons," in *Progress in Arms Control?*, ed. Russett and Blair.
10. Carl Sagan, "Nuclear War and Climatic Catastrophe: A Nuclear Winter," *Foreign Affairs* 62 (Winter 1983/84).
11. Theodore Draper, "Nuclear Temptations," *The New York Review of Books*, vol. 30, nos. 21 and 22 (1984).
12. Keeny and Panofsky, "MAD Versus NUTS."
13. *Ibid.*
14. Draper, "Nuclear Temptations."

15. Sidney D. Drell and Frank von Hippel, "Limited Nuclear War," in *Progress in Arms Control?*, ed. Russett and Blair.
16. False alarms were common during the Cold War. Once or twice each year, U.S. early warning radar picked up signals that could have been misinterpreted as a Soviet nuclear attack. These false alarms were caused by things as harmless as flocks of geese or the radar picking up its own signal when reflected by things orbiting the Earth. Such false alarms led to fears that a nuclear war could begin accidentally, when one side or the other misinterpreted a misleading but benign radar signal as an attack, leading to a nuclear launch in response. One of the primary reasons for the 1987 agreement on risk reduction centers was to share information so that false alarms would not lead to accidental nuclear war.
17. "The Newest Y2K Fear: A Mistaken Missile Launch," *Wilmington* (Del.) *News Journal,* February 26, 1999.
18. Arms control has not been limited to efforts to control weapons of mass destruction. There have been many important agreements on limiting conventional weapons as well, but it is beyond the scope of this text to review all areas of arms control. Therefore, the discussion in this chapter will be limited to arms control as it relates to weapons of mass destruction.
19. Harvey Sicherman, "Defeat in the Senate," Foreign Policy Research Institute, October 20, 1999, available online at *www.fpri.org*.
20. Sicherman, "Defeat."
21. *The Poetry of Robert Frost*, ed. Edward C. Latham (New York: Rinehart and Winston, 1969), 399.
22. The Soviet launch of the Sputnik satellite in 1957 led to American fears of a "missile gap." Because the Soviets had rockets capable of putting a satellite into orbit and the United States did not, John Kennedy criticized Richard Nixon and the rest of the Eisenhower administration for allowing the USSR to create a missile gap (allegedly giving the USSR an advantage). We now know that the "missile gap" of which Kennedy spoke never existed. American fears of the original missile gap were unfounded, but no one in the United States knew so at that time. The Soviets did not have a significant advantage in long-range missiles during the 1950s, even though they had the technology at the time to gain an advantage.

    After he defeated Nixon in the 1960 election, President Kennedy financed a crash program to develop and deploy U.S. missiles. By 1962, there was an actual missile gap, but it was in America's favor. By that time the United States enjoyed an advantage in long-range missiles that was almost 4 to 1. To counter this disadvantage, the USSR smuggled many of their medium-range nuclear missiles into Cuba during 1962. In October of that year, the Cuban missile crisis brought the two superpowers to the brink of nuclear war. Kennedy imposed a naval blockade (that he called a "quarantine") around Cuba, and Soviet leader Khrushchev threatened war in response. The definitive study of this period is Allison's *Essence of Decision*.

    The Cuban missile crisis ended when Khrushchev backed down and promised to withdraw his nuclear weapons from Cuba. In response to their humiliation during the Cuban crisis, the Soviets developed a crash program of their own to deploy ICBMs after 1962. By 1970, the Soviet Union reached nuclear parity with the United States.
23. The term "nuclear parity" means that the two sides had a roughly equivalent nuclear strike force. Parity does not indicate a numerical equality. The USSR did not have to match the United States weapon-for-weapon in order to achieve parity. Parity refers to the fact that the two sides could inflict a similar amount of damage on each other with their strategic weapons.
24. The cheapest and easiest way to overcome any so-called defensive system, such as an array of ABMs, is to throw so many offensive weapons at it (e.g., missiles and warheads) that the defensive shield cannot hope to knock them all down. Deployment of missile "defenses," therefore, almost always stimulates potential enemies to escalate their offensive arsenals, which then require more defensive weapons, and so on *ad infinitum*. In other words, an offensive-vs.-defensive spiral leads to unchecked arms races. These considerations led the United States and the USSR to negotiate limits of ABMs in the first SALT treaty. The same considerations are still relevant to current plans by the United States to develop, and possibly deploy, a new generation of missile defenses (see following discussion).

25. A MIRV is a multiple independently targetable reentry vehicle. MIRVing places more than one warhead on a nuclear missile.

26. The original SALT treaty allowed two ABM systems for each side; this was later amended and reduced to one ABM system each. The United States used to have a single ABM system deployed around a missile base. It was closed down long ago. The Russians built their lone ABM system around Moscow, and it is still in operation.

27. A strategic weapon has a range that is greater than 3,000 miles.

28. An ICBM is an intercontinental ballistic missile. They are launched from a land-based missile silo. An SLBM is a submarine-launched ballistic missile.

29. President Reagan threatened to "break out" of the limits of SALT II on several occasions—it was a treaty that he opposed—but Reagan never carried through on these threats, and American foreign policy remained loyal to the SALT II limits in practice.

30. An LRB fitted with air-launched cruise missiles (ALCMs) was counted as one MIRVed weapon for the purposes of SALT II.

31. The Soviet SS-18 was the largest nuclear missile ever deployed. It had the capability of carrying thirty warheads on a single missile. The SS-18, however, was limited to no more than ten warheads by SALT II.

32. SALT and other treaties prior to INF were verified via nonintrusive "national technical means." Each side relied on its own spy satellites to verify whether or not the other side was living up to its treaty commitments. On-site verification is much more reliable than technical verification.

33. START I cut the numbers of SS-18s from 308 to 154. America's best ICBM of the day, the MX, was exempted from START I reductions.

34. SLBMs is an area of nuclear deterrence in which the United States has always had the clearest advantage. U.S. SLBMs were exempted from the START I cuts. Under START II, American SLBMs had to be cut from 3,456 down to 1,728.

35. See "Selections from ABM Treaty and Related Documents," in *Progress in Arms Control?*, ed. Russett and Blair, 106–08.

36. The Pentagon estimates that at least 30,000 U.S. soldiers were exposed to highly toxic sarin nerve gas and to lethal cyclosarin chemical agents while demolishing Iraqi munitions and rockets at the Khamisiyah weapons depot in March 1991. See "Gulf Vets Get News on Nerve Gas," *Wilmington* (Del.) *News Journal*, October 28, 2000.

37. "Arsenal Workers Shocked by Bomb Discovery," *Wilmington* (Del.) *News Journal*, December 4, 2000.

38. "U.S. Move Ends Bioweapons Session," *Wilmington* (Del.) *News Journal*, December 8, 2001.

39. *Ibid.*

40. Stansfield Turner, *Caging the Genies: A Workable Solution for Nuclear, Chemical and Biological Weapons* (Boulder, Colo.: Westview, 1999).

41. Senator Joseph R. Biden Jr. (Democrat, Del.), Chairman of the Foreign Relations Committee, "Missile Defense Is a Risky Delusion," *Wilmington* (Del.) *News Journal*, December 30, 2001.

42. Keith B. Payne, "National Missile Defense: Why Now?" *Foreign Policy Research Institute Wire* 8, no. 1, (January 2000).

43. Avery Goldstein, "Why Nukes Still Trump: Deterrence and Security in the Twenty-first Century" (public talk presented to the Foreign Policy Research Institute, September 20, 2000), available online at *www.fpri.org* (October 15, 2000).

44. "Missile-Defense Cost Could Be $60 Billion," *Wilmington* (Del.) *News Journal*, April 26, 2000.

45. Michael O'Hanlon, "Star War Strikes Back," *Foreign Affairs* 78, no. 6 (November/December 1999), 80.

46. "Putin Proposes Deeper Nuclear Cuts," *Wilmington* (Del.) *News Journal*, November 14, 2000.

47. O'Hanlon, "Star Wars," 81.

48. Keith B. Richburg, "Russia Gains Role in NATO," *Washington Post*, May 29, 2002.

49. William J. Broad, "Call for New Breed of Nuclear Arms Faces Hurdles," *New York Times*, March 11, 2002.

50. Michael R. Gordon, "Nuclear Arms: For Deterrence or Fighting?" *New York Times*, March 11, 2002.

51. William M. Arkin, "Secret Plan Outlines the Unthinkable," *Los Angeles Times*, 10 March 2002, *www.latimes.com* (March 21, 2002).
52. Gordon, "NuclearArms."
53. Sagan, "Nuclear War."
54. *Ibid.*

Chapter 4

1. I use the term "Middle East" here in its most commonly accepted form: it includes the geographic area stretching from North Africa to Pakistan (from west to east), and from the Arabian Sea to the Caspian Sea (south to north). It therefore incorporates the vast majority of the Arab world as well as non-Arab states such as Turkey and Iran.

2. In August 1941 British and Soviet forces invaded Iran following that country's refusal to expel a large number of German advisors and businessmen from its territory. Iran subsequently agreed to grant the Allies the unrestricted right to control its roads, railways, airports, and communications for the duration of the war in order to allow them to directly supply the USSR with war supplies.

3. "Message from President Truman to the Congress on the Truman Doctrine," in *The Dynamics of World Power: A Documentary History of United States Foreign Policy, 1945–1973*, vol. 1, *Western Europe*, ed. Robert Dallek (New York: Chelsea House Publishers, 1973), 111–15.

4. The NSA of 1947 established the institutional basis for U.S. foreign policy during the Cold War. It created the Central Intelligence Agency, the Department of Defense, the Air Force as an independent service, and the National Security Council as an advisory council to the president. NSC-68 articulated the United States's strategy for fighting the Cold War and called for massive increases in military spending and readiness in order to maintain superiority over the USSR.

5. Thomas Bryson, *American Diplomatic Relations with the Middle East, 1784–1975: A Survey* (Metuchen, N.J.: Scarecrow Press, 1977), 176. Point Four was basically a revival of the wartime Lend-Lease program and the Marshall Plan, and its establishment made the United States the first nation to employ economic aid as a Cold War diplomatic tool. The Technical Cooperation Administration was established to implement Point Four throughout the region through bilateral agreements.

6. Shafeeq Ghabra, "Kuwait and the United States," in *The Middle East and the United States: A Historical and Political Reassessment*, 2d ed., ed. David Lesch (Boulder, Colo.: Westview Press, 1999), 297; Daniel Yergin, *The Prize: The Epic Quest for Oil, Money, and Power* (London: Simon & Shuster, 1991), 591. European and Japanese dependence on imported oil was even higher; the former imported sixty percent (up from thirty-seven percent in 1962), and the latter imported seventy-three percent of its oil needs by 1972. Japan also imported forty-four percent of its oil from Arab countries and was far more dependent on oil as a source of energy (seventy-seven percent of its total energy, as compared to forty-six percent for the United States).

7. Amitav Acharya, *U.S. Military Strategy in the Gulf: Origins and Evolution under the Carter and Reagan Administrations* (New York: Routledge, 1989), 15.

8. Maya Chadda, *Paradox of Power: The United States in Southwest Asia, 1973–1984* (Oxford, England: ABC-CLIO, 1986), 141. In 1981, another secret agreement obliged the United States to purchase $200 million worth of Israeli military goods annually. This was reaffirmed later in 1981 and again in 1983.

9. The Shi'a branch of Islam is the minority sect, accounting for approximately twenty percent of all Muslims. Sunni Muslims are the majority worldwide (roughly eighty percent of all Muslims). Shi'a Islam is concentrated primarily in Iran (where it constitutes the majority), Iraq, and Azerbaijan.

10. Chadda, *Paradox of Power*, 27. The Carter Doctrine mirrored a similar declaration in 1903 by the British foreign secretary asserting that Great Britain would oppose the advances of any other power in the Persian Gulf. In this sense, it can be viewed as the final chapter of the evolution of the United States during the twentieth century from disinterested

observer to regional hegemon. It is also the historical continuation of the pattern exhibited by any Western power that exerted a strong influence over the Persian Gulf: that of a policy warning other outside powers to abstain from aggressive designs upon it.

11. Steve Yetiv, *America and the Persian Gulf: The Third Party Dimension in World Politics* (Westport, Conn.: Praeger, 1995), 55.

12. Acharya, *U.S. Military Strategies*, 65–70. By definition, a joint task force (such as the RDF) is a temporary arrangement composed of a joint force assigned by the joint chiefs, with a limited, specific objective—in this case, to serve as a tripwire for U.S. interests in the Persian Gulf. In times of peace, a joint task force did not retain control over its assigned forces and had a complicated chain of command. The RDF, in particular, was assigned an area of geographic responsibility that was awkwardly and arbitrarily divided between the U.S. European Command and the U.S. Pacific Command. A unified command, on the other hand, has a broad, continuing mission, is composed of significant elements of two or more services, and has an area of geographic responsibility in its own right.

13. "Memorandum of Understanding between the Government of the United States and the Government of Israel on Strategic Cooperation," November 30, 1981, *www.israel.org* (March 14, 2000).

14. George Lenczowski, *American Presidents and the Middle East* (Durham, N.C.: Duke University Press, 1990), 261.

15. In December 1987, Palestinian protests (i.e., the Intifada) broke out in the Gaza Strip and West Bank in response to the killing of four people by an Israeli truck. The uprising rapidly evolved into a period of sustained popular revolt against the Israeli occupation of those territories, resulting in more than fifteen hundred (mostly Palestinian) deaths. This escalated the Palestinian–Israeli conflict to unprecedented levels: Palestinian protests involved thousands of people, widespread economic strikes, and violent resistance. Israel imposed curfews, sealed off entire towns, and used increased troop deployment to maintain control. The United States remained largely on the sidelines during this episode.

16. Acharya, *U.S. Military Strategies*, 129. The E-3 Sentry is an airborne warning and control system (AWACS) aircraft that provides all-weather surveillance, command, control, and communications that are crucial for modern air defense and aircraft operations. The naval force that was dispatched included two aircraft carriers task forces. Its mission was to sweep mines, assist tankers hit in any attack, and/or confront any vessels that tried to harass oil ships. Its activities were expanded by the Reagan administration until 1987 when the entire operation was upgraded into an escort mission for tanker traffic.

17. *Ibid.*, 82.

18. Yetiv, *America and Persian Gulf*, 130.

19. Lenczowski, *American Presidents*, 236–37. Through Israel, more than 500 tube-launched, optically tracked, wire-guided (TOW) missiles were transferred to Iran in August and September 1985; in January 1986 the United States committed itself to transferring 4,000 TOW missiles to Iran directly, and throughout that year additional missiles and spare parts were also provided to Iran. In the end, only three American hostages were released during this period. The entire operation ended when it was exposed by a Lebanese magazine on November 3, 1986.

20. Michael Palmer, *Guardians of the Gulf: A History of America's Expanding Role in the Persian Gulf, 1833–1992* (New York: Free Press, 1992), 123. As noted earlier, since 1980 the U.S. Navy had been escorting U.S.-flagged shipping through the Gulf. The U.S. decision was primarily motivated by a desire to ensure access to the region's oil but was also made to deny the Soviets a foothold; however, the USSR also agreed to escort Kuwaiti tankers (a total of three were reflagged by them compared with eleven by the United States) and built up their navy in the region along with the British, French, Belgians, Italians, and Dutch.

21. *Ibid.*, 149–50.

22. Majid Khadduri and Edmund Ghareeb, eds., *War in the Gulf, 1990–1991: The Iraq-Kuwait Conflict and Its Implications* (Oxford, England: Oxford University Press, 1997), 94. By 1987, Iraq had become one of the main U.S. customers of agricultural and food products—a process facilitated by the extension of U.S. agricultural credits of $1 billion. By 1990, bilateral trade had increased from the early 1980s' level of $500 million to more than $3.5 billion.

23. Lawrence Freedman and Efraim Karsh, *The Gulf Conflict, 1990–1991: Diplomacy and War in the New World Order* (Princeton, N.J.: Princeton University Press, 1992), 26.
24. *Ibid.*, 39. Approximately $30 billion of that debt was owed to Arab countries ($10 billion to Kuwait alone) that had supported it during the war, and the remaining $50 billion to Western (including $5 billion to the United States) and Soviet creditors.
25. Khadduri and Ghareeb, *War in the Gulf*, 153. The year of 1990 also witnessed mounting tensions due to Iraq's execution of an Iranian-born British journalist on charges of espionage, the seizure [in March] of contraband parts for the development of a "supergun" that had the capability of targeting Israel from Iraq and generally increasing concerns regarding the pace and scale of Iraq's development of unconventional weapons.
26. Freedman and Karsh, *Gulf Conflict*, 345–61, and Lester Brune, *America and the Iraqi Crisis, 1990–1992* (Claremont, Cal.: Regina Books, 1993), 57. The GCC states of Qatar, Oman, Bahrain, and the United Arab Emirates (UAE) sent a joint force of fifty-five thousand to join the Saudi army. Egypt sent two divisions and a regiment (40,000), and Syria sent a division and a regiment (21,000); Great Britain contributed an armored division with numerous planes and ships, as did France; Italy provided four ships and ten aircraft, Denmark and Norway a ship each, and Belgium sent four ships and eighteen aircraft.
27. Anthony Lake, "Confronting Backlash States," *Foreign Affairs* 73, no. 2 (1994): 45.
28. Text of Martin Indyk's speech at the Washington Institute for Near East Policy on May 18, 1993, as quoted in *Middle East International*, no. 452 (1993): 3–4.
29. The United States has consistently objected to three main dimensions of Iranian behavior since 1979: its support for terrorist groups, its alleged drive to develop weapons of mass destruction, and its opposition to the Arab–Israeli peace process (Iran does not recognize Israel's right to exist).
30. Peter Rudolf, "Critical Engagement: The European Union and Iran," in *Transatlantic Tensions*, ed. Richard Haas (Washington, D.C.: Brookings Institution Press, 1999), 86–87.
31. In the mid-1980s, Palestinians in the Occupied Territories of the West Bank and Gaza Strip rose up in revolt against Israeli military occupation; the uprising was called the Intifada (rebellion) and lasted for three years.
32. Sunni Islam is adhered to by approximately eighty percent of all Muslims; the minority branch, Shi'ism, accounts for most of the rest and is concentrated in countries such as Iran, Iraq, and Azerbaijan—although Shi'is exist in almost every Muslim country. Pashtuns are the largest single ethnic group in Afghanistan, comprising thirty-eight percent of the population, with Tajiks (25%) and Hazaras (19%) forming the other large groups. The opposition Northern Alliance is overwhelmingly formed by Tajiks and Hazaras.
33. "Bush Says Arafat Must Go," Wilmington (Del.) *News Journal*, June 25, 2002.
34. *Ibid.*
35. *Posture Statement* of General Henry Shelton, Chairman of the Joint Chiefs of Staff, before the Armed Services Committee of the U.S. House of Representatives, February 2, 1999. (Washington, D.C.: Government Printing Office, 1999; also available via the Office of the Chairman of the Joint Chiefs of Staff; available online at *www.dtic.mil/jcs/core/nms.html*). For an excellent review of the negative implications of these budget reductions, also see Anthony Cordesman, *Trends in U.S. Military Forces and Defense Spending: Peace Dividend or Underfunding?* (Washington, D.C.: Center for Strategic and International Studies, 1999).
36. Anthony Cordesman, *The U.S. As a 'Superpower': Comparative National Military Forces and Defense Spending Efforts* (Washington, D.C.: The Center for Strategic and International Studies, 1998), 5.
37. These FSRs include Armenia, Georgia, Azerbaijan, Turkmenistan, Kazakhstan, Uzbekistan, Kyrgyzstan, and Tajikistan.

Chapter 5

1. Herbert S. Parmet, *George Bush: The Life of a Lone Star Yankee* (New York: Lisa Drew/Scribner), 483.
2. Most infamous were his remarks from February 15, quoted in the *International Herald Tribune*, February 16, 1991. "There's another way for the bloodshed to stop, and that is for

the Iraqi military and the Iraqi people to take matters into their own hands to force Saddam Hussein the dictator to step aside and to comply with the United Nations resolutions and then the family of peace-loving nations."

3. Parmet, *George Bush*, 482. Bush made this clear on numerous occasions including in his press conference on April 16 when he said "I think that the American people want their sons and daughters to come home, and they're going to come home. . . . The fundamental policy is to bring our men and women home."

4. Jane E. Stromseth, "Iraq's Repression of Its Civilian Population: Collective Responses and Continuing Challenges," in *Enforcing Restraint: Collective Intervention in International Conflicts*, ed. Lori Fisler Damrosh (New York, Council on Foreign Relations Press, 1993), 84–85. One and a half million Kurds and Shiite Muslims from southern Iraq fled to Iran. But because OPC covered only northern Iraq and the Iraqi-Turkish border, the important role Iran played in addressing the plight of these victims will not be addressed. Interestingly, morbidity rates were worse near Turkey in the early stages of the crisis, partly because the Iranian efforts were better managed and supplied. Strained relations between Iran, its Arab neighbors, and the West seem to have tempered any vigorous international assistance.

5. Daniel Bolger, *Savage Peace: Americans at War in the 1990s* (Novato, Calif.: Presidio Press, 1996), 233.

6. See John Bulloch and Harvey Morris, *No Friends but the Mountains: The Tragic History of the Kurds* (London: Viking, 1992), 27–28; Gerard Chaliand, *The Kurdish Tragedy* (London: Zed Books, 1992), 70–72

7. David Hoffman and Ann Devroy, "Allies Urged Bush to Use Land Forces," *Washington Post*, April 18, 1991, A1.

8. Bolger, *Savage Peace*, 234.

9. Ted Koppel, *Nightline*, April 4, 1991.

10. Lawrence Freedman and David Boren, " 'Safe Havens' for Kurds in Post-war Iraq," in *To Loose the Bands of Wickedness: International Intervention in Defense of Human Rights*, ed. Nigel S. Rodley (London: Brassey's, 1992).

11. Quoted in Freedman and Boren, "Safe Haven," 54.

12. Walter Clarke, "Failed Visions and Uncertain Mandates in Somalia," in *Learning from Somalia: The Lessons of Armed Humanitarian Intervention*, ed. Walter Clarke and Jeffrey Herbst (Boulder, Colo.: Westview Press, 1997), 5.

13. Thomas Weiss, *Military-Civilian Interactions*, (Oxford, England: Rowan and Littlefield, 1999), 77; Alex de Waal, "Dangerous Precedents? Famine Relief in Somalia, 1991–93," in *War and Hunger: Rethinking International Responses to Complex Emergencies*, ed. Joanna Macrae and Anthony Zwi (London: Zed Books, 1994), 139–59.

14. Chris Seiple, "The U.S. Military/NGO Relationship in Humanitarian Interventions" (Carlisle, Penn.: US Army Peacekeeping Institute, Center for Strategic Leadership, Carlisle Barracks, no date), available online at *http://carlisle-www.army.mil* (March 21, 2000), 53.

15. Seiple, *Military/NGO*, 53.

16. Trevor Rowe, "Aid to Somalia Stymied," *The Washington Post*, July 29, 1992, A1.

17. John L. Hirsch and Robert B. Oakley, *Somalia and Operation Restore Hope* (Washington, D.C.: U.S. Institute of Peace Press, 1995).

18. James L, Woods. "U.S. Government Decisionmaking Processes During Humanitarian Operations in Somalia," in *Learning from Somalia: The Lessons of Armed Humanitarian Intervention*, ed. Clarke and Herbst (Boulder, Colo.: Westview Press, 1997), 158.

19. Thomas Weiss, "Rekindling Hope in UN Humanitarian Intervention," in *Learning from Somalia*, ed. Clarke and Herbst, 220, cites $1.5 to $2 billion, but in a later publication, Weiss, *Military-Civilian Interactions*, 91, he cites a $1 billion figure.

20. Weiss, *Military-Civilian Interactions*, 85.

21. Including in the north, which declared independence as "Somaliland" in 1991.

22. *United Nations and Somalia* 1992–1996 (New York: UN Department of Public Relations, 1996) 43–44, 261–263; Weiss, *Military-Civilian Interactions*, 88; Allard, *Somalia Operations*, 18.

23. Clarke, "Failed Visions," 9. The ambassador elaborated on this point in a personal conversation at the Third Cornwallis Group meeting in Nova Scotia, April 1998.

24. See Mark Bowden, *Black Hawk Down: A Story of Modern War* (Boston: Atlantic Monthly Press, 1999); Frontline, *Ambush in Mogadishu* (Boston: PBS, 1998), videocassette.

25. America sent in reinforcements to beef up force protection efforts and promote withdrawal. In March 1994, it also sent in 1,800 soldiers to cover the withdrawal of the remaining UN forces. By the end of March 1994, all U.S. forces were out. UNISOM II moved out in March 1995. Since then, Aidid has died (in August 1996), but the country still struggles with conflict, governance, and poverty.

26. J. Matthew Vaccaro, "The Politics of Genocide: Peacekeeping and Disaster Relief in Rwanda," in *Enforcing Restraint: Collective Intervention in International Conflicts*, ed. Lori Fisler Damrosh (New York: Council on Foreign Relations Press, 1993), 378.

27. Vaccaro, "Politics of Genocide," 384.

28. Weiss, *Military-Civilian Interactions*, 149.

29. Tutsi refugees also served to complicate regional politics, not only via their anti-Rwandan activities but also activities in Uganda (support for Musuveni), Zaire (support for Kabila's rebels), and Burundi (where they would get involved in national politics).

30. See Gerard Prunier, *The Rwanda Crisis: History of a Genocide* (New York: Columbia University Press, 1995), 127–90, for an account of negotiations and failed implementation of the Arusha Accords.

31. Weiss, *Military-Civilian Interactions*, 144; Vaccaro, "Politics of Genocide," 373; Frontline, *The Triumph of Evil* (Boston: PBS, 1998), available at *www.pbs.org/wgbh/pages/frontline/shows/evil.* But a new UN report discloses evidence that an elite hit squad working under the direction of the RPF and with assistance from "a foreign government" was responsible for the killing. Reportedly, this information (the testimony of three Rwandans claiming to be part of the hit squad) was available to UN investigators from early on but was buried. Apparently, the assassination was motivated by RPF frustration with the slow pace of power-sharing negotiations. See Steven Edwards, "'Explosive' leak on Rwanda genocide: Informants told UN investigators they were on squad that killed Rwanda's president—and a foreign government helped," *National Post*, March 1, 2000, available at *www.nationalpost.com.* The UN report is titled "Report of the Independent Inquiry into the Actions of the United Nations during the 1994 Genocide in Rwanda, 15 December, 1999," and is available on the UN website at *www.un.org.*

32. United Nations, *The United Nations and Rwanda, 1993–1996* (New York: Department of Public Information, United Nations, 1996), 37. Prunier, *Rwanda Crisis*, 213–311, offers a detailed account of the genocide, resumed war, refugee flows, and French intervention.

33. Larry Minear and Philippe Guillot, *Soldiers to the Rescue: Humanitarian Lessons from Rwanda* (Paris: OECD, 1996), 58.

34. Ten Belgian soldiers guarding the prime minister were slaughtered when they laid down their weapons in what one observer calls "an unwise extrapolation of traditional peace-keeping principles." Weiss, *Military-Civilian Interactions*, 144. The Belgians quickly pulled all their troops out of Rwanda, and Bangladesh declared its plans to follow suit, contributing to the UN Security Council's reduction of UNAMIR in the early stages of the violence.

35. *United Nations and Rwanda*, 422.

36. Minear and Guillot, *Soldiers to the Rescue*, 61.

37. An international tribunal for Rwanda was mandated in November 1994 (UNSC Resolution 955, November 8, 1994) but with little funding and personnel. Many tens of thousands have been arrested by Rwandan authorities and are being held in squalid conditions, but the Rwandan government and the tribunal have limited resources and an often-tense relationship, making their Herculean task even more daunting. It is unclear if, when, or how justice will ever be paid. See *Leave None to Tell the Story: Genocide in Rwanda* (Human Rights Watch, March 1999), available online at *www.hrw.org/reports.*

38. Alain Destexhe, *Rwanda and Genocide in the Twentieth Century* (New York: New York University Press, 1995), 30–34, 54–55, 66; Minear and Guillot, *Soldiers to the Rescue*, 60; *United Nations in Rwanda*, 37–48; Vaccaro, "Politics of Genocide," 372. In the Balkans, media outlets also seemed to play large roles in fanning ethnic hatreds. Moreover, many of the killings in Rwanda were by machete, which made for gruesome coverage by Western visual media.

Still, as those who insist the CNN effect is overrated like to point out, gory scenes of unarmed men, women, and children being hacked to death wasn't enough to trigger sufficient popular outrage and force an armed intervention by the West/United States. It should also be noted, however, that it was the media images of American soldiers dragged through the streets of Mogadishu that triggered an American pullout of Somalia and that most consider the major factor in explaining why America did little in response to the Rwanda crisis.

39. In most of the refugee and internally displaced camps, there were large numbers of Hutus who had participated in the genocide, presenting the international community with some difficult moral and practical dilemmas surrounding the provision of aid to these camps. See Prunier, *Rwanda Crisis*, 312–28; Destexhe, *Rwanda and Genocide*, 55–60; Minear and Guillot, *Soldiers to the Rescue*, 167–70; *United Nations in Rwanda*, 76–90; Thomas Weiss and Cindy Collins, *Humanitarian Challenges and Intervention: World Politics and the Dilemmas of Help* (Boulder, Colo.: Westview Press, 1996), 99–108.

40. Minear and Guillot, *Soldiers to the Rescue*, 125.

41. International responses to the Rwandan crisis can be divided into three categories— conflict resolution efforts via diplomatic negotiations, civilian humanitarian relief operations, and armed peace support operations. Unfortunately, all these efforts were either untimely, insufficient, or both. Space limitations allow us to concentrate only on U.S. activities in this chapter.

42. See Appendix A. Many of the conditions are open to a wide range of interpretation and so the relative ease or difficulty of meeting them depends largely on how they are applied. For example, how does one define "U.S. interests" and "acceptable risk"? Obviously one would be more willing to incur higher risks in pursuit of what one considers a vital national interest than in pursuit of something seen as of secondary or tertiary importance. But where does the prevention or halting of genocide lay within the spectrum of national interests? Apparently, in respect to Rwanda at least, it wasn't a top priority for Clinton.

43. Ivo H. Daalder, "Knowing When to Say No," in *UN Peacekeeping, American Policy, and the Uncivil Wars of the 1990s*, ed. William Durch (New York: St. Martin's, 1996).

44. Clinton's stay in Kigali lasted three hours, during which he never left the airport and the engines of Air Force One never shut down.

45. "Remarks by the President to Genocide Survivors, Assistance Workers, and U.S. and Rwandan Government Officials, March 25, 1998," available online at *www.pbs.org*

46. UNAMIR was also directed to share the info with Habyarimana, who denied any knowledge of such plans and vowed to investigate. It is still unclear exactly what role he played in the planned genocide. On early warning signs, see especially the videos *The Triumph of Evil, Anatomy of a Genocide*, and *Rwanda: Genocide Foretold*, as well as the joint evaluation, *International Response to Conflict and Genocide and Human Rights*, Human Rights Watch, *Leave None to Tell the Story*, and Philip Gourevitch, We Wish to Inform You That Tomorrow We Will Be Killed with Our Families (New York: Farrar, Strauss, and Giroux, 1998), ch. 8. The infamous Dallaire cable is available at *www.pbs.org*

47. Michael Kelly, "Words of Blasphemy in Rwanda," National Journal 28 (March 1998).

48. These quotes are also available at Frontline's *Triumph of Evil* web page in the section titled "100 Days of Slaughter," available online at *www.pbs.org/wgbh/pages/ frontline/shows/evil/etc/slaughter.html.*

49. Weiss, *Military-Civilian Interactions*, 165.

50. "Testimony, May 5, 1998, Jeff Drumtra, Africa Policy Analyst, U.S. Committee for Refugees, House International Relations, International Operations and Human Rights, Genocide in Rwanda," Federal Document Clearing House, Congressional Testimony, May 5, 1998.

51. Domingo Acevedo, "The Haitian Crisis and the OAS Response," in *Enforcing Restraint: Collective Intervention in International Conflicts*, ed. Lori Fisler Damrosh (New York: Council on Foreign Relations Press, 1993), 119.

52. In 1981, the Reagan administration secured from Haiti, in exchange for continued economic aid, the right to interdict and search and turn back Haitian boats suspected of carrying refugees.

53. Randall Robinson was the head of TransAfrica, a Washington-based lobby group. He held a hunger strike in April 1994 in protest of Clinton's forced repatriation policy. This is further discussed later.

54. Thomas Carothers, "Democracy Promotion under Clinton," *Washington Quarterly* 18, no. 4 (autumn 1995): 15–16.

55. Morris Morley and Chris McGillion, "'Disobedient' Generals and the Politics of Redemocratization: The Clinton Administration and Haiti," *Political Science Quarterly* (fall 1997): 383.

56. UNSC Resolution 940, July 31, 1994.

57. Some argue that international intervention (manifested primarily through UN, EU, and later American negotiation efforts, and UNPROFOR and NATO on the ground) helped prolong the war by encouraging the Muslims to hold out when they might otherwise have sued for peace earlier. Though certainly true, it was better this than an outright Serb/Croat victory as the intervention afforded the Bosnian government the time to create a more effective military, ally with Croatia, and push its Serb enemies back.

58. Weiss, *Military-Civilian Interactions*, 107.

59. James Gow, *Triumph of the Lack of Will: International Diplomacy and the Yugoslav War* (London: Hurst and Company, 1997), 2.

60. Montenegro was the only republic in which nationalists did not have a sweeping victory.

61. Milosevic refused to accept confederation unless borders were redrawn to ensure all Serbs lived in Serbia, which was, unsurprisingly, unacceptable to Croatian and Bosnian leaders.

62. Milosevic annulled Kosovo and Vojvodina's autonomy in 1989. He also ensured supporters took control in these two regions, as well as Montenegro, ensuring control over half the votes on the collective presidency.

63. Much ethnic cleansing went on in Serb-held parts of Croatia while UNPROFOR was deployed there. See Richard Holbrooke, *To End a War* (New York: Macmillan Publishing, 1993), 33. See William Durch and James Schear, "Faultlines: UN operations in the Former Yugoslavia," in *UN Peacekeeping, American Policy and the Uncivil Wars of the 1990s*, ed. Durch (New York: St. Martin's Press, 1996), on the actions of, and challenges to, UNPROFOR in Croatia.

64. Some even assert the Serbs wanted to exterminate all Bosnian Muslims, though this author rejects the argument. Genocidal acts certainly occurred, and authoritative international organizations have declared Serb actions attempted genocide, but whether or not there was a concerted and widespread plan to exterminate the Muslim population of Bosnia remains unclear.

65. Prior to the outbreak of war, Serbs were a majority in only about 31 of 110 districts—approximately thirty percent of Bosnian land. See Susan Woodward, *Balkan Tragedy: Chaos and Dissolution after the Cold War* (Washington D.C.: Brookings Institute, 1995), 226–27.

66. Weiss, *Military-Civilian Relations*, 114.

67. Gow, *Triumph of Lack of Will*, 40–45. If Serb strategy was well understood by European and American political and military leaders at the time, it might have been easier to convince them of the possible effectiveness of using force (including ground troops). If Serb forces shied away from direct confrontation with the ragtag Muslim "army," imagine their hesitation to engage well-armed NATO troops covered by heavy air support.

68. Gow, *Triumph of Lack of Will*, 203.

69. This section draws heavily on the work of Durch and Schear, "Faultlines;" 227–52.

70. Wayne Bert, *Reluctant Superpower: United States' Policy in Bosnia, 1991–95* (New York: St. Martins Press, 1997), 189.

71. President Clinton's appearance on CNN in early May 1994 to defend his foreign policy and the embarrassing "town hall meeting" of his foreign policy team weeks later are evidence that the Clinton administration was aware and concerned about the foreign policy credibility issue.

72. See David Rhode, *Endgame: The Betrayal and Fall of Srebrenica, Europe's Worst Massacre since World War II* (New York: Farrar, Strauss and Giroux, 1997), for an in-depth account.

73. Bert, *Reluctant Superpower*, 221–22; Holbrooke, *To End a War*, 68–70; Bob Woodward, *The Choice* (New York: Simon and Schuster, 1996) 259–60.

74. Holbrooke, *To End a War*, 72–73; Bert, *Reluctant Superpower*, 47.

75. Lester Brune, *The United States and Post–Cold War Interventions: Bush and Clinton in Somalia, Haiti, and Bosnia, 1992-1998* (Claremont, Calif.: Regina Books, 1998), 111.

76. Warren Strobel argues convincingly that it was during the summer and fall of 1992, when the war was still fresh and Gutman and others had just exposed the Serbian concentration camps, that the U.S. government faced the greatest pressure to intervene. Administration officials admit that the reports forced the government to respond, but because Bush was dead set on nonintervention, the responses were aimed less at the actual events and more at the political problems created by the stories and pictures. Public denunciations of the Serb camps and violence were made and even some minor policy initiatives were pursued to make it appear that the administration was responding appropriately. Bush's call for access to and closure of the camps and increased international humanitarian access to war victims in August seems to fit this description. In the end, though, Bush did not change its Bosnia policy, even in the face of such intense media-driven public pressure. The same analysis seems appropriate to the Clinton administration, which had a tendency to respond to the latest Serbian outrage with heated rhetoric, threats, and calls for peace, all the while refusing to take forceful action to resolve the crisis.

Strobel argues that "Bosnia also provides a specific case in which the power of televised images to pressure US foreign policy officials diminishes over time, especially when the leadership itself does not act or send some other signal of the issue's significance. 'This is the limited influence the media have,' said Gutman. 'You can have an impact at times.' But if governments do not take action, 'it dissipates.' By March 1995, Deputy Secretary of State Strobe Talbott could say that 'the "don't just stand there, do something!" instinct'— the public's unspecific demand for some kind of policy action—no longer applied in Bosnia. It is not that officials felt some countervailing pressure, he said, but that public pressure was absent altogether. After four years, he said, Americans now knew where Bosnia was and that there were no simple solutions. This, Talbott believes, diminishes the CNN effect. The United States did send troops to Bosnia later that year to enforce the Dayton accords, but . . . did so for reasons that had little to do with media or public opinion pressures." Warren P. Strobel, *Late-Breaking Foreign Policy, The News Media's Influence on Peace Operations* (Washington D.C.: United States Institute for Peace, 1997), 153.

77. Holbrooke, *To End a War*, 91–152. Prior to the bombings, UNPROFOR troops had been regrouped to promote force protection against possible Serb retaliation.

78. Bert, *Reluctant Superpower*, 176. The Clinton administration turned a blind eye to arms shipments into Croatia from Iran and from elsewhere in violation of the arms embargo. See note 20. Moreover, Croat forces received training from a private organization of former American military officers. See Bradley Graham, "U.S. Firm Exports Military Expertise; Role in Training Croatian Army Brings Publicity and Suspicions," *Washington Post*, August 11, 1995, A1. This assistance helped turn the tide of wár in Croatia and Bosnia.

79. See Holbrooke, *To End a War*, 161, for a map of the offensive.

80. See Holbrooke, *To End a War*, 186–374, for details of the negotiations.

81. "NATO's role in Bosnia and Herzegovina," at NATO's website at *http://www.nato.int/docu* (September 18, 2000).

82. Linda D. Kozaryn, "NATO Approves Bosnia Troop Cut," *American Forces Press Service*, from U.S. Department of Defense's Defense Link website at *http://www. defenselink.mil* (September 18, 2000).

83. It is likely that the cumulative effects of intensified bombing and the growing threat of a ground campaign were most responsible for Milosevic's decision. See Steven Erlanger, "NATO Was Closer to Ground War in Kosovo Than is Widely Realized," *New York Times*, November 7, 1999, A6. Other likely influences included Milosevic's inability to split NATO, Russia's reluctant support of NATO's position, and the ICTY's (International Criminal Tribunal for the Former Yugoslavia) May 24 indictment of Milosevic. See the Frontline documentary "War in Kosovo: NATO's 1999 war against Serbia over Kosovo," available online at *http://www.pbs.org/wgbh* (May 28, 2000). Apparently, Milosevic was so worried that he had been secretly indicted by the tribunal that he refused to go to Paris for the Rambouillet negotiations. See Jane Perlez, "The Terrible Lesson of Bosnia: Will It

Help Kosovo?" *New York Times,* February 1, 1999, A15. This public indictment occurred just days before he capitulated to NATO demands.

84. Apparently, the Church was not founded in Kosovo—rather, it moved there after its original foundation in central Serbia was burnt down. See Noel Malcolm, *Kosovo: A Short History* (London: MacMillan, 1998), xxxi.

85. Barton Gellman, "The Path to Crisis: How the United States and Its Allies Went to War," *Washington Post,* April 18, 1999, A1.

86. Gellman, "Path to Crisis," A1.

87. Serb officials, including Milosevic, insist this was a staged attack by the KLA on its own people to draw NATO into Kosovo or that the unarmed elderly farmers and children were really fighters dressed in civilian clothes. One of the most remarkable aspects of the Balkan conflicts were Serb efforts to challenge Western media reports and historical accounts of events. Often, Serbs accused Bosnian Muslims of bombing themselves to gain international sympathy. More recently, Network Bosnia reports "Reuters quotes Yugoslav Information Minister Goran Matic as saying that France planned and masterminded the Srebrenica massacre of 1995. Matic told a Belgrade news conference the mass murder of 8,000 Bosniak males after Bosnian Serb forces overran the town was initiated by the French secret service, working with 'their Muslim counterparts' and part of the Bosnian Serb army, the 10th anti-terrorist brigade. . . . Matic has challenged the common wisdom before, last year arguing alternately that Kosovo Albanian displaced persons were paid Hollywood actors or just families out for a walk." *Bosnia Daily* 2:26, February 14, 2000, at *www.networkbosnia.org* (June 7, 2000).

88. Quoted in Elaine Sciolino and Ethan Bronner, "How the President, Distracted by Scandal, Entered Balkan War," *New York Times,* April 18, 1999, A1.

89. Though there seems to have been much exaggeration by Western governments, media, and NGOs. See the January 7 report "The Kosovo Death Count," from *On the Media* available at *www.wnyc.org/talk*

90. "KFOR Objectives/Mission," from KFOR Online at *http://kforonline.com/kfor/objectives.htm* (September 20, 2000).

91. Quoted in Ivo H. Daalder and Michael O'Hanlon, "Unlearning the Lessons of Kosovo," *Foreign Policy* (fall 1999), 128.

Chapter 6

1. F. H. Hinsley, *Power and the Pursuit of Peace* (Cambridge, England: Cambridge University Press), 1967.

2. Paul R. Pillar, *Terrorism and U.S. Foreign Policy* (Washington, D.C.: Brookings Institution Press, 2001).

3. Joseph Kahn, "U.S. Rejects Bid to Double Foreign Aid to Poor Lands," *The New York Times,* January 29, 2002.

4. Lex Takkenburg, *The Status of Palestinian Refugees in International Law* (New York: Oxford University Press, 1998), 17.

5. Claire Sterling, *The Terror Network* (New York: Holt, Reinhardt and Winston, 1981).

6. See generally Helena Cobban, *The Palestinian Liberation Organization* (Cambridge, England: Cambridge University Press, 1984), particularly chapter 3.

7. See John Gray, *False Down* (New York: New Press, 1998), especially chapter 5.

8. Neil MacFarquhar, "To U.S., a Terrorist Group; To Lebanese, a Social Agency," *The New York Times,* December 28, 2001, and John Kifner, "Lebanon to Resist U.S. Sanctions on Hezbollah, *The New York Times,* November 6, 2001.

9. David Gilmour, *Lebanon: The Fractured Country* (Oxford, England: M. Robertson, 1983).

10. John Esposito, *The Islamic Threat: Myth or Reality?* 3d ed. (New York: Oxford University Press, 1999), especially chapter 3.

11. Barry Rubin, *Paved with Good Intentions* (New York: Oxford University Press, 1980).

12. Hala Jaber, *Hezbollah* (New York: Columbia University Press, 1997).

13. Avi Shlaim, *War and Peace in the Middle East.* chap. 6 (New York: Penguin, 1995).

14. U.S. Department of State, *Patterns of International Terrorism (April 1998)*, Department of State Publication 10610, 82.
15. Timothy Egan, "Man Caught in 2000 Plot Is Giving Investigators Information on Suspects," *The New York Times*, September 27, 2001.
16. Philip L. Martin and Susan Martin, "Managing Migration to Prevent Terrorism," *Migration World* 24, no. 5 (2001): 20.
17. *Ibid*, 21.
18. See, for instance, Jean-Marie Guéhenno, *The End of the Nation-State* (Minneapolis: University of Minnesota Press, 1993).
19. Alison Mitchell, "Disputes Erupt on Ridge's Needs for His Job," *The New York Times*, November 4, 2001, B7.
20. Martin and Martin, "Managing Migration," 1.
21. *Ibid*, 21.
22. *Ibid.*, 20.
23. *Ibid*, 20.
24. Robin Toner, "Civil Liberty vs. Security: Finding a Wartime Balance," *The New York Times*, November 18, 2001, A1, B4.
25. Mark J. Miller, "A Durable Migration and Security Nexus: The Islamic Periphery in Transatlantic Relations," in *Migration, Globalization and Human Security*, ed. David T. Graham and Nanak. Poku (London: Routledge, 2000).
26. "Text of President Bush's State of the Union Address to Congress," *The New York Times*, January 30, 2002, A22.

Introduction to Part II

1. Grace G. Roosevelt, *Reading Rousseau in the Nuclear Age* (Philadelphia: Temple University Press, 1990), 56.
2. *Ibid.*
3. Stanley Hoffman, *The State of War* (New York: Frederick Praeger, 1965), 85.
4. Roosevelt, *Reading Rousseau*, 190, 196.
5. Hoffman, *State of War*, 68.
6. *Ibid.*, 69.
7. Peter J. Schraeder, *African Politics and Society* (New York: St. Martin's, 1999), 325.
8. Classical realist analysis such as that developed by Morgenthau, Kennan, and Kissinger was limited almost exclusively to the study of nation-states, while ignoring other international actors.
9. Keohane and Nye, *Power and Interdependence*.
10. Paul Kennedy, *The Rise and Fall of Great Powers* (New York: Random House, 1987).
11. Joseph Nye, *Bound to Lead* (New York: Basic Books, 1990); Henry Nau, *The Myth of America's Decline* (New York: Oxford University Press, 1990), Duncan Snidal, "The Limits of Hegemonic Stability Theory," *International Organization* 39, no. 3 (1985); Gilpin, *War and Change in World Politics*.
12. George Modelski, "Long Cycles of World Leadership," in *Contending Approaches to World System Analysis*, ed. William R. Thompson (Beverly Hills Calif.: Sage, 1983); Joshua Goldstein, *Long Cycles: Prosperity and War in the Modern Age* (New Haven, Conn.: Yale University Press, 1988); Raymond Vernon, "The Product Cycle Model," in *Transnational Corporations and World Order*, ed. George Modelski (New York: W. H. Freeman, 1979).
13. Stephen D. Krasner, *International Regimes* (Ithaca, N.Y.: Cornell University Press, 1983); Robert O. Keohane, *After Hegemony: Co-operation and Discord in the World Political Economy* (Princeton N.J.: Princeton University Press, 1984); Oran R. Young, "International Regimes: Problems of Concept Formulation," *World Politics* 32, no. 3 (1980); John Gerard Ruggie, "International Responses to Technology," *International Organization* 29, no. 3 (1975).
14. David Held, ed., *A Globalizing World? Culture, Economics, Politics* (London: Open University, 2000); R. Moore, *Globalization and the Future of US Human Rights Policy* (Washington D.C.: Center for Strategic and International Studies, 1998); D. Rodrik, *Has Globalization Gone*

Too Far? (Washington D.C.: Institute for International Studies, 1997); P. Hirst and
G. Thompson, *Globalization in Question: The International Economy and the Possibilities of Governance* (Cambridge, England: Polity Press, 1996); James N. Rosenau and Ernst-Otto Czempiel, eds., *Governance without Government: Order and Change in World Politics* (Cambridge, England: Cambridge University Press, 1994); James N. Rosenau, *Turbulence in World Politics* (Princeton, N.J.: Princeton University Press, 1990); C. Hewitt de Alcantara, "Uses and Abuses of the Concept of Governance," *International Social Science Journal* 50, no. 2 (1998).

15. Samir Amin, *Imperialism and Unequal Development* (New York: Monthly Review Press, 1977); Johan Galtung, *The True Worlds* (New York: Free Press, 1980); James Caporaso, "Dependence and Dependency in the Global System," *International Organization* 39, no. 4 (1978); Fernando H. Cardoso and Enzo Faletto, *Dependency and Development in Latin America* (Berkeley: University of California Press, 1979); Immanuel Wallerstein, *The Modern World-System* and *The Modern World-System II* (New York: Academic Press, 1974 and 1980).
16. R. H. Chilcote, ed., *Dependency and Marxism* (Boulder, Colo.: Westview Press, 1982); J. F. Becker, *Marxian Political Economy* (Cambridge, England: Cambridge University Press, 1977); Michael B. Brown, *The Economics of Imperialism* (London: Penguin, 1974).

Chapter 7

1. Margaret Garristen DeVries, *The IMF in a Changing World* (Washington, D.C.: International Monetary Fund, 1986), 5.
2. See William H. Meyer, *Transnational Media and Third World Development* (Westport, Conn.: Greenwood, 1988) chapter 3 for an example of such imperial trade patterns taken from my prior research on flows of international information (news, print media, broadcasting, etc.).
3. Although Cuba was not officially a colony per se, policies such as the Platt Amendment meant that U.S. hegemony made Cuba a virtual colony.
4. The only marginal exception to the lack of room for expansion would be the last few bits of Africa that were carved up at the 1885 Berlin conference. See Hermann Kinder and Werner Hilgemann, *Anchor Atlas of World History, Vol. 2* (New York: Anchor/Doubleday, 1978), 97, 109.
5. DeVries. *IMF in a Changing World.*
6. *Ibid.,* 9.
7. United Nations, *Human Development Report 2000,* 206.
8. Lester Thurow, *Head to Head* (New York: William Morrow, 1992).
9. Nau, *Myth of America's Decline.*
10. Thurow, *Head to Head.*
11. Isaak, *Managing World Economic Change.*
12. Nye, *Bound to Lead.*
13. Thurow, *Head to Head.*
14. Helen V. Milner, "International Political Economy: Beyond Hegemonic Stability," *Foreign Affairs* 77 (spring 1998).
15. Stephen D. Cohen, *The Making of U.S. International Economic Policy* (Westport, Conn.: Praeger, 2000).
16. Robert S. Walters and David H. Blake, *The Politics of Global Economic Relations* (Englewood Cliffs, N.J.: Prentice Hall, 1992).
17. *Ibid.*
18. Joan E. Spero and Jeffrey Hart, *The Politics of International Economic Relations* (New York: St Martin's Press 1997), 10–13.
19. *Ibid.,* 14.
20. The classic statement of interdependence theory is Keohane and Nye, *Power and Interdependence.* Interdependence theory itself is closely related to, and helped to spawn, subsequent theories of international "regimes" and global "hegemonic stability." See Keohane's *After Hegemony,* Nye, *Bound to Lead,* Gilpin, *War and Change in World Politics;* and Kennedy, *Rise*

and Fall. Also see chapter 11 in this text for more on regime theory. The most recent developments in this intellectual history are theories of "globalization" and "global governance" from the 1990s.

21. Walters and Blake, *Politics of Global Economic Relations,* 80. Although the Jamaica Agreement of 1976 made floating exchange rates the "official" policy for the IMF, in practical terms, all major currencies were already floating on international markets by 1973.

22. Executive Office of the President, United States Trade Representative, *1999 Annual Report of the President on Trade Agreements* (Washington, D.C.: Government Printing Office, 2000).

23. "Patent Violators Warned," *Wilmington (Del.) News Journal,* March 13, 1992.

24. See William H. Meyer, *Human Rights and International Political Economy in Third World Nations,* [chap. 5] (Westport, Conn.: Praeger, 1998), for more detail on NAFTA, especially how the provisions for free movement of investment capital have impacted human rights. The same text details the pro-NAFTA and anti-NAFTA literatures.

25. *Ibid.*

26. *Ibid.*

27. U.S. State Department, *Dispatch* (July 1995), 2.

28. "Grain Subsidies Expected to Rise," *Wilmington (Del.) News Journal,* July 13, 2000.

29. "World Trade Fifty Years On," *The Economist,* May 16, 1998.

30. "Trade Group's Ruling Stirs Trouble for U.S., Europe," *Wilmington (Del.) News Journal,* February 2, 2000.

31. *Ibid.*

32. Charlene Barshefsky, "Toward Seattle: The Next Round and America's Stake in the Trading System," public address presented to the Council on Foreign Relations, New York City, October 19, 1999, available online at *www.usia.gov* (November 4, 2000).

Chapter 8

1. *Washington Post,* September 27, 2001, A14.

2. Paul Mosley, Jane Harrigan, John Toye, *Aid and Power: The World Bank and Policy-Based Lending,* vol.1 (London: Routledge, 1991), 22–23.

3. Mosley, Harrigan, and Toye, Aid and Power, vol. 1, 39.

4. With a respectable impact in some areas. In 1999, the bank estimated that it had been the pivotal force in eliminating seventy percent of all ozone depleting substances, mainly through financing the closing of thirty-six CFC factories in China and Russia.

5. For example, since 1994 the deputy director of the IMF has been Stanley Fischer, a naturalized American born in Northern Rhodesia and appointed to his post by Larry Summers, his own former grad student and protege who was then deputy secretary of the treasury. As a result, connections between the treasury department and the IMF were particularly strong in their tenures in office; the two were said to speak to each other on a daily basis. *Financial Times,* October 2, 1998.

6. The American contribution was especially vital because it would release an additional $100 billion already pledged by other countries.

7. Graham Hancock, *Lords of Poverty: The Power, Prestige and Corruption of the International Aid Business* (New York: Atlantic Monthly Press, 1997).

8. William Greider, *One World, Ready or Not: The Manic Logic of Global Capitalism* (New York: Simon and Schuster, 1997), 262.

9. In 1962, all of sub-Saharan Africa had $3 billion in external debt; by 1996 this figure was $227 billion.

10. "IMF Role in World Economic Woes Is Hotly Debated," *New York Times,* October 2, 1998.

11. See, for example, the address by Deputy Director Alassane Ouattara, "The IMF and Developing Countries: From Myths to Realities," November 10, 1998. Available online at *www.imf.org/external/np/speeches/1998/111098.HTM* (November 3, 1999).

12. Harald Malmgren, "Dollar Politics," *The International Economy* (January/February 1999), 10–13.

13. Owen Ullmann, "Mad Dog," *The International Economy* (March/April 1999), 24–27.

14. Others have argued that this a clear misunderstanding of the east Asian situation, that moral hazard played little role in east Asia because investors were lured to those markets

by their seemingly unstoppable growth, not the prospect of quick profits secured by international guarantees. More generally, skeptics observe that moral hazard is only one of many problems in the modern global economy. More serious are contagion and rippling meltdowns, both of which imply a compelling need for an institution like the IMF.

15. Though counterinitiatives are always present. In late 2000 there were moves afoot, suppressed for the moment by new IMF managing director Horst Kohler, to make borrowing from the IMF more expensive and difficult, to discourage casual reliance upon it.

16. For example, C. Fred Bergsten, "Empire Strikes Back," *The International Economy* (May/June 2000).

17. They have reason to be: in the 1990s alone, the number of the world's poorest rose by 100 million.

18. See, for example, Vinod Thomas "Why Quality Matters," *Economist*, October 7, 2000, 92.

Chapter 9

1. Charles P. Kindleberger, *The World in Depression, 1929–1939* (Berkeley: University of California Press, 1973).

2. Theodore H. Cohen, *Global Political Economy: Theory and Practice* (New York: Addison Wesley Longman, Inc., 2000), 205.

3. Terence P. Stewart, "Dispute Settlement" in *The GATT Uruguay Round: A Negotiating History, 1986–1992*, vol 2., ed. Terence P. Stewart (Boston: Klewer Law Publications, 1993), 2672.

4. T. N. Srinivasan, *Developing Countries and the Multilateral Trading System: From the GATT to the Uruguay Round and the Future* (Boulder, Colo.: Westview Press, 1997), 56–58.

5. Cohen, *Global Political Economy*, 332–34; see also Walden Bello and Stephanie Rosenfeld, *Dragons in Distress: Asia's Miracle Economies in Crisis* (San Francisco: Institute for Food and Development Policy), 90.

6. John Croome, *Reshaping the World Trading System* (Brussels: World Trade Organization, 1995), 262–63.

7. World Trade Organization, "Overview of the State-of-Play of WTO Disputes," available online at *www.wto.org* (August 1, 2000).

8. *Ibid.*

9. Executive Office of the President, U.S. Trade Representative, "USTR Announces Procedures for Modifying Measures in EC Beef and Bananas Cases," May 26, 2000.

10. Missy Ryan, "10 Sovereignty Issues Now before the WTO," *National Journal*, November 20, 1999, 3385.

11. U.S. Trade Representative, "Measures in EC Beef and Bananas."

12. Executive Office of the President, U.S. Trade Representative, *1999 Annual Report of the President of the United States on the Trade Agreements Program* (Washington, D.C.: Government Printing Office, 2000), 55.

13. *Ibid.*, 44.

14. *Ibid.*, 44.

15. "Fruitless but Not Harmless (World Trade Organization Rules Against European Union's Banana Import Rules)," *The Economist*, April 10, 1999, 18.

16. Executive Office of the President, U.S. Trade Representative, *2000 Trade Policy Agenda* (Washington, D.C.: Government Printing Office, 2000), 3–4.

17. House Joint Resolution 90 was introduced March 6, 2000. See *The Congressional Record* available online at *http://thomas.loc.gov* for March 6, 2000.

18. House, Representative Jack Metcalf of Washington addressing the U.S. House of Representatives in favor of House Joint Resolution 90, "Any Participation in Multilateral Organizations That Affects the Independence and Sovereignty of the United States Is Wrong and Should be Discontinued," in *The Congressional Record*, 106th Congress, 2d sess., April 10, 2000, H1989 (*http://thomas.loc.gov*).

19. House, Representative Thomas Reynolds of New York addressing the U.S. House of Representatives opposing House Joint Resolution 90, "Withdrawing Approval of the United States from the Agreement Establishing the World Trade Organization," in *The Congressional Record*, 106th Congress, 2d sess., June 21, 2000, H4788 (*http://thomas.loc.gov*).

Introduction to Part III

1. Critical theories of international relations and U.S. foreign policy, such as dependency theory, argue that poor nations are poor because rich nations are rich. In other words, these critical views lay the blame for Third World poverty on the alleged exploitation of those nations by the United States and the other Western powers during the age of imperialism. "Neo-imperialism" during the Cold War and post–Cold War eras only serves to exacerbate the international injustice and inequality between nations that was inherited from the colonial era, according to this view. For a sampling of such views, see the endnotes for the introduction to part II.
2. Lawrence Summers, treasury secretary for the Clinton administration, comments on the CSPAN television network, September 22, 2000.
3. Matthew Hoffman, "Going Global: The Complexity of Constructing Global Governance in Environmental Politics," Ph.D. diss., George Washington University, 2000; Martha Finnemore, *National Interests in International Society*, Ithaca, N.Y.: Cornell University Press, 1996; Martha Finnemore and Kathryn Sikkink, "International Norm Dynamics and Political Change," *International Organization* 52, no. 4, 1998; Audie Klotz, *Norms in International Relations*, Ithaca, N.Y.: Cornell University Press, 1995.
4. Robert Axelrod, "The Emergence of Cooperation among Egoists," *American Political Science Review* 25, no. 2, 1981.
5. Edna Ullman-Margalit, *The Emergence of Norms*, Oxford, England: Claredon Press, 1977; Margaret Keck and Kathryn Sikkink, *Activists beyond Borders: Advocacy Networks in International Politics*, Ithaca, N.Y.: Cornell University Press, 1998; Ann Florini, "The Evolution of International Norms," *International Studies Quarterly* 40, no. 2, 1996; Gary Goetz and Paul Diehl, "Toward a Theory of International Norms," *Journal of Conflict Resolution* 36, no. 4, 1992; Ethan Nadelmann, "Global Prohibition Regimes: The Evolution of Norms in International Society," *International Organization* 44, no. 4, 1990.

Chapter 10

1. James E. Dougherty and Robert L. Pfaltzgraff, *Contending Theories of International Relations* (New York: Harper and Row, 1990), 81–83.
2. Calvocoressi, *World Politics since 1945*, 282.
3. *Ibid.*, 90 ff.
4. Niccolo Machiavelli, *The Prince*, chap. 15 (New York: New American Library, 1952).
5. *Ibid.*, chap. 18.
6. E. H. Carr, *The Twenty Year Crisis* (New York: Harper, 1939).
7. Quoted in David P. Forsythe, *Human Rights and World Politics* (Lincoln: Nebraska University Press, 1989), 3.
8. Quoted in LaFeber, *America, Russia, and the Cold War*, 258.
9. *Ibid.*, 3.
10. Alan Tonelson, "Human Rights: The Bias We Need," *Foreign Policy* 78 (Winter 1982).
11. Jack Donnelly, *International Human Rights* (Boulder, Colo.: Westview, 1993), 32–34.
12. See John A. Vasquez, *Classics of International Relations* (Englewood Cliffs, N.J.: Prentice Hall, 1987), 18–19.
13. See Kinder and Hilgemann, *Anchor Atlas*, vol. 2, 187.
14. David P. Forsythe, *The Internationalization of Human Rights* (Lexington, Mass.: D.C. Heath, 1991), 61.
15. *Ibid.*, 122.
16. Vernon Van Dyke, *Human Rights, The United States and World Community* (New York: Oxford University Press, 1970).
17. Richard Falk, *Human Rights and State Sovereignty* (New York: Holmes and Meier, 1981), 13.
18. Lars Schoultz, *Human Rights and U.S. Policy toward Latin America* (Princeton, N.J.: Princeton University Press, 1981).
19. *Ibid.*, 179.

20. See Meyer, *Human Rights*, chap. 4.
21. Schoultz, *Human Rights*, 232.
22. *Ibid.*, 181.
23. *Ibid.*
24. Falk, *Human Rights*, 13.
25. Quoted in Schoultz, *Human Rights*, 110.
26. Schoultz, *Human Rights*, 191.
27. *Ibid.*, 111.
28. Forsythe, *Human Rights*, 108.
29. Schoultz, *Human Rights*, 112.
30. Forsythe, *Human Rights*, 109.
31. See Hugo Adam Bedau, "Human Rights and Foreign Assistance Programs," in *Human Rights and U.S. Foreign Policy*, ed. Peter Brown and Douglas MacLean (Lexington Mass.: D.C. Heath, 1979); and Douglas MacLean, "Constraints, Goals and Moralism in Foreign Policy," also in *Human Rights and U.S. Foreign Policy*.
32. See Brown and MacLean, *Human Rights and U.S. Foreign Policy*, xi.
33. Schoultz, *Human Rights*, 195.
34. Brown and MacLean, *Human Rights and U.S. Foreign Policy*, xiii–xiv.
35. U.S. Department of State, annual country reports on human rights in foreign countries, available online at *www.state.gov*.
36. Donaldson, *America at War* 123.
37. The final drafts of the two covenants were approved by the UN General Assembly in 1966 and then offered to all members for ratification. No U.S. president before Carter was willing to sign the treaties. Carter signed them in 1977 and then turned them over to the Senate for ratification. The treaties remained on a congressional back burner until 1992 when the Civil and Political Covenant was finally ratified by the Senate. The International Covenant on Economic, Social and Cultural Rights remains unratified by the Senate, and there is little chance that this will change in the foreseeable future.
38. Tonelson, "Human Rights," 53–54.
39. Forsythe, *Human Rights*, 110 ff.
40. Cyrus Vance, "Human Rights and Foreign Policy," *Georgia Journal of International and Comparative Law* 7, Supplement (1977).
41. Schoultz, *Human Rights*, 205.
42. Matthew Lippmann, "Multinational Corporations and Human Rights," in *Human Rights and Third World Development*, ed. George Shepherd and Ved P. Nanda (Westport, Conn.: Greenwood), 256–59; Tonelson, "Human Rights," 63.
43. Tonelson, "Human Rights" 55.
44. *Ibid.*, 63; Falk, *Human Rights*, 23.
45. Jacobo Timerman, newspaper publisher and noted dissident in 1970s Argentina, was arrested in 1977 by the military junta there. He was tortured and imprisoned until 1979. After his release, he publicly thanked Carter and gave the president credit for forcing the generals to let him go. For more on his case, see his *Prisoner without a Name, Cell without a Number* (New York: Random House, 1981).
46. During 1976 and 1977, twenty-seven black leaders died of suspected torture in RSA jails. This number includes Biko's death in 1977. After the evidence proving Biko's murder was smuggled out of the RSA, and after Carter began applying public pressure to the RSA, deaths of black leaders in South Africa's prisons dropped to a total of four between 1978 and 1980 (the remainder of Carter's tenure). During the Reagan administration's policy of constructive engagement toward the RSA, including a return to quiet diplomacy and no public criticisms of the RSA (see the following discussion), deaths of blacks in confinement escalated to a total of twenty-eight in six years (1981–1986, inclusive). All of this is documented in "Cry Freedom," the film about the life and death of Steven Biko (Universal Studios, 1988). Details on each death and the number of deaths per year are listed at the film's conclusion.
47. David Carleton and Michael Stohl, "The Role of Human Rights in US Foreign Assistance Policy," *American Journal of Political Science* 31, no. 4 (1987).

48. Of course, Carter is also honored for the Camp David accords under which he negotiated a peace treaty between Egypt and Israel.
49. Falk, *Human Rights.*
50. Ole R. Holsti, "Public Opinion and Human Rights in American Foreign Policy," *American Diplomacy*, 1, no. 1 (1996), available online at *www.unc.edu/depts/diplomat* (March 16, 1996).
51. Jeane Kirkpatrick, "Dictatorships and Double Standards," *Commentary* (November 1979).
52. Jeane Kirkpatrick, "Establishing a Viable Human Rights Policy," *World Affairs* (spring 1981).
53. Kirkpatrick, "Dictatorships and Double Standards," 44.
54. *Ibid.*
55. Kirkpatrick came under much post hoc criticism in academic circles after the breakup of the Soviet Union and the democratization of Eastern Europe. These were events that her 1979 article seemed to hold as impossibilities. Despite the unprecedented turn of events and the scholarly critiques, Kirkpatrick refused to recant her earlier assertions on the impossibility of liberal reforms inside totalitarian states.
56. In the early 1980s, Congress had subjected El Salvador to a human rights review every six months (instead of just once a year as with other nations). Reagan and his advisors persuaded Congress to remove these additional human rights restrictions on aid to El Salvador after 1985.
57. "Further US Help Is in Abeyance Until Polish Situation Is Clarified," *New York Times*, December 15, 1981.
58. Donnelly, *International Human Rights*, 73.
59. "Reagan, in Reversal, Orders Sanctions on South Africa," *New York Times*, September 10, 1985.
60. This study was released by Bankorp of Cape Town (a financial institution) in December 1989.
61. Sanford Unger and Peter Vale, "South Africa: Why Constructive Engagement Failed," *Foreign Affairs*, 64, no. 2 (1985–86).
62. The Reagan administration also gave indirect support to the Aquino faction by allowing pilots who were defecting from the Marcos regime to land their aircraft at Clark Air Base in the Philippines.
63. Andrew Boyd, *Atlas of World Affairs* (New York: Routledge, 1990).
64. Although I have no desire to debate the many possible reasons for the end of the Cold War here, suffice it to say that, in the opinion of this author, Reagan's military budgets were only one of the contributing factors and perhaps not even the most important one at that. Other causes for the end of the Cold War in 1989 would involve the impending merger of the economies of the EU in 1992 and the very complicated internal dynamics in the political economies and party elites of both Poland and the Soviet Union. The mass exodus in 1989 from East Germany through Hungary (the first communist nation to open its borders with the West in 1989) and into West Germany was another crucial triggering factor for the fall of the Berlin Wall and the delegitimization of communist leaderships. Hence the end of the Cold War is a classic case of an international event that is "overdetermined." A number of contributing causal factors (such as economics, military spending, changes in leadership, migration, etc.) interacted at a key time in history to bring about a reshaping of the political landscape in Europe.
65. Forsythe, *Human Rights*, 120–121
66. *Ibid.*
67. Reagan gave this speech in Chicago on May 4, 1988.
68. Richard Schifter, "The Semantics of Human Rights," *Department of State Bulletin* (Washington, D.C.: Bureau of Public Affairs, 1988).
69. *Country Reports on Human Rights Practices for 1989* (Washington, D.C.: Government Printing Office, 1989).
70. *Ibid.*, 4.
71. In 1975, the United States and thirty-four other parties to the Helsinki Accords, including the Soviet Union, agreed to recognize the existing borders in all of Europe. At that time, existing European borders placed the Baltic states de facto within the Soviet Union. The United States therefore at least implicitly acknowledged the Baltics as part of the Soviet state. The Helsinki Accords themselves were part of 1970s détente policy.

72. "Moscow Putting Added Pressure on Lithuania," *New York Times,* March 20, 1990.
73. LaFeber, *America, Russia, and the Cold War,* 344. Bush advised Ukrainians and other non-Russian groups against seceding from the USSR.
74. "Leader of Party in China Is Ousted for His 'Mistakes,' " *New York Times,* January 17, 1987.
75. "US Voices Regrets at Events in China," *New York Times,* May 20, 1989.
76. For more on the number and location of casualties during the Tiananmen Square massacre, see the documentary "Gate of Heavenly Peace," (San Francisco: Maata Distribution, 1996).
77. "2 US Officials Went Secretly to Beijing in July," *New York Times,* December 19, 1989.
78. Aron Hadar, *The US and El Salvador* (Berkeley, Calif.: US-EL Salvador Research and Information Center, 1981); Human Rights Watch, *El Salvador's Decade of Terror* (New Haven, Conn.: Yale University Press, 1991).
79. "6 Priests Killed in Campus Raid in San Salvador," *New York Times,* November 17, 1989.
80. "Bush Lifts Ban on Economic Ties to South Africa," *New York Times,* July 11, 1991.
81. "Mandela Group Votes to Retain Curbs," *New York Times,* July 7, 1991.
82. "Candidates Stick Mostly to Facts, but Disputes Arise over China," *Washington Post,* October 12, 1992.
83. "Trade Privileges for China's Goods: A Policy Reversal," *New York Times,* May 27, 1994.
84. "Bush's Talk on Somalia," *New York Times,* December 5, 1992.
85. "US Troops in Somalia," Access Information Service *Resource Brief* 8, no. 4 (1994).
86. "Showdown in Haiti," *New York Times,* September 19, 1994.
87. "Excerpts from the Clinton News Conference," *New York Times,* April 24, 1993.
88. For more on the realist nature of Clinton's policies for Bosnia, see "Blank on Bosnia," *New York Times,* October 16, 1996; and "Plan to Limit US Forces' Stay in Bosnia," *Philadelphia Inquirer,* October 29, 1996.
89. Aristide Zolberg and Robert Smith, *Migration Systems in Comparative Perspective* (New York: International Center for Migration, 1996).
90. Bruce W. Jentleson, "Who, What, Why and How: Post–Cold War Military Intervention," in *Eagle Adrift,* ed. Robert Leiber (New York: Longman, 1997).
91. "Clinton's Words on Mission to Bosnia," *New York Times,* November 28, 1995.
92. "Backing Away Again, Secretary of State Christopher Says Bosnia Is Not a Vital Interest," *New York Times,* June 4, 1993.
93. Human Rights Watch, *El Salvador's Decade of Terror.*
94. Susan L. Woodward, *Balkan Tragedy* (Washington, D.C.: Brookings, 1995).
95. For an empirical assessment of the relationship between U.S. aid and human rights in recipient nations, see Meyer, *Human Rights,* chap. 4.
96. Paul Lewis, "UN and US Pressed on Rights Stance," *New York Times,* February 2, 1997.
97. *Ibid.*

Chapter 11

1. A brief note on nomenclature. There is far more diversity separating the nations of the Third World than there are similarities that unite them. Therefore, it is somewhat misleading to lump all nations in Africa, Asia, and Latin America into a single grouping and refer to them collectively as the "Third World." The term itself has its roots in the Cold War. Third World nations were set apart from the "first world" (the nations of the West) and distinct from the "second world" (the communist bloc of the East). Third World nations were given this label in large part to highlight their "nonaligned" status (i.e., they preferred not to take sides in the Cold War). Although the term "Third World" has its drawbacks, the alternatives are no better. Third World nations are also referred to as less-developed countries (LDCs) or as "developing nations." LDCs has a somewhat pejorative connotation ("less developed" implies some degree of inferiority), although all nations (in some sense) are "developing" at any given time. Because most LDCs are in the southern hemisphere, they are also often referred to collectively as "the South," especially to distinguish them from the more advanced industrialized nations of "the North" (e.g., the United States, Western Europe, and Japan).

   Although each term has strengths and weaknesses, for the purposes of this text these terms are roughly synonymous. Furthermore, there is some utility in treating these nations as a single group while studying American foreign policy (AFP). AFP has often been based on the assumption that these nations simply are a single grouping in terms of U.S. foreign relations.

2. Krasner, *International Regimes*, 1. For other classic texts from the regime theory literature, see Keohane, *After Hegemony*; Ruggie, "International Response,"; Susan Strange, "A Critique of Regime Analysis," in *International Regimes*, ed. Krasner; and Young, "International Regimes."

3. Krasner, *International Regimes*.

4. U.S. Department of State, "Generalized System of Preferences," *Gist* (September 1990).

5. *Ibid.*

6. Walters and Blake, *Politics of Global Economic Relations*.

7. The United States alone has more than nineteen percent of the total votes on the board of governors. *Ibid.*, 69.

8. It is beyond the scope of this chapter to discuss the complicated political and economic reasons for the failure of nonpetroleum Third World cartels. In brief, cartels work only when there is no easy-to-develop substitute for the raw material in question and when cartel members can effectively create and manage buffer stocks. A buffer stock requires withholding goods from the market during times of low prices, and increasing the cartel's exports in times of high prices. Oil producers are perhaps the only Third World nations with the wealth needed to forgo sales of their primary product in order to drive up prices on the international market. Copper exporters in southern Africa, by contrast, are so badly in need of export earnings that they cannot afford to halt sales of copper, even when prices hit rock bottom on the international market. Nearly all Third World nations that enter cartels are in a situation much closer to that of the copper exporters than that of OPEC.

9. Indexing means that any increase in prices paid for LDC imports would be offset by equal increases in the profits made from LDC exports.

10. The United States did pay into a special fund set up by the NIEO to aid the poorest of LDCs who were hit the hardest by the massive increases in oil prices.

11. For more background on the NIEO and the NIIO and for a longer discussion on the connections between these new orders, see William H. Meyer, *Transnational Media and Third World Development* (Westport, Conn.: Greenwood, 1988) 3–6.

12. William Drozdiak, "UN Summit on Poverty Hit by Critics," *Washington Post*, March 9, 1995.

13. "AI and the UN World Summit for Social Development," *www.amnesty.org/library/engindex*, March 8, 1995.

14. Gareth Porter and Janet Welsh Brown, *Global Environmental Politics* (Boulder, Colo.: Westview, 1991). See also Oran R. Young, *The Effectiveness of International Environmental Regimes* (Cambridge, Mass.: MIT Press, 1999).

15. "U.S. and Third World Disagree," *Wilmington* (Del.) *News Journal*, June 11, 1992.

16. "North Meets South," *Wilmington* (Del.) *News Journal*, May 24, 1992.

17. "Bush Defends U.S. Policies," *Wilmington* (Del.) *News Journal*, June 13, 1992.

18. Biliana Cicin-Sain, "Environmental Policy," public talk presented at the University of Delaware, September 1992.

19. Carbon dioxide emissions from burning fossil fuels are the major culprit.

20. Chlorofluorocarbon (CFC) gasses such as Freon are thought to be the cause for ozone depletion.

21. "Chasing Smuggled CFCs," *Wilmington* (Del.) *News Journal*, March 26, 1996.

22. "The Road to Rio's Earth Summit," *Wilmington* (Del.) *News Journal*, May 24, 1992.

23. "UN Implementing the Earth Summit," *New York Times*, December 1, 1992.

24. Jean-Pierre Ple, a member of the State Department's environmental policy staff, expressed his high hopes to this author that the SDC would be an effective new regime for promoting environmentally sound public policies. Ple was later disappointed by the SDC's lack of power and ineffectual nature. In that respect, State Department staffers such as Ple shared the disappointment felt by most Third World leaders regarding the failure of the SDC.

25. "US Seeks Support on Global Warming Issue," *Wilmington* (Del.) *News Journal*, June 9, 1992.

26. "Bush Defends US Policies."

27. "U.S. Signs Pact on Global Warming," *Wilmington* (Del.) *News Journal*, October 19, 1997.

28. "Countries Argue over Global Warming," *Wilmington* (Del.) *News Journal,* April 6, 1995.
29. "World Officials Agree to Share Clean Energy Technology," *Wilmington* (Del.) *News Journal,* April 14, 1995.
30. "Emissions Curb Would Put U.S. in Economic Shock," *Wilmington* (Del.) *News Journal,* December 19, 1997. See also "Squandering the Surplus: $11 Billion on the Unratified Kyoto Protocol," *Heritage Members News,* Autumn 1999, available online at Heritage Foundation, *www.heritage.org.*
31. Upon taking office, President George W. Bush announced in 2001 that, in his opinion, the terms of the Kyoto Protocol no longer apply to American policy. In that sense, the Kyoto agreement is now "dead" as far as the Bush administration is concerned.
32. Melinda Kimble, Assistant Secretary of State for Oceans, the Environment and Scientific Affairs, "U.S. Policy Approaches to the Climate Change Debate," public talk presented at the University of Delaware, May 1999.
33. It was relatively easy for Argentina to be the first Third World nation to commit to carbon dioxide reductions. Argentina is blessed with large reserves of natural gas. Natural gas burns much cleaner than other fossil fuels such as oil or coal. Therefore, Argentina can produce its own energy without emitting high levels of carbon dioxide. In fact, Argentina is already producing carbon dioxide at a level that is below the Rio target of 1990 levels.

Chapter 12

1. Michael H. Glantz, "The Global Challenge," in Annual Editions: Environment 00/01, ed. John L. Allen (Sluice Dock, Guilford, Conn.: Dushkin/McGraw-Hill, 2000) 8–11.
2. Oran R. Young, "Rights, Rules, and Resources in World Affairs," in Global Governance: Drawing Insights from Environmental Experiences, ed. Oran R. Young (Cambridge, Mass.: MIT Press, 1997) 5.
3. Lawrence E. Susskind, Environmental Diplomacy: Negotiating More Effective Global Agreements (New York: Oxford University Press, 1994) 7.
4. *Ibid.,* 6.
5. *Ibid.,* 3.
6. *Ibid.,* 6.
7. Lamont Hempel, Environmental Governance: The Global Challenge (Washington, D.C.: Island Press, 1996) 31.
8. *Ibid.*
9. *Ibid.,* 141.
10. Walter A. Rosenbaum, Environmental Politics and Policy, 4th ed. (Washington, D.C.: CQ Press, 1998) 359.
11. Hempel, *Environmental Governance,* 180.
12. Marc Allen Eisner, "Green from Greed? Corporate Environmentalism and the Future of Regulation," presented at the annual meeting of the American Political Science Association, August–September 2000, 9.
13. *Ibid.*
14. Hempel, *Environmental Governance,* 182.
15. Eisner, "Green from Greed?" 9–10.
16. David Vogel, "International Trade and Environmental Regulation," in Environmental Policy, 4th ed., ed. Norman J. Vig and Michael E. Kraft (Washington, D.C.: CQ Press, 2000) 352–53.
17. *Ibid.,* 352.
18. Hempel, *Environmental Governance,* Table 7.1, 189
19. *Ibid.,* 188.
20. *Ibid.,* 187.
21. Our Common Future: The World Commission on Environment and Development (New York: Oxford University Press, 1987).
22. *Ibid.*
23. Bob Hall, Gold and Green (Durham, N.C.: Institute for Southern Studies, 1994).
24. Eisner, "Green from Greed?" 1.
25. *Ibid.,*

26. Brian Tokar, Earth for Sale: Reclaiming Ecology in the Age of Corporate Greenwash (Boston, Mass.: South End Press, 1997).
27. Thomas L. Friedman, The Lexus and the Olive Tree (New York: Farrar, Straus, Giroux, 1999) 32.
28. Hempel, *Environmental Governance*, 195. See also Table 7.2, 193.

Conclusion

1. "Colin Powell Maps out an Activist Foreign Policy," *Wilmington* (Del.) *News Journal,* January 18, 2001.
2. Lawrence J. Korb, "Bush's First Battle Is His Own Military Myths," *Wilmington* (Del.) *News Journal,* March 17, 2001.
3. Michael O'Hanlon, "Military Can Be a Lean, Mean Fighting Machine," *Wilmington* (Del.) *News Journal,* February 1, 2002.
4. "Fighting the Next Battle," *US News and World Report,* January 3, 2000.
5. "Rumsfeld Likely to Militarize Space," *Wilmington* (Del.) *News Journal,* January 12, 2001.
6. George Gedda, "UN, Often Seen as Adversary, Becomes Key Ally," *Wilmington* (Del.) *News Journal,* October 6, 2001.
7. Holger Jensen, "Bush Foreign Policy Prides Itself on Going Solo," *Wilmington* (Del.) *News Journal,* August 1, 2002.
8. *Ibid.*
9. William M. Arkin, "CentCom Plans an Iraqi War but No Outcome," *Wilmington* (Del.) *News Journal,* May 13, 2002; Nicholas Lehman, "The Next World Order," *The New Yorker,* April 1, 2002.
10. Arkin, "CentCom Plans Iraqi War."
11. See the comments by Haas in Lehman, "The Next World Order."
12. *Ibid.*
13. Georgie Anne Geyer, "Bush Pushed to Escalate War in Middle East and Beyond," *Wilmington* (Del.) *News Journal,* April 10, 2002.
14. William M. Arkin, "Secret Plan Outlines the Unthinkable," *Los Angeles Times,* March 10, 2002, available online at *www.latimes.com* (June 4, 2002).
15. "Jordan Pact to Be Renegotiated," *New York Times,* April 12, 2001.
16. "US and Europeans Try to Head off a Trade War," *Wilmington* (Del.) *News Journal,* May 3, 2002.
17. *Ibid.*
18. "Bush Offers Alternative to Kyoto," *Wilmington* (Del.) *News Journal,* February 15, 2002.
19. *Ibid.*
20. "US Signs Treaty for UN Tribunal," *Wilmington* (Del.) *News Journal,* January 1, 2001.
21. "US Pulls out of International Court Treaty," *New York Times,* May 6, 2002, available online at *www.nytimes.com* (June 15, 2002).
22. *Ibid.*

INDEX

Intermediate nuclear force (INF), 40, 59,
68–71, 74
Intermediate Nuclear Force (INF) treaty,
45–46, 64
International Atomic Energy Agency (IAEA),
22, 66
International Bank for Reconstruction and
Development (IBRD). See World Bank
International Bill of Human Rights (IBHR),
247, 249
International Criminal Court (ICC), 307–308
International Criminal Tribunal, 142
International Development Association (IDA),
204
International Finance and Monetary
Committee (IFMC), 197
International Financial Architecture, 207
International Financial Institutions Advisory
Council (IFIAC), 212
International financial institutions (IFIs), 215
International Forum on Globalization Web
site, 168
International Human Rights Day, 247
International Human Rights Law Group Web
site, 239
Internationalism, isolationism and, 178–179
International Labor Organization (ILO), 223
International Military Education and Training
program, 249
International Monetary Fund (IMF), 171,
173–174, 180–186, 194–204, 274, 282,
297
American foreign policy (AFP) regarding
trading regime under, 272
Camdessus, Michel, 195
Clinton and, 195
created to, 179
devaluation of Mexican peso, 206–208
development of Structural Adjustment
Facility (SAF), 201
dollar crisis and, 181–183
floating rates, 184
as "handmaiden" to America and American
policy, 198
possible changes to, 212–213
post-World War II foundations, 219–220
protesters to annual meetings of, 194
recent presidents of, 198
Schroeder, Gerhard, 195
Summers, Larry, 195
tensions with World Bank, 211–212
Wolfensohn, James, 194–195
See also Bretton Woods Institutions (BWIs)
International Monetary Fund Web site, 168
International Panel on Climate Change,
292–293
International Police Academy (IPA), 249, 252
International regime, 272–273

International Standards Organization (ISO),
297
International Straits agreement, 1936, 10
International Trade Organization (ITO),
219–220, 273
Inter-University Center for Terrorism Studies
(George Washington University) Web
site, 4
Intifada I, 95
Intifada II, 107–108, 110
IPA. See International Police Academy
Iran, 10–11
accidental shooting down of passenger
plane by U.S.S. Vincennes, 97
Americans taken hostage in, 40
anti-Americanism as cornerstone of, foreign
policy, 92
Antiballistic missile (ABM), 76
dual containment and, 103
Islamic Revolution, 158
map of, 1946–1948, 11
secret negotiations with United States, 96–97
Shah of, 85, 89, 158
war with Iraq, 95–97
Iran-Contra scandal, 42–43, 97
Iranian hostage crisis, 242–243, 256
Iranian Revolution, 92
Iranian Revolutionary Guards, 158
Iran-Iraq War, 91, 95–97
Iran-Libya Sanctions Act (ILSA), 104–105
Iraq
Antiballistic missile (ABM), 76
dual containment and, 103
government view of events in Iraq, 158
inspection of biological weapons, 73
invasion of Kuwait, 99–102, 159
no-fly zones to protect Kurds and Shi's, 101
Operation Desert Shield, 99–100
Operation Desert Storm, 100–101
relationship with United States, 98–99
war with Iran, 95–97
Iraq, Northern, 116–120
Iraqi Kurdish, 116–119
Irish Republican Army, 154
Islamic fundamentalism, 158–159
Islamic Palestinian groups. See Hamas
Islamic political activism, 112
Islamic Republic, 158
Islamic Revolution, 158
ISO. See International Standards Organization
Isolationism, 15
from 1776–1941, 176–178
foreign economic policy during, 177–178
internationalism and, 178
nationalism and, 177
U.S., 246
Israel, 51
Camp David Accords, 91–92

arms reduction, 68–69, 74–78
deterrence, 53–78
proliferation, 65–66
temptations, 61
weapons, 55, 66–68
Nuclear Nonproliferation Treaty (NPT), 112
Nuclear utilization theories (NUTS), 58–64
advantages and disadvantages of, 60–61
criticisms against, 77–78
versus Mutual assured destruction (MAD),
74–75
policy fixes for problems with, 63–64
Nuremberg Tribunal for World War II, 307
NUTS. *See* Nuclear utilization theories
NWO. *See* New world order

OAS. *See* Organization of American States
OAU. *See* Organization of African Unity
Occupied Territories, 87–88
OECD. *See* Organization of Economic
Cooperation and Development
Office of Homeland Security, 161
Office of Public Safety (OPS), 249, 252
Oil, 91
embargo, 1973, 276
See also Organization of Petroleum
Exporting Countries (OPEC)
Oklahoma City, Federal Courthouse in, 161
Olympics
Moscow, 1980, 38
Seoul, 1998, 261
Omnibus Trade and Competitiveness Act,
1988, 188
OPC. *See* Operation Provide Comfort
OPCW. *See* Organization for the Prohibition of
Chemical Weapons
OPEC. *See* Organization of Petroleum
Exporting Countries
Open markets, 176
Operation Defensive Wall, 108, 110
Operation Desert Shield, 99–100
Operation Desert Storm, 100–101
Operation Enduring Freedom, 109
Operation Horseshoe, 147
Operation Provide Comfort (OPC), 116–120
Operation Provide Relief (OPR), 121–122
Operation Restore Hope, 120–123
Operation Rolling Thunder, 27
Operation Support Hope (OSH), 126–127,
130
OPR. *See* Operation Provide Relief
OPS. *See* Office of Public Safety
Organization for Economic Cooperation and
Development (OECD) Web site, 168
Organization for the Prohibition of Chemical
Weapons (OPCW), 71–73
Organization of African Unity (OAU), 125
Organization of American States (OAS), 131,
179, 251

Organization of Economic Cooperation and
Development (OECD), 154
Organization of Petroleum Exporting
Countries (OPEC), 90, 184, 276–278
embargo on oil exports to United States, 90
impact of embargo, 278
oil embargo, 1973, 276–278
Organization on Security and Cooperation in
Europe (OSCE), 35
OSCE. *See* Organization on Security and
Cooperation in Europe
OSH. *See* U.S. Operation Support Hope
Oslo Accords, 105–108
Oslo II, 106
Ottoman Empire, U.S. signed treaties of trade
and friendship with, 81
Our Common Future, 296
Ozal, Turgut, 118–119

Pakistan, 66, 159
Palestine
dividing, between Jews and Arabs, 84
selected as Jewish state, 84
terrorism against British in, 153
terrorism against Israel in, 153
See also Arab-Israeli conflict
Palestine Liberation Organization (PLO), 51,
90
challenged by Hamas, 106
Israel invasion of Lebanon, 94–95
recognition of Israel's right to exist, 95
Palestine Mandate, 84, 87
Palestine Question, 83–84
Palestinian Authority, 106, 111
Palestinian Interim Self-Government
Authority, 106–108
Palestinian-Israeli issues, 156
See also Arab-Israeli conflict
"Paper gold," 182
Paris, peace talks in, 1973, 29
Partial Test Ban Treaty (PTB) of 1963, 65
PDD25. *See* Presidential Decision Directive
Peace Corps, 249–250
"Peace dividend," 165
Pearl Harbor, Japanese attack on, 160
People's Liberation Army (PLA), 21
People's Republic of China (PRC), 19, 21–22,
32, 264
Clinton human rights approach, 270
economic sanctions against, 265
Soviet Union and, 33
See also Nixon, Richard; Reagan, Ronald
Persian Gulf, 81–82
Persian Gulf Service Command (PGSC), 82
PFPs. *See* Policy Framework Papers (PFPs)
PGSC. *See* Persian Gulf Service Command
Philippines
currency devaluation, 208–209
Marcos dictatorship in, 261